PARTY POLITICS

VOLUME III

THE STUFF OF POLITICS

BY THE SAME AUTHOR

Parliament
Cabinet Government
The British Constitution
The Approach to Self-Government

PARTY POLITICS

BY

SIR IVOR JENNINGS

K.B.E., Q.C., Litt.D., LL.D., F.B.A.

Master of Trinity Hall, Cambridge
Bencher of Gray's Inn

VOLUME III

THE STUFF OF POLITICS

CAMBRIDGE

AT THE UNIVERSITY PRESS

1962

PUBLISHED BY
THE SYNDICS OF THE CAMBRIDGE UNIVERSITY PRESS

Bentley House, 200 Euston Road, London, N.W. 1
American Branch: 32 East 57th Street, New York 22, N.Y.
West African Office: P.O. Box 33, Ibadan, Nigeria

©

CAMBRIDGE UNIVERSITY PRESS

1962

Printed in Great Britain at the University Press, Cambridge
(Brooke Crutchley, University Printer)

CONTENTS

v

CONTENTS

CONTENTS

PREFACE

This volume completes not only *Party Politics* but also the survey of British political institutions begun with *Cabinet Government* in 1936 and continued with *Parliament* in 1938. The termination of a project formulated more than a quarter of a century ago perhaps excuses a little sentiment, and one's mind turns to the famous Epilogue of Littleton's *Tenures*, which begins: 'Ore jeo ay fait a toy, mon fils, trois livres.' The reference is apt because Littleton continues with an apology: '...I would not have thee beleeve, that all which I have said in these bookes is law, for I will not presume to take this upon me. But of those things that are not law, inquire and learne of my wise masters learned in the law.' There is high authority (Co. Litt. 395 a) for following 'the grave and prudent example of our worthy author'. In relation to *Party Politics* the advice is very relevant; for the book is founded not only on the learning of 'my wise masters learned in the law', but also on that of many wise masters learned in other disciplines.

Cabinet Government was designed as a law book, and on the argument expressed in *The Law and the Constitution* it was such a book, though the argument was not widely accepted in the thirties. *Parliament* was more difficult to classify, since it was necessary to use material which could hardly be brought even within the broad definition of the *lex et consuetudo Parliamenti*. *Party Politics* could not be written unless the conventional boundaries of academic learning were ignored. It was obviously necessary to make use of the learning of historians and political philosophers. This third volume betrays my profession in several chapters; but my reliance on experts in other fields of knowledge is even more obvious than in the earlier volumes. Almost every conclusion has to be checked by reference to wise and learned masters. The technique which I have used is not, however, original. It is constantly in use by civil servants and legal advisers. Every political decision is, or at least ought to be, based upon a vast accumulation of knowledge and experience; but every adviser has to pick out what seems to him to be relevant and to emphasise what seems to him to be important. This volume uses the same technique, but I have had to learn how to omit both in reading and in writing, and it would be surprising if many of my judgments were not challenged by those more competent to judge.

Littleton ended his Epilogue with the line ' *Lex plus laudatur quando ratione probatur*'; and Coke displayed his remarkable capacity for deflating histrionics by adding, 'This is the fourth time that our author hath cited verses'. Perhaps it is as well, therefore, that political principles cannot be proved by reason.

TRINITY HALL W. I. J.
CAMBRIDGE

CHAPTER I

POLITICAL CONFLICT

I. POLITICS AND PRINCIPLES

The stuff of politics consists of the ideas and prejudices in the minds of politicians. What it is in their minds is, however, not very different from what is in the minds of their constituents. Though the *corpus* of knowledge and experience in the mind of one man differs from that in the mind of another, there is in our modern society a large common element, due to the fact that parents, schools and churches teach very much the same things and that newspapers, magazines, books and broadcasts publish much the same ideas. There are of course variations between one family and another, one school and another, one newspaper and another, and so forth. Personal experience is more varied: but ease of communication in modern Britain has tended to diminish variations in the environment. We recognise at once the different environmental influences on, let us say, Mr Harold Macmillan and the late Mr Aneurin Bevan, but they would have been far greater if they had been born a century earlier. What is more, they would probably have been less if both had been born forty years later, because both would probably be distinguished members of the Oxford Union Society. Mr Macmillan at Eton would have obtained even the higher qualifications which Balliol College now insists upon; and Mr Bevan would have obtained very similar qualifications at his grammar school and have been very acceptable to an Oxford college.

This increasing uniformity of opinion is politically important. It helps, for instance, towards the stability of the party system. It is not so important in relation to the stuff of politics because politicians have always been drawn from the educated class, among whom there always have been methods of communication. Possibly we tend to assume too readily that the members for the Cornish boroughs and those for the Yorkshire boroughs in the Long Parliament had identical ideas. Clearly they had much in common because the invention of printing in the fifteenth century and the growing circulation of literature, the development of the grammar and other schools under the Tudors, the use of the universities and the inns of court for the education of laymen, the circuits of the judges and the meetings in quarter sessions, and above all the comparatively frequent meetings of Parliament since Henry VIII had enabled ideas to be shared. Even if there were greater differences among the country gentry than there are now among the members of the Conservative party, however, there was a very solid core of common ideas. Much of it came from the universities and the inns of court, where people chatted over their drinks much as they do now. Nor were there divergences at later times. It is not at all easy to separate the 'landed interest' from the 'mercantile interest'. There were eccentrics like John Wilkes in one century and Keir Hardie in the next, but even they shared most of their ideas with their contemporaries. The essential factor in the rise of the Labour party is that the trade-union leaders had been to board schools and could read newspapers. Most of the active politicians have in fact read the same sort of literature as the Conservative and Liberal politicians, even though they had much less formal education.[1]

Because party politics gives an impression of perpetual conflict, it is necessary to insist upon the solid core of accepted ideas. It is perhaps more obvious to one who has lived in an Asian country in which there is a large English-educated class. At first he seems to be, at least intellectually, very much at home. Further experience qualifies this impression. First, he finds that the ideas which he shares are limited to the English-educated class. Indeed, the gulf which separates the ideas of those educated in English and those not so educated is an important political factor which has no parallel in Britain. Secondly, he finds that there are important differences relating to family life, social relations, religion, communal relations, relations with servants, etc. Ceylon politics had a distinct flavour even in the quiet days after Independence, when the leading politicians were doing their best to run a democratic system on the best models. The flavour was not due

---

[1] See, e.g. Thomas Burt, *My Autobiography*; Lord Elton, *Life of James Ramsay MacDonald*; Viscount Snowden, *Autobiography*; Lord Snell, *Men, Movements and Myself*; Herbert Morrison, *An Autobiography*; and even Alan Bullock, *Life and Times of Ernest Bevin*.

to personal factors. There was a variation in assumptions which would probably be noticeable in most other countries to those who had an intimate knowledge of their politics. It is equally noticeable at different stages of British history. Indeed, one of the main difficulties of the student of politics who is not a professional historian is to appreciate the degree to which social ideas have changed. Some examples appear in Volume I of this work—the conversion of land from the foundation of the social order to a mere commodity, the change in the concept of the family which occurred when people began to congregate in towns, and what Coleridge called the 'spirit of commerce', which has spread even to labour relations.

It must not be thought that prejudices and ideas change as rapidly as events. Even the most active student of politics, whether he be a practical politician or not, faces new problems and new conditions with old assumptions. Most of those who merely take a daily dose of politics from a newspaper and broadcasts will not even notice that such problems and conditions exist. Startling events like the Spanish Armada, the Gunpowder Plot, the Civil War, the Revolution, the loss of the American colonies, the French Revolution, Peterloo, the Chartist agitation, the Irish famine, the two great depressions, and the two great wars lived long in the memory and created prejudices for decades. Less startling events, such as the invention of printing, the rise of a critical theology, the development of new forms of literature, the voyages of the great navigators, the development of historiography, the discoveries of scientists, the inventions of the industrialists, though they altered the environment profoundly, altered ideas and prejudices very slowly. There is usually a considerable time-lag between the cause of a social change and its consequences in terms of accepted ideas.

This time-lag is due in the main to the fact that the ordinary citizen is not consistently engaged in the adaptation of his ideas to the changing environment. Even the professional scholars, the poets and prose writers, the artists, the inventors, the propagandists and the *entrepreneurs* tend to have their minds concentrated on their own work and do not appreciate its cumulative effect on social attitudes. It is easier to write history than to write prophecy. The ordinary citizen does not even realise that some at least of the assumptions by which he is

3   I-2

regulating his life are being undermined. Even the young—if one may judge from the universities, in which there is usually more exacting analysis of beliefs than elsewhere—are not able to explain the variations between their own views and those of their fathers. Where they conform with the social attitudes of their environment, as they usually do, there is variation in their conformity due to their shorter memories. Undergraduates of this generation know about Hitler, but any repugnance that he produces in them is second-hand. If they know about the Great Depression, and they may not, it will be a bit of economic history. An effort of imagination is needed to think of undergraduates of a generation for whom there were no jobs. These are examples only. The environment has changed in many ways; and, though the public-school men generally conform with the conservatism of their parents and schoolmasters, the ideas and prejudices implicit in that conservatism are slightly different. They probably find themselves more in sympathy with the Bow Group than with Cabinet Ministers; and even the Bow Group is beginning to 'date'.

This reference to 'conservatism'—which has a small 'c' of deliberate purpose—is by way of example only. We are at the moment less concerned with party politics than with general attitudes, the whole complex of ideas and prejudices with which the citizen is furnished. The fact that an undergraduate calls himself 'Liberal' or 'Socialist' does not in fact imply that he is failing to conform. Since nobody argues from first principles, nobody can have taken all knowledge to be his province, and nobody under fifty (and not many over that age) can have much political experience, most ideas and prejudices are second-hand. The young man who calls himself 'Socialist' has, in the main, the same ideas and prejudices as the young man who calls himself 'Conservative'. They seem to him—unless he is a mere careerist, which rarely happens—to lead to different conclusions. Even the conclusions are really not very different, for there is a large measure of agreement.

Undergraduates are a small and unrepresentative section of the population. There is no reason to suppose that the process is very different in other sections. Those who leave school at the age of 15 and go into industry probably have (under the post-war educational system) less

4

native ability than those who go to the universities; they are thrust into an environment where ideas are not so frequently argued over and where the men in the 'shop' determine 'public opinion'; and there is consequently an even greater pressure towards conformity. Politically speaking it is probably 'Labour'; but the *corpus* of ideas and prejudices is for all practical purposes the same.

We have so far avoided discussion about the nature of these ideas and prejudices. If it be true that at any given point of history they are in all essentials common, the reader can answer that question by answering the question about the nature of his own ideas and prejudices. Let us, however, take a fairly typical young man. He began to acquire doctrine as soon as he was born. He learned to behave in the way in which his parents wanted him to behave. Both at home and at school he has been encouraged to conform. He comes, let us suppose, from a most respectable professional family. His parents have shown no signs of eccentricity, whether by voting Labour or otherwise. By careful housekeeping and a limitation on luxuries, they have sent him to a school which has never been corrupted by public money. He is about to acquire those marks of competence which are accepted by universities as sufficient evidence of intellectual merit. He has played for the house, if not for the school. He has been a fag and he looks forward to becoming a prefect. He is 'C. of E.' because his parents are; and when he was 'confirmed' he accepted all the parson's assurances. He is, in fact, a credit to his school, and, as his housemaster has already indicated in a confidential letter to the tutor of St Jude's, he has every prospect of becoming a useful member of that ancient foundation if he is admitted to it.

There are, however, other types. Our young man is even more likely to come from a most respectable working-class family. His father is a trade unionist in good standing who pays the political levy. His mother shops at the 'co-op' and does not bother the officials by attending meetings. Our young man passed into the county grammar school at what is called, in the jargon, 11 +. His football has received favourable attention from the 'scout' of Coventry City, but his father doubts if he ought to become a professional footballer because, though 'there's money in it', the prospects are poor. He has, therefore, been apprenticed at the 'shop', has joined the trade union, and will in due course pay the political levy.

It is not really as simple as these hypothetical examples suggest. There is a divergence between one generation and another because conditions have changed since the fathers learned to conform thirty years ago. Moreover, family life may set up, not a desire to conform, but a pressure to rebel. One way to annoy the 'old man', who sometimes acts the heavy father, is to deny his political principles. Also, the schoolboy who does not quite fit the pattern may well want to distinguish himself by joining the Communist party so that he can talk darkly about 'bloody revolution'. If the boy in the 'shop' is being pushed around by the men it is pleasant to spite them all by joining the Young Conservatives.

On the other hand, it would be wrong to under-estimate the generous sentiments which so often sweep the young. The French Revolution stimulated English minds more than any event since the Civil War. The Cambridge evangelicals produced a reaction in the Oxford Movement, and both profoundly influenced the opinion of undergraduates, though neither movement went very deep among the rest of the population: but the Oxford Movement, in turn, aroused the relics of the old anti-clerical tradition and helped to establish the reign of a non-theological (and sometimes atheistic) 'science'. Intellectual activity encouraged the study of political economy in the early years of the nineteenth century and the reaction took two forms, an emotional nationalism and an emotional socialism (originally a wider term than now, and including what we call the Welfare State). In our own day the economic depression of the thirties, Hitler's attack on the Jews, the rape of Ethiopia, the Spanish Civil War, the exhilarations of 1940, the Suez attack of 1956, the destructive power of nuclear weapons, and the return to racialism, have caused waves of emotion. Such emotions are particularly strong among the young, partly because they are not experienced enough to keep a wary eye on their own impulses, partly because they have not always learned the cautious cynicism which enables one to appreciate how mixed are people's motives, especially those of professional propagandists like parsons, professors and politicians.

In any event the environment is constantly changing in ways too numerous to mention. The physical environment changes because of increased population, higher standards of living, new means of transport, new tastes in gardens, houses, furniture and clothes. Changes in the physical environment produce changes in social convention; and conventions change even when there are no very evident changes in the physical environment. There is, too, a constant development of knowledge, which forces changes not only in the physical environment and in social conventions but also in apparently stable doctrines like those of the Christian sects. There is indeed nothing that does not change, for even Homer reads differently to one who has studied elementary physics. The environment for one generation is different from that of the preceding generation. The circumstances which give rise to political ideas are in continual flux. The emotions which develop out of them are necessarily different.

We are apt to think of these changes as occurring in generations, and there is some justification for this oversimplification. The changes are of course constant, but men's ideas are less elastic. Ideas are not fixed, but they tend to run on tram-lines. A young man, born into conditions different from those of his father, lays his own lines. Even if he is by nature or environment a conformist, his lines start in a different place, run into a different direction, and end in a different place, from his father's lines. It may be that in due course he gets back to what were the ideas of his great-grandfather, making all allowances for time and circumstance; and there is some evidence that this does happen frequently. Nevertheless, there is a clear distinction between the fundamental assumptions of the father and those of his conforming son, deriving from the changed environment, and evident because the ideas of the father have not changed as quickly as the environment.

There is, of course, no such thing as a generation. Children are being born every hour of every day. Nevertheless, external events provide a framework of reference. If those born in the last decades of the nineteenth century, in the early decades of this century, between the wars, and since 1939, are regarded as 'generations', the differences in the environment, and therefore in their political ideas, are marked. One can, therefore, speak of a cycle of generations. On this basis, the adult life of a politician may spread over two generations. So does the adult life of an elector, and this is even more important because in all probability his political ideas, being more rarely expressed and less often attuned to current problems, are more likely to be comparatively fixed. It must be remembered that one third of the electorate is over 48, one third under 38, and one third between 38 and 48. The politics of the Government and the Opposition is the politics of the oldest of these three age-groups. The 'Edwardians', born before 1914, dictate politics to those who have never heard of Lloyd George, except in the history books. The 'inexorable march' of the Labour party before 1951 was clearly due to the fact that what was called 'socialism' (whose vagueness we shall discover in a later chapter) appealed to a majority of the young men and women put on the register each year, of whom there were about 300,000. The 'swing of the pendulum' is caused partly by the same phenomenon. The young men and women who vote for the first time (and normally they are approximately eight per cent of the electorate) tend to have views different from those of their fathers and grandfathers. The balance then tends to shift against the Government, merely because the Government is in office.

We are not yet ready, however, to discuss conflicts of opinion. We have first to ask whence came the political principles which politicians profess. Clearly they do not come from the politicians, from whom capacity for independent thought is not required. Men of originality seldom get into Parliament, and this has especially been so since party organisations developed. One cannot imagine, say, John Locke, or even Edmund Burke, satisfying a selection committee in ten minutes that he was a good party man. The old theory, that anybody with ideas must be a heretic, has been carried from religion into politics. Nor, indeed, is it likely that a person with original ideas would be successful in Parliament. It is perhaps useful to have a Ricardo, a John Stuart Mill, or a Sidney Webb on the back-benches: but a political leader must, according to convention, make 'party political' speeches, and any originality, except in methods of expression, 'lets the party down'.

Political philosophers, using that phrase in a rather broad sense, are undoubtedly influential, though progressively less so as British politics has developed. In the eighteenth century Locke and Blackstone were particularly influential. Burke and Adam Smith were relevant for something like a century. Bentham's ideas seeped into public discussion, though in large measure through his disciples. Later in the nineteenth century the apostles of nationalism and socialism became prominent, though they are seldom read today. It is indeed doubtful if any author has had any considerable influence on politicians since Lloyd George. Nor, indeed, was there very much originality in most of the writers who have influenced policy. Adam Smith was an exception, but even he gathered up ideas and applied them to the new conditions of the industrial revolution whose consequences few had seriously considered. Blackstone was at the other extreme, for he never said anything original, though he synthesised legal and political knowledge and made it accessible.

In the eighteenth century the politicians could be expected to have read Locke; and until well into the nineteenth century they had read Burke and Blackstone also. Adam Smith was regarded, in some quarters, as seditious, though strong-minded men like Huskisson and Peel could trust themselves to read the *Wealth of Nations*. Only bits of Bentham were readable, and not much more was accessible. On the other hand, nearly everybody in the later nineteenth century had read Mill. We must not, however, place too much emphasis upon this branch of learning. Ideas percolate through many channels. The romantic reaction to the industrial revolution, which had a profound influence on British politics, was better portrayed by the poets and novelists than by political philosophers and economists. The political notions to which it gave rise were in fact neither philosophical nor economic, but emotional. Whatever Adam Smith might say of natural liberty, what he meant by it was abhorrent to an increasing number of thinking people. Democracy, nationalism, the Welfare State and socialism may have had rational explanations, but it was never necessary to produce them because, if the politicians had understood them, the electors would not. A good piece of Disraelian rhetoric was worth all the pamphlets of the Fabian Society.

It is, however, easy to exaggerate. Behind the Cabinet 'minute' of a few lines is the memorandum submitted by the Minister; behind the memorandum submitted by the Minister is the memorandum

9

submitted to the Minister; behind the memorandum to the Minister is a bulky file; behind the file is a mass of miscellaneous reading and all the talk in pubs and clubs, debating societies and trade associations, professional conferences and trade-union meetings. A policy is possible because it looks practicable, it looks practicable because it seems sensible, and it seems sensible because there has been enough argument over it and writing on it to make it generally acceptable. The sum of all these policies, or strictly speaking the ideas behind those policies, is the current political philosophy, not the philosophy of the schools (which has become increasingly denuded of practical value, except as a critical apparatus) but the philosophy of the Clapham omnibus or the Southend train.

2. THE CONFLICT OF OPINION

It is necessary to emphasise the general acceptance of this current philosophy, because the politicians do their best to persuade us that there is a great gulf fixed between the two sides of the House of Commons, not merely a gangway designed to prevent the clashing of swords. The swords are wooden because the battle is something of a sham. Arrows fly across but they are only words, too few of them being tipped with gold.

It is obvious that even within the framework of accepted ideas there is ample scope for differences of opinion, relating for instance to emphasis, practical application, or timing. Even if parties were always based on principle and not on personalities there could be a host of parties. 'Principle' is a bad word, for it assumes something fundamental. The fact is, however, that any difference of opinion becomes fundamental if any group feels sufficiently strongly about it. For instance, there is broad agreement that limitations should be placed on the sale of alcoholic liquor, this broad agreement being based on the assumption that 'temperance' is a social good and that, so far as is practicable, the law should enforce it. Some think, however, that 'intemperance' is so harmful socially that the inhabitants of a district ought to be able, by majority vote, to forbid altogether the sale of alcoholic liquor in their district. If this opinion is strongly held by enough people it forms a distinction of sufficient importance to be the fundamental principle of a political party. There has indeed been a Prohibitionist party, which actually held a seat in Parliament—for Dundee, of all places—though it may be suspected that Mr Scrimgeour was a good enough Liberal to secure, not merely the votes of the Prohibitionists, but also the votes of the Liberals. Similarly, Home Rule for Ireland, Home Rule for Scotland, and Home Rule for Wales have been thought sufficiently important to justify the establishment of separate parties. On the other hand, Home Rule All Round, which would have implied Home Rule for England as well as for the Celtic fringe, was never sufficiently strongly supported to justify a separate party. This does not mean that Home Rule for Wales is intrinsically more important than Home Rule for England: it means only that emotional support for Home Rule for Wales is strong among a minority. There is no strong emotional support for Home Rule for England, though there is strong emotional support for Home Rule for nobody.

The political philosophy of those who support Home Rule for Wales does not, if nationalism be excluded, differ from that of other people in Wales. Indeed, many people in Wales may support Home Rule for Wales without feeling strongly enough about it to justify their withdrawal from the conflict between the Conservative and Labour parties. What this implies is substantial agreement with the philosophy of people in England. In fact, however, the Welsh nationalists are similarly agreed. Their point of disagreement, Home Rule for Wales, is for them significant and for others insignificant.

The difference between the Conservative and the Labour parties is not quite of the same order. It is true that some of the more active members of the Labour party believe passionately in the principle of the nationalisation of the means of production, distribution and exchange and that, because of their advocacy, this principle has been inscribed in the party's Constitution. In their view the Labour party differs from all other parties because it is a socialist party, in the narrow sense which the word 'socialist' has received since Karl Marx. On the other hand, the Labour party was in origin not a socialist party but the workers' party, the party of organised labour. A great many of its active members, while subscribing to the socialist formula in principle, have not in practice proposed, and do not in practice propose, anything more than the nationalisation of a few basic industries and the regulation of the rest of the means of production, distribution and exchange. There is evidence from polls and surveys that the mass of Labour voters has been, and is, even less enthusiastic about nationalisation. In their view the Labour party is not the socialist party, but the party which favours social equality, that is, socialist in the broad sense which obtained before Karl Marx.

Similarly, the Conservative party is not an anti-socialist party, in the narrow sense. It has always supported the nationalisation of the postal, telegraphic and telephonic systems. It was responsible for the nationalisation of electricity supply through the 'grid'. It nationalised the coal deposits and has retained the nationalised coal industry. It did not nationalise the railways, but it created a group of monopolies under close public control and has since 1951 retained the nationalised system. It did not nationalise the Bank of England, but it placed it under close regulation. It has supported marketing schemes and schemes of 'rationalisation' whereby competition was eliminated without nationalisation. The real characteristic of the Conservative party is that it has the almost unanimous support of the wealthier section of the population and that its active members are drawn almost exclusively from that section. On the other hand, it would never secure a majority if it relied on that support alone, and its programmes are formulated to attract the support of persons drawn from all sections of the population.

Accordingly, neither party—and we may now include the Liberal party—is a party of one idea, or monolithic, like the Welsh Nationalist party or the Communist party. Each of the three major parties is anxious to obtain power in order to put into operation a wide range of proposals covering all aspects of political life, internal and external. Fundamentally the policies are the same because they arise out of the social structure as it now exists, are based on a broad area of agreement on fundamental ideas, and are formulated to appeal to the same people, the whole body of electors. There are differences of emphasis, in priorities, and about details, and the elector takes his choice. The elector may disagree with most of the proposals of one party and yet vote for that party because he feels strongly about one aspect of its policy. A Labour voter may, for instance, feel strongly about the nationalisation of certain industries, and be prepared to put up with Labour men at the Foreign and Colonial Offices, though he would prefer to have Conservatives in external affairs; or he may eagerly support Labour policy on defence and be prepared to put up with the rest of its policy; or he may feel strongly about self-government for Africans and be indifferent to all else.

Indeed, no sensible person, who seeks to make up his own mind on public issues, can expect to agree with all the policies of any of the parties. From his point of view those policies are like the curate's egg, good in parts. They have been formulated, to obtain the widest possible support, by persons who have collected a miscellany of ideas and think that they can persuade enough electors to agree with them. The policies are a compromise of competing ideas, and probably of competing interests, within the party. Only a party hack agrees with them all, or at least says he does. What is more, the average elector pays little attention to the policies. He supports a party because he has always supported it, or because he believes that, in the long run if not the short run, it is more favourable than any other to people like him, or because he believes that it has in the past done a better job than any other, or because it seems to him to have better leaders. In his view an election is not a choice of policies but a choice of Governments, though he knows that, in making the choice of a Government, he also chooses a series of policies, which he probably has never bothered to read.[1]

The party conflict being a competition for power, the differences are emphasised and even exaggerated. Parliamentary debate is discussion of differences. It used to be complained that the Mother of Parliaments paid little attention to colonial affairs; but she does give such attention when parties are divided upon them. There is the same lack of attention to home affairs when the Opposition can find nothing to criticise. The only difference is that changes in home policy require legislation, and therefore some discussion, though there is little discussion if the measure is agreed; whereas changes in colonial policy can usually be effected either by legislation in the colony or by Orders in Council,

[1] See generally, Volume I, ch. x.

13

and accordingly no discussion takes place unless the Opposition disagrees. Thus, Parliament gives the impression of a regular conflict between Conservative and Labour. The large measure of agreement does not appear, especially in newspapers for which the only news is a 'crisis'; the small measure of disagreement is exaggerated. The sham battle goes on.

The large measure of agreement is due to the slow development of ideas, which are the result of experience of changing physical and social phenomena. This book is concerned with that development in fields in which there has been conflict; it seems to prove that the conflicts are over the frills and fringes. If Ireland be omitted, except in so far as it was a factor in politics in Great Britain, there has never been a fundamental cleavage since the Civil War; and the Civil War was not so much a conflict of opinions as a conflict of loyalties.

For most of the history of British politics the fundamental agreement on broad issues has been due to the homogeneity of the governing class. The enfranchisement of the workers in 1867 and 1884 did not immediately affect the situation because the middle class continued to govern. When working-class votes did begin seriously to affect political opinion—which was not until 1906—the increasing homogeneity of the British peoples (omitting the Irish) enabled this broad agreement to continue. As has so often been pointed out, Great Britain is a small island, densely populated, and with excellent communications. Except in Wales, there are no barriers of language; and in Wales language is not much of a barrier because nearly all the Welsh-speakers are also English-speaking and because, in spite of nationalist efforts, the ideas which circulate among Welsh-speakers through the newspapers and the chapels are essentially the same as those circulating in England. There are, too, no great economic divergences. The prosperity of some depends on the prosperity of all. There are local 'issues', which the parties play up, but in all essentials what is said at Land's End has also to be said at John O'Groats, because the interests and prejudices of Cornishmen are fundamentally no different from the interests and prejudices of the highlanders of Caithness.

There are enough differences to justify a host of parties, and from time to time these 'splinter parties' exist. It happens, however, that

14

the greater part of the politicians have coalesced into two parties, the whigs and the tories, the Liberals and the Conservatives, and (since 1922) Labour and Conservative.

3. THE TWO-PARTY SYSTEM

There is a logic in the two-party system. If political ideas be generally common, the party conflict on any particular issue is a question of more or less: the policies may be expressed as $x \pm$. On other issues they will be $y \pm$ and $z \pm$. There is some reason for assuming that politicians will divide, on the one side $x +, y +$ and $z +$, and on the other side $x -, y -$ and $z -$. This is, very largely, a matter of temperament. Those who are conservative in politics tend also to be conservative in other matters; those who are radical reformers in politics tend also to be radical reformers in other matters. It is also a matter of class-interest, because those who are doing well out of a particular situation think it excellent and wish to preserve it, while the underdogs are satisfied that it needs radical reform.

This is not, however, a complete explanation, for it might produce a multiplicity of parties, each stressing a particular aspect of public policy. The area of disagreement being very much smaller than the area of agreement, however, it is not worth while to establish a separate party to agitate for, say, increased pensions for old-age pensioners, or compulsory insurance against burglary, or the independence of Malta, or federation for Western Europe. These hypothetical examples show, however, what is the most important factor. Because the parties have coalesced into two, the one party in office and the other in Opposition, the task of the enthusiast for any particular reform is to convince one of the major parties.

This coalescence came about because, as we have seen in Volume II, the men in office after 1783 had to face what the eighteenth century called a 'formed opposition', a body of men who were anxious to replace the Cabinet as a body. Moreover, Government and Opposition were given 'ideologies' by the French Revolution. This did not mean that the House of Commons split into Loyalists and Jacobins. All members of the governing class were agreed that the English Revolution had already occurred in 1688, and that the British Constitution was, in its essential characteristics, admirable. There were, however, some who believed with Burke that any tampering with existing institutions would lead to chaos, and some who had sympathy with the *sansculottes*, the underprivileged, especially in the great cities. The latter were prepared for modest reforms which would not affect the dominance of the landed interest, which everybody regarded as admirable. The difference between Government and Opposition was, therefore, a difference between conservative and liberal, without capital letters. Party lines were by no means rigid. Indeed there were no party lines at all, but merely two nuclei consisting of the Cabinet on the one side and the friends of Mr Fox on the other. Groups were detached and attached from time to time. But anybody who wanted office had to be attached, or at least semi-attached, to one of the nuclei. When at last the Peelites were absorbed, the Conservatives were on the one side and the Liberals on the other: and this time capital letters have to be used. Anybody who had a particular nostrum, like Henry George or Charles Bradlaugh, had either to try to sell it in the wilderness or to persuade one of the parties to adopt it. Nor was this arrangement modified by the development of the Labour party. Its influence was small and depended on a tacit alliance with the Liberals, until after 1918 it was able to supplant the Liberal party as the major Opposition to a Conservative Government, and therefore as the alternative Government. The two-party system contains within itself the source of its own strength. Even the enthusiast for a cause has to be a party man.

In its early years, when the Conservative and the Liberal parties formed alternative Governments, there were some in the Labour party who thought that it should concentrate on particular issues affecting the organised working class, like trade-union and factory legislation. There were others whose main concern was socialist propaganda, that is, propaganda for the nationalisation of the means of production. This concentration on particular issues, which would have made the Labour party into a monolithic party like the Welsh Nationalist party, did not happen. Nearly all the Labour members were elected by Liberal voters by the tacit agreement (suggested by Liberal headquarters) of the Liberal associations. Their constituents expected them to support the

Liberal Government and, after 1910, that support was necessary for Liberal measures. Members had thus to take sides—and generally they took the Liberal side—on all public issues. The Labour party, in other words, became polylithic. Accordingly, when the Labour party forms Her Majesty's Opposition, the task of the leaders is to examine, with a suspicious eye, all the proposals emanating from, and all the executive actions of, the Conservative Government. They pick on those proposals or actions, or those details of proposals or actions, which seem to them to be objectionable or capable of being used as political ammunition. In the result the large element of agreement is suppressed and the small element of disagreement overemphasised. Indeed, many members of the Labour party may agree with the Conservative Government in a particular debate, but, since the party is polylithic and depends for its effectiveness as an Opposition on party discipline, the dissidents have either to keep silent or to make 'party political' speeches of the worst kind, those in which the speakers not only exaggerate, but express notions with which they do not agree.

On the other side the Conservative Ministers and their henchmen do not need to bother to explain the proposals with which everybody agrees. Their task is to defend themselves against Labour attacks. On their side, too, are some who agree with the Labour criticisms, when expressed with moderation, but they too have to speak and vote 'party political'. Hence the sham fight appears to be a genuine conflict of principle.

4. THE CYCLE OF OPINION

A political scientist has written a book of 450 pages on the particular problem which led to the fall of the Labour Government and the establishment of the National Government in 1931.[1] A similar book could be written about the short period in which the Liberal party broke up over Gladstone's Home Rule Bill of 1886. On this scale two volumes would be needed for the dispute between the Liberal Government and the Conservative peers in 1909–11. The historians, too, are producing work of the same kind. Mr John Brooke, for instance, has written nearly 400 pages on the Chatham Administration of 1766–8.

[1] R. Bassett, *Nineteen Thirty-One*.

There are dangers in this close attention to detail because it is necessarily based upon documentary evidence. That evidence can never be complete or accurate. Frequently no record is made of oral discussions; frequently such records as are available were made after the event by persons who relied on their memories. A conversation recorded as having taken place after an event when it actually occurred before may produce a completely false impression. Indeed, Mr Bassett occupies a substantial part of his space by showing inconsistencies in the documents and criticising those who have drawn conclusions from them. It is, however, reasonable to assume that he has not seen all the documents that exist and that a great many significant events went unrecorded.[1]

The older historians were content to paint on a smaller canvas. This method has the advantage of avoiding the confusion of probably inaccurate detail but has compensating disadvantages. Particular events or documents are often given undue significance, as if they indicated the character of the whole transaction. Purely temporal and personal factors having to be ignored, a process of continuous development, following a sort of historical pattern, is seen to emerge because the accidents of history, which may in fact have been significant, have been ignored. Moreover the progress of events is related to the ultimate development, the germ of an idea or of an institution having been discovered because ultimately that idea was accepted or that institution established. There may, however, have been no causal or even historical connexion between the germ and the idea or institution.

Both methods create difficulties for the student of politics, but he cannot be in any doubt that ideas and institutions, and even policies,

---

[1] The official documents of the Pakistan crisis of 1954–5, many of which were drafted by me, would give a very inadequate picture of events, though they could be supplemented by my contemporary notes. Those notes were sometimes written three or four days after the events recorded, and may therefore be inaccurate. In any case I sometimes received oral instructions based on discussions which I did not attend; there were discussions of whose existence I knew without knowing the details and, no doubt, discussions of which I was completely ignorant. I do not, for instance, know why, after *The Times* had announced that Mr Suhrawardhy had been appointed Prime Minister, the appointment was in fact offered to and accepted by Mr Chaudhri Mohamed Ali. I can guess; and, unless there are documents available, the historians will have to do the same. The newspaper reports gave something like a correct general impression, but were inaccurate in detail, especially when politicians were flying kites.

do grow. Indeed, if he be a practical politician or civil servant or constitutional lawyer he may find himself to be one of the gardeners, for he seizes upon ideas and institutions invented and developed by others in order to adapt them to his own purposes. Since he is also projecting those ideas and institutions into the future he needs to know something of the process of development in order that he may estimate, so far as his knowledge and experience allow, what effect they may have upon future generations. For this purpose he has to rely on the historians who have examined the evidence for earlier developments. Inevitably the historians differ among themselves, for they have not merely to record but to interpret. From the point of view of the student of politics the differences are not always significant. The more detail there is the less important it probably is. The anxiety of a Ph.D. student to find an unpublished document which proves a reputable historian to be wrong in his facts or erroneous in his interpretation, seldom holds terror for the student of politics, for the latter is concerned only with the broad lines of development. Nevertheless, historians do have their ideas corrected by later research; and the student of politics may have been relying on false evidence.

This book seeks to examine certain ideas, of a broad and general character, which have apparently played the most important part in British politics. The scale being small, the technique of generalisation has had to be adopted. The scale made it impossible to read all that had been written on a particular topic. A synthesis was more useful than a monograph, and little attention has been paid to primary sources—none whatever to manuscript sources. The possibilities of error have therefore been multiplied, especially in the last stage, when the work of historians is interpreted by a modern constitutional lawyer.

This attempt at a synthesis may possibly be of interest to historians, but it is intended primarily for political scientists and constitutional lawyers. It does not seek to prove anything, but it may suggest to the instructed reader that most political controversies have emotional foundations, or at least emotional reactions; that ideas take a long time to soak in, perhaps a whole generation; that most political controversies are exaggerated by rhetoric; that politicians are adapters rather than innovators, and that there is a remarkable continuity in British politics.

Other conclusions may be drawn to suit the readers' prejudices which will, probably, justify criticism of the exposition from every possible point of view.

Is it possible to find a pattern in the development of political ideas? If there is, it ought to be exhibited by a synopsis of British politics. Nothing very definite emerges, but there are signs of a sort of wave motion, with a wavelength of roughly a hundred years. It would be bold to say that it can truly be discerned, for a wave of opinion would inevitably be distorted by such events as wars and trade cycles. There can be no doubt, however, that periods of high emotion, especially those associated with religion and nationalism, are followed by periods of comparative quiescence. If these periods are associated with changes in the generations, one would expect a recurrence of high emotion in every third or fifth generation; and three generations make a hundred years. One can, in fact, make up pretty theories by the appropriate selection of dates, such as:

1639		Treaty of Berwick
1689	Bill of Rights	
1739		War of Jenkins's Ear
1789	French Revolution	
1839		Bedchamber Question
1889	London Dock Strike	
1939		Hitler's War

A wavelength of exactly a hundred years has been taken so as not to cheat, though nobody would expect a cycle to be so exact. This is, however, a fascinating game which the reader should play for himself.

CHAPTER II

THE WHIG CONSTITUTION

I. THE PROPAGATION OF LEGAL IDEAS

Constitutional law differs from other branches of the law in that some knowledge of it, perhaps distilled by some lay writer like John Locke or Walter Bagehot, has always been common among educated men. In the process of distillation the technical detail is eliminated, and what is left is the collection of general ideas which may perhaps be called the contemporary political philosophy. In the Middle Ages these general ideas came mainly from the canon law, the more general parts of the civil law, and the Latin versions of Aristotle. The canon law ceased to be taught in the universities after the Reformation, but its political assumptions continued to be argued about as theology. The teaching of civil law continued, and indeed Henry VIII founded the Regius Chairs of Civil Law in order to perpetuate it. As late as 1944 it was claimed by a learned civilian that it was part of a liberal education to know something about Roman law.[1] The claim was, however, more than a century out of time. From the second half of the sixteenth century the civil law was studied mainly for professional purposes, to enable graduates to join what a Master of Trinity Hall called in 1740 'that honourable and useful profession of civilians, the advocates of Doctors' Commons, a College of gentlemen regularly bred, too little esteemed, and too industriously depressed'.[2] The civil law has been outside the main stream of education for more than a century.

The vaguer ideas which came through the study of theology, philosophy and classical literature were more important. Until late in the fifteenth century the colleges of Oxford and Cambridge were occupied mainly by fellows and scholars, most of whom expected to take holy orders. With the settled conditions and the rising prosperity created by the Tudors it became fashionable for young men of good

[1] R. W. Lee, *Elements of Roman Law*, p. iv.
[2] Sir Nathanael Lloyd, King's Advocate, quoted in A. W. W. Dale, *Warren's Book*, p. 321.

21

family to go to the universities to acquire at least a veneer of culture, and they became pensioners at Cambridge or commoners at Oxford.[1] Few of them could read Greek until the seventeenth century: Sir Edward Coke, for instance, quoted Aristotle from Latin texts. But the theory of the law of nature which the Greeks had initiated and the Romans developed (and, by Justinian's time, nicely confused) had been worked out by theologians and canonists in the Middle Ages[2] and had become part of the inheritance of the educated class. It was, for example, quoted on both sides in the *Case of Shipmoney*. The idea of an all-pervading law, founded on reason, ordained by God, and binding on princes as well as on their subjects, was an important influence in the process of subordinating the Stuarts to the law of England.

It is probable, however, that the universities had less influence on the British Constitution than the inns of court. The inns had from the fourteenth century been collegiate bodies much like the colleges of Oxford and Cambridge. They provided excellent training in the law by way of lectures and moots, but residence was necessary and care was taken over the religion, morals and social training of the students.[3] In the sixteenth century the sons of the nobility and gentry, most of whom did not intend to practise at the Bar but merely wanted education for the unpaid magistracy, flocked to the Inns.[4] This educational system reached its fullest development in the first half of the sixteenth century and was still in existence at the outbreak of the Civil War, though it was already in decline.[5] Nevertheless, of the members of the Long Parliament who sat before the outbreak of civil war, 310 had been to one of the inns of court, whereas only 169 had been to Oxford and 111 to Cambridge.[6] It is perhaps significant that only 120 of the 310 became Royalists. Whatever the quality of the education given, it is plain that the inns of court were important disseminators of ideas in the first half of the seventeenth century.

[1] The first Cambridge college to mention pensioners in its statutes was Christ's (founded under that name in 1505): but older colleges already had pensioners.

[2] A. J. Carlyle, *Mediaeval Political Theory in the West*, I, pp. 102–10; II, pp. 5–33, 50–5, 96–116.

[3] Holdsworth, *History of English Law*, II, pp. 509–12.

[4] *Ibid.* IV, p. 267.   [5] *Ibid.* VI, p. 481.

[6] D. Brunton and D. H. Pennington, *Members of the Long Parliament*, pp. 6–7. About half of those who had been to a university or an Inn had been to both.

The main reason for the decline of the inns as educational establishments[1] is, however, itself significant. To learn the common law before printed books became available it was necessary to attend the lectures delivered by the readers and to listen to argument in Westminster Hall. Many of the old law books were printed in the middle of the sixteenth century, and nearly all the great classics had been printed by 1640.[2] The earliest collection of Acts of Parliament was published in 1482 or 1483, and the first complete edition of the statutes was published in English in 1543.[3] Some of the Year Books, which contained notes of the arguments and judgments in the courts at Westminster Hall, were published in 1482,[4] and the 'nominate' law reports began with Plowden's in 1571.[5] Above all, there was a great output of new legal and historical writing, the catalogue including some of the greatest names in English law, William Lambard, John Selden, Francis Bacon and Edward Coke.

Those were days in which it was possible for a lawyer like Francis Bacon to take all knowledge to be his province, and even lesser lawyers like Sir Robert Filmer could be well read in a sense which is no longer possible. That a knowledge of the law was widespread is shown by the works of William Shakespeare, which indicate not only that, even if they were not written by a trained lawyer, at least the author knew a great deal of law,[6] but also that his audience could take a legal point without having it explained in words of one syllable. The constitutional controversies of the early Stuarts were inevitably matters of public concern; and the fact that there had been such an output of legal literature, old and new, under Elizabeth I made it possible for the discussion to be founded on genuine learning. Indeed, the constitutional debates in the Parliaments of James I and Charles I were usually not about what the law ought to be, but about what the law was. The first great political dispute of modern English history, the dispute over prerogative, was in the beginning a lawyers' dispute.

[1] Holdsworth, *op. cit.* VI, pp. 482–4. [2] *Ibid.* V, pp. 378–9.
[3] *Ibid.* IV, p. 308.
[4] *Ibid.* II, p. 528.
[5] *Ibid.* V, p. 458. 'Nominate' reports, unlike the Year Books, were published under the editor's name.
[6] G. W. Keeton, *Shakespeare and his Legal Problems.*

2. PREROGATIVE

The greater part of English law arose out of the fusion of English customs with feudal ideas and institutions, especially in the first century after the Norman Conquest. The law has always given the Sovereign something of the character of a feudal monarch. He was an 'absolute monarch' in the sense of our law books: that is, except when John or Henry III did homage to the Pope, and except in relation to the King's French dominions, he had no feudal superior as, for instance, the Duke of Normandy had. The word 'absolute' did not involve unlimited power, whether it was used of the King or of the High Court of Parliament. The King was absolute because he had no superior to whom he owed suit of court; the High Court of Parliament was absolute because its decisions were not subject to appeal or to challenge by writ of error.[1]

The King could not be absolute in any other sense so long as feudal ideas were dominant. The obligations of king and vassal or, to use the formula more common in England, the obligations of king and tenant-in-chief, were mutual. The tenant had rights against his lord, the King, and duties towards his own tenants. The King was therefore subject

---

[1] Cf. L. Alston, in Sir Thomas Smith, *De Republica Anglorum* (1906 ed.), pp. xxix–xxxiv; C. H. McIlwain, *Growth of Political Thought in the West*, pp. 365–83. Sir William Holdsworth (*History of English Law*, IV, p. 206), said that the term 'absolute' meant 'an authority the exercise of which cannot be called in question by any legal process': but 'legal process' is, in this context, anachronistic. The King was an 'absolute King' because he had not to do homage or suit of court; and that is what Coke meant when he said in *Caudrey's Case* (1591), 5 Co. Rep. (Part 1), 1 a at 40 b, that 'the kingdom of England is an absolute monarchy, as well over ecclesiastical persons, and in ecclesiastical causes, as temporal, within this realm, to the due observation of which laws both the King and the subject are sworn'. See also *Darnel's Case* (1627), 2 St. Tr. 1 at 37, where Heath, A. G., arguing for the Crown, said: 'The King cannot command your lordship, or any other court of justice, to proceed otherwise than according to the laws of this kingdom; for it is part of your lordship's oath, to judge according to the law of the kingdom. But, my lord, there is a great difference between these legal commands, and that *absoluta potestas* that a sovereign hath, by which a king commands; but when I call it *absoluta potestas*, I do not mean that it is such a power as that a King may do what he pleaseth, for he hath rules to govern himself by, as well as your lordships, who are subordinate judges under him.' He went on to say, 'shall not we generally, not as subjects only, but as lawyers, who govern themselves by the rules of the law, submit to his commands, *but make inquiries whether they be lawful*, and say that the King doth not this or that in course of justice' (italics present author's).

24

to law, as Bracton said: *Lex non debet esse sub homine, sed sub Deo et lege.* That did not mean what Coke thought it meant, that the King was under the common law: it meant that he was subject to the customary law of England, which accorded rights to everybody, from the King to the meanest villein, and imposed corresponding duties on everybody, from the meanest villein to the King. There was even a 'sanction' if the King broke faith with his tenant-in-chief, a *diffidatio* or 'defiance' (the word has since changed its meaning) whereby the vassal denounced his allegiance, was no longer bound to render the customary services, and could even wage war against the King. We must also remember that Glanville had given what was in form, at least, the exact opposite of Bracton's assertion. He quoted Justinian's Institutes, *quod principi placuit legis habet vigorem.* These phrases gave trouble when Glanville and Bracton were printed in the Tudor reigns and learned lawyers began to interpret them according to ideas which were four centuries distant from Angevin feudalism.

It is a pleasing paradox that what pleased the King is best illustrated by Magna Carta. The assembly of the clergy and the barons at Runnymede in 1215 was in substance (though not in law) a feudal court, an unusually large one because so many people had grievances against the King. He had broken the law as clergy, barons, merchants and common people understood it: and, as Bracton said forty years later, the King was subject to the law. But the King with the assent of the barons and others present could, to use a modern term which is nevertheless appropriate, settle the law. For instance: 'No scutage nor aid shall be imposed in our kingdom, unless by common counsel of our kingdom, except for ransoming our person, for making our eldest son a knight, and for once marrying our eldest daughter; and for these there shall not be levied more than a reasonable aid'.[1] Other ages might claim that this meant no shipmoney except by Act of Parliament,[2] or even no taxation without representation. To the barons it had a precise feudal meaning.

More often, however, the decisions of the King in his court dealt

---

[1] W. S. McKechnie, *Magna Carta*, p. 274.
[2] Oliver St John *arguendo* in *Case of Shipmoney* (1637), 3 St. Tr. 825 at 896: he translated '*auxilium*' as 'supply'.

not with the rights of the members of a class but with individual rights.[1] The distinction between the legislative, the executive and the judicial functions had not been drawn. If it could have been explained it would not have been understood. What the King did was to take a decision in council and, if necessary, to give effect to it. There were, of course, many innovations, particularly under Henry II and Edward I.

Those who advised Henry II, among whom was Glanville, knew some canon law and some civil law. Even so, Henry's reforms depended on power and persuasion, not on a theory of monarchy. Many of his reforms were approved in Magna Carta and not many were disapproved. Neither John nor Henry III had as wide a power as Henry II, and Bracton wrote under Henry III. Edward I had: indeed he was so powerful that he could follow a precedent set by Simon de Montfort and require the counties, cities and boroughs to send representatives to Westminster to tell him what was going on in their communities, to consent to the levy on their communities of 'extraordinary aids' which were not the customary aids of feudal law, and to receive the King's commands as to how their communities should behave. One of the advantages of this system of afforcing the King's court by the 'commons' was that petitions (bills) could more easily be presented to him and he could give decisions (acts) on them. He had no intention of setting up a legislature called the King in Parliament, or even a new court called the High Court of Parliament. As Fleta (who wrote under Edward I) put it: the King holds his court in his council in his parliaments.[2] It was his court, but a particularly numerous assembly might be summoned in order to have general discussions (in French, *parlements*). All the seeds of the King in Parliament are here, but they grow as slowly as the giant oaks; and even for Coke more than three hundred years later Parliament is still the High Court of Parliament, whose power is 'absolute' because it has no superior—though it is equally permissible to say that the King is 'absolute' because he, too, has no superior.

We have, then, a customary law which is settled in the King's court in so far as it is within the King's jurisdiction. It was, however, also

[1] F. M. Stenton, *The First Century of English Feudalism*, p. 36.
[2] Pollard, *Evolution of Parliament*, p. 24.

settled in the lords' courts—the future courts baron and customary courts—in so far as the lords had jurisdiction. Henry II was careful not to interfere with the lords' jurisdiction, and Magna Carta provided that 'the writ which is called *praecipe* shall not for the future be issued to anyone, concerning any tenement whereby a freeman may lose his court'.[1] The writ called *praecipe* was a royal order to a royal officer which had the effect of bringing a dispute within royal jurisdiction and therefore (where it was a claim to hold of a mesne lord) deprived the lord of his jurisdiction. As it happened, other means were found for bringing suits relating to land within royal jurisdiction, and so the prohibition was, in substance, nugatory. The point is, however, that customary law was not exclusively a matter for the King's court. On the other hand the customary courts of the Anglo-Saxons, the county courts and the hundred courts, except where they had become 'franchises' or liberties of mesne lords, were under royal control through the sheriffs of counties and the bailiffs of towns within the royal demesne.

What complicated the matter, especially when studied by lawyers like Coke centuries later, was that new subordinate courts were established to exercise royal jurisdiction. Their jurisdiction was based on writs issued from the Chancery and was therefore limited. It did not extend to matters ecclesiastical, which included wills and intestacies of personalty, nor to matters covered by maritime law or the law merchant. Nor did it cover matters within the equitable jurisdiction of the Chancery. By means of procedural devices, much of the jurisdiction of the three courts of Common Pleas, Exchequer and King's Bench became common; and the law developed by them became the common law. But even in Coke's day it was far from true that the common law made up the whole of English law. Coke as Chief Justice of the King's Bench did a good deal of empire-building by means of writs of prohibition: but the supervising authority was not the Court of King's Bench but the King in Council.

Nor had the common-law courts supervision over the King's rights, or prerogatives. It was, of course, part of their duty to enforce his prerogative at his request: that was the essential function of the Court

[1] W. S. McKechnie, *Magna Carta*, p. 405.

27

of Exchequer, and both the *Case of Impositions* (Bates' Case)[1] and the *Case of Shipmoney* (Hampden's Case)[2] were proceedings instituted in that court on behalf of the King. Proceedings could not be brought against the King because these were inferior courts taking jurisdiction by reason of the King's writ, and no theory had yet developed by which the King could issue a writ to himself. Pollock and Maitland agreed with Francis Bacon that the story that there had been a writ beginning *praecipe Henrico Regi Angliae* was an old fable.[3] With the customary exaggeration of monarchical attributes, the King's immunity from suit or prosecution in his own common-law courts was put in the form 'The King can do no wrong': but the King could do wrong, and the way to draw attention to it was to bring a complaint by petition to the Curia Regis, the Council, or the High Court of Parliament.

The factors which brought the royal prerogative into the political arena in the reigns of the Stuarts were many. First, however, it should again be emphasised that initially it was a lawyers' dispute, a dispute about what rights the King had, not about what rights he ought to have in a well-conducted seventeenth-century monarchy. The point may be best put by quoting the preface, published in 1641, to the text of William Hakewill's speech on Impositions delivered in the House of Commons in 1610:[4]

The endeavour of it is to prove that the just Prerogative of our Kings never warranted them to raise monies at their pleasure, by laying a charge on merchandize to bee exported or imported, without assent of Parliament. But, on the contrary, the settled lawes of the land, the presidents of former ages, the acts of our most necessitous and powerfull Princes, and indeed every thing requisite to make the truth apparent, do as it were unanimously consent to discharge us of this unjust and heavy burthen.

Only in the Long Parliament did the lawyers give place to the politicians, and the change occurred because the Long Parliament set out on a course which was not according to precedent.

---

[1] (1605) 2 St. Tr. 371. [2] (1637) 3 St. Tr.
[3] Pollock and Maitland, *History of English Law*, I, p. 517.
[4] *The Liberties of the Subject against the Pretended Power of Imposition* (1641), p. 2; the speech is also in 2 St. Tr. 407.

28

The emphasis upon precedent is in part a consequence of the training which so many active politicians had received in the inns of court. It is, however, also a relic of customary law. If a person's rights and duties depend upon customary law, he must be able to cite a precedent for any action which he proposes to take, to show that a claim of right has been made in the past and, as far as records show, was not contested. The Curia Regis, in which the King's rights as well as other rights were settled, had become the High Court of Parliament, and it was so treated both by Sir Thomas Smith, writing in the reign of Elizabeth I, and by Sir Edward Coke, writing in the reign of James I. It was a court giving judgment, as Sir Thomas Smith put it,[1] 'betweene private man and private man, or betweene the prince and any private man, be it in matters criminall or civill, for land or for heritage', but by Bill read thrice in each House and assented to. But Smith adds that 'that great counsell being enough occupyed with the publique affaires of the realme, will not gladly intermeddle it selfe with private quarels and questions'. What it generally did is thus described by Smith:[2]

The Parliament abrogates olde lawes, maketh newe, giveth orders for thinges past, and for all thinges hereafter to be followed, changeth rightes, and possessions of private men, legittimateth bastards, establisheth formes of religion, altereth weightes and measures, giveth formes of succession to the Crowne, defineth of doubtful rightes, whereof is no law alreadie made, appointeth subsidies, tailes, taxes, and impositions, giveth most free pardons and absolutions, restoreth in bloud and name as the highest court, condemneth or absolveth them whom the Prince will put to that triall.

Whether Parliament acted, to use our more precise language, as court or as legislature there was a record of its decision. So, too, there were records of all the other courts, the Council, the Star Chamber, the King's Bench, the Exchequer, the Common Bench, the Chancery, and so forth. Nor were all the records those of 'judicial' decisions. The record of a writ was as good to found a claim of right as the record of a decree, provided that it had not been contested—in which case there ought to be a record of a decree. Nor was a record essential. It was the best evidence of a claim of right, and hence of customary or

---

[1] *De Republica Anglorum*, Lib. 2, ch. 6.
[2] *Ibid*. Lib. 2, ch. 1.

common law, but neither Coke nor any other lawyer or judge neglected to call upon history to supply precedents, whether they were matters of record or not. It is necessary to emphasise these points because the practice of law reporting has given rise to the view among common lawyers (but not necessarily among constitutional lawyers) that a valid precedent is a note of a judicial decision, taken by a barrister in open Court. The earliest 'law reports', the Year Books which began in Edward I's reign and ended in Henry VIII's reign were, strictly speaking, not precedents at all, but notes of the arguments used by counsel and the observations of the judges. The precedents which Bracton had used in the thirteenth century were taken from the records. The precedents which Coke preferred nearly three centuries later were matters of record,[1] though this preference did not prevent him from quoting many other sources, including the Bible, the classical authors and the reporters. The development of law reports into works of authority, 'binding precedents', did not occur until the late eighteenth or early nineteenth century.[2]

The reason for the development was that the record was conclusive only as to what it said. If the record (e.g. an Act of Parliament) said that no tenant for life of land should commit waste it was binding on all tenants for life. But if the record said that John Doe was seised of Blackacre it did not necessarily imply that Richard Roe was seised of Whiteacre. John Doe's case was a precedent for Richard Roe only if Richard Roe's case was similar: and 'similar' meant not that all the

---

[1] In Co. Litt. 260*b*, after saying that records are the rolls of Parliament and of the proceedings and acts of courts of justice, Coke adds: 'The rolles being the records or memorialls of the judges of the courts of record, import in them such incontrollable credit and veritie, as they admit no averment, plea or proofe to the contrarie....' See also Co. Litt. 117*b* and 3 Inst. 71. In 4 Inst. 4 Coke praises the records of Parliament because there is set down 'not only the judgment, or resolution, but the reasons, and causes of the same by so great advice'. He adds that under Edward I & II this was also done in the courts, and then there was no need of law reports: but since it was not done from Edward III 'certain grave and sad men' published reports. But these 'though of great credit, and excellent use in their kind, yet far underneath the authority of the parliament rols, reporting the acts, judgements and resolutions of that highest court'. See also Coke's adverse criticism on a report of a case when the reporter had not seen the record: 4 Inst. 17.

[2] Sir Carleton Allen, *Law in the Making* (6th ed.), pp. 183–250, though it seems to me that the learned author does not sufficiently emphasise the distinction between the record and the report.

facts were the same but, as we should put it, that the relevant facts were the same. This was, however, to imply a rule of law, what the common lawyers call a 'principle', by which certain of the facts in John Doe's case were excluded as irrelevant. This could not be done simply by looking at the record in John Doe's case: it was necessary to know why John Doe's case was so decided, and so it was important to have not merely the decree on the record but also the argument or opinion of the court which led to that decree.

The fact that common law was founded on customary law and therefore on precedents thus gave every constitutional dispute an appearance of legalism. It was, however, far from true that the law was inferred inductively from the decided cases. Learned judges and counsel would have a series of propositions in their memories and could on occasion quote arguments or decisions in preceding cases. Those propositions were, however, based not merely on legal learning but also on experience and reason. This would perhaps have been so if Rome had never been built. It did not require a *jus naturale* to distinguish commonable beasts from beasts not commonable, because every countryman knew which beasts manured the soil and which fouled it. The assumption of a natural law, derived via the canonists and the civilians from the Roman law was, however, an important factor in the development of law.

'The law of nature,' said Coke,[1]

is that which God at the time of his creation of the nature of man infused into his heart, for his preservation and direction: and this is *lex aeterna*, the moral law, called also the law of nature. And by this law, written with the finger of God in the heart of man, were the people of God a long time governed, before the law was written by Moses, who was the first reporter or writer of law in the world. The Apostle in the Second Chapter to the Romans saith, *Cum enim gentes quae legum non habent naturaliter ea quae legissunt faciunt.*[2]...And Aristotle, Nature's Secretary, lib. 5. Aethic. saith, that *jus naturale est, quod apud omnes homines eandem habet potentiam.*[3] And herewith doth agree Bracton, lib. 1, cap. 5. and Fortescue, cap. 8. 12. 13. and

---

[1] *Calvin's Case*, 7 Co. Rep. 1a, 12a.

[2] [Rom. ii. 14: 'For when the Gentiles, which have not the law, do by nature the things contained in the law, these, having not the law, are a law unto themselves.']

[3] *Ethics*, 5, VII, 1. See D. P. Chase's translation (Everyman, Dent), at p. 117, where it is said that the Social Just is natural or conventional, the natural Just being 'that which has everywhere the same force and does not depend on being received or not'.

16. Doctor and Student, cap. 2 and 4.[1] And the reason hereof is, for that God and nature is one to all, and therefore the law of God and nature is one to all.

To the modern lawyer this is a magnificent farrago: but Coke never wrote nonsense. Natural law, as he and his contemporaries understood it, was part of the law of England: and if his citations strike us as a little forced, in that they make Aristotle and St Paul agree with Ulpian, we must remember the weight of tradition which the Roman Church had bequeathed to the Church of England and above all remember that lawyers read Latin but not Greek: for both reasons even the common lawyers thought like civilians and in civilian terms.

Examples of this combination of precedent and natural law or right reason are scattered throughout the great constitutional cases, but it will be enough to quote from the argument of Sir Edward Little-ton, S.G., in the *Case of Shipmoney*:[2]

The method whereby I may maintain the right of my Master, and the Crown, is this: I shall first ground it upon reason; every human proposition is of equal authority, only reason makes the difference.—I shall ground my reasons, *First*, upon the law of nature; *Secondly*, of State; and *Thirdly*, of Public safety, necessity and conveniency. Neither shall it be against the statute law, common law, or any of the hereditary rights and liberties of the subjects of England, but consonant to, and warranted by all. I shall not only prove it *ex rationibus cogentibus*, or as lawyers say, *ex visceribus causae*, but *de similibus ad similia*. I shall confirm it by a beadroll of examples and precedents of former ages, and compare them with this, and see if the case be altered.

These 'examples and precedents' were not necessarily judicial decisions. They included examples in which subjects had been required, at their own charge, to guard the sea and the land: 'I conceive that though I find not direct authority in printed books, yet records are as good testimonies, and greater than reports, that are but extracts, and second authorities drawn out of them.'[3]

These quotations are from the case for the Crown; but the case for Hampden was similarly compounded. What we have, in fact, is a common law which regulates every person and authority from the

[1] [Justinian's Inst. lib. 1, cap. 2, is given as a marginal reference.]
[2] (1637) 3 St. Tr. 825 at 925.   [3] *Ibid.* at 930.

32

King and the High Court of Parliament to the court leet and the village copyholder. It is founded upon precedents, especially the records of Parliament and the King's courts, but it is essentially rational. When James I pointed out that he and others, as well as the judges, had reason, Coke replied that causes which concerned the life, or inheritance, or goods, or fortunes of his subjects, were 'not to be decided by natural reason but by the artificial reason and judgment of law, which law is an act which requires long study and experience, before that a man can attain to the cognizance of it...'.[1] What that meant was clear from the case itself. The King cannot arrest any man, as the book says in 1 Hen. 7, because the party cannot have remedy against the King; similarly, if the King give judgment, what remedy can the party have? In other words, our books say that there cannot be a remedy against the King, but every man ought to have a remedy for a wrong; therefore the King can neither arrest nor give judgment, because if he did there would be no remedy. Here we have what may be called a principle of natural law, *ubi jus ibi remedium*, and perhaps a second principle of natural law, that the King can do no wrong. Our books therefore say that the King cannot arrest; and we, the judges, conclude that he cannot give judgment either. It is all very rational, but within a framework of law illustrated by precedents.

This extension of the common law into the field of public law was new in legal history. It was made possible by the publication of the ancient law books and their misinterpretation by lawyers on both sides. For Coke and the parliamentary lawyers, Parliament was a High Court established by the Anglo-Saxon kings under the name of Witanagemot or *conventus sapientum* and continued by the Normans under different names.[2] The Great Charter of 1225 was an Act of Parliament which was 'for the most part declaratory of the principall grounds of the fundamentall laws of England, and for the residue it is additionall to supply some defects of the common law...'.[3] Oliver St John, arguing for Hampden, was prepared to assert that even the Magna Carta of 1215 was an Act of Parliament.[4] The records of Parliament, or of anything

---

[1] *Prohibitions del Roy* (1607), 12 Co. Rep. 63 at p. 65.
[2] 1 Inst. 164; 4 Inst. 2.   [3] 2 Inst. Proeme.
[4] *Case of Shipmoney* (1637), 3 St. Tr. 825 at 896, quoted *ante* p. 25.

that could be alleged to be a Parliament, were of the highest possible authority. The common law, too, was not an invention of the thirteenth and fourteenth centuries, but had existed from time immemorial, though unfortunately 'the books and treatises of the common laws in [the Anglo-Saxon] and other kings times, and specially in the times of the ancient Brittons (an inestimable loss) are not to be found'.[1] It follows that any reference to *lex* in Glanville or Bracton must be a reference to a common or statute law. Similarly, taxes might be covered by different names, such as scutages, aids, tallages and the rest. Oliver St John could argue that levying of shipmoney was forbidden by Magna Carta (1215), Article 14, because 'scutage or aid' was supply for defence and 'common counsel' meant Parliament.[2] The alleged statute *De Tallagio non concedendo* (it was actually a draft which somehow got enrolled) was held by several judges in the *Case of Shipmoney* to be a statute; and in forbidding tallages it forbade shipmoney, or so it was alleged.

Even so the Parliamentary lawyers must have found difficulties in their records. The Crown lawyers could have defeated them by the same sort of historical precedents, which could have shown them that there was no Parliament before Edward I; that kings had 'legislated' before there were Parliaments and continued to do so afterwards; that the King, though subject to feudal law, was not subject to common law, because no writ ran against him; that the common law courts, like all subordinate authorities, were subject to the control of the King in his councils as well as of the King in his Parliaments, and indeed that Parliaments were merely afforced councils; that kings had been used to suspend and dispense with laws, issue charters *non obstante* Acts of Parliament, and grant pardons for breaches of the law; and, in short, that the statute law and the common law came from the royal prerogative, not the royal prerogative from the common law.

This line of defence was not seriously developed. The Tudor lawyers had been most assiduous in the collection of precedents, and Stuart lawyers like William Prynne emulated them. But our great lawyers were not good historians, and they interpreted the ancient

---

[1] 2 Inst. Proeme. Coke, as a good Cambridge man, put in a special mention for King Alfred who, on the persuasion of a couple of learned monks, 'founded the famous university of Cambridge'. [2] *Loc. cit.*

34

records much as we modern lawyers tend to misinterpret the Stuart decisions, by reference to contemporary ideas. Also it was essential to a historical interpretation to recognise that the whole concept of kingship in English law, the greater part of the land law, the typically 'English' ideas of the inquest and the jury, and much else in the common law, were Norman importations. Such a recognition would have led to the French and Scots historians of feudal law. The common lawyers were, however, insular people, bred for the most part in inns of court where the rest of the world was virtually ignored. There was, too, a strong national prejudice against the Norman Conquest, as Coke shows in some of his asides. The Parliamentary lawyers honestly believed that English institutions came from the Anglo-Saxons if not from the ancient Britons, but they also wanted to believe it. They could and did read Latin, but they preferred Aristotle (in Latin), the Bible (in Latin), the classical writers of Rome, and the *Corpus Juris Civilis* to the work of the more modern civilians. They read the *Grand Custumier* of Normandy—or at least Coke did— but only to find out laws and institutions which were, as they thought, common to the Normans and the Anglo-Saxons. There was a strong xenophobic tradition derived from the anti-clerical movement under the early Tudors, the corruption of the Church of Rome, the persecu- tions under Mary, the Spanish Armada, the popular nationalism of William Shakespeare, and the Gunpowder Plot. It had its influence on the interpretation of English law as it had on English Protestantism.[1]

The civilians were less insular, and Cowell quoted from contemporary writers on feudalism: but he, too, had studied the common law and accepted much of the common law tradition.[2] It seems, indeed, that the historical interpretation was making some way under James I and Charles I. The man who brought it into English history, Sir Henry Spelman, published only part of his *Archaeologus* before the Civil War and it went only up to the letter L, so that it did not include the article on *Parliamentum*. Spelman read at Lincoln's Inn but left at the age of 20 and became not a lawyer but a historian.[3] His work had influence after the Restoration and was completed—if historical analysis ever is

[1] Chapter III.
[2] J. G. A. Pocock, *The Ancient Constitution and the Feudal Law*, pp. 91–2.
[3] *Ibid.* pp. 93–4.

3-2

complete—not by a lawyer but by a Cambridge Professor of Physic, who was appropriately enough Master of Gonville and Caius College, Dr Robert Brady.[1] Before the Civil War, however, the lawyers' interpretation of history reigned supreme.

The Royalists—if we may so term them before the great division of 1642 had been brought about—used not history but canon law. We must not say too much about 'divine right', because every person had a rank or station to which God had been pleased to call him,[2] and the question at issue was what power God had been pleased to attribute to the office of King. That there was by divine authority some law above an Act of Parliament was obvious enough, not only because the Mosaic law and the Gospels were above secular law, but also because James VI of Scotland had become James I of England non obstante the Act of 1543. That Act had declared that, in the event of the deaths of Edward, Mary and Elizabeth, the children of Henry VIII, the Crown should descend to the person selected by that King by his letters patent or will. Henry VIII's will had in fact designated his younger sister Mary, Duchess of Suffolk, who had issue surviving in 1603. Nevertheless, James VI of Scotland, who was descended from Henry VIII's elder sister Margaret, was selected by Elizabeth I shortly before her death and succeeded without opposition. The first Parliament of James I, in its first Act, recognised the validity of his succession 'by inherent birthright and lawful and undoubted succession'.[3] The situation was capable of interpretation in several different ways. The only question raised immediately was whether James I was 'complete and absolute king' before his coronation, and the judges ruled that he was.[4] But the general trend of the argument in Calvin's Case was that James I had succeeded under fundamental law, by inherent right, and that forthwith every person born in England, as well as every person born in Scotland, owed him personal allegiance. It was on the basis of this fundamental law, this law of reason, that Francis Bacon argued for Calvin:[5] but what was argued for Calvin might also be argued for

[1] Pocock, op. cit. pp. 193–4.
[2] Hence a de facto king could be said to rule by 'divine right': cf. J. N. Figgis, Divine Right of Kings (2nd ed.), p. 139.
[3] G. W. Prothero, Select Statutes and Other Constitutional Documents, p. 251.
[4] 3 Inst. 7 and Calvin's Case (1609), 7 Co. Rep. 1a, at 10a.   [5] 2 St. Tr. 559 at 578.

King James, with this difference, that whereas the law of reason and the common law were alleged to be consistent in the case of Calvin, the fundamental law by which James I succeeded was contrary to an Act of Parliament. Indeed, though Bacon did not specifically mention that Act, he went far towards asserting that the King's succession, like the subject's allegiance and the child's obedience, came from nature and not from the law, that is, it came from the law above the law:[1] though he also quoted the phrase of a judge then present, in a previous case, 'that he would never allow that Queen Elizabeth...should be a statute queen, but a common law queen'.[2] That complicated the argument, though in such a manner as to appeal to Coke, C.J., and Bacon put himself logically in order by adding, 'as the common law is more worthy than the statute law, so the law of nature is more worthy than them both'.

This neat little sentence put into a nutshell the broader issue between Bacon and Coke. Whatever the common lawyers proved from their records to have been accepted as common law or customary law, the King had prerogative, regality, *majestas*, sovereignty,[3] power and authority by the law of nature which, of course, came from God. This did not mean that the property and other rights of the King could not be settled or regulated by common or statute law: it meant only that neither the Crown itself nor the inherent attributes of monarchy or sovereignty could be taken away by common or statute law. Finch, C.J., put the point admirably in his judgment in the *Case of Shipmoney*:

Acts of parliament may take away flowers and ornaments of the Crown, but not the Crown itself; they cannot bar a succession, nor can they be attainted by them, and acts that bar them of possession are void. No act of parliament can bar a king of his regality, as that no lands should hold of him; or bar him of the allegiance of his subjects; or the relative on his part, as trust and power to defend his people; therefore acts of parliament to take away his royal power in the defence of the kingdom are void (as my Lord Chief

[1] *Ibid.* at 580.
[2] *Ibid.* at 581.
[3] Another word which must not be misunderstood. When English lawyers spoke of 'sovereignty' they meant not supreme power but the power and authority of the Sovereign, that is, the King.

Baron said);[1] they are void acts of parliament, to bind the king not to defend the subjects, their persons and goods, and I say their money, too: for no acts of parliament make any difference.[2]

This made the issue one of principle, and of a very simple principle which every educated person could understand. It needed no burrowing into records. *Jus naturale* was in the Latin versions of Aristotle; *salus populi suprema lex* came from Cicero;[3] kings were instituted by God, as the Old Testament made plain; and Jesus Christ told all Christians to render unto Caesar the things that were Caesar's. Being an issue of elementary principle, too, it was easily emotionalised. Royalty was already something in a story book. Henry VIII's pomp and bonhomie, coming in a period of prosperity, had made the monarchy popular; and the popularity that it lost under Edward VI and Mary I was more than regained under Good Queen Bess. James I could hardly be described as lovable and Charles I was a shifty sort of person. But the popularity of monarchs depends less on their characters than on their 'public faces'. Before the days of the photograph they were little more than abstractions, though those who saw the portraits of King Charles would think him a fine figure of a man. There was in any case a vast emotional content in loyalty to the Crown. Shakespeare had played on it and, in playing so finely, had enhanced it. There was deep Royalist sentiment before King Charles made his reputation safe by being executed. Most of those who fought for him were fighting not for Charles Stuart but for King Charles.

There was, however, sentiment on the other side. The curious connexion between nationalism and fictitious history put nationalism on the side of the common law and Parliament.[4] The common law and

---

[1] Davenport, L.C.B., gave judgment for Hampden, 3 St. Tr. 825 at 1202, because the county could not provide a ship and the sheriff was required to levy a tax, which was unlawful; also, the writ did not aver sufficient cause. But he admitted that an Act of Parliament which prevented the King from defending the country in time of danger (e.g. the Spanish Armada) would be '*felo de se* and void'.

[2] (1637) 3 St. Tr. 825 at 1235.

[3] Though Francis Bacon thought it came from the XII Tables: *Of Judicature* (*Essays*, E. H. Blakeney's ed. p. 223). The reference is to *De Legibus*, III, 3: see G. W. Prothero, *Select Statutes*, p. 408.

[4] Theoretically the common law and Parliament were in conflict; but the question whether the common law was a fundamental law which controlled statute law, though

38

Parliament were Anglo-Saxon institutions, if not ancient British. The notions which James I published (before he became King of England) in the *True Law of Free Monarchies* were alien importations. The early Stuarts were Scots and their wives were Roman Catholics; and Roman Catholicism was not merely, in the eyes of Stuart Protestants, perverted Christianity; it was also, for those who remembered the Spanish Armada, alien and hostile.

Religion was, however, a source of emotion in itself, as we shall see in the next chapter. It is difficult for us to realise the detestation in which the doctrines, and especially the politics, of the Church of Rome were held at the beginning of the seventeenth century and the fear which the Counter-Reformation inspired. It is perhaps best illustrated in the debate in *Floyd's Case* in 1621.[1] Edward Floyd was a Roman Catholic who had made slighting remarks about the Princess Elizabeth (Stuart) and her husband, the Calvinist Elector Palatine. The House of Commons assumed a jurisdiction which Coke, who was a member, would have found hard to justify from his precedents. Members vied with each other in the savagery of the sentences which they proposed for him; and the severe and unlawful punishment decreed by the Commons was increased by the Lords.[2] In this case there was no controversy with King James, but in the next reign there was strong suspicion that the King, under the influence of his papist wife, intended to restore the old religion. Religion was not the cause of the Civil War, but the hatred of popery was a material factor in cementing opposition to Charles I.

James I helped to build up a Parliamentary opposition by the stupid sermons which he read to the House of Commons about the privileges of that House and of its members. Linguistic conventions change imperceptibly, and those used by and to royalty are always a little peculiar. It is, however, difficult to read the petitions from the Commons as anything worse than courteous and loyal but firm, whereas the King's speeches and replies denote an arrogance of mind which an

argued (*ante*, p. 37), never came to issue in any case of political importance: cf. J. W. Gough, *Fundamental Law in English History*.

[1] Notestein, Relf and Simpson, *Commons Debates, 1621*, III, pp. 123–6; C. H. McIlwain, *Constitutionalism and the Changing World*, pp. 187–90.

[2] J. R. Tanner, *English Constitutional Conflicts of the Seventeenth Century*, p. 48.

assembly of country gentlemen must have found galling. There were frequent meetings of Parliament between 1621 and 1629, and many members were re-elected in successive Parliaments. A common tradition of opposition, especially to the constant demands for money followed by exactions of uncertain legality or even of certain illegality, led to a 'public opinion' among the country gentlemen antagonistic to the Court, but by no means antagonistic to monarchy as such. The cessation of Parliaments after March 1629, and the extension of illegal taxation from indirect taxes to direct taxes, seem to have made that opinion almost unanimous, at least in the south and east. John Hampden thus became a popular hero when he refused to pay shipmoney, and many others did the like. The Parliaments of 1640 did not intend civil war, but they did intend to cut down the King's powers. Given the assumptions on which the Crown lawyers worked, even when they were not so extreme as Finch, C.J., it was not enough to pass Acts of Parliament, for they might be declared invalid. Nor indeed was it at all certain, even after the execution of the Earl of Strafford, the imprisonment of Archbishop Laud, and the flight of Secretary Windebank and Lord Keeper Finch, that the law would be observed. There was an English army in the north and an Irish army oversea.

It was, however, accepted law at the Restoration in 1660 that the Acts of the Long Parliament which had received the assent of Charles I were valid, though they had seriously restricted the royal prerogative. They had, *inter alia*, abolished the power of the King to do without a parliament for more than three years; legalised impositions levied in the past but forbidden them for the future; abolished the power of the Council to give judgment in any civil or criminal case and abolished the prerogative jurisdiction of the Court of Star Chamber, the Courts of the North and of Wales, the Court of the Duchy of Lancaster, and the Exchequer Court of the County Palatine of Chester; abolished the Court of High Commission and restricted the powers of the ecclesiastical courts; and declared unlawful and void the proceedings in the *Case of Shipmoney*.

This legislation considerably strengthened the common law. What was the effect of reversing the *Case of Shipmoney* was arguable; certainly wide powers of acting in an emergency were left to the King; but the opinions of the majority of the judges and barons were expressly overruled. The abolition of the Court of High Commission left the King with no superior ecclesiastical court, and there could be no doubt that the prerogative courts of Canterbury and York and the diocesan courts were subject to the jurisdiction of the Court of King's Bench. Above all, the abolition of the jurisdiction of the Council (except to commit, subject to *habeas corpus*) and the Court of Star Chamber abolished all control over the King's Bench, except in Parliament, and left only the Courts of Chancery and Admiralty as competitors with the courts of common law. The Court of King's Bench thus became *primus inter pares*.

The problem of the relation between common law and statute law was complicated by two new factors, the claim of Parliament to legislate without the King's assent, and the importation of the doctrine of sovereignty. The Long Parliament had reversed Finch, C.J., but it had not denied the existence of a fundamental law. On the contrary, the Earl of Strafford's Act of Attainder[1] accused the Earl of high treason, *inter alia*, 'for endeavouring to subvert the ancient and fundamental laws and government of His Majesty's realms of England and Ireland'. The Grand Remonstrance of December 1641[2] accused the King's advisers and others of a 'malignant and pernicious design of subverting the fundamental laws and principles of government, upon which the religion and justice of this kingdom are firmly established'. But Charles I also could appeal to the fundamental law; and in his answer to the Grand Remonstrance[3] he insisted that the right of bishops was grounded on the 'fundamental law of the kingdom and constitution of Parliament'. He claimed, too, an undoubted right to call such persons as he thought fit to his secret councils. Further, high treason was alleged against John Pym, John Hampden, William Strode, and others because, among other things, they had 'endeavoured to subvert the fundamental laws and government of the kingdom of England, to deprive the King of his regal power, and to place in subjects an arbitrary and tyrannical power....'.[4]

[1] S. R. Gardiner, *Constitutional Documents of the Puritan Revolution* (3rd ed.), pp. 156–8.
[2] *Ibid.* pp. 205–32.   [3] *Ibid.* pp. 233–76.   [4] *Ibid.* p. 236.

This bandying of 'fundamental laws' as a prelude to a civil war must not be taken too seriously. It might be likened to modern electioneering. Nevertheless, it was for the time being generally accepted that there were fundamental laws which neither King nor Parliament could overthrow. In substance, Parliament appealed to them when it raised the militia in 1642[1] and declared James II to have abdicated in 1689. Nor was the assumption quite so ridiculous as it seemed to those bred in the fashionable 'sovereignty' theory of the nineteenth century. Every Constitution, written or unwritten, revolutionary or evolutionary, is founded ultimately on acquiescence or custom;[2] and what is acquiesced in is a set of simple propositions expressing fundamental constitutional relationships. The realisation of this fact produced the theory of the social contract;[3] but both Hobbes and Locke used that theory to produce a single constitutional authority, the 'sovereign'. Jeremy Bentham derided the social contract and John Austin produced a 'sovereign' sitting somewhere in Purgatory because it came neither from natural or divine law nor from popular assent in a social compact. Austin did not say that Parliament was sovereign, and Dicey distinguished 'legal sovereignty' from sovereignty in fact. The Stuart disputes need not, however, have produced the present constitutional law. The fundamental law could have developed into a more complicated system of relationships including, for example, some fundamental liberties enforced by the courts as part of the common law and incapable of being taken away by Act of Parliament or otherwise. What happened in fact was that the concept of the fundamental law withered away, leaving only the supremacy of Parliament. Even now, probably, Bill Bloggs has not quite accepted the latter theory. Some things which Parliament might legally do would bring him to the barricades.

The attitudes of the parties to the Civil War can be rationalised because anybody who fought for the King or for the Parliament must, unless he were a mere adventurer, have had some 'reason' for so doing.

[1] Gardiner, *op. cit.* pp. 245–7. See the defence of the Lords and Commons, *ibid.* pp. 254–8, especially p. 257. And cf. J. W. Gough, *Fundamental Law in English History*, pp. 81–2.

[2] Jennings, *The Law and the Constitution* (5th ed.), Appendix IV.

[3] J. W. Gough, *The Social Contract.*

It is, however, dangerous to go further and motivate behaviour by economic interest. It is no doubt true that a wealthy member of the new middle class had a fiercer hatred of arbitrary taxation than one of Prince Rupert's retainers had; and it is true that independent East Anglia, where the Parliament was strong, was wealthier than the rude and barbarous north, where the King was strong. But East Anglia had more independent landowners, and was closer to Martin Luther, while Cambridge was the mother of the English Reformation; the north was still dominated by great landowners and favourable to the old religion. If the loyalties of a body of men, like the members of the Long Parliament, be considered, it is impossible to find an economic motivation.[1] The inarticulate major premise might be founded on money, or on religion, but it might also be merely the result of a complicated human personality. Just as the modern Conservative may love a fictitious 'Empire' without having shares in South African gold or Canadian oil, so our ancestors might love King Charles or hate tyranny without being either money-changers or religious enthusiasts.

The Declaration of Breda issued by Charles II in 1660[2] was a carefully drafted formulation founded on the lessons of the Civil War as seen by a moderate Royalist. It claimed the King's rights 'which God and nature hath made our due' but promised 'that all our subjects may enjoy what by law is theirs, by a full and entire administration of justice throughout the land, and by extending our mercy where it is wanted and deserved'. Thus the King (or to be more accurate Lord Clarendon) reverted to the older interpretation of the law, whereby the King's prerogatives and his subjects' rights came from the fundamental law, not the law and his subjects' rights from the prerogative. It was, in other words, a return to the conception of Magna Carta as originally understood and not as distorted by Coke: the conception of *jus cuique*. Indeed, the King called the people's rights 'their just, ancient and fundamental rights'. On the other hand, it was politic to mention the powers and privileges of Parliament, if only to enable the King to qualify his promises. There was to be a general pardon 'excepting only such persons as shall hereafter be excepted by Parliament'; the just

[1] D. Brunton and D. H. Pennington, *The Members of the Long Parliament.*
[2] Gardiner, *op. cit.* pp. 465–7.

43

rights of the King and his subjects would be resettled in a free Parliament; the King would be ready to consent to 'a liberty to tender consciences' if an Act of Parliament was offered to him; and all differences over titles to land and all things relating to grants, sales and purchases during the troubles, would be 'determined in Parliament'. Yet this, too, was but a modification of a feudal concept. There were to be a 'resettlement', a new 'determination' of rights, a grant of liberties, and an exception from a general pardon, in the body which had grown out of and superseded the *Curia Regis*, the High Court of Parliament.

The obverse of this Declaration was the Act for the Preservation of the King, 1661 (13 Car. II, st. 1, c. 1), which made it unlawful to maintain that both Houses of Parliament or either House had a legislative power without the King, and declared that all orders and ordinances of both or either of the Houses of Parliament, for imposing of oaths, covenants or engagements, levying of taxes, or raising of forces, to which the royal assent had not been given, were void *ab initio*. Even so, the Civil War had permanent effects upon constitutional law. Like the Act just quoted, we speak now not of the High Court of Parliament but of the legislative power of the King in Parliament. The High Court of Parliament, by a fiction similar to that by which the court *coram rege* became a court independent of the King, became the House of Lords sitting in its judicial capacity. It was, in fact, the court *coram rege in parliamento.*[1] The legislative power of the King in Parliament, on the other hand, is exercised by a Bill passed by both Houses and assented to by the King. It is, of course, subject to law, the *lex et consuetudo parliamenti*, which arises out of the fundamental law of England.

That fundamental law had been much discussed by pamphleteers during the Civil War. Moderate men like Judge David Jenkins on the Royalist side and Philip Hunton on the Parliamentary side[2] had agreed in principle to a formulation which obviously derived, perhaps at second or third hand, from Jean Bodin's *Six Livres de la République*,

---

[1] *Skinner* v. *East India Co.* (1666), 6 St. Tr. 709.
[2] For Judge Jenkins, see J. W. Gough, *Fundamental Law in English History*, pp. 103–4, and *Judge Jenkins' Case* (1647), 4 St. Tr. 921. For Philip Hunton, see C. H. McIlwain, *Constitutionalism and the Changing World*, pp. 196–230.

published in French in 1576 and in English in 1606. Our fundamental or constitutional law (which perhaps arose out of custom, convention or 'compact') provided the heirs of Henry VII with 'inalienable rights' which included all the rights necessary for the conduct of executive government, vested judicial authority in a series of professional courts with appeal (except in ecclesiastical and admiralty cases) to the House of Lords, and conferred legislative power on King, Lords and Commons acting together in accordance with the law. Since the powers of the King and the jurisdiction of the courts could be modified by the King in Parliament, one might say with Bodin that the King in Parliament was a 'sovereign' authority, *legibus soluta*, or free of laws other than the fundamental law which created and empowered it.[1] Where moderate men differed was in their interpretation of the consequences of a break between the King on the one side and the Lords and the Commons on the other. That problem was not solved by the Civil War. Worthy men for another hundred years thought that no power existed to overthrow the Lord's anointed; but other worthy men—and they were converted into a majority by James II—thought that if a King broke his coronation oath the Lords and Commons were absolved from their allegiance.

There were of course more extreme views. The one side may be represented by the 'Act' of the Rump of the Long Parliament under which Charles Stuart was tried and condemned: it declared that the people were (under God) the original of all just power and that what was enacted by the Commons in Parliament had the force of law.[2] The other side is represented by Sir Robert Filmer's *Patriarcha*, which was not published until 1680, though it had been circulating in manuscript before 1642. Filmer was a reasonably typical country gentleman, cultured, well-read and thoughtful. He was educated at Trinity College, Cambridge, and at Lincoln's Inn, and had mixed with men of culture both in Cambridge and in London.[3] It is because he was an

[1] McIlwain, *op. cit.* pp. 53–5.

[2] *Trial of Charles Stuart, King of England* (1649), 4 St. Tr. 989 at 990. See also *Captain Streater's Case* (1653), 5 St. Tr. 365 at 387, where the doctrine of the 'sovereignty of Parliament' as enunciated by A. V. Dicey in 1886 was laid down by Rolle, L.C.J., though the validity of an Act not assented to by King and Lords was not discussed.

[3] Peter Laslett's Introduction to Sir Robert Filmer, *Patriarcha* (1949 ed.), pp. 1–2.

unusually articulate member of the class of ordinary country squires that his work is one of the few which have directly influenced English politics. He built a political theory out of their prejudices and thus made himself the political philosopher of the landed interest. To understand those prejudices, we must remember three major changes of ideas since the Industrial Revolution. First, because of the development of natural science since Sir Isaac Newton hardly anybody interprets literally the stories of the Old Testament. Filmer and the generations of landed proprietors who succeeded those of his age did so interpret them. Secondly, the character of the family has changed. The family in nearly all agricultural societies consists of all the male descendants of a known male ancestor and their wives, so that a remote cousin is a member of the family, or strictly speaking of as many families as he has known ancestors in the male line. This is so whether the family owns land or not, and whether descent is by primogeniture or not: but the family so defined is a very cohesive unit among landed proprietors whose estates descend to heirs male by primogeniture: and it was especially so in England where, until 1882, two-thirds of all the land descended to heirs male of the body by strict settlements renewed in every generation, and where younger sons had interests charged on the land. The English family was thus a 'patriarchy' in which the tenant for life in possession was 'head of the family' or patriarch. This idea of the family began to break down as choses in action replaced lands as the principal components of wealth. The earlier merchants and manufacturers bought land and founded families in the old sense: the merchants and manufacturers who moved to the suburbs in the nineteenth century were, for the most part, strong family men, but their family consisted of their own progeny and the wives of their sons. The third change was the deposition of land from its station as the determinant of the political and social hierarchy. This was not a mere question of family, though of course when the eldest son succeeded to the headship of the family he also succeeded to his father's status in the county and the parish. The landowner was, so far as the inhabitants of his manors were concerned, *parens patriae*: and his own *parens* was his lord the King. On the other hand the wealthy merchant or manufacturer was head only of his own household, which would include his domestic servants and possibly his apprentices and journeymen.[1]

It is easy enough so to interpret the Bible as to prove that kingship, the family and property are institutions of divine origin, for the Old Testament, like the Quran, assumes a patriarchal society founded on private property. The analogy of the State and the family was, too, a commonplace of political theory since Aristotle:[2] what Filmer suggested was that they were in fact organically connected. Nor was this idea unknown to English law, for it was often said that the King was *parens patriae*. Above all, though the Roman system of inheritance was quite different from the Frankish primogeniture of English law, the power of the head of the family, *patria potestas*, was at once a power over persons and a power over property.

These were the materials from which a well-read country gentleman, who had studied at Cambridge and an Inn of Court and had hobnobbed with clerics and historians, could produce a political theory which seemed plain commonsense to his peers. Its tendency was, of course, to benevolent autocracy, the sort of autocracy on the national plane which existed, as every decent landowner knew, in his own village. Also, it described society as it actually existed, as a consequence of feudalism, over the greater part of Europe. It therefore did not involve a bandying of texts, which could be done by Puritans and Royalists alike. It was common to Christendom; it was, to all appearances, a natural phenomenon; and therefore it was of divine origin. As Dr Figgis points out,[3] it proved the divine right of kings out of nature. It was of course easy for this argument to be turned into a theory of natural rights, life, liberty and property if not the pursuit of happiness, and Locke did so turn it—but it was for the time being an attractive theory for Royalist landlords. It was a political theory for the landed interest. 'His was the genuinely conservative mind', says Mr Laslett,[4] 'the sort of mind that so much wanted to prove that the traditional reality was the only conceivable political order, that he looked no further than to its vindication in just the form in which it existed.' The conservative

---

[1] P. Laslett in Filmer, *Patriarcha*, pp. 24–5.   [2] *Ibid.* pp. 27–8.
[3] *Divine Right of Kings* (2nd ed.), pp. 148–52.
[4] *Loc. cit.* p. 32.

mind would have existed if Filmer had never written or his manuscript had remained in the library of his country house: but conservatives are always grateful for those who find means for defending them rationally, since inherently conservatism is emotional.

They needed defence, or at least they needed to be fortified in their conservatism. Filmer became a cult between 1679 and 1796, when the tories were defending James, Duke of York and King of England, and were losing. It was therefore to Filmer that the first book of the bible of Whiggism, John Locke's *Two Treatises of Civil Government* (1690), was devoted.

3. THE GLORIOUS REVOLUTION

The Cavalier Parliament elected in 1661 was originally *plus royaliste que le roi*, but it was far from subservient. Over a hundred of its members had been members of the Long Parliament; and, though it did not attempt to limit the powers of the King, it assumed as a matter of course that he had legislative power only in Parliament and that the Commons had the right to discuss not only the King's measures but also his policies. It was not dissolved until 1679, but by then the reaction to the Restoration had set in and the numerous changes in membership—only 200 of the original members remained in 1678— 'reflected the growing discontent of the country with the royal policy'.[1] There was, too, a leader of the opposition. The Earl of Shaftesbury was dismissed from the office of Lord Chancellor at the end of 1673 and at once began a movement to organise extreme Protestant opinion. The cavalier cloak of 'Church and King' was wearing a little thin. The extravagance of the court was no doubt exaggerated in political discussion, but Parliament was not yet used to the notion that an annual vote of supplies was essential; and it was obvious enough that some of the moneys voted for the Dutch wars had been spent on the King's mistresses. Cavalier sentiment against the Puritans was still strong, but there was unanimous antagonism to popery, except in the court. Though it was not definitely known until 1678 that the King was in the pay of Louis XIV and had entered into an agreement to declare his adhesion to popery, his motives were suspect, and the influence of his

[1] G. N. Clark, *The Later Stuarts*, p. 54.

48

son James, Duke of York, was clearly on the side of the Church of Rome. The Declarations of Indulgence and the financial straits of the court had renewed the fear of government by prerogative. Economic rivalry with the Dutch, a legacy from the Commonwealth, had become less acute and there was growing fear of the power of the French king. 'From about this time for many years to come it was one of the constant factors in English history that a solid body of Englishmen, who disagreed about many other things, were agreed in fearing three things which they believed to be closely allied—popery, France and arbitrary power.'[1]

This was the environment when Titus Oates and Israel Tonge invented the Popish Plot. It was a plot by the Jesuits to assassinate Charles II and bring the Duke of York to the throne; and as the story developed the Duke himself was implicated. The lies were made credible by a genuine mystery, the sudden death of Sir Edmund Godfrey, the justice before whom Oates and Tonge had sworn their first depositions. The plot is of no interest to us except as evidence of the ferocity of anti-papal sentiment, to which we shall return in the next chapter, and except as the immediate cause of the movement to exclude the Duke of York from the succession. The movement failed, perhaps because Shaftesbury supported the claims of the Duke of Monmouth, Charles' natural son, instead of William of Orange. Seeking to placate the Parliamentary opposition and get more money, the King had in 1677 consented to a marriage between William and the Princess Mary, the elder daughter of the Duke of York. Unless the Duke had sons by his second wife, Mary of Modena, Princess Mary was next in succession to the throne. William of Orange was himself in the line of succession, since he was the son of the elder sister of the King. Nevertheless, some of the exclusionists (or whigs) supported Monmouth, and a few were implicated in the Rye House Plot, this time a genuine plot to assassinate the King.

There was an immediate reaction, which was used to break up the opposition, oppress dissenters, and dissolve corporations. Charles II was able to ride out his reign, which ended in 1685, without calling a Parliament after that of 1681. James II had to call on Parliament to

[1] *Ibid.* p. 76.

secure the revenues voted for life, and it was more favourable to the Crown than Charles II's later parliaments. Monmouth's attempt to raise rebellion failed, his supporters were suppressed with ruthless severity, and the loyalty of Parliament was assured. In the second session, however, James II asked for a standing army, while admitting that some of the officers had not taken the oath under the Test Act. Opposition developed forthwith, but Parliament was prorogued without a vote and did not meet again, for it was dissolved in 1687 without a third session. In *Godden* v. *Hales*[1] the right of the King to appoint papist officers *non obstante* the Test Act was upheld. The case brought into practical politics once more the academic arguments. It was argued by all the judges except Street, J.—

1. That the kings of England are sovereign princes.
2. That the laws of England are the king's laws.
3. That therefore 'tis an inseparable prerogative in the kings of England, to dispense with penal laws in particular cases, and upon particular necessary reasons.
4. That of those reasons and those necessities the king himself is sole judge: and then, which is consequent upon all,
5. That this is not a trust invested in, or granted to the king by the people, but the ancient remains of the sovereign power and prerogative of the kings of England; which never yet was taken from them, nor can be.[2]

This case was part of a deliberate attempt to romanise the army, and similar attempts were made to romanise the universities of Cambridge and Oxford.[3] These and other proceedings not only aroused anti-papist sentiment; they also threatened interference with property rights under pretence of prerogative.[4] Charles II's policy of revising corporation charters was continued, and an attempt was made to get favourable county officers in order to have a pro-papist Parliament elected. The

---

[1] (1686) 11 St. Tr. 1165.   [2] *Ibid.* at 1199.

[3] *Case of Dr Peachell, Vice-Chancellor of the University of Cambridge* (1687), 11 St. Tr. 1315; *Magdalen College (Oxford) Case* (1688), 12 St. Tr. 1. These cases were decided by the new Court of High Commission, set up in flagrant breach of the Act of 1641 which had abolished the old Court.

[4] James II said in his second Declaration of Indulgence, 1687, that the free exercise of religion and the perfect enjoyment of their property were the two things men value most: *E.H.D.* VIII, p. 395.

support of dissenters was sought by the *Declarations of Indulgence,* which provided toleration for papists and dissenters alike as well as for the Church of England. The second Declaration was ordered to be read in the churches, but the archbishop and six other bishops petitioned the King to withdraw the order, on the ground that it seemed to them to be illegal. These bishops were charged with seditious libel,[1] but were acquitted by the jury. Meanwhile Queen Mary had produced an heir, James Edward Stuart, afterwards called the Old Pretender, to distinguish him from his son, Charles Edward Stuart, the Young Pretender.

The Old Pretender was born on 10 June 1688. The formal invitation to William of Orange to land an army in England, for months in contemplation, was sent on 30 June. It was signed by four peers (Shrewsbury, Devonshire, Danby and Lumley), the Bishop of London, Edward Russell and Henry Sidney. In the language which became settled after the Revolution, four were 'whig' and three 'tory'. Many thousands were in the secret.[2] It was known that there was disaffection in the army, which could not be trusted to obey the King's orders if William landed in force. The invitation expressed no 'ideology', and the signatories themselves did not know what the sequel would be if William's invasion were successful. The Revolution was premeditated, but not the Revolution Settlement. Even in July or August James could have saved the situation by a policy of moderation,[3] but he went blithely on his way, making arrangements for the calling of a parliament in which, if his electioneering proved successful, the House of Commons would favour the King's measures. Not until the end of September, apparently, did the Council learn what everybody else knew, that an invasion was in preparation. James made some concessions, but they were grudging and came too late to be useful, since they were thought to be empty gestures which would be repudiated as soon as the threat of invasion was removed. James had almost lost before the 'Protestant wind' began to blow on 1 November. The army would not

---

[1] Copies of the petition had been sold in the streets: K. Feiling, *History of the Tory Party,* p. 224.
[2] *Ibid.* p. 227.
[3] David Ogg, *England in the Reign of James II and William III,* p. 203.

fight and the navy either would not or could not—probably both. Nobody wanted to fight, on either side. There was no exaltation of any kind. Had the King been willing to compromise, even after William landed in Torbay on 5 November, there was enough loyalist sentiment to provide him with support; and if William had proved recalcitrant there might have been a civil war. The compromise would have been humiliating for the King because William was strong enough to dictate strong terms. James refused to take the lead offered to him on such terms. No doubt he was right, though probably he acted more on impulse than on reason. His real object had been to bring the English back into his own Church, and he had merely succeeded in making enemies of his daughters.

It is odd that a revolution so judicious and pedestrian should be called 'glorious'. From June to December 1688, when James left the country openly and without obstruction, everybody was engaged in a cool calculation of advantages and disadvantages. There was nothing glorious except the bonfires on the night of 11 December, the night on which England had no ruler and the mob took charge of London. The only battle was the exchange of proclamations and declarations.[1] It is odd, too, that so little was said about the principles of political obligation about which so much had been written since the death of Elizabeth I. Men of different philosophies and of none took political action because it was necessitated by the circumstances.

The tradition of legalism which inspired the subsequent proceedings of Lords and Commons is noteworthy. They had, of course, a political motive. It was important that all English subjects should accept William and Mary as King and Queen: but the fact that so much effort was made to legalise the succession shows how profoundly the legalism of the Stuart lawyers had sunk in. For those who considered that the Stuarts ruled by right of inheritance—and generally the supporters of the theory of divine right considered that only a king by inheritance had such a right—there was no means by which James II, or his son James Edward, could be deprived of his throne. Even if James II could abdicate, he could not deprive his issue of their inheritance: and even if the Stuarts in the male line could be disinherited by Act of Parliament,

[1] Ogg, *op. cit.* pp. 222–3.

52

that Act had to be passed by a Parliament summoned by him and to be assented to by him.[1] Many worthy peers, prelates and others could not swear an oath of allegiance to William and Mary, though many of the non-jurors recognised a duty of obedience to a *de facto* monarch, saving their allegiance to their lawful King across the water.

Even for the mere formalist there were difficulties. If it could be assumed, as the Bill of Rights claimed, that James II had abdicated, the person next entitled was the infant James Edward. Hence many tories wanted a regency, to be exercised by William of Orange: but William himself answered that point by refusing to contemplate a regency. If it could also be assumed that Mary of Modena never gave birth to a son, but that James Edward was smuggled in by a conspiracy, as was rumoured at the time of the birth, Mary of Orange was Queen and William was prince-consort. Again William answered that assertion by refusing to be prince-consort. Hence the good tory lawyer had not a leg to stand on unless he was willing to agree that a *de facto* King, recognised as such by the peers and a freely elected House of Commons, was lawfully King: and this seemed to suggest that rebellion was in some circumstances lawful, or could be made so by *ex post facto* legislation. Perhaps the Scots produced the best theory. King James VII, said the Claim of Right,[2] being a professed papist, acted as king without taking the oath, required by law, to maintain the Protestant religion and to rule according to the laudable laws; and by the advice of wicked and evil counsellors he invaded the fundamental constitution of the kingdom and altered it from a legal, limited monarchy to an arbitrary, despotic power (and so forth); whereby he forfeited his right to the Crown and the throne became vacant.

However the lawyers explained the situation, it clearly had to be accepted by those who remained in either kingdom. Jacobite sentiment was nevertheless strong, and there were rebellions in 1715 and 1745. The defeat of Charles Edward Stuart at Culloden in 1746 virtually ended the legitimist movement, though the Young Pretender lived until 1788 and his brother Henry, Cardinal of York, lived until

---

[1] As was the case with Edward VIII: see His Majesty's Declaration of Abdication Act, 1936.
[2] *E.H.D.* VIII, pp. 635–9.

1807. The tories as a body were split between the Jacobites and the conformists. Their situation was made easier by the accession of Queen Anne because she was, next to the Old Pretender and his issue, the lawful heir of Henry VII. Their position was worsened again, however, by her death without issue surviving. In contemplation of that event, the Act of Settlement of 1701 vested the Crown in Sophia, Electress of Hanover, and the heirs of her body. This limitation excluded not only the issue of James II, but also the issue of Henrietta, Duchess of Orleans, youngest daughter of Charles I, who had a numerous and distinguished progeny, though all Roman Catholics. Sophia's claim was as a daughter of Elizabeth, daughter of James I: but Elizabeth had also had two sons, both of whom had issue.[1] Hence Sophia's son, who ascended the throne of Great Britain and Ireland in 1714 as George I, had but a remote claim by descent, and his title depended upon the Act of Settlement and the Bill of Rights.

Thus, though the tories had helped to bring about the deposition of James II, many of them were not happy about it. Some of them went back to their estates because they would not swear oaths to William and Mary. Others followed their example when George I came to the throne. This had important effects, for it stimulated the tradition of the independent country gentleman who would not take office under, or receive favours from, a Hanoverian King. If elected to Parliament, or if a peer, he would consider a measure on its merits, and could not be bribed with office or honours. There was no tory party in 1760, though many people—Samuel Johnson and Sir William Blackstone, for instance—called themselves tories because they were against the whigs. The tory party of the late eighteenth century was an offshoot of the whigs, started by William Pitt and the Portland whigs, but inspired mainly by reaction to the French Revolution.[2] Edmund Burke, man of business to the second Marquis of Rockingham (who had been bred in the strictest whig principles),[3] became the philosopher of the new tory party.

Meanwhile the whigs had appropriated the revolution to themselves.

[1] See the tables in *E.H.D.* VIII, pp. 125, 127, 131 and 133.
[2] Volume II, ch. I.
[3] He was out with the Duke of Cumberland in '45: see *D.N.B.*

Some of them did very well out of it. Charles Talbot, Earl of Shrewsbury, became Duke of Shrewsbury; William Cavendish, Earl of Devonshire, became Duke of Devonshire; Edward Russell became Earl of Orford, and Henry Sidney became Earl of Romney. To them were added William's Dutch companions: the Keppels became Dukes of Albemarle and the Bentincks became Dukes of Portland. It was indeed, from their point of view, a glorious revolution. Moreover it had a philosophy given by John Locke, physician to the first Earl of Shaftesbury, the leader of the opposition to Charles II and therefore the first whig.

Locke's political influence throughout the eighteenth century and well into the nineteenth was immense, for every educated man was expected to have read at least his *Essay concerning Human Understanding* (1690) and probably his *Essay on Toleration* (1689) and his *Two Treatises of Civil Government* (1690). He probably had more political influence than any other political writer, not excluding Edmund Burke, for Burke's works enjoyed similar prestige but for a shorter period. Locke was born in 1632 and died in 1704, and thus lived through both revolutions. His home environment was Puritan and his father was a lawyer who joined the Parliamentary army in 1642. The son was sent to Westminster School in 1646, where the environment was parliamentary. In 1652 he went up to Christ Church, Oxford, where he came under some Royalist influence, though in religion he was influenced by the Cambridge Platonists and in philosophy by Descartes.[1] In 1659 he was elected Student of Christ Church and lectured on Greek and Moral Philosophy. He also studied medicine, though not until 1674 was he granted a faculty to practise. He was, however, also involved in public affairs. He was secretary to a diplomatic mission to Brandenburg in 1665 and he became associated with Lord Ashley, afterwards Earl of Shaftesbury and Lord Chancellor, in 1667. He therefore held official positions while Shaftesbury was Lord Chancellor in 1672-3. From 1675 to 1679 he was in France, mainly on account of his health, though he was able to resume his Cartesian studies. Shaftesbury was back in office when Locke returned

[1] J. W. Gough in his edition of *The Second Treatise of Civil Government*, p. viii; and see D. J. O'Connor, *John Locke*, pp. 14-15.

to England, and for a short time Locke was employed on secret political business: but his health broke down and he returned to Oxford. Whether he had any part in the intrigues for bringing the Duke of Monmouth to the throne is not clear, but he was under suspicion and thought it wise to go into exile in 1683. His health improved, and in Holland he was able to resume writing. He returned to England early in 1689 but did not go back to Oxford. From 1696 to 1700 he was a Commissioner of Trade, but mainly he spent his time revising his books for publication, producing new editions, and writing more books. His most influential work, though written earlier, was published immediately after the Revolution, in 1689–90.

With Locke's theory of knowledge we are not concerned. It was important that he had a philosophy to operate as a frame of reference for his constitutional theories, and undoubtedly *Human Understanding* helped towards the rationalist approach to political and social problems which dominated eighteenth-century practice. His direct influence flowed, however, from his *Essays on Toleration* and his *Two Treatises of Civil Government*. The former must be mentioned later: with the latter we are immediately concerned because it set out the foundations of the Whig Constitution.

The belief that the purpose of the *Two Treatises* was to justify the Revolution of 1688[1] is erroneous. Locke was not trying to formulate the case for the whig politicians but to ascertain the assumptions or principles from which he himself concluded that the removal of James II was justifiable. He was 'party political' only in the sense that he asserted doctrines which would favour the whigs, and therefore those doctrines were widely accepted and became the whig interpretation of the English Constitution. He was, however, not 'party political' in the sense that he sought to provide arguments for the whigs. It was not a party manifesto like John Milton's *Eikonoklastes* or the pamphlets issued by the party machines since 1868. These seek to show that the action taken was right: what Locke showed was that the Revolution of 1688 could be justified in principle.

Locke was not a lawyer, and accordingly he broke away from the common-law view of the Constitution which had prevailed under the

[1] W. S. Carpenter in *Of Civil Government* (Everyman ed.), p. vii.

56

earlier Stuarts and which had been weakening under the later Stuarts. He accepted the idea of a perpetual law of nature, arising out of the state of nature which had, in his view, preceded political society. That law of nature provided for the preservation of life, liberty and property. He did not, however, effect the transition from the law of nature to the common law, as a lawyer might have done. On the contrary, he generally thought of positive law in terms of legislation, as his successors the Benthamites did. This was mainly due to his concept of the 'social compact' by which the authorities of the commonwealth were established. Common law was not for him, as it was for Coke, an emanation from immemorial custom. It had been enacted by legislative authority to protect life, liberty and property in accordance with the law of nature. The fact that he gave so much emphasis to legislative power is, however, evidence of a great change of outlook since the Civil War. Coke, as a lawyer taking his law from precedents, was necessarily conservative in these matters; for him Parliament was still the High Court of Parliament. The Long Parliament and the legislative reforms of the Commonwealth and the Protectorate had, however, put the judicial aspect of the King in Parliament entirely in the shade.[1] A layman like Locke, using few if any law books, simply assumed that Parliament was a legislature, called together at frequent intervals exclusively for that purpose.

Hence legislation was the most important function of the commonwealth, and legislative power was supreme power, subject to the law of nature. The social compact had established the 'legislative' to make positive law, the 'executive' to enforce the positive law, and the 'federative power' to conduct relations with other peoples in accordance with the law of nature. Very little was said about the judicial power. It was said that the state of nature lacked a 'known and indifferent judge, with authority to determine all differences according to the established law',[2] and accordingly one of the purposes of government was to supply this want. Locke distinguished this power from the power of executing the laws, but he did not say that the judicial power and the executive power were or ought to be vested in different

[1] C. H. McIlwain, *High Court of Parliament*, p. 103.
[2] *Of Civil Government*, II, § 125.

57

hands. Indeed, he was so little concerned with the judicial power that he may have intended to include the judicial power within the executive. In any event the supreme power was the legislative power, which was subject to the law of nature. He neither said nor, apparently, implied that the legislative power was subject to the common law. On the other hand, the first and fundamental positive law was that which established the legislative power; and this fundamental law was unalterable. Nor could the legislative power be 'absolutely arbitrary over the lives and fortunes of the people', because it continued to be subject to the law of nature: but he did not say or imply that legislative power was subject to positive law.

Applying all this generalisation to England itself, we may say that the King summoned Parliament from time to time to make laws. It was a breach of the fundamental law to legislate except in Parliament, to dispense with Acts of Parliament, or to tax without consent of Parliament. The King was, however, not merely part of Parliament; he also controlled the executive authority and conducted foreign relations. By the 'common law of nature' the King had wide discretionary authority 'for the good of the society'. Locke even went so far—in a rather faint echo of the *Case of Shipmoney*—as to suggest that when all the members of the society have to be preserved 'the laws themselves should in some cases give way to the executive power, or rather to this fundamental law of nature and government'.[1] Evidently *salus populi suprema lex* had some meaning, though Locke did not use that phrase. Apart from this, prerogative was not above the law: it was available only when the law was silent: but Locke did a good deal of hedging on this subject, especially when he discussed the question of a conflict between the legislature and the executive.[2] What he had in mind was not the kind of conflict which, had Coke's line of thought been developed, could have been settled by courts of law, but the sort of conflict which had developed between the Long Parliament and Charles I, or between the political leaders and James II. He thought of the problem, therefore, in terms of the right of rebellion. This caused him to consider the nature of tyranny,[3] which he defined as 'the

[1] *Of Civil Government*, II, §159. [2] *Ibid.* §§167-8.
[3] *Ibid.* ch. XVIII.

58

exercise of power beyond right'. Opposition to tyranny is justified because the orders are unlawful. This is, however, something of an interjection, because the government is dissolved (or, as we should put it, the Constitution is overthrown) in three circumstances: First, when the legislature is changed, because then the fundamental law is broken; Secondly, when 'he who has the supreme executive power neglects and abandons that charge'; Thirdly, when the legislature, or the prince, acts contrary to the trust placed upon it or him. Thus, it could be held that James II had broken the fundamental laws, and had caused a breakdown in the Constitution, by exercising arbitrary power outside the law, hindering Parliament from assembling, and interfering in elections.

The analysis is not wholly satisfactory, even on Locke's own premises. The weakness arises especially from the consideration of positive law as consisting of rules enacted by the legislature, which in turn implies that the royal prerogative and the composition and power of Parliament arise out of fundamental law or the law of nature. This is almost exactly the reverse of the extreme common-law theory, that the positive law is common law, modified by statute, that the prerogative of the Crown and the power of Parliament derive from the common law and are subject to fundamental law or the law of nature, which is consistent with and embodied in the common law. No doubt the complication arose because Locke accepted some of Hobbes' premises but resisted his conclusions.

4. THE SOVEREIGNTY OF PARLIAMENT

Practice suggests theory; and theory helps to mould practice if it seems to accord with political conditions. The provisions of the Bill of Rights and the Act of Settlement, carefully limiting the succession to the Crown and the powers of its wearer, and providing for the independence of the judges, were more important than Locke's theories; but those theories, not being inconsistent with the Revolution Settlement, helped to mould opinion during the next hundred years. We can see their influence in Blackstone's *Commentaries*, the work not of a whig but of a person who, as a son of Oxford and the Middle Temple, was a good liberal-minded tory. Blackstone was the country gentleman's lawyer, the scholar who 'first made English law speak the language of the scholar and the gentleman'. He was not a great scholar; still less was he a great lawyer. He had a considerable and well-digested knowledge, not merely of the law books, but also of all the literature from Aristotle to Locke which a well-read lawyer of his age ought to have studied. He wrote gracefully and had a remarkable facility for making legal absurdities look almost sensible. His explanations were sometimes so far-fetched as to be almost ludicrous, but he did seek to explain, and that had not been done before. Whereas before him there had been only abridgements, dictionaries and treatises, he digested the whole of the law into four readable volumes. Therefore his *Commentaries* became not merely the standard text-book for all law students and a work of authority in the courts of law, but also the sort of book which every gentleman ought to have in his library and every discriminating country justice ought to have read. As his first editor, Professor Christian, put it in the fourteenth edition:

The Commentaries on the Laws of England form an essential part of every gentleman's library: the beautiful and lucid arrangement, the purity of the language, the classic elegance of the quotation and allusion, the clear and intelligible explanation of every subject, must always yield the reader as much pleasure as improvement; and wherever any constitutional or legal question is agitated, they are the first, and, in general, the best authority referred to.

For the moment, however, we are concerned only to demonstrate from Blackstone how firmly the principles of the Revolution Settlement had been accepted and how stable was the British Constitution (as it must be called after the Union with Scotland in 1707) during the Hanoverian reigns. So stable was it that it survived the French Revolution and the French wars, the industrial revolution, the agitation for reform, the development of democracy, and two world wars: and in the second half of the twentieth century we constitutional lawyers quote Magna Carta and Coke's *Institutes*, the *Case of Ship-money* and the *Case of Prohibitions*, the Bill of Rights and the Act of Settlement, and much more besides, to explain and illustrate the modern law. Nor must we forget that over the water there operates the oldest surviving written Constitution, founded in the main on the

60

same sources, assisted by French interpretations of liberty, but essentially English in its texture. These are remarkable examples of constitutional stability arising out of three revolutions, though the United States, unlike Great Britain after 1689, had to suffer a civil war.

Blackstone was a diligent compiler, and he ignored few ideas of the previous century and a half. We must not assume that his analysis was universally accepted. As he tells us in the later editions, 'no sooner was the work completed, but many of its positions were vehemently attacked by zealots of all (even opposite) denominations, religious as well as civil; by some with a greater, by others with a less degree of acrimony'. Among these zealots was an Oxford pupil of Blackstone's named Jeremy Bentham, who poked such fun at his professor's 'law of nature' that ever since it has had to wander round in disguise.[1] Accordingly, we merely note in passing that laws contrary to the law of nature are void,[2] though there are many 'indifferent points' in which both the divine law and the natural leave man at his liberty, but in which he may be restrained for the benefit of society. Municipal or positive law is 'a rule of civil conduct prescribed by the supreme power in a State'.[3] This child of Hobbes and Locke of course presupposes that the common law was at some time or other prescribed by the supreme power.[4] This supreme power or authority is placed in those hands wherein, according to the founders of the several States, the qualities requisite for supremacy, wisdom, goodness and power, are the most likely to be found.[5] In the British Constitution this supreme power or sovereignty is lodged in three independent bodies, the King, the Lords Spiritual and Temporal, and the House of Commons, wherein the three great qualities of government are so well and so happily united.[6] If ever it should happen that the independence of any one of the three should be lost, or that it should become subservient to the views of the other two, there would soon be an end of our Constitution.

The legislature would be changed from that, which (upon the supposition of an original contract, either actual or implied) is presumed to have been

---

[1] Its present disguise is 'The Rule of Law'.
[2] 1 Bl. Comm. 41.   [3] 1 Bl. Comm. 46.
[4] But see the analysis of the common law in 1 Bl. Comm. 63–73, where this idea is dropped.
[5] 1 Bl. Comm. 49.   [6] 1 Bl. Comm. 51.

originally set up by the general consent and fundamental act of the society: and such a change, however effected, is according to Mr Locke (who perhaps carries his theory too far) at once an entire dissolution of the bonds of government; and the people are thereby reduced to a state of anarchy, with liberty to constitute to themselves a new legislative power.[1]

This supreme power is not, however, supreme over God and nature. There are natural rights, such as life and liberty, which no human legislature has power to abridge or destroy, unless the owner shall himself commit some act amounting to a forfeiture. Similarly, there are divine or natural duties, such as the worship of God and the maintenance of children, which receive no stronger sanction from being declared by the law of the land. Also, there are crimes and misdemeanours which are *mala in se*. In all these cases the legislature acts only in subordination to the great lawgiver, transcribing and publishing his precepts.[2] Things indifferent, however, become right or wrong, just or unjust, according as the municipal legislator sees proper.

The application of these principles to the law of England gave Blackstone great trouble, and his views were not firmly settled until the ninth edition. Even then his learned editor found it necessary to dissent.[3] This is, however, not a matter which came into political con-

[1] 1 Bl. Comm. 52.   [2] 1 Bl. Comm. 54.

[3] Though it is not part of the story because it never came into controversy (except incidentally during the American Revolution and the Home Rule dispute) something more should be said about the development of the doctrine of the sovereignty of Parliament. As has been seen, it was not one of the theories of the Stuart lawyers, who indeed had never heard of sovereignty except as an attribute of monarchy. It was, however, developed from Bodin by Hobbes in *De Cive* (1642) and *Leviathan* (1651). These books were written during the Civil War, after Parliament had seized power, and accordingly they stressed and justified absolute power. Though Locke did not mention sovereignty, he took the idea of supreme legislative power from Hobbes and thus distorted the idea of the Constitution as it actually operated in 1690. Positive law was far from being an emanation of supreme legislative authority, because the greater part of it was common law, much of which was founded on customary law. The emphasis upon legislation was due to the reforming zeal of the Parliament men between 1640 and 1660, to Hobbes's absorption in the problem of power, and to the Bill of Rights. Parliament was not 'sovereign' in the eyes of the law, though a record in Parliament had the highest possible authority and Coke had stated correctly in his context that one Parliament could not bind another. There was authority in *Doctor Bonham's Case* and possibly elsewhere for the view that an Act of Parliament could be declared void. Blackstone had difficulty over this problem, because Locke, from whom Blackstone took much of his political theory, asserted the supremacy of Parliament without reference to the common law, whereas the common law as enunciated by Coke and other Parliamentary lawyers

troversy. The British Constitution as Blackstone understood it was in all essentials the English Constitution which Locke had justified three-quarters of a century before. The executive authority was vested in the King, the legislative power in a Parliament consisting of the King, the Lords and the Commons, and the judicial authority in the courts of law. Parliament had (subject to a qualification taken from Coke which caused the difficulty mentioned above) supreme power, though limited by the law of God and nature. The Whig Constitution had become the British Constitution, and we hear no more of Filmer or divine right: the Tory Constitution had disappeared.

Political controversy, in so far as it related to constitutional matters, centred not upon the power of Parliament but upon its composition

could control Acts of Parliament. At first he correctly stated the law, while at the same time asserting Locke's theory of supreme power. He gradually watered down his statement of the common law until it became in the ninth and subsequent editions a mere statement that 'Acts of Parliament that are impossible to be performed are of no validity' (1 Bl. Comm. 91).

Even this statement was objected to by his editor, Christian, in the 14th edition. Also, his editor quoted a dictum of Hobart, L.C.J., in *Day* v. *Savadge* (1615), Hob. 87, to the effect that an Act of Parliament contrary to natural equity, as to make a man a judge in his own cause, was void. That, too, he expressly repudiated. Bentham's attack on natural law and natural rights in the *Fragment of Government* (1776) (the *Comment on the Commentaries* was not published until 1928) was so devastating that in the nineteenth century we hear little more of them, though the common law, which Bentham also attacked, survived the reforming zeal of that century. Indeed, we continue to hear of 'natural justice' as part of the common law. Also, John Austin, one of the Benthamites, lifted from the last pages of Bentham's *Principles of Morals and Legislation* (1789) a whole new science of Jurisprudence which was explained in the *Province of Jurisprudence Determined* (1832). Bentham and Austin belonged to a group of radical reformers for whom natural law was a fiction and the common law a lot of mumbo-jumbo. Hobbes's theory of sovereignty and his assumption that law rested on force (both of which had recently been illustrated in the French Revolution) were attuned to their prejudices and to the times in which they lived. The Austinian theory of law as a command issued by a sovereign to subjects dominated legal thought in the nineteenth century. Though neither Austin nor anybody else succeeded in finding where this sovereignty lay, the lawyers ignored the practical problem and simply assumed that, as a legal fiction, sovereignty lay in the King in Parliament: or, as A. V. Dicey put it in *The Law of the Constitution* (1885) that Parliament was 'legally sovereign'. Since this notion of sovereignty is a recent importation into legal discussions, any competent lawyer could, for an adequate fee, demonstrate at least to his own satisfaction, if not to that of a court bred on Dicey, that it was a modern heresy and not part of the law at all. Indeed, the arbitrary actions of some party majorities in some Commonwealth legislatures have induced some to hope that law courts would go back to the older orthodoxy. Cf. Jennings, *The Law and the Constitution* (5th ed.,) ch. IV and appendix III; and see Geoffrey Marshall, *Parliamentary Sovereignty and the Commonwealth*.

and the relations of its parts. In spite of the emphasis placed upon the legislative power by Locke and Blackstone, the older tradition, represented especially by Coke, that the common law regulated human relationships and that the statute law merely remedied its defects, continued throughout the eighteenth century. The reforming zeal of the Long Parliament, the Commonwealth and the Protectorate was not again exhibited until the dawn of the nineteenth century, when the social consequences of the industrial revolution became so obvious that substantial legislative changes were needed: and this was even more so after 1832, when the balance of political power began to shift. There were, of course, important legislative measures in the eighteenth century, and by the end of the century the justices of the peace found themselves administering 'stacks of statutes'. There was, too, an enormous amount of legislation by private Act, especially for the inclosure of common fields and manorial waste, the provision of canals and turnpikes, and the regulation of the towns.

These consequences of the great economic changes of the eighteenth century were, however, not in political controversy, partly because the Houses of Parliament became more unrepresentative of the people at large as the century progressed. Indeed, we who are accustomed to our great cities and a complex system of production, distribution and exchange, tend to exaggerate the degree of change. The great whig lords and the country gentlemen were not wrong in thinking of England as primarily an agricultural country. The landed interest was dominant politically, socially and economically; and this dominance was maintained not only by the interest of the landowners in mineral royalties and urban rents, but also by the anxiety of the urban middle class to become country gentlemen. Not until after Waterloo did the 'condition of the people' become a live political issue. Politics related primarily to executive government, to foreign affairs, relations with Ireland and the American colonies, the slave trade, and above all jobs for the boys.

The disappearance of the constitutional dispute after the death of Queen Anne—except for a pathetic fragment at the Pretender's court and the loyalty of some of the Highlanders to the Stuart clan—was mainly responsible for the fragmentation of the Whig party. They were all whigs when the Revolution Settlement appeared to be in danger, but there never had been any real organisation of either party and there was nothing to keep the whigs together, or to bring them together when they parted. The Government could not put on the whips, appeal to party loyalty, or proscribe the unfaithful. Somehow it had to get a majority out of a heterogeneous collection of 'connexions' and independent country gentlemen. Parliament had to be in regular session because neither George I nor George II could 'live on his own', or indeed had any ambition to do so. Accordingly, politics became a process of controlling elections and managing enough of the waverers in the House of Commons to secure a majority for the King. It was the age of the wire-puller, whose technique was worked out by Sir Robert Walpole, developed by the Duke of Newcastle, and operated by George III. The elder Pitt discovered a new device, though it was in fact a reversion to the seventeenth century, that of stimulating the quiescent nationalism of the backwoodsmen; but he had not the ambition to found a party, nor the peculiar political sense required to operate party government, nor the health to keep up the persistent propaganda required for government by oratory. George III's intervention in political management did raise a constitutional issue, for it seemed to alter the balance of power established by the Revolution. If the King was not merely the executive and an equal partner in Parliament, but the manager of complaisant party majorities in the House of Commons and the House of Lords, the whig theory of the Constitution was overthrown. Edmund Burke realised that this was an issue which ought to unite the whigs: but the matter was complicated not only by the assumed influence of Lord Bute but also by the complete failure of the whig leaders to appreciate that politics was anything more than acquiring influence, prestige, power and jobs for the boys. Party came back through the younger Pitt and Charles James Fox, though because of the French Revolution the development was slow.

5. PARLIAMENTARY REFORM

The basis of the Whig Constitution, up to the Reform Act and even later, was the landed interest. The House of Lords consisted almost exclusively of those considerable landowners who had influence in their counties and who had either placed that influence at the disposal of Ministers or had become Ministers themselves. As the eighteenth century advanced, however, the House of Lords gradually lost its hegemony. The great men were usually willing, and often anxious, to take office; but even then they spent months in their country houses; and the greater part of the practical work of government was done by the 'men of business' in the House of Commons. Though the great men were in the House of Lords, the great statesmen were in the House of Commons. Sir Robert Walpole's great advantage over his opponents was that he was a House of Commons man. The elder Pitt became an almost extinct volcano, occasionally emitting fire and smoke, when he became Earl of Chatham. The first great gladiators, the younger Pitt and Charles James Fox, fought in the House of Commons. There were Prime Ministers in the House of Lords until 1902 and all Cabinets were 'aristocratical' until 1880: but the House of Commons, as a House, had dominated the Constitution for a hundred years. But that House, too, was dominated by the landed interest. The county members, who were in fact nominated by the great landowners or by groups of smaller landowners, played a far more important part than would be warranted by their mere numbers. As a body and as individuals they prided themselves on their independence. The great majority of the borough members, too, were returned by the influence of landowners. In the eyes of contemporaries this was no perversion of the electoral system. The right of property arose by divine law and the law of nature and was therefore part of the fundamental law of the Constitution. An educated person would have been surprised if this had been questioned, at least before the French Revolution. Borough patrons accepted the duties of their station by returning 'men of business', lawyers, ambitious younger sons, and such like, in order that the King's service might be carried on. The mercantile interest was adequately represented in the City of London and the other great towns; and indeed it was able by reason of its wealth to purchase or win seats elsewhere. Even the general population of the towns was represented through great open boroughs like those of Westminster and Preston.

When Parliamentary reform did become a political issue it was not because of any theory of representation. The system of electoral management which the Duke of Newcastle had developed and John Robinson had perfected depended mainly on obtaining borough seats for Government supporters, by securing the adhesion of borough patrons, by using the Government influence in the seaports and other places, and by supplying money to fight elections which otherwise would go by default. By those who had been kept out of office by Lord North's long period of office and those who criticised the conduct of the American war, these methods were regarded as having increased the power of the Crown and destroyed the traditional independence of the House of Commons. The complaint was not that the system of representation was in itself bad, but that the decay of so many small boroughs (and, be it added, though the history was not so well known as it is now, the creation of pocket boroughs under the Tudors and the Stuarts and the restriction of the effective franchise by Parliamentary committees) placed too much power in the hands of the King and his Ministers. Though Burke was, even before the French Revolution, against Parliamentary reform, both young Pitt and Charles James Fox thought of it as part of the policy of economical reform, a necessary sequel to the reforms effected by the Rockingham whigs in 1782. There was, at this stage, no suggestion whatever that there was anything wrong in the dominance of the landed interest.

In the main, the election of 1784 was won by Pitt by the methods which he had condemned in his speech of 1783 on Parliamentary reform. It was at least as much a triumph for the King and John Robinson as a triumph for Pitt. The Prime Minister did bring in a very modest scheme of reform in 1785, providing *inter alia* for compensation for disfranchised boroughs, on the ground that the franchise was property. Fox supported the principle while objecting to the details, but the proposal was heavily defeated. Henceforward Pitt was an opponent of Parliamentary reform, which in effect became a party question after the French Revolution, though the Foxite whigs were so few that it was not a serious issue. On the other hand, Fox was not a full-blown democrat. His main purpose was to strengthen the House of Commons against the King. He did believe, after 1789, that political power ought to be more widely distributed. He thought that political liberty in France had strengthened French power and authority.[1] In the reaction against the French Revolution he was, however, crying for the moon. Pitt could never have persuaded either the King or his colleagues, and a disrupted Opposition could do nothing.

In the long period of tory rule from 1784 to 1830, broken only by the Ministry of All the Talents in 1806, there was no real prospect of Parliamentary reform, if for no better reason than that both George III and George IV were against it. In that period, however, the face of much of England had changed. We must not think of the industrial revolution as a revolution. The process was more like the rising of the tide on an irregular, sandy beach than the sweep of the bore up the River Severn. Even at the beginning of the present century there were villages where the squire and the parson could sway the vote, though by that time few county divisions were completely rural and none was under the control of landlords as such. The depression in agriculture in the eighties had completed a process which had begun over a century before. Nor was the encroachment of the towns the only social change. Land had become a commodity even where it was strictly settled, and the Settled Land Act, 1882, completed that process by enabling the tenant for life in possession to sell the land.

Fifty years before, however, much of England was still essentially rural and dominated by the landed interest. Nor was this thought undesirable. What was objected to by the whigs was the existence of the proprietary boroughs, which could be bought and sold in the market (though sales were infrequent) and meanwhile provided personal representation for wealthy individuals; the dominance of so many boroughs by self-perpetuating corporations (usually tory) or hand-picked freemen; the corruption employed in so many of the smaller boroughs, in which the vote had become a commodity saleable to the highest bidder; and the lack of representation for so many industrial towns which were still parts of the counties in which they were situated.

These rational objections to the system of representation would not in themselves have caused the sweep of opinion which carried Reform in 1832. The tories were defending the Whig Constitution against the

[1] J. L. Hammond, *Charles James Fox*, pp. 78–80.

68

economic power of the industrial middle class, of whom the ten-pound householder was thought to be typical. The whigs' proposals tended to weaken the landed interest and the working class but to strengthen the middle class and thus to overthrow the Revolution Settlement and follow the French Revolution.[1] On the other hand, the whigs themselves had no very clear idea of what they were proposing to do. The pressure came from the great cities, where the pretensions of the tory justices and corporations, and the interests of whig manufacturers and shopkeepers, created a complex of local animosities. Generally, too, the tory Church and the whig chapels were in conflict, though this also was mainly a class distinction. Nor must it be forgotten that in many places the working class was on the side of the whigs. Except under local initiative, which had generally resulted in the establishment of public services under independent statutory authorities, no attempt had been made to regulate the new urban masses, who were living in narrow, unpaved, unpoliced, undrained, unlit and unsavoury streets and working excessive hours in insanitary and overcrowded factories with unprotected machinery. The conditions revealed by the great investigations of the thirties and forties were appalling, and in due course Parliament legislated on public health, factory conditions, the

[1] Cf. the Duke of Wellington's comment, made in 1833 before anybody had much experience of the effect of the Reform Act:

'The revolution is made, that is to say, that power is transferred from one class of society, the gentlemen of England, professing the faith of the Church of England, to another class of society, the shopkeepers, being dissenters from the Church, many of them Socinians, others atheists.

'I don't think that the influence of property in this country is in the abstract diminished. That is to say, that the gentry have as many followers and influence as many voters at elections as ever they did.

'But a new democratic influence has been introduced into elections, the copyholders and freeholders and leaseholders residing in towns which do not themselves return members to Parliament. These are all dissenters from the Church, and are everywhere a formidable active party against the aristocratic influence of the Landed Gentry. But this is not all. There are dissenters in every village in the country; they are the blacksmith, the carpenter, the mason, etc. The new influence established in the towns has drawn these to their party; and it is curious to see to what a degree it is a dissenting interest. I have known instances of a dissenting clerk in the office of an agent in a county of an aristocratical candidate, making himself active in the canvass of these dissenters, to support the party in the towns at the election.'

See *Croker Papers*, II, p. 206. Wellington exaggerated the influence of the dissenting interest, taking the country as a whole, though what he said was probably true of Middlesex and Yorkshire.

employment of women and children, police, and so forth: but these conditions existed in many places in the twenties. Moreover the villagers—and many of the artisans were migrated villagers—had been able, if the harvest was bad, to fall back on the philanthropy of squire and parson and wealthier neighbours. For the artisan there was nothing save the inefficient poor law between employment and starvation. But employment was regulated by the market, and post-war dislocation produced booms and slumps in bewildering succession, the booms attracting workers into the towns and the slumps sending them to the poor law. The artisans had not read Adam Smith and indeed most of them could read nothing at all; but from time to time their voices were raised, and sometimes their arms too, against those in authority. Peterloo in 1819 was significant only because the crowd was so badly handled and the massacre got into the newspapers. Manchester was not the only town with a disaffected populace.

Thus the agitation for Parliamentary reform in 1830–1 was not a mere struggle for power between party groups. Strong emotions were engaged on both sides. Indeed, the pressure of public opinion forced the whigs to produce a more radical Bill than many of them wished. Nor were the tories wrong in believing that the balance of the Whig Constitution was being disturbed. The system could be defended on conservative principles. It had a prescriptive foundation; it had brought the country through the French wars and helped to defeat Napoleon; it had enabled Britain to lead the world in industrial development and the provision of new means of communication. Whether the British Constitution had had anything, or much, to do with it did not matter. In spite of the American and French Revolutions it was still the admiration of the world, or so it could be thought. Now the whigs were overthrowing it by vesting power in one class instead of giving each of the classes its proper representation. They were making England a nation of shopkeepers.

The immediate effect of the Reform Act was, however, small.[1] There

---

[1] As *Blackwood's Magazine* remarked, with some surprise, 'The great institutions of society, the church, the funds, the corn laws, primogeniture, though threatened, are not overthrown': quoted by R. B. McDonald, *British Conservatism, 1832–1914*, p. 20.

was a change of theory. Bagehot, writing in 1859, said that the object which the whigs had in view was 'to transfer the predominant influence in the State from certain special classes to the general aggregate of fairly instructed men'.[1] Actually, the whigs had had no such object, but the fact that by 1859 an acute constitutional observer thought they had is significant. The Reform Act had increased the electorate by one per cent of the population, or about one-quarter of the pre-reform electorate. Its more important effect, however, was to strengthen the representation of the landed interest on the one hand and that of the urban middle class on the other. It had simply shifted the balance of power. In particular, by weakening the representation of the smaller boroughs and giving representation to the newer towns it had weakened party control through borough proprietors and patrons and thus made it necessary for the parties to appeal on grounds of policy. By 1859 this could be converted into a theory of the representation of the educated, or 'instructed', classes. It could therefore be argued that the franchise could be lowered, especially in the towns, so as to enfranchise the 'respectable' workers. This was not a matter of principle, and there was no emotion in it. Hence in 1866–7 the questions could be discussed in terms of party advantage. Would the urban workers, if enfranchised, vote Liberal or Conservative?

Workers' representation had been in issue twenty-five years earlier. Though in most of the great cities the Reform Bill agitation had had the support of the unorganised 'mob', the Bill was a great disappointment to the radical politicians, who were generally middle class but whose ideas had been moulded by the French Revolution, Tom Paine's *Rights of Man*, and the pamphleteers who had fought for the liberty of the press after Waterloo. The theory of government of the people, by the people, for the people was not invented by Abraham Lincoln. It was not even a product of the American Revolution, though that event had important effects on English opinion. It might be read into John Locke's *Two Treatises on Civil Government*. For practical English purposes, however, the theory of equal representation began in the early years of George III's reign. In 1771, for instance, the Society of the Bill of Rights instructed its members to work for 'a complete and

---

[1] W. Bagehot, *Parliamentary Reform*, p. 3.

71

equal representation of the people in Parliament'.[1] After the French and American Revolutions (neither of which proclaimed the theory of equal representation) the opinion began to spread, but even in 1830 it was still a small minority opinion. The advantages and disadvantages were coolly considered by J. S. Mill in *Representative Government* in 1861: but he was expressing a minority opinion even at that late date.

The idea had in fact been put back by the Chartist Movement. The Parliaments of 1832 and 1835 had been dominated by the 'governing class' as before 1832. The whigs had had to lean over backwards to show that they were not democrats. The suppression of the trade unions and particularly the transportation of the 'Tolpuddle Martyrs' had sown distrust of the Whig Government in the small section of opinion which was concerned with these matters. The poor law of 1834 had created great distress and, to those who generalised about these questions, produced something of the idea of a class war. The enforcement of the 'principle of less eligibility'—the principle, that is, that the position of the rate-aided pauper should be deliberately made less attractive than that of the worst employed worker—was in many places applied in conditions of trade depression, which started in 1836 and was not substantially relieved until near the end of the forties. This depression produced two great agitations, that against the Corn Law and that for the People's Charter. The one succeeded and the other failed. Both gave great stimulus to political education; but the success of the one led, after the Peelites had been absorbed, into the great battle between the Liberal and the Conservative parties. The failure of the other took Parliamentary reform out of the realm of emotional politics. Since the great change between the eighteen-fifties and the nineteen-fifties is the acceptance of the principle of one person, one vote, one value, there ought logically to be a chapter of this volume on

---

[1] E. Halévy, *The Growth of Philosophic Radicalism*, p. 123. The idea is, however, much older. It was discussed by the Army in 1647: see Firth, *Clarke Papers*, I, pp. 299–307; and Mark Howell, *The Chartist Movement*, p. 4. The Heads of Proposals offered by the Army were less radical and in fact said nothing about the franchise, though they did recommend redistribution: S. R. Gardiner, *Constitutional Documents*, p. 317. In the 'Agreement of the People' (1649) the franchise was conferred upon all persons assessed to poor relief but not servants to and receiving wages from any particular person: *ibid.* p. 363. The 'Instrument of Government' (1653) provided for a property qualification of £200: Gardiner, *op. cit.* p. 411.

the 'Coming of Democracy'. After 1848, however, there never was a great popular movement for popular representation; and Parliamentary reform was, so to speak, one of the incidentals of party politics; one party was prepared to extend the franchise if it thought that it would thereby win more seats, and the other was prepared to acquiesce, or even to agree, if it thought that, on balance, it would win. Nobody thought it worth while to bring out the great battalions of the unenfranchised for a mass demonstration.

The assumption behind the Chartist Movement was that the grievances of the urban workers could be remedied by legislation, that such legislation would not be forthcoming from Parliaments which represented the employers, and accordingly that the workers must be given the vote and Parliament otherwise reformed. In Radical London there had been in 1830–2 some working-class opposition to the Reform Bill on the ground that it would strengthen the employers.[1] In general, however, it had been thought that the reforms of 1832 would benefit the people as a whole. The attack on trade unionism in 1833–4 showed that they had not helped the workers; and the drafting of the People's Charter by Francis Place and its publication by the London Working-Men's Association in 1838 was a direct result.[2] Copies were sent to all Working-Men's Associations in Great Britain asking for comments, and a revised edition was published later in the year. It demanded a franchise based on residence for three months, the ballot, equal constituencies, annual Parliaments, no property qualifications, and payment for Members. The London Radicals were not, however, the best people to organise a mass movement, and in any case nobody had any money. For a time it looked as though Thomas Attwood and the Birmingham Political Union (which had been revived) would lead the movement. But when the National Chartist Convention met in London in 1839, Feargus O'Connor and the men from the North took the lead. In the North and in South Wales were the ingredients of a real revolutionary movement of a highly class-conscious type. In this respect the Convention was not representative:

Nearly one-half the assembly belonged to the non-artisan classes. Some, like O'Connor and John Taylor, were sheer demagogues; others, such as

[1] G. Wallas, *Life of Francis Place*, p. 353.   [2] *Ibid.* pp. 359, 365, 367.

73

O'Brien and Carter, were doctrinaire social revolutionaries. The Birmingham delegates, except Collins, were prosperous fellows who had drifted into political agitation. Hadley was an alderman of Birmingham and a warden of St Martin's Church in the Bull Ring. Douglas was the editor of the *Birmingham Journal* and Salt was a lamp manufacturer on a considerable scale. Wade was a kind of Christian Socialist, a predecessor of Charles Kingsley. James Taylor was a Methodist Unitarian preacher who lived at Rochdale, and preached on a Methodist Unitarian circuit in East Lancashire. There were several medical men, inspired, no doubt, by similar motives, several booksellers, a lawyer, and a publican or two.[1]

This would not have mattered if the delegates had been in agreement, for all revolutionary movements are led by the heretics of the middle class. The delegates were, however, not agreed. There was behind them a vast, disturbed public opinion which wanted to do something or other, it knew not what, about something or other about which it had no idea: nor had the delegates, but the agitation in the provinces inflated their ideas. The one thing on which everybody agreed was in condemning the Anti-Corn Law League, which was holding its initial conference in London at the same time. After that the Convention descended into futility. There was much talk of arming the people, which led to resignations; there was a suggestion of a general strike: and in the end they merely delivered the petition for the Charter at Attwood's house.

Meanwhile conditions were going from bad to worse in the industrial areas.

From Bristol to Edinburgh and from Glasgow to Hull rumours of arms, riots, conspiracies, and insurrections grew with the passing of the weeks. Crowded meetings applauded violent orations, threats and terrorism were abroad. Magistrates trembled and peaceful citizens felt that they were living on a social volcano. The frail bonds of social sympathy were snapped, and class stood over against class as if a civil war were impending.[2]

Fortunately, this potentially revolutionary situation was well handled. The danger lay not with the braggarts of the Convention but with the desperate men in the provinces, who had no leaders. There were riots at Birmingham, but wholesale arrests broke up the second Convention held there and such local organisations as existed. There followed an

[1] Mark Howell, *The Chartist Movement*, p. 122.   [2] *Ibid.* pp. 136–7.

ineffectual rising at Newport (Monmouthshire), put down by the troops, and a few small outbreaks elsewhere, but the first period of Chartism ended in futility.

There was renewed activity in 1840, based this time on Birmingham and professing to attain the Charter by wholly peaceful and legal means. It was easier to be illegal than legal, for the law on corresponding societies and conspiracy, designed to prevent unlawful agitation, made almost any kind of organisation for political ends unlawful. The widespread distress and the sense of grievance under which the workingmen laboured, if dammed, would force an outlet and lead to sporadic, though undirected, violence. In some places even the Church was taking part, though in rebellion against the general Conservative tendencies of the Church of England and the Wesleyan Methodists. We have from Paisley a Chartist version of Ecclesiastes iv. 1:[1]

There is then one master grievance, one all-reaching, all-blasting evil: one enormous, atrocious, monstrous iniquity: one soul-blighting, heart-breaking, man-destroying, heaven-defying sin, which fills the earth with bondage and with blood, which aids the powerful and strikes the helpless, which punishes the innocent and rewards the guilty, which aggrandises the rich and robs the poor, which exalts the rich and beats down the humble, which decries truth and pleads for falsehood, which honours infamy and defames virtue, which pampers idleness and famishes industry, one GIGANTIC VIL-LAINY, the root and cause, the parent and protector of a thousand crimes ...committing wrong and miscalling it right, committing robbery and calling it LAW, nay, in the sight of heaven, committing foul murder and calling it JUSTICE.

In fact, however, the Christian Chartists had little influence, except by giving an air of comparative respectability to what was in large part plain demagoguery.

Feargus O'Connor, who had been arrested in April 1840 for a libel which had little to do with Chartism, was released in August 1841 and forthwith claimed martyrdom in a poem, written by himself, which contained the verse:

> O'Connor is our chosen chief,
> He's champion of the Charter;
> Our Saviour suffered like a thief
> Because he preached the Charter.[2]

---

[1] *Ibid.* p. 202.   [2] *Ibid.* p. 222.

75

He was one of those magnificent rogues, occasionally thrown up by politics, who love the limelight and have no scruples about the means by which it is played. He cared as little for the truth as for the Charter, but he loved the glory while it lasted and was prepared to work hard for it. He proceeded to eliminate all rivals, and he himself led the procession carrying the giant petition which Thomas Duncombe presented to the House of Commons in May 1842. The debate was noteworthy for a great speech by Macaulay, defending the foundation of the Constitution on property. It was, however, the Radical Roebuck who, supporting the petition, provided the theme of the debate by admitting that it was drawn up by 'a malignant and cowardly demagogue'. Never was truth so devastating; but it did not help the petition, which was defeated by 287 votes to 49. There remained only the remedy of 'physical force', or rebellion, which O'Connor had neither the courage to try nor the ability to lead. There was some disorder, put down by vigorous action by the Government. There was a revival of Chartism in 1843, under O'Connor's direct management, but there was a gradual decline thereafter due not merely to the bad management of the leaders but also to returning prosperity and the remedial legislation of Peel's Ministry. A new petition, said to contain six million signatures, was taken to Parliament in 1848 in three hansom cabs—the police had forbidden a procession—and it was found to contain less than two million signatures, many of which were obviously false. Chartism was not dead, but it was very, very feeble. O'Connor became insane in 1852.

In point of fact, Chartism succeeded. The franchise was based on occupation of land in 1884 and on residence in 1918; the ballot was adopted in 1872; annual Parliaments were never approved, but the life of a Parliament was reduced to five years in 1911; the principle of equal electoral districts was accepted in 1885; the property qualification for members was abolished in 1858 and allowances have been paid since 1911. Bagehot's approach to the problem of representation in 1859 was quite different from Macaulay's in 1842. Macaulay was no diehard; but he repeated the old theory that the Constitution was founded on property. Bagehot was no Radical, but he was a banker, accustomed to property in more intangible forms than land, and he was writing only three years before the Companies Act of 1862 authorised the formation of companies with limited liability: as W. S. Gilbert put it

> Some seven men form an Association
> (If possible, all Peers and Baronets)
> They start off with a public declaration
> To what extent they mean to pay their debts.
> That's called their Capital.[1]

When peers and baronets were forming companies, there was not much to be said for the divine right of the landed interest. We are nearer the age of the divine right of Capital, which because of its diffusion could not be given representation in the House of Commons (it had plenty in the House of Lords), except by giving directorships to members of the House and getting seats in the House for directors, a two-way traffic which has continued to this day.

Bagehot's emphasis was therefore placed not on land but on education. It was, however, a little difficult to argue that the level of education was determined by owning land worth forty shillings a year, by farming land worth £50 a year, and by occupying urban property worth £10 a year. Even Robert Lowe, leading the Cave of Adullam against the Liberal Bill of 1866, did not say that: what he said was that a lowering of the franchise, as proposed in the Bill, would vest power in the working class, the most venial, the most ignorant, the most drunken, the most impulsive, corrupt and violent people.[2] The average working man (he said on Baines' Bill of 1865) who lived in an £8 house and drank 600 quarts of beer a year at 4d. a pot, had only to drink 120 quarts a year less and rent a £10 house to acquire the franchise. Hence these proposals to lower the franchise would let in the improvident.[3]

This is perhaps to caricature the Adullam case; but in any event it was a rearguard action by a minority. A great many wage-earners had the vote in 1865 because money values had been lowered and rents and wages increased, so that the £10 occupier of 1865 was not the same as the £10 occupier of 1832. Neither party saw any particular virtue in the £10 limit, and both thought that they would gain more votes if

---

[1] Quoted by J. H. Clapham, *An Economic History of Modern Britain*, II, p. 137.
[2] *E.H.D.* XII (1), p. 162. [3] *Life of Lord Sherbrooke*, II, p. 259.

it were lowered. It was no longer a question of principle, but simply a 'party political' question; nobody, except the last-ditchers in both parties, was particularly excited about it, not even the working-men who were offered the vote. The emotions of Chartism had been swamped in the rising tide of Victorian prosperity. There was even less objection to the lowering of the county franchise in 1884, and to more or less equal single-member constituencies: it was just a question of doing sums with inadequate data in order to guess which party would gain the more.

6. THE HOUSE OF LORDS

The Whig Constitution of 1830, which the whigs were accused of overthrowing by the Reform Act, was defended because it was 'mixed', since it was at once monarchical, aristocratical and democratical. 'Democratical' here meant that the House of Commons was dominated by the landed interest but had some representation of the rest of the population. Similarly 'aristocratical' needed definition. The numerous creations of peerages in the eighteenth century, especially after William Pitt became Prime Minister in 1783, had considerably altered the composition of the House of Lords. If it was an aristocracy, it was artificially created. This is especially true if only the active politicians be considered. In Wellington's Cabinet of 1828–30 were nine peers, only two of whom (one a Scot) held peerages created before 1689, and only two others held peerages created before 1784. The Whig Government of 1830–4 was more aristocratic, but of its twelve peers only two held peerages created before 1689, and only one other held a peerage created before 1784. In other words it was a new aristocracy, created for what should properly be called political services.

As a debating assembly, the House of Lords was less important than the House of Commons. The elder Pitt lost a great deal of his effective power by having himself created Earl of Chatham, and his younger son never repeated the error. The five Prime Ministers in office from 1812 to 1834 (excluding Canning's short Ministry in 1827) were all peers, but they depended heavily on their lieutenants in the House of Commons— Viscount Castlereagh, Canning, Huskisson, Peel, and Lord Althorp; and the fact that Lord Althorp went to the House of Lords as Earl Spencer broke up Lord Melbourne's Government of 1834.

The standing of the House of Lords declined even more rapidly after 1834. As the opponents of the Reform Bill had feared, the extension of the franchise, the abolition of the pocket boroughs, and the consequent weakness of the Government had altered the balance of the Constitution. The balance had in fact been shifting since 1783, and especially since 1815; but after 1832 political issues had to be fought in the House of Commons, if not in the constituencies, and could no longer be settled in country houses. Moreover, the decline in the political influence of the landed interest gradually weakened the power even of the Russells and the Cavendishes who had had the foresight to invest in urban property. Lord John Russell and Disraeli took peerages, but right at the end of their political careers. Lord Derby, the Earl of Aberdeen, the Marquis of Salisbury, and the Earl of Rosebery became Prime Ministers, but all depended on their henchmen in the House of Commons. The end of the House of Lords as an effective institution might have been foreseen in 1886, when most of the Liberal peers went Unionist.

This became obvious in 1906, when the Conservative party, heavily defeated at the general election, sought to use the House of Lords as a means for rendering the Liberal Government ineffective and so enabling the Conservatives to win the next election. Had there been no war in 1914 the stupidity of this procedure, looking at the matter from the Conservative point of view, would have been apparent. Because the peers obstructed Liberal legislation between 1906 and 1909, Lloyd George was able to waggle a juicy carrot before their lordships' noses in the Budget of 1909, to attack 'the Dukes' as prehistoric animals when they seized the carrot, and to deprive the peers of effective power before another Home Rule Bill was introduced. By that time nobody was prepared to defend the existence of hereditary legislators, and the whole problem became 'party political'.

The House of Lords has survived, with no powers worth mentioning, though something like one-tenth of the House does useful public service by considering Government Bills, sitting on numerous committees, and holding interesting but not very important debates. In 1958 even a Conservative Government had to give the House an injection by asking Parliament to authorise the creation of life peers.

CHAPTER III

CHURCH AND KING

I. NO POPERY

When the 'Reformation Parliament' summoned in 1529 slowly and
even gently deprived the Pope of his claims to right, power and jurisdiction in England, no dog barked, and there was no very joyous chorus
when they were restored under Mary I. This was only partly due to the
corruption and worldliness of the Church. To the ordinary individual
in the town or the village the parson was the Church; and to the parson,
the bishop and the university were the Church; to whom the bishop
owed allegiance was, for most, a matter of indifference. In the conditions of the sixteenth century there could be no sense of the unity of
Christendom. For the comparatively small wealthy class the Church
had offered, not merely a refuge for the saint and the scholar but also
a career for the ambitious. It was the instrument by which an active
and not too scrupulous man could hope to rise to the highest position
in Church and State, as Cardinal Wolsey above all demonstrated. The
bishops were, on the whole, worldly men, politicians, not fathers of
their flocks. Clerics and laymen competed for power and prestige,
especially after the accession of Henry VII, when the Church ceased
to be the sole avenue of advancement for ambitious men. Nor were
the clerics all holy men, devout scholars, or learned theologians. The
tradition of the disreputable cleric was widespread. The Pope himself
was an Italian prince and the scandals at his court were notorious. The
archbishops, bishops and abbots were great landowners, seeking to
secure the largest possible profit from a large part of the land of
England. The lesser clergy levied the most objectionable of all taxes,
the tithe. In the towns there was constant conflict over franchises.
Nor were the theological dogmas of the Church, which had been
worked out in a feudal society, attuned to the new mercantilism
founded on profit and interest.

In any case the Church was already very English. Control by the
papacy had rarely been strong, and the higher ranks of the clergy owed

80

more to the King than to the Pope. Of the seventeen diocesan bishops in England at the accession of Henry VIII, fifteen had been active in State affairs, one was the step-brother of Henry VII, and the other, Fisher, had been confessor to the Lady Margaret.[1] Wolsey's attempt to use papal power in order to aggrandise himself had appeared to be a threat not only to the laity but also to the Church. The use of the word 'Reformation' to cover the whole period from the termination of papal authority under Henry VIII to Elizabeth's ecclesiastical reforms (omitting the reaction under Mary) is politically misleading. Thomas Cromwell can hardly be described as a theologian and he was not proposing to reform the Church. His initial task was so to alter the ecclesiastical establishment as to secure a divorce for Henry VIII of a kind which the King, as an amateur theologian, and his people would recognise as valid. The anti-clerical traditions of English landowners, and the social ambitions which were a marked feature of the Tudor reigns, enabled him to go further and suppress the monasteries and chantries; but this, too, was essentially a political reform, designed mainly to fill the King's coffers. It did more than that, for it completed the extinction of the feudal system. In the Middle Ages the Church had been competitor with the barons. After the Wars of the Roses there were no longer great barons, though a new nobility was in process of development. The 'Reformation', by abolishing whatever remained of the independent authority of the Church, resulted eventually in the Church becoming a part, though a significant part, of the landed interest.

Meanwhile, the papacy had become a national enemy, if not the national enemy, and 'No Popery' was a constant factor in English politics for nearly three hundred years.

It would be wrong to attribute the development exclusively to the Popes, though Pius V (1566–72) and Gregory XIII (1572–85) could hardly have done more to attract the responsibility. The reigns of Mary and Elizabeth Tudor were periods of great economic and intellectual progress in which English nationalism was strongly developed. England was a small country, competing in a world dominated by great Roman Catholic countries. The Roman Catholics themselves, both inside and

[1] H. Maynard Smith, *Pre-Reformation England*, p. 21 n.

outside the country, properly felt themselves bound to restore the English to the old religion. Much of the effort was entirely non-political, but religion and politics were inextricably mingled in a warring society. It was impossible, at this stage, to regard religion as a personal belief of no concern to anybody else. Moreover a substantial body of Puritan opinion had developed in the later Tudor reigns, especially in Cambridge, and had spread widely. To this body of opinion the Church of Rome was not merely a corrupt Christian Church, as it was to Anglicans; it was the Antichrist of the Bible and therefore the cause of the evils which vexed the world.

Mary Tudor's campaign to restore England to the bosom of the Roman Church was her own idea. She was assisted by her relative, Reginald, Cardinal Pole, but he was sent as legate *a latere* at her request. Both her cousin, the Emperor Charles V, and her Lord Chancellor, Stephen Gardiner, Bishop of Winchester, tried to damp down her impolitic enthusiasm. She proceeded on her way with the zeal of a Tudor who was half Spanish, with the result that history knows her, a little unfairly, as 'Bloody Mary'. The merits of her victims were extolled, and sometimes exaggerated, in Foxe's *Book of Martyrs*, one of the best pieces of Protestant propaganda ever penned. Moreover Queen Mary had lost Calais, which had been English for two hundred years.

Of the numerous plots in which the Roman Catholic powers, Mary of Scotland, and some of the English and Scottish Roman Catholics were involved in the reign of Elizabeth I it would be impossible to speak. Their connexion with religion was often peripheral. Sometimes religion was just a device for gaining allies, a cloak for personal ambition. After 1570 all plots could be attributed to the Pope because the Papal Bull of that year[1] condemned Queen Elizabeth as a heretic, excommunicated her and deprived her of her rights and dignities. The people of England were absolved from their allegiance to her and forbidden to obey her laws and orders. That this made every good Roman Catholic in England a traitor was perhaps not appreciated in Rome, and ten years later Gregory XIII issued an explanation which was even

[1] G. W. Prothero, *Select Statutes and other Constitutional Documents* (4th ed.), pp. 195–6.

worse. The Bull of 1570 did not bind Catholics except when its execution became possible. In other words, a good Roman Catholic was to keep his treason secret until it became politic to come into the open. Few English Catholics were traitors in fact, but they were always under suspicion of secret plotting. The suspicion was enhanced by the activities of the Jesuits. The first English College for training priests for missionary work in England was set up in Douai in 1568, and three others were established by 1592. A Jesuit mission to England was organised in Rome in 1579. There was a secret Roman Catholic printing press in London in 1581, though most Catholic propaganda was smuggled in. There were plots to assassinate the Queen and put Mary of Scotland on the throne; and Mary herself was executed for being involved in one of them. In such an atmosphere suspicion was inevitably rife. Some of those condemned were no doubt innocent; some condemned for treason were guilty only of propagating religion; but even so the total number of persons executed for treason or religious nonconformity during Elizabeth's long reign was much less than the total number executed for religious nonconformity during five years under 'Bloody Mary'.[1] The most famous plot, however, came after the death of Elizabeth, the Gunpowder Plot of 1605. 'Guy Fawkes' Day' has long lost its association with anti-papist agitation; but its popular institution as a day of remembrance and celebration bears witness to the strength of anti-papist feeling. That feeling was in the background of all political conflict over religion. It helps to explain the Civil War and the almost unanimous dismissal of James II, the last papist king. It has given a peculiar tinge to British nationalism, particularly in its relation to Ireland; and to this day 'No Popery' is chalked in the streets of Belfast on 12 July (the anniversary of the defeat of James II at the Battle of the Boyne). It provided one of the elements of the common heritage which made the Union of England and Scotland possible.

The close association of 'no popery' with nationalism was strengthened by the defeat of the Spanish Armada in 1588. The attempted invasion by Philip II of Spain was primarily a move in power politics; but the Pope's contingent promise of financial support and the

[1] On all this, see J. B. Black, *The Reign of Elizabeth*, pp. 137–48 and 326–35.

Spanish king's insistence on his religious aims made Elizabeth's victory over Spain the defeat of popery. The whigs and tories of 1688 had been told about the Armada by their grandfathers, and one of the Inns of court (Gray's Inn) still drinks to 'the pious, glorious and immortal memory of Good Queen Bess'.

2. THE ENGLISH REFORMATION

As has been said, the English Reformation was by origin a purely political movement, and in the hands of Thomas Cromwell it remained political. There was, however, a small intellectual movement, imported into Cambridge from the Low Countries, and transported to Oxford by Cardinal Wolsey's appointments to his new foundation, now Christ Church. It began, surprisingly enough, in conservative Trinity Hall, the English home of the canon law, whose Master, after 1525, was Stephen Gardiner. Thomas Bilney of Trinity Hall, the first of the Protestant martyrs, converted Hugh Latimer of Clare, Robert Barnes of the Austin Friars (behind Corpus Christi), and John Lambert of Queens', all of whom later became martyrs. They formed the nucleus of the coterie of Protestants known as 'Little Germany', which met in the White Horse Inn, behind what is now the Bull Court of St Catharine's. They were not seditious conspirators, but the suppression of papal authority brought into question the doctrine of the Church of England and created a party conflict which ended only with the Restoration of Charles II.

The first steps taken by the Reformation Parliament were not suggested by King Henry VIII. He simply allowed the anti-clericalism of the House of Commons to express itself in legislation. That anti-clericalism was stronger in 1529 than it had ever been before, or became afterwards, because Wolsey had made the Church so unpopular. In due course this anti-clerical sentiment turned into anti-papist sentiment, which was strengthened in the reigns of 'Bloody Mary' and 'Good Queen Bess'; but in 1529 it was directed against the Church of England. Nor were the clergy themselves firm in their allegiance to Rome. The papacy had done no great harm while it was remote and weakened by its political difficulties. When Wolsey exercised his power as legate, however, the papacy became close and powerful. 'When the attack on the Church came after Wolsey's fall, resistance was in part weakened by the thought that the king's rule could not be worse—might indeed be lighter—than papal rule as exemplified by the Pope's legate.'[1]

Moreover the Church could be cowed by threats, for the Pope had no means of protecting it against royal extortion, and bishops, abbots and the higher clergy had much more to lose than their reputations for learning and piety. At the critical moment it was easy to resort to the Statutes of Praemunire, which had forbidden recognition of papal jurisdiction, though they had rarely been enforced.[2]

After the appointment of Thomas Cromwell to minor office in 1532 the breach with Rome and the dissolution of the monasteries were carried through with ruthless efficiency. Not all the later legislation went through Parliament without some opposition, but it was never very strong. Nor was there much opposition outside, though Sir Thomas More, Bishop Fisher, and a few monks suffered martyrdom. The dissolution of the smaller monasteries helped to produce in 1536 the rising in the north usually known as the pilgrimage of grace, but even this movement arose out of other grievances.

So far the problem was essentially political, but the battle between Anglican Catholicism and Lutheran Protestantism, which had been going on in Cambridge from 1521, became evident in the Church in 1539. On the one side were the Duke of Norfolk and Stephen Gardiner, who was Bishop of Winchester as well as Master of Trinity Hall. On the other side were Thomas Cromwell and the younger Cambridge men, including Thomas Cranmer, Archbishop of Canterbury, Hugh Latimer, who was Bishop of Worcester, and Nicholas Shaxton, Bishop of Salisbury. For the time being the conservatives triumphed, and indeed Latimer and Shaxton were accused of heresy. Cromwell himself was executed in 1540, less because of the treason and heresy of which he was accused by the Act of Attainder than because he had persuaded the King to marry Anne of Cleves and would not help to replace her by Katharine Howard, a niece of the Duke of Norfolk.

---

[1] G. R. Elton, *England under the Tudors* (2nd ed.), pp. 87–8.
[2] May McKisack, *The Fourteenth Century*, pp. 280–3.

There followed 'eighteen years of somewhat purposeless turmoil',[1] dominated by the conflict between Catholic and Protestant, but ending in the Elizabethan settlement. Cromwell was not replaced, and for the remainder of the reign of Henry VIII the conservatives triumphed, though they were weakened by the discovery of Katharine Howard's unchastity and by the King's last marriage to Katharine Parr, who was somewhat of a Protestant but kept herself out of politics. Even so, the statements of doctrine in the 'King's Book', published in 1543, were orthodox Catholic, subject of course to the acceptance of royal supremacy over the Church. On the other hand, Gardiner and his friends were unable to unseat Cranmer, and Prince Edward was brought up as a reformer. On the King's death in 1547 a council of moderate men assumed what was in effect a regency, but it was dominated by Edward Seymour, Earl of Hertford, who became Duke of Somerset and Lord Protector. The Protestants were now in the ascendant and a host of continental refugees poured in. Cranmer was one of the Council and Gardiner had gone back to Cambridge.[2] Cranmer's views became more Protestant under the influence of the reformers, though he was always a moderate man. The first Prayer Book, that of 1549, was a compromise which could be read by Gardiner and by Cranmer in quite different senses. The revised Prayer Book of 1552 'marked the arrival of the English Church at Protestantism'.[3] It was followed by an Act of Uniformity, which imposed penalties upon those who failed to use it, and the Forty-two Articles to which the clergy were required to subscribe.

The reformers had, however, gone far ahead of popular sentiment, which was little concerned with ecclesiastical ceremonies or their deeper implications. The attempt to set up Lady Jane Grey as successor to Edward VI failed because of the popular support for a real Tudor. Mary I ascended the throne not because she was an adherent of the Church of Rome but because she was the daughter of Henry VIII. She probably did not realise this; but if she did it made no difference,

---

[1] G. R. Elton, *op. cit.* p. 193.

[2] He was, however, imprisoned in the Fleet and in the Tower of London from 1548 to 1553. He was ejected from the Mastership in 1552 but restored in 1553 on the accession of Mary I.

[3] G. R. Elton, *op. cit.* p. 212.

for her main aim was to restore the English Church to the bosom of her own Church. She was, indeed, more papist than the Pope, for some kind of compromise was politically essential. Though she was bound to regard the anti-papist and protestant legislation of Henry VIII and Edward VI as invalid, since it was contrary to the canon law, even Stephen Gardiner, who became Lord Chancellor, realised that the only way to get rid of it was to repeal and replace it by Act of Parliament. Nor could the endowments of which the Church had been despoiled be replaced, for Parliament was not persuadable. New laws against heresy—the old sort of heresy—were passed with reluctance, and their execution was largely responsible for the tradition of 'Bloody Mary'. Some two thousand clergy were extruded, but there were no replacements, and many of them obtained benefices where their acquiescence in protestantism was unknown. Mary's insistence on marrying Philip, Archduke of Burgundy and afterwards King of Spain, was thoroughly unpopular; and Parliament insisted that, though he became King, he should not have a right of succession to Queen Mary. Anti-clericalism, protestantism and nationalism were stimulated by her short reign, and everybody welcomed the accession of her half-sister, Elizabeth, the daughter of Anne Boleyn. She could not be a papist because the Church of Rome said she was illegitimate; she was the ablest of the Tudors; she could play off her marriageability among the royal families; and for nearly the whole of her long reign she had the wise advice of Sir William Cecil, Lord Burghley. The traditions of 'Bloody Mary' and 'Good Queen Bess' persist to this day.

In the reign of Elizabeth I began the grand alliance between Church and Crown which was broken by James II, a breach which cost him his throne; but the alliance otherwise continued until the death of Queen Anne. To achieve this alliance Queen Elizabeth had to root out Roman Catholicism and to produce a settlement which would be regarded as reasonable by reasonable men. There was no difficulty about rooting out Roman Catholicism. Queen Mary had helped to make that easy, and Elizabeth had every assistance from the Roman Catholic powers and from the Pope himself. To produce a reasonable settlement was more difficult. On the death of Mary the exiles came trooping back, many of them full of Lutheran or Calvinistic doctrine.

The violent aversion to papist ideas which Mary and the Roman Catholic powers produced stimulated extreme Protestantism. Queen Elizabeth herself had no very strong views, but what views she had inclined her to support rather the anti-papist Catholicism of her father's ecclesiastical establishment than the doctrines of Geneva. On the other hand, a substantial minority of the clergy, probably the more zealous minority, wanted to purify the Church of the corruption associated with Roman practices. This minority had the support of a strong and vocal minority in Parliament: and the most significant development of Elizabeth's reign was the growth of independent ideas in the House of Commons. The 'opposition' members, if we may so call them, were loyal to the Queen; but they could not always be managed by privy councillors, especially after 1572, when Cecil went to the House of Lords as Lord Burghley. They insisted on debating matters which the Queen thought to be her 'prerogative', especially her marriage, the succession, and the Church settlement. They even had support among the councillors. Elizabeth was not only imperious but also wise, and she never made the same mistake twice. Nevertheless, she had to pay attention to the strength of feeling in the House of Commons.

The settlement of 1559 was therefore a compromise. The new Prayer Book was, in substance, that of 1552, though somewhat modified to make it more acceptable to Catholic opinion; and legal effect was given to it by a new Act of Uniformity. The Act of Supremacy revived the legislation of Henry VIII, repealed Mary's heresy legislation, abolished papal jurisdiction and vested jurisdiction in the Crown. It also required all ecclesiastical and civil authorities to make, take and receive a 'corporal oath upon the Evangelist', testifying that the Queen was 'the only Supreme Governor of this realm and of all other her Highness's dominions and countries, as well in all spiritual or ecclesiastical things or causes as temporal...'.[1] The Church of England thus became Protestant by Act of Parliament.

Though the Marian bishops refused to take the oath of supremacy, their places were filled, in part by bishops deprived in 1553, and in part by Marian exiles. Matthew Parker, a Cambridge man in the Cranmer tradition, became Archbishop of Canterbury. 'A believer in authority

---

[1] J. R. Tanner, *Tudor Constitutional Documents*, pp. 130–5.

88

and monarchy, opposed to all extremes and disorder, and one who devoted his intellectual abilities to history rather than theology, he was at the same time an admirably firm and dispassionate administrator.'[1] Though the Convocation of Canterbury had in 1559 asserted the full Catholic position both on papal authority and on dogma,[2] only two or three hundred of the lesser clergy were deprived for refusal to take the oath. The Elizabethan settlement was cemented by the nationalism which grew out of Roman Catholic threats and intrigues, but they also encouraged Puritanism. The death of Parker in 1575 brought to the see of Canterbury a mild Puritan, Grindal of York; and the very moderation of the bishops stimulated not only a presbyterian minority within the Church but also the development outside the Church of sects which may be described as 'congregationalist' or 'independent'. From 1580, and especially after Whitgift succeeded Grindal in 1583, an attempt was made through the Court of High Commission to stamp out non-conformity. It became in fact a minority outside the Church, though it remained strong in Parliament.

Nevertheless, Puritanism remained strong within the Church, and under James I it produced a conflict between the bishops, who were supported by the King, and many of the clergy. Though the new Archbishop, Bancroft, was a Cambridge man, he had no Puritan sympathies, and he sought to enforce the canons of 1604, in which the Puritan claims were rejected. What is more, the alliance between the bishops and the King resulted in the bishops supporting the King's claims to prerogative. The conflict within the Church therefore became part of the battle over prerogative which led to the Civil War. Indeed, it became impossible to separate the spiritual from the temporal. Though some Puritans left the Church, or were extruded, because they could not support either the canons of 1604 or an ecclesiastical order based upon bishops, others accepted episcopacy on the basis that bishops were royal officers. The acceptance of Arminian doctrines—under which the bishops claimed divine authority through apostolic succession—by Charles I and some of his bishops, sharpened the contest. Also, the laity came into it. The raising of clerical pretensions

[1] G. R. Elton, *England under the Tudors*, pp. 275–6.
[2] *Ibid.* p. 271.

89

aroused the old anti-clerical antagonism. Indeed it did more; for the claim associated the Church of England with the Church of Rome and gave the Puritans the support of anti-papist and nationalist sentiment. The Counter-Reformation was having considerable success on the continent and in Ireland. Queen Henrietta Maria was thought to be a centre of Roman propaganda. The King's own position seemed to sturdy Protestants, who knew no theology but objected to popes and Jesuits, to be moving towards Rome. The Oxford Calvinist, George Abbot, had succeeded Bancroft in 1611, but he had little influence after 1627, and the enforcement of Church discipline was left to another Oxford man, William Laud, Bishop of London from 1626 and Archbishop from 1633, perhaps the most hated prelate that ever was. The Court of High Commission, over which he presided, was regarded by the Parliament men as an instrument of oppression second only to the Court of Star Chamber.

The alliance between Church and King and the intransigence of Charles I converted the Civil War from a battle between prerogative and Parliament to a battle between the Church and Puritanism. Yet the Elizabethan settlement, the establishment of a national church on an Anglican doctrine which Richard Hooker had no difficulty in defending, was as sensible as most of the things that Elizabeth and her advisers initiated. It harnessed three strong emotions, religion, personal loyalty and nationalist sentiment. Clerics, especially donnish ones, could not start a revolution because laymen would have stopped their quarrels by giving them, where necessary, a choice between their careers and their consciences. As things were, the alliance of Church and King necessarily implied that those who were against the bishops were against the King, and vice versa.

Popular history has sharpened the distinction between Cavalier and Puritan. According to real history people of much the same type were active on both sides, and the vast majority of the people were passive. In politics, however, popular history is more important than real history. On the one side is 'romance', the dashing cavalier of Prince Rupert's army, loyal to his king, embodying in himself the colour and imagination of the better Tudors. On the other side is the dour Puritan of Oliver Cromwell's New Model, preparing himself for the fray by listening to a long sermon and singing psalms, and then riding inexorably upon the Royalist flank. It was a conflict between twopence coloured and penny plain; and when schoolboys of subsequent generations have been asked to take sides, the majority has chosen not religious zeal and plain efficiency, but romance, illusion and scatter-brained inefficiency, the cheerful 'sinners' rather than the grim 'saints'.

This contrast has had many political repercussions, and the fact that it is overdrawn does not matter. Indeed, it was enhanced by experience under the Commonwealth and the Protectorate. As in all revolutions, the extremists took charge; and even Oliver Cromwell, who was not an extremist, had not the power to resist extremist pressure. The shifty and narrow-minded King Charles saved his reputation by being executed. The honest and comparatively broad-minded Lord Protector lost his by being relatively successful. Neither side favoured toleration, though Cromwell, as an independent, was far more tolerant than Archbishop Laud had been. What the population suffered, however, was the intolerance of the Puritan Army, the futility of the rule of the 'saints', and the stupidity of compulsory conformity with the Puritan way of life. Almost everybody welcomed Charles II, and the excesses of Restoration England were a relief after the excesses of Puritan England.

The Church was restored with the King, and it had advantages as a political instrument that dissent and Nonconformity have never been able to claim. Cromwell's men had smashed or mutilated 'superstitious' monuments, but they could not destroy the beauty of the great cathedrals and parish churches, our most precious heritage from the Middle Ages. Indeed, the inhibitions against superstitious uses have given the English churches a dignity of which so many of the Roman churches have been robbed by garish images, while at the same time the Church has preserved the association of religious and artistic emotion with which the dissenters had necessarily to dispense. It happened, too, that the prayers, the psalms and the Bible itself were translated in the vintage years of the English language, when the vernacular and the numerous importations of the learned had been moulded by a series of great poets and dramatists into a flexible and expressive speech. The Authorised Version of the Bible is common to all English sects and was in fact the primary weapon of the dissenters against the Church. By the end of the seventeenth century, however, its phrases had been embodied in common speech; its lessons fitted more perfectly into the services prescribed by the Book of Common Prayer than into the extempore prayers of Puritan divines as the common speech diverged from that of the Elizabethan and Jacobean period. The services of the Church of England, in fact, are as a whole period pieces, in broad outline reasonably intelligible to the uninstructed laity, and yet so constructed and expressed that they give the impression of an ancient ritual in which the congregation shares by responses, prayers, psalms and hymns.

After the extravagances of Puritan rule the Church of England gave an impression of stability and dignity. It provided shelter for those who were weary of controversy and wanted not theology but peace. It was, too, the national Church. The Puritans helped to develop the incipient nationalism of the Elizabethan age, but their religion came from Germany, Geneva and Scotland; and dissent had not yet settled down into the very English tradition of the Nonconformist sects. The influence of the profligate Court and the obscene Restoration stage must not be exaggerated. Bunyan's *Pilgrim's Progress* (1678) is far more typical of the age and had a much wider influence. It was, of course, Puritan propaganda and it helped to fill the dissenters' chapels: but to those not concerned with theological controversy (and they always have been the vast majority) it was propaganda for religion against irreligion.

James II disrupted the alliance between Church and King by attempting to restore popery. The Church of England was no longer in the forefront of battle: but Archbishop Sancroft and six other bishops went so far as to petition against the second Declaration of Indulgence and became popular heroes when the jury acquitted them in the *Case of the Seven Bishops*; and Henry Compton, Bishop of London, was one of the seven men who signed the invitation to William of Orange. Probably few cared very much for the politics of bishops, and the dissenters had been cool towards James II's promises of toleration. Many of the most worthy of the clergy could not swear allegiance to William and Mary after they had sworn allegiance to James Stuart.

On the other hand, most of the non-jurors went quietly into retirement and took no part in the activities of the Jacobite party. Mary II was a good Protestant, and the alliance between Church and Crown was cemented by Queen Anne strongly enough to withstand the shock of the accession of George I.

3. CHURCH AND CLASS

In a book on politics it is wise to emphasise that those who take religion seriously are a minority. Perhaps this is especially so in a Protestant country. Where the Church of Rome (or, for that matter, any other religious institution) has a monopoly it can establish itself in all spheres of social life from the family to the monarchy, from the trade union and the co-operative society to the Houses of Parliament. Under such a monopoly excommunication is a potent social sanction even against those who fail to take it seriously as a religious sanction. There are great social pressures towards conformity in all societies; but in a country in which religious freedom prevails in fact as well as in law there are competing sects and therefore competing conformities; and because there are competing conformities the great institutions of social life, other than the religious institutions, have to be almost, if not quite, neutral. Consequently, the ordinary man can go about his daily life without bothering about religion.

Of religious liberty something must be said in the next chapter. After the Restoration nonconformity was not merely heresy, it was closely allied with treason.[1] Compulsory conformity takes its origin from the character of religion in general, whether Christian or otherwise, as an expression of ultimate truth. To deny that there is one God or that Muhammad is his Prophet is as offensive to a Muslim as the denial of the Holy Trinity is to a Roman Catholic or an Anglican. Mahayana Buddhism is as objectionable to a Theravada Buddhist as the doctrines of the Church of Rome are to a Quaker. In Christendom,

---

[1] Cf. the preamble to the Five Mile Act, 1665, which refers to 'the poisonous principles of schism and rebellion' which are distilled into the minds of His Majesty's subjects by dissenting ministers, 'to the great danger of the Church and Kingdom'. See also the Conventicle Act, 1670, which referred to 'seditious sectaries and other disloyal persons, who under pretence of tender consciences have or may at their meetings contrive insurrections'.

however, the close association of Church and State made the position of the dissenter from the established religion particularly difficult. Under Elizabeth I the attitude of the Church of Rome compelled the devout Roman Catholic to choose between his loyalty to his Church and his loyalty to the Crown. The end of the Civil War similarly associated Puritanism and treason. Thus, the concept of religious uniformity which ecclesiastical politicians took over from the pre-Reformation monopoly of the Church of Rome became firmly fixed in law and practice. The efforts of the Stuarts to introduce toleration were universally regarded as efforts to introduce popery and were firmly resisted.

Even so, Puritanism did not disappear with the Restoration. There were even Puritans among the landed classes, especially in Yorkshire.[1] The general effect of the Civil War had been, however, to create among the landed gentry a detestation of Puritanism as a political movement even if, as Lord Macaulay suggested,[2] many of them had no great love for the Church of England as such. In the towns the dissenters were much stronger, especially in London and Bristol and in unincorporated towns like Birmingham and Manchester, to which the Five Mile Act did not apply.[3] Even in the towns, however, there was pressure towards conformity. It was assumed that a dissenter was disloyal; the holding of a corporate office was difficult for him because of the oaths required by the Corporation Act, 1661; and the Test Acts made it virtually impossible for him to hold office under the Crown or be elected to Parliament. It was possible to engage in trade or banking: but as soon as a wealthy dissenter wanted to found a family in the eighteenth-century manner, by buying land and making himself 'gentry', the forces of society were arrayed against him. Moreover most schools were, nominally at least, associated with the Church, while the two English universities were closed to dissenters.[4] Excellent

[1] C. E. Whiting, *Studies in English Puritanism*, pp. 415–24.

[2] *History of England* (1903 ed.), I, p. 68.

[3] C. E. Whiting, *op. cit.* ch. VIII. The Five Mile Act of 1665 forbade preachers who had not assented to the Prayer Book to come within five miles of a corporate town without taking an oath.

[4] All tests were abolished by Act of Parliament in 1871. Until then a dissenter could matriculate in Cambridge if he could find a college, but could not proceed to a degree: in Oxford he could not even matriculate.

dissenting academies were established, but their pupils were necessarily segregated from the landowners' sons, who went to the universities.

Thus, dissent tended to have a class basis, and was found mainly among the shopkeepers and journeymen of the towns, while the landed interest was almost solidly 'Church', except in Lancashire (where there were strong relics of Romanism among the landowners) and Yorkshire (where dissent was quite strong among the landowners). The farmers and labourers were generally 'Church'; and though in the towns the workers were more closely associated with the dissenters, any active propaganda among them by the dissenters would have been regarded as the preaching of sedition, at least under the later Stuarts.

The situation of the dissenters was eased immediately after the Revolution by the Toleration Act, 1689. Under it persons 'dissenting from the Church of England' who were prepared to take the oaths under 1 W. & M. c. 1 and to subscribe the declaration against transubstantiation under the Test Act, 1678, were exempted from the requirements of several other Acts. They were, too, authorised to build conventicles and, after registration, to worship in them. On the other hand, there were still serious disabilities imposed upon them. In particular, they could not be elected to corporations or hold corporate office unless they took the sacrament in the Church of England; and the Occasional Conformity Act, 1711, made it unlawful to take the sacrament annually in order to qualify.[1] Also, the Schism Act, 1714, was designed to make it impossible for dissenters to have their own schools, though owing to the death of Queen Anne it never operated. This legislation of 1711 and 1714, enacted under Queen Anne, was part of the tory reaction to the Revolution Settlement and it was, in fact, the last legislation in Great Britain limiting religious liberty.[2] The whigs were more liberal. In general their views derived from genuine sympathy with dissenters if not with dissent. Some of those who showed such sympathy had fought for the Parliament, but some had not.[3] This initial sympathy was not lost when the dissenters supported the Revolution, the accession of George I, and the defence of the Hanoverian

---

[1] B. Williams, *The Whig Supremacy*, pp. 66–7.
[2] H. S. Skeat and C. S. Miall, *History of the Free Churches of England*, p. 220.
[3] C. E. Whiting, *op. cit.* p. 416.

monarchy in 1715, when the Old Pretender made an effort to recover his patrimony. Toleration became whig doctrine and was indeed made part of the whig theory of the Revolution Settlement by John Locke. The Schism Act was repealed in 1718 and the Occasional Conformity Act in 1720. From 1727 an annual Indemnity Act enabled a dissenter to qualify for office, in spite of the Test and Corporation Acts, by taking the sacrament after election or appointment: and this process continued for a hundred years.[1]

This toleration did not mean, however, that the whigs were all dissenters: far from it. Nor did it mean that the dissenters were acceptable in polite society. On the contrary, there was a deterioration in their social status after 1700. Under William III they enjoyed royal favour and were patronised by the great men. Under Anne the Court turned against them. Under the Georges the Church became part of the social hierarchy and a barrier was set up between the landed interest and the dissenting interest, the former including the Church. That barrier was almost impregnable.[2] Nor was toleration due mainly to sympathy with dissent: on the contrary, it was also due to indifference to, or contempt of, the Church of England. That Church had suffered severely in a series of purges. Many of the Royalist clergy had gone abroad, or given up their livings, during the Civil War, the Commonwealth and the Protectorate. The legislation of Charles II had extruded some two thousand clergymen, perhaps a fifth of all the clergy, because they could not assent to the revised Prayer Book or repudiate the Solemn League and Covenant. On the other wing some five hundred clergymen lost their benefices because they would not take the oath of allegiance to William and Mary or deny the doctrine of transubstantiation; and there were others after the death of Queen Anne who would not take the oath of allegiance to George I. Many of those extruded by these purges were among the most zealous, the most learned or the most saintly of the clergy. Moreover the reaction to the excesses of the Puritan regime had led not only to a recourse to the Church as the embodiment of order and stability, but also to a contempt for religious enthusiasm and Christian morality. The extravagances of the Court

[1] B. Williams, *op. cit.* pp. 68–9.
[2] H. S. Skeats and C. S. Miall, *op. cit.* pp. 76, 196.

and the profanity and obscenity of the Restoration stage were part of this reaction to Puritanism. Irreligion, probably, was the exception; but the popular religion, which often differs so much from institutional religion, might be, and perhaps usually was, nothing more than a vague deism combined with some measure of conformity with the services of the Church. Nor was it to the advantage of the Church that bishops were so often appointed for their political support, that the Church was used to provide careers for younger sons, that absentee rectors and vicars had their duties performed by ill-paid and ill-educated curates, that the holding of benefices in plurality was a common practice, and that so many of the country parsons were worldly men.[1]

The Church of England was therefore at its lowest in the first half of the eighteenth century. Nor must it be forgotten that this was also a period in which mere antiquity was not a merit. It had its own standard of taste, which was high; but it was, artistically, an innovating age. The antiquarianism of the nineteenth century, which justified an institution or work of art by its antiquity, was one of the many products of the industrial revolution. Even so, nationalism was strong, and the combination of Church and King was strong even when the Church was languishing and the King was George I. More often, probably, the 'good old tory' was a landowner who supported the Church and would have nothing to do with the Court, a landowner, maybe, from the champion counties or the Welsh Marches or Lancashire. The whigs accepted the whole Revolution Settlement, including a limited toleration for dissenters. This ideological distinction was merely nominal under George III, until after the French Revolution parties in a new alignment adopted the old names.

4. METHODISM

John Wesley's background was a curious mixture of Puritanism and Anglicanism. His father was a High Church parson whose father and grandfather had been Puritan ministers extruded for dissent in 1662; he had been educated at a dissenting academy, but had subsequently

---

[1] William Grimshaw, afterwards a famous Evangelist, was thus described when he was a young parson: 'He refrained as much as possible from gross swearing unless in suitable company, and, when he got drunk, would take care to sleep it out before he came home': Middleton, *Biographia Evangelica*, IV, p. 398, quoted by Balleine, *History of the Evangelical Party*, p. 65.

accepted the theology of the Reformed Church, had gone to Oxford to take holy orders and had become Rector of Epworth. John Wesley's mother was the daughter of another extruded Puritan minister, but she too had rejected the 'stern Calvinism' of the presbyterians and had joined in communion with the Church. Indeed, after the Restoration she was caught using the peculiar technique of the superficially conforming non-juror, refusing to say 'Amen' to the prayers for William III. John Wesley was born in 1703 and was educated at the Charterhouse and Christ Church, though it was when he was Fellow of Lincoln from 1720 to 1735 that Oxford impressed itself upon him. His younger brother, Charles, had founded a 'Holy Club' of undergraduates who took part in regular devotions (hence they were dubbed 'Methodists' by irreverent Oxford men) and good works. John Wesley joined them on his return to Oxford in 1729 and took the lead. George Whitefield, of St John's College, also became a member.

The Wesleys joined the mission to Georgia in 1735 with the object of evangelising the Indians and preaching the Gospel to the colonists. The mission was a failure, not merely because John Wesley had an ill-managed love affair, but also because the earnest sacerdotalism and rigid discipline which so befit young High Churchmen in Oxford were ill-adapted to missionary effort in a pioneer environment. After disputes with the trustees and litigation over the expulsion from the Church of the young married woman who had, before her marriage, been the object of John's affections, the Wesleys returned to England in 1738. The experience had a revolutionary effect on John Wesley's attitude to his faith; and, after a period of doubt, he went through an emotional experience which the sects call 'conversion'. Though this was common among the Puritans, he was not persuaded by Puritan theology. The Cambridge reformers were theologians; they alleged that the Church as established had been perverted from the true faith over the centuries and should be reformed according to the principles which they derived from the New Testament. What John Wesley learned from the Moravians, after his experiences in Georgia, and when he was in a suitable emotional state, was the doctrine of justification by faith. It involved the assumption that every man was in a state of damnation until 'by a supernatural and instantaneous process wholly unlike that of human reasoning, the conviction flashes upon his mind that the sacrifice of Christ has been applied to and has expiated his sin'.[1] It was almost inevitable that he should himself suffer this experience, which can be described only by metaphor:

In the sunshine of a glorious spiritual morning, the fogs were lifted, mists were dispelled, the tempest was stilled; the heights were attained. Wesley, elevated now to the pinnacle of spiritual experience, breathed pure and fragrant air. Alone before the Holy One he stood. And there a live coal from Heaven's altar purged his dross, illumined his understanding and sealed him as a messenger of Grace.

But what language can ever explain the mystery and miracle of a soul re-born? Wesley, lifted to the Holy Mount, was endowed with new sensitivities; new faculties and powers. A revealing Faith became the eye of his soul, whereby he saw Him Who is invisible: it became to him a spiritual ear through which he heard the Still, Small Voice divine. On the Mount of Transfiguration, Wesley's spirit took wing to where the heavens rang with praise. There he peered forward, and life's horizons were strangely amplified. The wondrous awesome music of choirs celestial flooded his soul....[2]

Such a religious experience required no theology at all. Except, no doubt, that there would have been a chorus of saints, it could have been suffered by a Roman Catholic. It is equally in the tradition of *Paradise Lost* and *Pilgrim's Progress*. Wesley's immediate affiliations were with the Moravians, who have been sympathetic to all the Protestant sects, though he was less impressed by them than he had expected from his association with Peter Böhler. He and his conversion would be irrelevant to a book on politics were it not that John and Charles Wesley and George Whitefield (who had been 'converted' earlier and therefore made a success of his subsequent mission to Georgia) went out and preached to the people, were repudiated by the Church of England, and therefore had to found their own sect of Methodists. Though nonconformist only in the sense that the Church refused to accept them as conformist,[3] they ultimately strengthened the 'Nonconformist Conscience'.

[1] W. E. H. Lecky, *History of England in the Eighteenth Century* (1895 ed.), III, p. 45.
[2] J. Wesley Bready, *England before and after Wesley*, p. 189.
[3] Strictly speaking the Methodists did not 'dissent'; they did not conform to Church discipline. Hence in the nineteenth century the 'dissenters' were called 'Nonconformists' in order to include the Methodists.

The Wesleys and Whitefield had to preach in the fields partly because the Church would not allow them to preach from the pulpit, but also because only in the fields and the market place could one preach to the masses. The process of 'conversion' might be carried out, as with John Wesley himself, by prayer and quiet contemplation. It was, however, a slow process and rarely applicable to the working men and women whose souls were to be saved. Preaching fiercely against sin from the pulpit was not foreign to the tradition of the Church of England as elaborated by the Puritan divines, though it was not common in the early part of the eighteenth century because it savoured of Puritanism. The Church of England sermon was not the essential part of the service but an addendum to it, an exposition of doctrine to those who had already worshipped according to the form of the Book of Common Prayer. For the Methodist the sacraments and prayer were essential, but the frontal attack on sin and the development of religious emotion had to precede the 'conversion' which enabled the Christian genuinely to worship—as distinct from merely taking part in the service—in church. George Whitefield had begun to preach in the fields because he was not allowed to preach from the pulpit. John Wesley, though equally proscribed, was reluctant to follow his example because he was still affected by the notions of decency and order which he had acquired at Oxford. However, he was persuaded to attend one of Whitefield's mass meetings at Kingswood (now a suburb of Bristol) and saw for himself that this was the only way of reaching the mass of the people.[1] What the Methodists discovered, in fact, was the fundamental principle of crowd psychology, that emotion is contagious and that the emotion of the crowd is greater than the sum of the emotions of the individuals composing it. Since 'conversion' in the Methodist (or evangelical) sense was an emotional experience and not a rational process, it was easier to bring about in a crowd than in a church, particularly when the orator was George Whitefield.[2]

[1] B. Williams, *The Whig Supremacy*, p. 93.

[2] Garrick is reported to have said of him that he could pronounce the word Mesopotamia in such a way as to move an audience to tears: W. E. H. Lecky, *History of England in the Eighteenth Century* (1895 ed.), III, p. 60. See generally *ibid.* pp. 59–66, for a remarkable description of Whitefield's preaching. John Wesley was not such a golden-tongued orator, but he had learned the technique of revivalism at the 'love-feasts' of

The mass meeting was not, however, the only Methodist technique. Indeed, until the great civic halls were built (more for politics than for religion) in the nineteenth century, smaller meetings had to be held indoors when the weather was bad. The faithful had to be kept firm in their faith by constant intercourse in small 'classes', like the Quaker meetings, in which each could give testimony to his faith, confess his sins in public, and pray and be prayed for. Since neither the Church nor the dissenting sects would usually provide facilities, it became necessary to build meeting-houses; and such houses, which were not chapels, spread rapidly over the country, especially in the urban areas, after the first one was built in the Horsefair, Bristol, in 1739. Nor could the Wesleys and Whitefield and the few other clergymen who supported them, in spite of their valiant efforts, meet the demands of the Methodist Revival. It became necessary to appoint local and itinerant preachers, and before John Wesley's death in 1791 there were over seven hundred professional preachers, not to mention Whitefield's preaching assistants—he had become Calvinist in 1740.

Though John Wesley thought doctrinal differences unimportant, he never deviated from the fundamental doctrine of his own Church. Nor was there on his part any attack on the established order in Church and State. He was rebellious only in the sense that he preached with a strange fund of enthusiasm which the Church and the gentry found distasteful, that he founded what might in an earlier age have been called 'conventicles', and that he employed preachers who had not taken orders in the Church. There was no question of treason or sedition;[1] nor was there any attempt to overthrow the Church as by law established.

the Moravians, which lasted through the night. 'His preaching now began to be attended by those physical manifestations which have often accompanied revivals of religion. Strong men and women cried aloud, before assembled congregations, in the agony of their spirit. Fits were frequent amongst those who heard. By-and-by—sometimes in a few hours or even minutes—agony would give way to joy, terror to peace, the fear of hell to the transports of heaven, the service of the devil to an assured acceptance with God': H. S. Skeats and C. S. Miall, *History of the Free Churches in England*, p. 288. See also the lengthy description in Lecky, *op. cit.* III, pp. 77–85.

[1] The Wesleyan Statutes of 1792 declared that 'None of us shall either in writing or in conversation speak lightly or irreverently of the Government. We are to observe that the oracles of God command us to be subject to the higher powers; and that honour to the King is there connected with the fear of God': Halévy, *History of the English People in the Nineteenth Century* (2nd ed.), I, p. 427.

Nevertheless the Methodists were violently opposed, and the word 'violently' may be taken literally. In many parts of the country mobs were encouraged by the country gentry and even by the parsons to break up Methodist meetings and sack meeting-houses. It is difficult to believe that this was an echo of the Civil War, though 'folk memory' is long. We need not find a rational explanation at all; for anything new and demonstrative, not to say exhibitionist, arouses irrational antagonism. What the Methodists were really doing, for the first time since the Restoration, was to take religion to the common people and so to upset the social equilibrium. The Church of Rome had adapted itself to the later Roman Empire and to feudalism. After the Restoration the Church of England had adapted itself to the social hierarchy dominated by the landed interest. It was indeed one of the aspects of the supremacy of land. The squire instituted the vicar, the vicar appointed the curate, and the 'lower orders' were expected either to attend church and listen to a sermon designed to suit the prejudices of the squire, or to stay away. When the Methodists came near the parish, however, the 'lower orders' trooped out to listen, and perhaps to be converted. In other words, the Methodists, while themselves accepting the established social order, threatened to destroy the hegemony of squire and parson.[1]

There was less danger in the towns, particularly in those towns where a growing population made nonsense of the ancient parish boundaries. The parish was a unit of lay administration as well as a unit of Church ministration; and no alteration was possible before 1818,[2] except by private Act of Parliament. Even if the Church had been

---

[1] The Countess of Huntingdon persuaded Society to hear the Methodist preachers, but few were converted even to the belief that Methodism was tolerable. The Duchess of Buckingham replied to an invitation as follows: 'I thank your ladyship for the information concerning the Methodist preachers; their doctrines are most repulsive and strongly tinctured with impertinence and disrespect towards their superiors, in perpetually endeavouring to level all ranks and do away with all distinctions. It is monstrous to be told you have a heart as sinful as the common wretches that crawl on the earth. This is highly offensive and insulting; and I cannot but wonder that your ladyship should relish any sentiments so much at variance with high rank and good breeding. I shall be most happy to come and hear your favourite preacher.' See Charles J. Abbey and John H. Overton, *The English Church in the Eighteenth Century* (1896 ed.), p. 348.

[2] An Act of Anne authorised the creation of fifty new parishes in London, but only ten new churches were built in the whole of the eighteenth century. The Church Building Act, 1818, was the first of a lengthy series of Acts authorising the creation of new parishes by Order in Council.

willing to undertake the cure of souls in new industrial centres it would not have had either the finance or the machinery. It was, at least in theory, financed by the tithe or tenth part of the produce of agricultural land. Where there was a rector, the tithe was probably payable to him; but in other cases it was paid to the corporation or private person having the right of tithe, though often the vicar was entitled to a portion of the tithe. The creation of a new parish therefore adversely affected somebody's income—it might be the Crown, a bishop, a college, a private patron, or the rector. It was possible to establish a 'chapel of ease' (a chapel for prayer and preaching only) but only with the consent of the ordinary, patron and incumbent of the parish. In other words, until legislation began in 1818 the Church had no effective means of providing for the new industrial population, especially where (as in the North of England) populations had been sparse and parishes consequently large. The Methodists were under no such inhibitions. They could collect money to build a meeting-house (usually, but incorrectly according to ecclesiastical law, called a chapel), vest the land in trustees, provide for local services by lay preachers and circuit ministers and for religious ministrations generally, under the control of the superintendent of the circuit, who was directly responsible to John Wesley himself. Thus, Methodism became particularly strong in the industrial areas. It was very weak in the purely agricultural counties—Salop, Westmorland, Rutland, Cambridge, Huntingdon, Hereford and Dorset—and not much stronger in Cumberland, Derbyshire, Nottinghamshire, Suffolk, Essex and Devon. All Hampshire and large parts of Surrey and Sussex formed one circuit. Oxfordshire, Gloucestershire and Kent had few Methodist members. Methodism was strongest in Staffordshire, Durham, Northumberland, Lancashire, Yorkshire and Cornwall.[1] Almost all the circuits with more than a thousand members in 1791 were towns—London, Bristol, Redruth, St Ives, Birmingham, Burslem, Macclesfield, Manchester, Bolton, Liverpool, Colne, Nottingham, Sheffield, Leeds, Birstall, Bradford, Halifax and Sunderland.[2] By 1815 there had been added Bramley,

---

[1] Maldwyn Edwards, *After Wesley*, pp. 142–3.
[2] *Ibid*. p. 144. W. F. Hook, who became vicar of Leeds in 1837, said that in that city Methodism was 'the *de facto* established religion': C. S. Carpenter, *Church and People*,

Wakefield, Dewsbury, Epworth, York, Hull, Darlington, Barnard Castle, Newcastle, and Shields.[1] Wales is not included in these lists because Howell Harris, whose missionary efforts were so successful that Wales became predominantly Methodist, was a follower of Whitefield, and so the Methodism of Wales was Calvinistic.[2] We must of course appreciate that the great majority of the people, of all classes, except possibly in Wales and Scotland, were not actively religious; but all were affected in their ideas by the prevailing religious sentiment. If therefore we leave out for the moment the Roman Catholics (who were strong only in Lancashire) and the dissenting sects, we may say that the southern counties, except Cornwall, Bristol and London (with Middlesex), were dominated by the Church of England, while Cornwall, Staffordshire, Lancashire, Yorkshire, Durham and Northumberland were dominated by the Methodists.

It is difficult to estimate the political effects of Methodism because for the most part they were indirect. John Wesley himself was not a student of politics. He had a mass of ill-digested tory prejudices which he did not hesitate to express. He wrote against John Wilkes, criticised Junius, argued the case against the American colonies, and criticised Dr Price's views on liberty.[3] He was also against Catholic emancipation. On the other hand he criticised rotten boroughs without being a reformer, felt strongly on the slave trade, encouraged industry and

1709–1809, p. 390. As to Sheffield, see E. R. Wickham, *Church and People in an Industrial City.*

[1] Edwards, *op. cit.*

[2] *Ibid.* p. 142. Howell Harris was preceded by Griffith Jones (1684–1761), who preached a revivalist religion before the Methodists, but whose main contribution was the establishment of 'circulating schools' in which the people were taught to read the Bible in Welsh. Howell Harris was an English-speaking Welshman who went to Oxford, but left after a term because of 'the irregularities and the wickedness which surrounded him'. He began evangelistic preaching in Wales in 1725 and extended it after the Methodists made contact with him. He was more effective than Whitefield and the Wesleys because he could preach in Welsh, and he founded a mass of local societies, with no kind of organisation except an occasional assembly. Though Harris was always sympathetic to the Church he was refused ordination; and his colleague Daniel Rowlands, who was a priest and often administered the sacrament to thousands, was deprived of his licence. Accordingly the Calvinistic Methodists separated from the Church in 1811 and made Wales almost exclusively Nonconformist. See Lecky, *op. cit.* III, pp. 104–8; and H. S. Skeats and C. S. Miall, *History of the Free Churches of England*, pp. 316–30 and 440–3.

[3] Maldwyn Edwards, *John Wesley and the Eighteenth Century* (1955 ed.), pp. 63, 66, 71, 76.

104

money-making (though he had strong views on the right way to spend money), attacked the drink trade fiercely, and generally said enough to make his protagonists believe that he was something of a social reformer.[1] All this is not, however, very important. He was a great propagandist and a first-class administrator, not a political theorist or a practical politician. More important is the fact that Methodism by its very nature had a conservative bias. Though repudiated by the Church, there was nothing in its doctrine which was unacceptable to the Church. Because it was outside the Church, however, Methodism also influenced Nonconformity and did much to produce the 'Nonconformist Conscience'. Perhaps its greatest influence on politics, nevertheless, was to keep the working classes of the towns outside politics by providing excitement of a non-political kind during the early part of the industrial revolution. The excitement diminished after the French Revolution, but it is important that, during a revolutionary period, so many members of the working class were concerned with religion and not with politics. Though it was not so designed, Methodism was 'opium for the people'.[2]

This attitude was tenable only so long as Methodism was a fighting religion and politics was a conflict of family connexions. Long before the end of the century neither requirement was satisfied. The second generation of revivalist preachers in Wales proved to be even more effective than the first, and then Calvinistic Methodism swept the country, so that in the early years of the nineteenth century Wales was nine-tenths Nonconformist. In England, however, Methodism became respectable, and Wesley died in 1791 not as a rebel but as a pillar of society. Meanwhile, however, political opinion had been developing in the towns, especially among the journeymen and labourers. As we shall see, the initiative then passed to the dissenters, though they too failed to capture the industrial workers. At the death of Wesley Methodism was still, in theory, part of the Church of England; though it had its own meeting-houses and preachers it did not claim that anybody not in holy orders could administer the sacraments. This

[1] E.g. J. Wesley Bready, *England Before and After Wesley*.
[2] The point is exaggerated by J. L. and B. Hammond, *The Town Labourer*, but it is nevertheless valid.

could not long survive, and in 1795 the Wesleyan Methodists broke away. The division did not at once lead to its reform as a popular Church. In spite of the reaction to the Terror, democratic ideas were floating in, and in 1797 a section which objected to the quasi-clericalism of the Wesleyan ministers broke away to form the Methodist New Connexion. There was another split in 1812, when the Wesleyan Methodists, now highly respectable, objected to open-air revivalist preaching, with the result that the Primitive Methodist Connexion was formed. In 1815 there was yet another split, for much the same reason, in Cornwall, and the Bible Christians were formed.

These divisions bear witness to the failure of Methodism to carry on the traditions of Whitefield, who first preached to the coal-miners of Kingswood and the tin-miners of Cornwall. Its conversion into just another ecclesiastical establishment was, however, due mainly to the predominance of comparatively wealthy men among the trustees of the chapels. There was no place for the working man in chapel, just as there was none in church. He had no Sunday clothes and could not afford a pew. Pew rents were brought in just before the death of John Wesley, and in due course they made up a large part of the annual income.[1] If he were a radical or a reformer, however—and after 1815, if not before, he was quite likely to be—he would not want to go to chapel to hear tory propaganda from the pulpit.

By the end of the eighteenth century the Methodist Church while still increasing greatly in numbers, and attracting artizans and workmen, had ceased to be the Church of the worker, and was controlled by respectable middle-class people of strong loyalist views. The leading ministers with few exceptions had tory affiliations: some...were most outspoken in their toryism.[2]

Methodism was against trade unionism, Catholic emancipation and the Reform Bill. Of the seven 'Tolpuddle Martyrs', six were Methodists and two of them were local preachers, but they received no support from their Church. So, too, most Wesleyan Methodists were against the Charter, though many of them supported the Anti-Corn Law League.

[1] Maldwyn Edwards, *After Wesley*, pp. 90–1.
[2] *Ibid.* p. 91.

The Primitive Methodists were more sympathetic to the Charter, and doubled their membership during the Chartist agitation, though most of the Chartists were 'infidels' or plain 'Christians' who supported, not priests and creeds, but 'pure, practical and undefiled religion'.[1]

5. THE DISSENTING INTEREST AND THE FRENCH REVOLUTION

The Methodists were not dissenters, for they differed from the Church about method rather than doctrine; and John Wesley always regarded himself as a priest of the Church of England. There was, however, still a large volume of dissent at the end of the eighteenth century. 'They are all whigs, enemies to arbitrary power', said Dr Richard Price, 'and firmly attached to those principles of civil and religious liberty which produced the Glorious Revolution and the Hanoverian Succession.'[2] They were not comfortable allies, however, for the memory of the Civil War lived long, and they were accused of being 'Commonwealth's men':[3]

> History thy page unfold:
> Did not their sires of old
> Murder the King![4]

They tried to make themselves thought of as men of '88; but good tories insisted on regarding them as men of '49.[5] This accusation was important. On the one hand it encouraged the weaker brethren towards conformity and kept down the size of the dissenting interest, in spite of the weakness of the Church. On the other hand, it encouraged those who would not give up the ancient beliefs to take a radical line and to welcome the French Revolution.

The dissenters were to be found chiefly among the wealthier inhabitants of the towns, the larger tradesmen and small manufacturers. Being dissenters, they had no ambition to be country gentry (though their wives often had); and, being proscribed by the 'respectable classes' who supported the Church, they formed a close fellowship whose tradition of fair dealing created a high standard of business

---

[1] *Ibid.* p. 93; N. U. Faulkner, *Chartism and the Churches*, pp. 15–20.
[2] A. Lincoln, *English Dissent, 1763–1800*, p. 4.
[3] *Ibid.* p. 5. [4] *Ibid.* p. 6 (1790).
[5] *Ibid.* p. 9.

morality. It was almost unknown for a dissenter to be a bankrupt or a pauper.[1] They were, for the most part, educated men, frequently men who had been taught in the dissenting academies, the best schools that England produced before the nineteenth century. The dissenters were, however, never very numerous. The Presbyterians went into rapid decline after 1660 and in 1808 there were only 270 congregations; the Independents (Congregationalists) kept their strength reasonably well, and in 1808 there were 1024 congregations; the Baptists increased somewhat, and in 1808 there were 708 congregations.[2] Middlesex and Yorkshire were the great counties of Nonconformity, while Westmorland had the fewest meeting-houses.

It must not be thought that the dissenters were unanimous, whether

---

[1] A. Lincoln, *op. cit.* p. 13.
[2] *Ibid.* pp. 15–16. The Religious Census of 1851 gives the following figures:

	Sittings	*Most numerously attended service*
Church of England	5,317,915	2,541,244
Methodists		
Wesleyans	1,447,580	667,850
Primitives	414,030	100,125
Calvinistic	211,951	125,244
Others	369,152	181,947
Independents	1,067,760	524,612
Baptists	752,343	365,946
Friends	91,599	14,364
Presbyterians	86,692	47,582
Unitarians	68,554	28,483
Roman Catholics	186,111	252,783

The total sittings for all denominations were:

Church of England	5,317,915
All other denominations	4,894,648
Total	10,212,563

The total attendance on census day was:

	Morning	*Afternoon*	*Evening*
Church of England	2,541,244	1,890,764	860,543
All other denominations	2,106,238	1,293,371	2,203,906
Total	4,647,482	3,184,135	3,064,449

The population of England and Wales in 1851 was 17,928,000. The figures are taken from H. S. Skeats and C. S. Miall, *History of the Free Churches of England*, pp. 523–5.

in respect of religion or in respect of politics. In respect of religion they tended to disintegrate into a multitude of sects. In 1851 there were thirty-five religious communities, including the Church of England, the Church of Rome, seven varieties of Methodists, nine foreign importations, and twenty sects derived from the old dissenters.[1] The only common element among the sects was their dislike of the Established Church, and even that dislike began to wane in the nineteenth century, though the Oxford Movement helped to perpetuate it. In respect of politics, the only common element was acceptance of the Revolution Settlement, the essential principle of which, as seen by the dissenters, was civil and religious liberty. On the other hand they were not likely to be democrats because so many of them belonged to a socially privileged class.[2]

The political influence of the dissenting interest began to show itself under George III. In the counties they were strong among the urban inhabitants who had votes as forty-shilling freeholders. In the corporation boroughs they were generally disfranchised, but they were strong in many freemen boroughs. In the scot and lot and potwalloper boroughs they were quite strong, but were probably swamped by the Methodists and the pagans. If we may judge from the pamphlets they mostly supported John Wilkes, and they were strong in Middlesex.[3] Wilkes may also have had support from the Methodists; but John Wesley wrote against Wilkes; and most of the Methodists of Middlesex, probably, were not forty-shilling freeholders. The dissenters seem to have been almost unanimous against the American War: here the principle of civil and religious liberty was involved and many preferred to support Puritan New England against George III's Old England. On the other hand, the effrontery of the Unnatural Coalition and the belief that Fox's India Bill was intended to create more corrupt patronage probably helped William Pitt to secure the dissenters' vote in 1784.[4] In 1787, however, the dissenters tried to obtain a repeal of the Corporation and Test Acts. Pitt was inclined to acquiesce, but he

[1] Voltaire's gibe that England had a hundred religions and one sauce was exaggerated both as to religion and as to sauce.
[2] E. R. Wickham, *Church and People in an Industrial City*, p. 68.
[3] A. Lincoln, *op. cit.* p. 26. Wilkes had dissenting parents.
[4] Earl Stanhope, *Life of Pitt*, I, p. 336.

did not want to lose the support of the Church, and the bishops were against. He therefore opposed on the ground that many dissenters were against the Establishment, and that accordingly 'the bulwark must be kept up against all'.[1] Fox, on the other hand, supported the Bill, and he did so again when the Bill was again presented in 1789. In 1790 he took charge of the Bill;[2] but the French Revolution had already destroyed the hopes of the dissenters.

The Terror and Napoleon have given the French Revolution a bad name in England, and the only pieces of English political writing, now remembered, which came out of it were Burke's polemical essays. It is therefore necessary to recall the extraordinary sympathy with which the Revolution was first received. 'Jacobin' became a term of abuse, but probably more than half the people welcomed the Revolution. To take a sort of random sample, Mr P. A. Brown[3] considered the attitudes of the poets. Cowper was by this time an elderly evangelical, concerned that the times were evil and reform impossible. Even he was shaken out of his 'pious scepticism'. Robert Burns, as an exciseman, had to keep his feelings under control, but in his cups he toasted 'the last verse of the last chapter of the last book of Kings'; and his patriotic verse, written after 1789, has a democratic tinge. William Blake wrote a poem on the French Revolution which was never published, and wore the cap of liberty in the streets of London. William Wordsworth, just down from Cambridge, went to France to draw inspiration from the new freedom. Coleridge, at Christ's Hospital, celebrated the fall of the Bastille in verse; and, when he went up to Cambridge, narrowly escaped being 'progged' for a demonstration in favour of liberty of opinion. Southey was still younger, and at Westminster; his early verse, written at Oxford, was on revolutionary themes. Hazlitt began his literary career with a letter to a newspaper on the persecution of the Birmingham reformers in 1791. Crabb Robinson, a clerk in articles, turned 'Jacobin'. Landor was sent down from Balliol for shooting at the shutters of a tory's rooms.

The ground for the reception of Revolutionary ideas by the Non-

---

[1] Earl Stanhope, *op. cit.* p. 337.
[2] H. S. Skeats and C. S. Miall, *History of the Free Churches of England*, pp. 391, 395, 396.   [3] *French Revolution in English History*, pp. 31–7.

conformists had been well prepared. They were all students of Locke, and they suffered from legal disabilities for which, by this time, nobody could find a justification save that they were said to protect the Establishment. Rousseau published *Contrat Social* in 1762 and thus provided an argumentative foundation for liberty. In 1768 Joseph Priestley, a Unitarian, published his Essay on the First Principles of Government. It was not a very original work, and indeed Professor Laski called it 'an edition of Rousseau for English Nonconformists'.[1] The emphasis was upon freedom not merely of religion but also from all unnecessary State interference, even in matters of trade. It was while reading Priestley's book that Jeremy Bentham thought of the 'principle of utility'. Richard Price, also a Unitarian, was another disciple of Locke and Rousseau. He was led to write on politics by the American Revolution, and his *Observations on the Nature of Civil Liberty* was published in 1776.

We shall have to say more about civil and religious liberty in the next chapter, for it was not a mere Nonconformist doctrine. What is important for present purposes is that the French Revolution, following so soon after the refusal to repeal the Corporation and Test Acts, tended to push the dissenters towards the radical wing of the whig party. Birley says that the Jacobins' struggle was the beginning of the class war:[2] but that is too simple an explanation. The first class war was between the landed interest and the industrial middle class, and it resulted in the first Reform Act and the Repeal of the Corn Laws. The Marxist class war, that between the capitalist and the working class, never got going, though in the Chartist Movement it looked as though it might. The French Revolution was, as Marx himself insisted, a *bourgeois* revolution. Its main effect in England was to stimulate sections of the working class in the great cities to believe in the virtues of Parliamentary reform: but in that respect they were allies of the industrial middle class. On the other hand, the middle class as a whole was not persuaded because, as so many of them believed, everything good in the French Revolution had been achieved in England in 1688. The exceptions were infidels like Thomas Paine and dissenters like

---

[1] *Political Thought from Locke to Bentham*, p. 149.
[2] R. Birley, *The English Jacobins*, p. 6.

Dr Priestley. Nor was the 'mob' entirely on the side of the reformers. On the contrary, it proved easy in 1791 to get the 'mob' of Birmingham to attack the meeting-houses of the dissenters. In other words, there was a tacit alliance among the left wing of the aristocratic whigs, led by Charles James Fox, the dissenters, and the politically conscious section of the urban working class, the alliance which produced the first Reform Act.

Meanwhile, the reaction was led by Burke's *Reflections on the Revolution in France* (1790), a remarkably forceful and emotional defence of Church and State as by law established. Since this essay (or letter) is the foundation of modern Conservatism, and the Nonconformists are now Conservatives, we are apt to forget that it was an attack on the dissenters. It was provoked by a message to the Convention from the Revolution Society, which Burke called 'a club of dissenters', and which did contain many dissenters, though there were some Churchmen also; and it was in form an attack on a sermon by Dr Price in the meeting-house at Old Jewry. Its substance, however, was an impassioned defence of the *status quo*:

We are not the converts of Rousseau; we are not the disciples of Voltaire; Helvetius has made no progress among us. Atheists are not our preachers; madmen are not our lawgivers. We know that *we* have made no discoveries; and we think that no discoveries are to be made, in morality; nor many in the great principles of government, nor in the ideas of liberty, which were understood long before we were born, altogether as well as they will be after the grave has heaped its mould upon our presumption, and the silent tomb shall have imposed its law on our pert loquacity. In England we have not yet been completely embowelled of our natural entrails; we still feel within us, and we cherish and cultivate, those inbred sentiments which are the faithful guardians, the active monitors of our duty, the true supporters of all liberal and manly morals. We have not been drawn and trussed, in order that we may be filled, like stuffed birds in a museum, with chaff and rags and paltry blurred shreds of paper about the rights of man. We preserve the whole of our feelings still native and intire, unsophisticated by pedantry and infidelity. We have real hearts of flesh and blood beating in our bosoms. We fear God; we look up with awe to kings, with affection to parliaments; with duty to magistrates; with reverence to priests; and with respect to nobility.[1]

[1] E. Burke, *Works* (1834 ed.), I, p. 413.

'We are resolved', said Burke a little later, 'to keep an established church, an established monarchy, an established aristocracy, and an established democracy, each in the degree it exists, and in no greater';[1] and there is a long defence of the Church, going even to the length of defending monastic orders. It was always Burke's way to exaggerate his propositions. In appealing to 'wise prejudice' he was going counter to the spirit of the age in which he had lived and helping to produce the romantic conservatism of the next generation. He accepted the Revolution Settlement and a somewhat modified version of Locke's social contract: and he was, apparently, unaware of the great social changes going on around him, which would necessarily overthrow all the 'establishments' as they then existed. By stating the conservative case so forcefully and emphatically, almost without qualifications, he helped to strengthen the opposition to conservatism. In particular, by standing pat on the Established Church he gave conservatism a religious bias to which all the free churches, Methodist as well as those of ancient dissent, must necessarily be opposed.

On the other hand, the French Revolution tended to send the sceptical country gentry back into the Church. In France Church and State had been overthrown together, as Burke had said they would be. Kings, bishops and aristocrats went to the guillotine together. We need not assert that the gentry became religious in order to save their necks: they would no doubt have put their necks at the service of Church and King. But the Terror showed that the social order was one and indivisible. Any reform in Church or State was therefore dangerous. The Established Church was part of the established order and had to be protected as such. Burke's extravagant theory 'not only embittered the Nonconformists, but it went a long way towards dividing the population into those who were for religion and those who were for freedom'.[2] 'The sudden revival of zeal for the Established Church...', says Sir Richard Coupland, 'was largely due to the belief that Jacobinism and Atheism were inseparable twins, that the rights of property would be remembered as long as Christianity was not forgotten.'[3]

[1] Ibid. p. 415.
[2] S. C. Carpenter, Church and People, 1789–1889, p. 11.
[3] R. Coupland, Wilberforce, p. 425.

The implications of the political distinction between 'church' and 'chapel' did not at once appear. The excesses of the French Revolution frightened the dissenters, who feared for their houses, shops and offices. There was, indeed, a period of quiescence among them until 1810, when Viscount Sidmouth introduced a Bill to restrict the liberty of preaching. This was not an attack on dissenters as such: it was simply an illustration of the prevailing belief that clergy of the Church of England were all responsible people, while among the dissenting ministers and Methodist preachers were young, dissolute and ignorant men.[1] It was, however, supported by churchmen and others because the preachers often alleged that the Church Catechism was '(in their coarse language) a heap of nonsense'[2] and because so many of them were alleged to be sowing the seeds of discontent and sedition.[3]

Viscount Sidmouth, indeed, had to be taught the difference between a Methodist and a dissenter, for the Toleration Act, by a rather broad interpretation, had been applied to both. His Bill therefore brought the Methodists and the dissenters together for the first time. The whigs, of course, cashed in, Lord Erskine declaring that the Bill was aimed at two million persons who had been in the bosom of the Church but had been driven from it by persecution.[4] The Bill was defeated, but the agitation resulted in the establishment of a Protestant Society for the Protection of Religious Liberty, which proceeded to attack all the restrictive laws. Within a year it succeeded in getting the Conventicle Act and the Five Mile Act repealed. In the following year the Unitarians were protected by an Act repealing the statutes making it blasphemy to deny the doctrine of the Trinity. In 1828 the Test and Corporation Acts were repealed, though with some restrictions. Though the Protestant Society disappeared before 1832, the close collaboration of dissenters and Methodists in an attack on the privileges of the Established Church had much to do with the development of Nonconformity as a political movement. It was, too, in association with the whigs, who gained considerably from such association when so many Nonconformists were enfranchised by the Reform Act.

So far as the Methodists were concerned, however, the movement

---

[1] *Life of Viscount Sidmouth*, III, pp. 43–4. [2] *Ibid*. p. 44.
[3] *Ibid*. [4] Skeats and Miall, *History of the Free Churches of England*, p. 449.

was slow. Though they were much stronger among the working classes and were therefore often regarded by timorous magistrates as seditious, their leadership for some considerable time remained tory. These tendencies were strengthened by the French wars; 'Boney' had no fiercer opponents than the working-class members of the Methodist connexions, and they were encouraged in their loyalty by the Methodist pulpit and press.[1] During the Luddite disturbances of 1811 and 1812, too, the Methodist preachers were on the side of law and order.[2] The political unions of the twenties and the thirties based themselves on the Methodist organisation and used the system of 'classes'. It was impossible for Methodist laymen, who were the most articulate members of the working classes, to keep out of the agitation for Parliamentary reform, but the political neutrality enjoined on Methodist preachers was, as usual, another expression for conservatism. The preachers did not take part in politics but disapproved of ill-disposed persons who wanted to subvert the British Constitution.[3] Opposition to Roman Catholic relief was not 'politics'; nor, oddly enough, was opposition to the slave trade.[4] On the other hand, the agitation for reform in 1831 was so strong that it was thought not objectionable for Christians to take part in it, though as soon as the Reform Act was passed there was an immediate reaction against party politics.[5] Jabez Bunting, who was the 'Pope of Methodism' for a long period at the beginning of the nineteenth century, is alleged to have said that 'Methodism hates democracy as much as it hates sin'.[6] This attitude of official Methodism was, however, largely responsible for the division of the Methodist connexion and the relative fall in the membership of the Wesleyans. Moreover opposition developed within the Wesleyan Methodist connexion itself, especially in the forties; and in the second half of the nineteenth century the Wesleyans were simply another Nonconformist sect, giving general support to the Liberal party under the influence of Hugh Price Hughes.[7]

---

[1] S. C. Carpenter, *Church and People, 1789–1889*, pp. 70–3.
[2] R. F. Wearmouth, *Methodism and the Working-Class Movements in England, 1800–1850*, pp. 56–62.
[3] *Ibid.* p. 286. [4] *Ibid.* p. 287. [5] *Ibid.* pp. 288–9.
[6] M. Edwards, *After Wesley*, p. 154. For the association of both the Church and the Wesleyans with conservatism in 1835 and 1837, see E. R. Wickham, *Church and People in an Industrial City*, p. 104. [7] Edwards, *op. cit.* pp. 160–1.

6. THE NONCONFORMIST CONSCIENCE

The term 'Nonconformist Conscience' is not so old as is commonly thought. It came into use in 1890, when Parnell was made co-respondent in the divorce suit brought by Captain O'Shea. Hugh Price Hughes and the Nonconformists in the National Liberal Federation then made it plain that they could not continue to support Home Rule if Parnell continued to lead the Irish Nationalist party. Since Parnell's adultery with Mrs O'Shea had been suspected for some years, there was something of a sneer in the phrase, though it was forthwith accepted by Hugh Price Hughes.[1] Nonconformity was always more concerned with individual sin than with social evils; 'an inflexible sabbatarianism, a stern condemnation of the sins of self-indulgence—sexual vice, drunkenness, gambling—and an ostentatious avoidance of every appearance of evil, which in this context connotes ball-room dancing, moderate drinking and card games'[2] were the Victorian manifestations, though one ought to add (to be truly 'puritan') condemnation of fine clothes and attendance at theatres.

That the major social evils as we now understand them—poverty, disease, illiteracy, slums, etc.—were not necessarily due to defects of character or to the failure of the churches to convert the mass of the people to an active Christianity was a discovery of the nineteenth century. Though they have existed from time immemorial, they were made both more obvious and more emphatic by the industrial revolution. The industrial towns were vast, disorderly, unplanned heaps of buildings and people, dependent on the local industry for their livelihood, with no means for policing, paving, lighting, drainage, refuse collection or education except that provided by co-operative initiative, and no provision for unemployment, sickness, old age, widowhood or orphanage except that provided by the poor law. Even when there were churches and chapels the incumbents and ministers could do

---

[1] The word 'conscience' was, however, much in use by Nonconformists long before 1890. A Nonconformist did not need to find reasons for deciding that drink, gambling and taxes on bread were wrong. His conscience told him that they were wrong. Cf. John F. Glaser, 'Nonconformity and the Decline of Liberalism', *American Historical Review*, LXI, p. 357.

[2] H. F. Lovell Cocks, *The Nonconformist Conscience*, p. 8.

little, except in co-operation with the local employers. The dissenting ministers were in any event inhibited from taking an attitude different from that of the employers, because their congregations consisted mainly of employers, shopkeepers and other members of the middle class, who provided for the maintenance of the chapels and the stipends of the ministers. This did not mean that nothing was done for the benefit of the local inhabitants as a whole. On the contrary, until the Poor Law Commissioners were set up in 1834 the problems of industrial England were all tackled locally and on the ground; and for the greater part of the nineteenth century and, in many places, well into the twentieth century, local initiative was the main spur to action. In that local initiative the clergy and the Nonconformist ministers often played a leading part. This was especially so in respect of education, where private and charitable enterprise (aided by a small national subvention after 1833) was the sole means available until 1870. The machinery of local government generally was built up slowly from 1834 to 1894 and the cost of 'social services' gradually transferred from charity to local taxation. It is significant that even in 1908 the majority of the Royal Commissioners on the Poor Laws thought that the main problems of the poor law ought to be met by a more intensive organisation of charitable enterprise.

The dislike of 'State interference' which was characteristic of most of the nineteenth century is discussed in chapter IV. It was exhibited most clearly by the urban middle class, the most active of whom were the Nonconformist ministers. In the main, they came from that class, their social relations were mainly in that class, they depended for their congregations and their stipends mainly upon that class, and accordingly they shared the ideas of that class. State interference was permissible for the enforcement of traditionally Nonconformist ideas, such as the 'English Sunday', the control of the sale of drink in ginshops and taverns, the control of gaming and lotteries, the prohibition of cock-fighting and bear-baiting, and, in short, most of the recreations of the working class.

There was a change towards the end of the century, by which time the working class had the vote, and broader objectives, such as those of the Radical Programme of 1884, had to be accepted by the urban middle class. Meanwhile Nonconformity had been consolidated as an ally of the Whig party, partly by anxiety to get all the discriminating laws repealed, and partly by the continued alliance of the Church with the Tory or Conservative party. The Nonconformist Conscience had no great interest in social reform until near the end of the century; but Nonconformity was strong enough in the whig politics of the earlier part of that century to justify the common usage, whereby the Nonconformist Conscience is dated back to 1810.[1]

7. THE CHURCHES SINCE 1832

The Church of England was never very strong politically. Its authority in England depended upon its alliance with the landed gentry. It had no jurisdiction in Scotland. In Wales and Ireland its jurisdiction was almost a fiction. The growing strength of Nonconformity made the Church a privileged sect, and it had already lost some of its privileges. The belief of the Reformers that it was a bit of 'Old Corruption' was confirmed by the votes of most of the bishops against the first Reform Bill. In the division in the House of Lords in which the Bill was defeated, twenty-one bishops voted in the majority of forty-one. Also, the clergy used their influence in the ensuing general election. 'In every village', alleged the whigs, 'we had the black recruiting-sergeant against us.'[2]

After the Reform Act the Reformers were dominant, and the fear of the tories in the Church was that the Reformed Parliament would reform the Church into something like a department of Government. The fear was exaggerated, but a great deal of emotion had been displayed during the Reform agitation; almost every assertion, on both sides, had been carried to the extreme; the Archbishop of Canterbury had been insulted and the palace of the Bishop of Bristol had been sacked by the mob. The Reformed Parliament had proceeded to amalgamate or, as the tories put it, to suppress, Irish bishoprics. Nobody could possibly defend the Irish Establishment as such, but an

---

[1] Indeed, Palmerston is alleged to have said that, in the long run, 'English politics would follow the consciences of dissenters': Skeats and Miall, *History of the Free Churches of England*, p. 595 n.

[2] C. S. Carpenter, *Church and People, 1789–1889*, p. 54.

important principle was involved, the right of the State, of its own motion, to interfere in the government of the Church.

Though it would be wrong to give the Oxford Movement a 'party political' connotation, it was no accident that Keble's sermon, which in effect transferred the movement from whiggish Cambridge to tory Oxford,[1] was delivered in 1833. It was preached while the Bill to amalgamate Irish sees was before the House of Lords.[2] The whole movement was directed against what Cardinal Newman called 'Liberalism'. By this he meant Liberalism in the Church. Nevertheless, of the eighteen propositions which he alleged to be Liberal,[3] more than half had political implications. This did not mean that the Tractarians formed a political party. They were merely a group of Oxford dons in Holy Orders who took their religion seriously and tried to seek out its foundations. In the result, even if they did not, like Newman, join the Church of Rome, they injected into the Church of England, and therefore into the Conservative party, an ultra-tory element. Its political importance was small because its doctrines were, to most Protestant Christians, either offensive or incredible. They implied, for instance, a rigid sacerdotalism in a country (even if one forgets Presbyterian Scotland and Calvinistic Wales) which had been traditionally anti-clerical and in which half the Christians refused to conform with the Church of England whether it was high, low or broad. In an age much concerned with the social consequences of the industrial revolution, the Tractarians devised the remedy of a restoration of the unity of Christendom on the basis of an alleged apostolic succession— a succession which, as the ribald pointed out, assumed that God had chosen some strange bishops to connect Keble with the apostles.[4]

It was, of course, even less true of the Conservative party than it was of the Liberal party that the tail wagged the dog: but it is true of all parties that the extremists strengthen the opposition. The Tractarians got the publicity, especially when Newman and some of his followers turned to Rome. Their doctrine clearly implied an end of civil and

[1] As a purely religious movement it had been started in Cambridge in 1826: S. L. Ollard, *A Short History of the Oxford Movement*, p. 23.
[2] *Ibid.* p. 9.
[3] *Apologia Pro Vita Sua* (1889 ed.), pp. 294–6.
[4] S. L. Ollard, *op. cit.* p. 23.

religious liberty;[1] and not only the Methodists and the dissenters but also the Evangelicals found it necessary to support the whigs against this new principle of 'Church and State'. On the other hand, Peel was strongly opposed to this brand of donnish politics.[2] Moreover, the second generation of Tractarian clergy were of a very different stamp, perhaps because in those days the industrial towns in which they preached Christianity were very different from Oxford. After 1850 the High Church party tended to be Liberal, or even socialist. Their ritualism came to be regarded as a harmless fad, and they joined the Evangelicals in the heavy work of the slums.

The Evangelical Movement was a development, within the Church, of some of the ideas of the Methodist Movement. Even in the early years of Wesley's ministry there were clergy who, while sympathetic to his objectives, did not find it necessary to follow him in all his methods. They provided Whitefield and Wesley with pulpits but, for the most part, kept their own preaching within their own parishes.[3] They were not much in favour with bishops and patrons of livings; but in some places, especially in London, there were endowed lecture-ships which were not subject to diocesan supervision so long as heresy was not preached; and there were proprietary chapels within parishes where evangelical preaching was sometimes possible. As the Wesleyan Methodists became more conservative and respectable, the Evangelical party in the Church increased in importance, especially because it obtained a footing in Cambridge through Isaac Milner, President of Queens' from 1788, and Charles Simeon of King's, Minister of Holy Trinity Church, Market Hill, from 1783. This produced a third generation of evangelical clergy, some of whom became missionaries in the foreign field, while others stayed in England. The problem of livings became less acute, partly because the prejudice against evangelicalism began to disappear, and partly because Simeon created a trust fund which, in due course, obtained something like a hundred livings. Moreover, there developed a band of eager evangelical laymen who formed an active and liberal wing of the Tory party.

[1] Newman, *Apologia Pro Vita Sua* (1889 ed.), pp. 295–6.
[2] Ollard, *op. cit.* p. 91.
[3] G. R. Balleine, *A History of the Evangelical Party in the Church of England*, pp. 50–1.

Perhaps too much emphasis has been laid on the 'Clapham Sect' of laymen who gathered in John Venn's parish of Clapham. They were influential people; through William Wilberforce they had associations with William Pitt; they took over from Granville Sharp ('the patriarch of the community')[1] and the Quakers the leadership of the attack on the slave trade; and they established Sierra Leone as a refuge for freed slaves. No doubt, too, they helped towards the development of liberal opinion in the nineteenth century. They were important in the second generation, which included Lord Macaulay, Bishop Wilberforce, Lord Glenelg and Sir James Stephen. They were, however, rather a close corporation,[2] and they probably had less influence on opinion than the worthy evangelical clergymen whose immediate achievements were less spectacular. They were consequences rather than causes of the Evangelical Movement.

Of the same type was Antony Ashley Cooper, styled Lord Ashley from 1811 to 1851, when he succeeded as seventh Earl of Shaftesbury. Having negligent parents, he was brought up as an evangelical by an old servant of the family; and his evangelicalism survived even residence at Christ Church, Oxford, where Pusey was a contemporary. Dicey may not be right in asserting that he might be mistaken for a Cambridge man who had listened to Simeon's sermons:[3] had he gone to Cambridge he might possibly have been a whig, though Wilberforce, the Stephens and the Venns were evangelical Cambridge tories. The fact that he was an evangelical tory and not a whig made it possible for him to brave the wrath of whig factory-owners and agitate for Factories Acts and other industrial legislation—though it should be added that when he succeeded to his father's estates in 1851 he also tried to improve the conditions of the agricultural labourers.

These examples and others—for instance, Richard Oastler and Michael Sadler—show that it was possible in the conditions of the first half of the nineteenth century for a tory to be very radical in respect

[1] R. Coupland, *Wilberforce*, p. 249; see also E. Lascelles, *Granville Sharp*, pp. 127-9.
[2] Sir James Stephen, *Essays on Ecclesiastical Biography* (1907 ed.), II, pp. 249-97.
[3] 'If Lord Shaftesbury's collegiate career were at some future time to be inferred from his tastes and from his opinions, the obvious surmise of an historical inquirer would be that his Lordship graduated at Cambridge and never missed a sermon of Simeon's': A. V. Dicey, *Law and Opinion in England* (1st ed.), p. 227.

of social reform. The dominance of the Conservative party by the landed interest up to 1880 must not blind us to the fact that that party also had strong support in the towns, especially after the working-class householders were enfranchised in 1867. It was probably due in part to the failure of the Chartist Movement; in part, too, it was due to a growing separation between Nonconformist employers and their employees; but the towns were the areas in which both the Evangelical party and the High Church party had most influence. The Evangelicals began active work in the industrial towns when the Church Pastoral-Aid Society was formed in 1836.[1] There they were joined by the second generation of the Tractarians.[2] Their propaganda had no political objectives: since the Reform Act the 'political parson' has always been an exception. But the clergy came from the comparatively wealthy families; they were usually Oxford or Cambridge graduates; their Church was fundamentally conservative, claimed a long historical tradition and relied on an emotional appeal. Without so intending, therefore, the Church of England was, in the towns as in the agricultural villages, a source of conservative propaganda.[3] It was, too, an important source until the end of the nineteenth century, when the trade-union movement and the socialist societies, which often had a Nonconformist background, began to influence opinion more strongly.

The first Reform Act enfranchised most of those dissenters who had not been enfranchised under 'Old Corruption'. Since the Methodists had large working-class support, especially in the sects which had broken away from the Wesleyans, they did not become really strong in the electorate until 1868. On the other hand, the Methodists were also strong in the industrial middle class, many other members of which were dissenters. We therefore find the Methodists and the dissenters moving towards a common front; and the common name 'Nonconformist' becomes more suitable. The whole body became politically more self-conscious, partly because it profited from the first Reform Act and could be a most valuable ally of the whigs, and partly

[1] Balleine, *History of The Evangelical Party*, p. 176.
[2] Ollard, *A Short History of the Oxford Movement*, p. 147.
[3] When Tait became bishop of London he was regarded with a certain suspicion by many of his clerical friends because of his association with the 'sacrilegious whigs': *Life of Archbishop Tait*, I, p. 194.

because of what Nonconformist ministers regarded as outrageous claims put forward by the High Church party.

We must not, however, press too far the idea of a common front. There was a gradation from the High Church party, who were often die-hard Conservatives, to the Unitarians and Quakers, who were often Radicals.[1] For some years after the Reform Act the Wesleyan Methodists were as Conservative as the Evangelicals.[2] What created the common front was the necessity for joint action against the political privileges of the Establishment. The most important of these was the power of the vestry and the churchwardens to levy a rate for church purposes. This was a relic of the idea, which many Churchmen insisted on perpetuating, that there was one Church to which the whole laity was attached as a matter of divine right and duty, or in other words a relic of the idea of Church monopoly. The remedy for non-payment of rates had been excommunication; but in 1815 the magistrates were empowered to enforce payment by distress. The Quakers took the lead in refusing to pay, but the Nonconformists as a whole objected to this imposition on behalf of what had become a minority Church. Thus church rates provided a solid reason for a common front until 1868, when they were made voluntary. The Church's monopoly of marriages was abolished in 1836, but divorce *a mensa et thoro*, without freedom to remarry, was a matter for the ecclesiastical courts; and divorce with liberty to remarry required an Act of Parliament, backed by a decision of an ecclesiastical court. This domination, by Anglican ecclesiastical law, of a population of whom only a proportion (say half the active Christians) was Anglican, was not removed until 1857, and even the Matrimonial Causes Act of that year was a compromise favouring the Anglican point of view. Burial in the churchyard, which was often the only burial-place, was another subject of controversy. These and other privileges, which many in the Church sought to retain from its ancient monopoly, led to a clear breach between Church and chapel.

On the other hand it must not be assumed that those of the people of England, or even of the electors, who were not active Anglicans, gave

[1] Gow, *The Unitarians*, pp. 70, 96–7.
[2] E. R. Wickham, *Church and People in an Industrial City*, p. 104. For the conflict which this set up within the Methodist Connexion, see *ibid.* p. 128.

firm support to the Nonconformists. All the denominational bodies were minorities, and indeed comparatively small minorities. The Church of England was, in England (but not Wales, Scotland or Ireland) the largest of the minorities; but its ancient monopoly, backed by traditional social habits (especially in respect of baptism, marriage and funerals) which derived from that monopoly, gave the minority the support of a great mass of people who were vaguely Christian but did not regularly attend either church or chapel. This became clear after 1885 when Nonconformity as a political force simply petered out, except in Wales. In the balance between parties the support of even a small minority is important, but by 1885 Nonconformity was weakening both absolutely and relatively. The old-style employer of labour, who had usually been a pillar of the chapel, was being replaced by the company director who had been to Rugby or Marlborough and Oxford or Cambridge, and who was vaguely 'C. of E.' because a rather jolly sort of 'Onward Christian Soldiers' Anglicanism was taught in his school and college chapel. Except in a few places like Cornwall, Bristol, London and Yorkshire, Nonconformity had no great hold on the mass of the electors.

There was, however, a short period between 1868 and 1885 when Nonconformity seemed to be important. Cobden and the Anti-Corn Law League in the forties had used the clergy, and especially the Nonconformist ministers, as instruments of propaganda against the Corn Law. Free trade in corn was particularly attractive to the middle-class industrialists because, as the Chartists realised, cheap bread helped to keep down wages. It was therefore not difficult to persuade Non-conformist ministers that any legislation which kept up the price of corn artificially was contrary to the divine law. Clearly, if God had wanted to protect English agriculture he would not have allowed the North American prairies to be opened to large-scale wheat production. Nonconformist ministers generally allowed themselves, even when they did not take an active part in politics, freedom to discuss public affairs in the pulpit because religion cannot be kept apart from morality, or morality from politics. Hence in the days when many illiterate electors had the vote the pulpit was a most valuable means of 'political education'.

Free trade having been established by divine law and the urban householders having been enfranchised in 1867, it was necessary for the Liberal party to retain the support of Nonconformity.[1] That support was, however, lost in 1870 because of the Education Bill. Since the early years of the century both church and chapel had been active in starting schools; and by 1851 there were over two million pupils in day schools, apart from another two-and-a-half million in Sunday schools. Of the two million pupils in day schools, about half were in schools provided by religious bodies; and of this million pupils about four-fifths were in Church schools. Even so, there were many boys and girls who never went to school; many more who attended for so short a period that they could not read or write, and indeed there were many schools where writing was not taught (in some the schoolmaster authenticated his return by his mark).[2]

Public opinion had now accepted the idea of the duty of the State to help in the provision of education, and indeed building grants had been available on an increasing scale since 1833, though most of the money had gone to Church schools. The Newcastle Commission, which reported in 1861, thought that the grant system had not effected 'a general diffusion of sound elementary education amongst all classes of the poor'.[3] A new grant system for schools inspected by the Committee of Council for Education was suggested, and these grants should be supplemented by subsidies from local rates. The Commission did not recommend compulsory education in State schools, because any attempt to do so would be met by objections, both religious and political. A revised grant system was in fact adopted in 1862 and resulted in an increase in average attendance with lower costs. It also resulted in increased controversy; for it failed to meet the problem, and inevitably produced argument as to how it should be solved. Figures from Birmingham in 1866 showed that of the children between the ages of three and twelve, eleven per cent were at work, forty-nine per cent

---

[1] In the debate on Disestablishment in May, 1871, Gladstone 'fully and frankly acknowledged the political strength of the Nonconformists, who had the power to shatter the whole Liberal party': Skeats and Miall, *History of the Free Churches of England*, p. 633.

[2] Frank Smith, *History of Elementary Education*, pp. 220–3.

[3] H. C. Barnard, *History of English Education*, p. 127.

were at school, and forty per cent were neither at work nor at school.[1] The Reform Act of 1867, which enfranchised a great many illiterate householders, induced even the most conservative to agree, in Robert Lowe's oft misquoted phrase, that it was necessary 'to compel our future masters to learn their letters'.[2]

The difficulty was to find out who are 'we', the Church, the Nonconformists, or a secular State? The Gladstone Government, which took office in 1868, having disestablished the Irish Church in 1869, proceeded to tackle the thorny problem of denominational education. The Radicals, most of whom were Nonconformists, decided to press for compulsory education in State schools, and an Education League was founded in Birmingham in 1869, among its members being George Dixon, Joseph Chamberlain, and Jesse Collings. Its view on religious education was that 'all dogmatic and theological teaching, and all creeds and catechisms, must be excluded from the schools, and that simple Bible reading, without note or comment, should be left to the decision of the ratepayers'.[3] In consequence a National Education Union, supported mainly by Churchmen, was set up to advocate the principle of the denominational school, with a conscience clause, and the payment of school fees out of public funds only in case of necessity.

The conflict was not exactly between the Church and Nonconformity, because some Nonconformists favoured Christian teaching in the schools. On the other hand, the Education Bill of 1870, when it appeared, was almost universally condemned by Nonconformists. A Central Nonconformist Committee was established in Birmingham and it proceeded to distribute a petition against the Bill among Nonconformist ministers: 7300 forms were sent out, and 5173 signatures were received in a few days. Even among the Wesleyan Methodist ministers there was a clear majority against the Bill. Among the other branches of Methodism, and among Congregationalists, Baptists, and Unitarians, the majority supporting the Committee was overwhelming.[4] We need not follow the course of the Bill, nor the subsequent battle

[1] Frank Smith, op. cit. p. 281; and see post, pp. 413-24.
[2] Life of Lord Sherbrooke, II, p. 330. It is usually quoted as 'We must educate our masters'.
[3] Frank Smith, op. cit. p. 284.
[4] A. W. W. Dale, Life of R. W. Dale, p. 276.

over 'rate-aided religion'. Some amendments were made to appease the Nonconformists, but their strength in the House of Commons was small, and the Government was supported by the Conservatives. The battle continued until the general election of 1874 at which, it was alleged, 'Nonconformist abstentions from the poll were amongst several principal causes of total Liberal defeat'.[1] Whether that was so we do not know, and probably never shall, for it was the first election under the ballot. Mr Garvin adds, however, that 'Nonconformity itself had lost, as events proved, its last fight for the leadership of national politics'. What is more, that ambitious young Unitarian, Joseph Chamberlain, who had taken the leading part in the battle, realised that he was backing the wrong horse. Even before the election he had written:

I have long felt that there is not force in the Education question to make it the sole fighting issue for our friends. From the commencement it has failed to evoke any great popular enthusiasm. Education for the Ignorant cannot have the meaning that belonged to Bread for the Starving...the assistance of the working-class is not to be looked for without much extension of the argument.[2]

Chamberlain turned from the Education League and the Central Nonconformist Committee to the Birmingham Liberal Association and the National Liberal Federation; and ten years later he produced the *Radical Programme*.[3] The fact that it includes a lengthy chapter on 'Religious Equality' (written by John Morley),[4] which makes a strong attack on the idea of a 'national church' and argues for disestablishment, shows that, in Chamberlain's opinion, the Nonconformist vote was worth keeping. It was, however, much less important after 1884 because under the third Reform Act equality of representation was at last conceded. The Nonconformists never had been strong in the

---

[1] *Life of Joseph Chamberlain*, I, p. 143.
[2] *Ibid.* p. 146.
[3] From 1874 to 1880 the Liberation Society, which contained most of the active 'political' Nonconformists, improved its organisation and raised funds for an attack on the Establishment as such. Of the 343 Liberals elected in 1880, over 100 were Nonconformists, including sixteen members of the Executive Committee of the Society. They were not strong enough, however, to carry Disestablishment: Skeats and Miall, *History of the Free Churches of England*, pp. 643, 669.
[4] *Life of Joseph Chamberlain*, I, p. 546.

English counties, except in Middlesex, Cornwall and Yorkshire: and the enfranchisement of the rural householder strengthened the parsons' political party. Moreover, Home Rule was not attractive to stern Nonconformists because it involved placing Ireland under the control of the Church of Rome. The middle classes were in any case going Conservative. After 1886, therefore, the Nonconformist vote was never again important, except in Wales and individual English constituencies. Its Indian summer was 1906, when it was thought to be more important than it actually was. The local preacher, of working-class origin, who had so strengthened Methodism in the eighteenth century, was quite frequently the local Labour leader, while the 'respectable classes' both in church and chapel were voting Conservative.

CHAPTER IV

LIBERTY

I. LIBERTY AND LIBERTIES

Since 'liberty' has been involved in political controversy for over three hundred years it has as many meanings as the Cheshire Cat might have had tails:[1] and when we tire of its infinite variety we drop into Anglo-Saxon and call it 'freedom'.[2] Both words, moreover, have acquired such an aura of sentiment that it is difficult to mention either without bursting into rhetoric. As his editor, Edward Christian, remarked in a comment on Blackstone's explanation of liberty:[3]

Though declamation and eloquence in all ages have exhausted their stores upon this favourite theme, yet reason has made so little progress in ascertaining the nature and boundaries of liberty, that there are very few authors indeed, either of this or of any other country, which can furnish the studious and serious reader with a clear and consistent account of this idol of mankind.

And forthwith Professor Christian, writing in 1803 during the reaction to the French Revolution, proceeded to declaim against Jacobins! Nevertheless, it is possible to sort out the dominant ideas behind the language of successive controversialists. It should first be noticed that in the language of the law a 'liberty'—the article is important—is a privilege conferred on a subject, the obverse of the 'prerogative' vested in the Crown, and indeed arising out of it. Its other Norman-French name is 'franchise'. Analytically it may be either a right, such as a right to levy a toll, to hold a court, to elect a burgess to Parliament, or an immunity, for instance from a tax or the jurisdiction of a court. So far there is no political controversy: but, as we have seen in chapter II of this volume, the controversies in which James I and Charles I were

---

[1] See, for instance, L. T. Hobhouse, *Liberalism*, ch. II, where it is classified under nine headings (and appropriated for the Liberal party).
[2] Sir George Cornewall Lewis said (*Use and Abuse of Political Terms*, 1898 ed., p. 151) that liberty and freedom are identical: but in politics all absolute statements are dangerous. I have heard nationalists under colonial rule assert that under that rule they had great liberty, but that what they wanted was freedom, that is, self-government.
[3] 1 Bl. Comm. 126.

involved were over rights, controversies in which Bacon was briefed against Coke. The word 'liberties' was used in the plural, and usually they were immunities. The King had no right to issue proclamations, to decide matters of law, to impose customs duties, to imprison the five knights, to levy shipmoney, and so forth. These alleged rights or prerogatives interfered with liberties.

There was, to the Stuart lawyers, a sound reason for this usage. Magna Carta, which the black-letter lawyers brought back into fashion after the old statutes were printed, was a charter of liberties. As the Charter of 1225 (when translated) put it:

In the first place we have granted to God, and by this present charter confirmed for us and our heirs for ever, that the English church shall be free, and shall have her rights (*jura*) entire, and her liberties (*libertates*) inviolate. ...We have also granted to all freemen of our kingdom, for us and our heirs forever, all the underwritten liberties (*libertates*), to be had and held by them and their heirs, of us and our heirs forever.[1]

Clearly there was no distinction between *jura* and *libertates*, except possibly a distinction between positive and negative; and in fact some of the *libertates* granted to all freemen were positive and some negative. The Stuart lawyers, therefore, referred to 'rights and liberties' without attempting to segregate them. For instance, the Petition of Right, 1628, demanded 'their rights and liberties according to the laws and statutes of this realm'; and Charles I conceded 'their just rights and liberties, to the preservation whereof he holds himself as well obliged as of his prerogative'.[2]

This concept of liberties as rights, privileges or immunities conferred by positive law is important because liberties are more concrete than liberty. The Stuart lawyers probably could not have explained exactly what these liberties were, though when it came to the point it was possible to argue whether James I or Charles I had tried, unlawfully, to subvert a particular liberty, or at least a particular liberty of a particular subject. Though it is not possible to say that liberty was the sum of individual liberties, it is nevertheless true that liberty involves

[1] McKechnie, *Magna Carta*, p. 222; the words in the Charter of 1215 which were not in that of 1225 are omitted, since the lawyers used the Charter of 1225 from the *inspeximus* of 1297.
[2] S. R. Gardiner, *Constitutional Documents of the Puritan Revolution*, pp. 69, 70.

130

individual liberties, specific rights or immunities which are part of the law of England. It is therefore not a mere abstraction or philosophical concept. Liberties are lawyers' concepts, often enforceable in the courts by appropriate remedies like the writ of *habeas corpus*. The philosophers and politicians use broader language and become vaguer: but behind that language are the liberties conferred by the law of England.

Nevertheless, Coke had been flirting with philosophy. He referred to liberty as 'that natural faculty which permits every one to do anything he pleases except that which is restrained by law or force'.[1] Force not authorised by law is of course illegal. We thus have a compound liberty. If I am arrested I have a writ of *habeas corpus*; but if I am forbidden to smoke the noxious weed imported by Sir Walter Raleigh I have no writ *de sigaro comburendo*: I go on smoking until somebody removes my cigar, when I begin to talk of trespass *vi et armis*.

A broader idea emerged with the Long Parliament. Until the Eleven Years' Tyranny the argument was over rights, and liberties involving rights. The Long Parliament, in pursuit of liberty, actually interfered with rights. The change can be seen in the 'Act for regulating the Privy Council and for taking away the Court commonly called the Star Chamber'.[2] The charters and the statutes were recited, and it was alleged that the powers under the Star Chamber Act had been exceeded; but the recital added that the proceedings of the Court had been found to be 'an intolerable burden to the subjects, and the means to introduce an arbitrary power and government'; and accordingly the Act took away what was, in some respects at least, a lawful jurisdiction. Though liberty was not mentioned, except in so far as a person was 'restrained of his liberty', the implication is that the Court of Star Chamber had, more or less lawfully, interfered with something which might be called liberty, which was desirable, and which was inconsistent with arbitrary government.

Thus, the phrase 'the laws and liberties of the kingdom' in the Grand Remonstrance of 1641[3] meant something more than the 'rights

[1] Co. Litt. 116.
[2] 17 Car. I, c. 10 (1641): S. R. Gardiner, *op. cit.* pp. 179–86.
[3] S. R. Gardiner, *op. cit.* p. 212.

and liberties' of the earlier Stuart legislation. Laws and liberties were opposed to arbitrary government. What, then, was arbitrary government? Clearly it meant making laws without Parliamentary authority, imposing taxes otherwise than by Parliamentary grant, and punishing offenders otherwise than through the King's justices. Liberty and absolute monarchy were incompatible: liberty meant Parliamentary government, though nobody denied the royal prerogatives so long as they were subject to law. Nor are we, as yet, in the realm of moral obligation. The flirtation with Romanism, civil and canon, nevertheless continued. Both John Milton and Algernon Sidney declared a law to be 'illegal' because it was contrary to the law of nature. The ideas on this subject were inchoate; but it was from the English Civil War that the Americans and the French drew the idea that liberties, or the rights implicit in liberty, are natural rights, fundamental rights laid down by the law of nature.[1]

The Parliament men were, however, concerned with another aspect of liberty, variously described as freedom of thought, liberty of conscience, or the right of private judgment. These descriptions go further than the liberties claimed. Many elements were involved in religious liberty, and few made clear which of them they meant. First there was belief in the facts, or assumptions, of Christianity itself. At this stage few, except the Jews, claimed liberty to deny them. Secondly, there was the ecclesiastical establishment, which had been placed in issue by the Reformation: if the Church of Rome was in error, the Church of England might be in error, so might the Presbyterian Church, the Baptists, the Independents, or the Friends. Accordingly, once it was admitted that the Church of Rome had no monopoly, there could be no end to the number of sects. Few, however, claimed liberty of conscience in this sense. Religion was not a matter of opinion but of fact. If the creeds of the Church of England, for instance, expressed truth, all the other creeds must express falsehood. Ought a man to have liberty to believe in falsehood? Besides, the unity of Christendom was usually part of the creed. Both the Church of Rome and the Church of England claimed to be catholic, though the Presbyterians pointed

---

[1] D. G. Ritchie, *Natural Rights* (3rd ed.), p. 10; T. H. Green, *Four Lectures on the English Revolution*, p. 20.

out that both were in error because there was no scriptural authority for bishops. But even Presbyterians did not accord liberty of worship.

What is more, this was no mere question of belief, it also involved questions of political obligation. The Pope was a foreign prince who claimed the right to absolve the King's subjects from their allegiance. According to Elizabeth's Act of Uniformity he had 'usurped' his powers and authorities, and they were 'restored' to the Crown. A loyal citizen, and especially a person holding authority, civil or ecclesiastical, had to take an oath acknowledging that the Queen was supreme governor, in spiritual as in temporal matters; and to deny the Queen's authority was a praemunire. It was, of course, one thing to deny that the Crown had authority in spiritual matters and another to assert that, even within the King's dominions, the Pope had it. Moreover 'spiritual' had a wide meaning, since it covered the whole realm of ecclesiastical jurisdiction and the control of ecclesiastical lands and revenues. It was therefore possible to claim liberty for dissenters but not for Roman Catholics, because the Church of Rome, unlike the Protestant sects, claimed to have rights under canon law which could not be controlled by English law, and because the Pope claimed powers which English law, as now established, vested in the King. In fact, however, most of the Protestant sects claimed not liberty but compulsory uniformity. The principal exceptions were the Independents, who were few in number before 1640,[1] but whose strength grew during the Civil War. Their political leader, Oliver Cromwell, pleaded for 'liberty of conscience', for instance in his report to the House of Commons after the Battle of Naseby:

Honest men served you faithfully in this action. Sir, they are trusty; I beseech you in the name of God, not to discourage them. I wish this action may beget thankfulness and humility in all that are concerned in it. He that ventures his life for the liberty of his country, I wish he trust God for the liberty of his conscience, and you for the liberty he fights for.[2]

So the Roundhead fought for liberty against arbitrary government: but he did not fight for liberty of conscience because that came from

[1] Lord Acton, *Lectures on Modern History*, p. 201.
[2] T. Carlyle, *Letters and Speeches of Oliver Cromwell* (ed. S. C. Lomas), 1, p. 205.

God. On the other hand, Cromwell was prepared for uniformity in forms of worship, for the sake of peace, so far as conscience allowed.[1]

In this matter the Baptists supported the Independents; and, after the appearance of William Penn, so did the Quakers (except, of course, as to forms).[2] But the Presbyterians had the same attitude as the Church of Rome and the Church of England to uniformity. Nor did Cromwell's toleration extend to Roman Catholics, at least in so far as concerned the external manifestations of their creed. He meddled not with any man's conscience, but accepted no liberty to 'exercise the mass'.[3] This is, of course, another element in religious liberty, and it is connected with yet another element, that of propaganda. Even if public celebration of the mass were not propaganda, it would be obnoxious to all Puritans as a public exhibition of Antichrist; but all religious groups (except perhaps the Quakers) had to be propagandist bodies because they took seriously the scriptural injunction to preach to all nations.

It was this problem of propaganda which produced the finest and most emotional defence of liberty in the English language, John Milton's *Areopagitica* (1644). Among all the masses of propaganda called forth by the Civil War, this pamphlet alone has survived outside the libraries, and its influence on opinion has for three centuries been profound. Liberty is an emotional concept because in one of its personal aspects it is opposed to slavery, in another it is opposed to forced conversion (and therefore leads to martyrdom), and in its national aspect it is opposed to tyranny. What Milton did was to harness emotion to what may be called liberty to print and publish. The occasion for it was the Order of Parliament of 14 June 1643, that no book should be printed or placed on sale unless it be licensed by a person appointed by both or either of the Houses of Parliament. The argument against the censorship of the press is, however, expressed in the finest prose, so that it is now read not only for the sake of the argument but also for the beauty of the language. Moreover the argument against censorship develops into an argument for liberty of

---

[1] *Letters and Speeches* (as above), 1, p. 218.
[2] Lord Acton, *Lectures on Modern History*, p. 201.
[3] T. Carlyle, *op. cit.* 11, pp. 325–6.

opinion, of which one short paragraph will suffice to indicate the quality and emotional appeal:

Well knows he who uses to consider, that our faith and knowledge thrives by exercise, as well as our limbs and complexion. Truth is compared in Scripture to a streaming fountain; if her waters flow not in a perpetual progression, they sicken into a muddy pool of conformity and tradition. A man may be a heretic in the truth; and if he believe things only because his Pastor says so, or the Assembly so determines, without knowing other reasons, though his belief be true, yet the very truth he holds becomes his heresy.[1]

The 'muddy pool of conformity and tradition' is capable of founding an accusation by all liberals against all conservatives for all time. The practice of the Commonwealth and the Protectorate was, however, far removed from the precepts of their more liberal preachers. Succeeding generations looked back upon the Puritan age not as an age of freedom and enlightenment, but as an age of tyranny and oppressive conformity. 'Puritan' became, and still is, a term of abuse. While the sects differed among themselves, they agreed in enforcing a rigid Sabbatarianism, in putting down popular recreations, in discouraging all religious emotion in architecture, art or music, in repressing the theatre, and generally in forcing social life into a rigid conformity such as not even the most extreme Protestant could accuse the Church of Rome of attempting.

Consequently, though the Restoration produced a reaction towards ecclesiastical conformity which was strengthened by the Corporation Act of 1662, the Test Acts of 1673 and 1678, the 'Five Mile' Act of 1665 and the Conventicle Act of 1670, it was in other respects a reaction towards liberalism. Indeed, in the small social circle which surrounded the profligate Court of Charles II it became licence. Puritanism survived as a system of social behaviour, and it was made more attractive by another influential piece of Puritan propaganda, John Bunyan's *Pilgrim's Progress* (1678 and 1684); but there was also a liberal stream —which after the French Revolution became mainly Conservative in politics—perhaps best represented by Samuel Pepys, though his *Diary* was not published until 1825. Social pressure has done much to enforce

---

[1] John Milton, *Areopagitica* (Everyman ed.), p. 27.

135

social conformity in England as elsewhere (though not as much as in Wales and Scotland): but there has been since 1660 a suspicion of all attempts to make the Englishman good by Act of Parliament. He found in experience under the Commonwealth and the Protectorate a new liberty, that of going to Heaven or the devil in his own way; and ever since he has been rather a difficult person to 'push around'.

The ecclesiastical reaction of the Cavalier Parliament could not last. It was inspired more by Royalist venom than by religious fervour. Indeed, religious 'enthusiasm' of all kinds became suspect as savouring of popery or Puritanism, even when exhibited within the confines of the Church of England. Also, there was a gradation from the cavalier who had come back with Charles II to the Quaker who refused all oaths. In the middle were not only all the vicars of Bray, but also all those who, for the sake of a quiet life, had conformed to the Covenant, and now conformed to the Church. The dissenters were not disfranchised, except in the corporation boroughs; and even there they could qualify by occasional conformity. They were few, though they became increasingly influential in the commercial cities; but many conformists had more sympathy with dissenters than with James II's popish Court. The Declarations of Indulgence were maladroit because they were so obviously directed towards a restoration of popery; and few sympathisers with dissent (Shaftesbury was an exception, but he was in French pay) were taken in. The dissenters supported William of Orange in 1688, George of Hanover in 1715 (more especially because there had been tory reaction under Anne), and George II in the '45. Toleration of dissent—though not of popery so long as either Pretender was alive—was not only essential politically, at least for the whigs, but also essential because religion had become a social bore unless it quietly accommodated itself, as most of the clergy did, to the atmosphere of the Augustan age. The people who mattered were building not churches but country houses; and they were reading (when hunting and drinking allowed) not theological polemics but good, quiet classical literature in which, fortunately, there was neither politics nor religion. What a decent man of good family ought to think about it all is shown by Lord Chesterfield's letters to his son. There was obviously not much to think, because the history of England could be compressed into twelve pages. The whole letter (no. XCIII) ought to be read, but a few extracts will indicate the tone:

In those days of Popery and ignorance, the Pope pretended to be above all kings, and to depose them when he thought proper.... To which unreasonable pretensions all princes had been fools enough more or less to submit. But Henry [VIII] put an end to those pretensions.... This was the beginning of the Reformation in England....

King Charles the First...would, by the advice of a hot-headed parson [Archbishop Laud], establish the Common Prayer through the whole kingdom by force, to which the Presbyterians would not submit. These, and many other noblemen, raised a civil war in the nation....[He was tried and beheaded]....This action is much blamed; but, however, if it had not happened, we had had no liberties left.

King Charles the Second...had no religion, or, if any, was a Papist; and his brother, the Duke of York, was a declared one. He gave all he had to whores and favourites....He lived uneasily with his people and his Parliament; and was at last poisoned....

King James the Second...resolved at once to be above the laws, make himself absolute, and establish Popery; upon which the nation very wisely and justly turned him out, before he had reigned quite four years....

The Prince and Princess of Orange were then declared, by Parliament, King and Queen...and this is called the Revolution.

King William was a brave and warlike king; he would have been glad of more power than he ought to have; but his Parliaments kept him within due bounds, against his will. To this Revolution we again owe our liberties....[1]

This is so charmingly ingenuous as to be almost a caricature: but Lord Chesterfield was no fool, and he simply put into words of one syllable what a noble lord should properly feel about the recent history of England. In four volumes of worldly advice little is said about religion. A noble lord would not teach religion to his son; that was a matter for the tutor, Mr Hatte; and Mr Hatte would no doubt teach a gentlemanly sort of religion. What Mr Hatte could not teach and Lord Chesterfield, as a man of the world, could, was the necessity of keeping up appearances:

When I say the appearances of Religion, I do not mean that you should talk or act like a Missionary, or an Enthusiast, nor that you should take up a controversial cudgel against whoever attacks the sect you are of; this would

[1] *Letters of Lord Chesterfield to his Son* (1800 ed.), I, pp. 277–83.

137

be both useless, and unbecoming your age: but I mean that you should by no means approve, encourage, or applaud, those libertine notions, which strike at Religions equally....Even those who are silly enough to laugh at their own jokes, are still wise enough to distrust and detest their characters; for, putting moral virtues at the highest, and Religion at the lowest, Religion must still be allowed to be a collateral security, at least, to virtue, and every prudent man will sooner trust to two securities than to one. Whenever, therefore, you happen to be in company with those pretended *esprits forts*, or with thoughtless libertines, who laugh at all Religion...let no word or look of yours intimate the least approbation; on the contrary, let a silent gravity express your dislike: but enter not into the subject, and decline such unprofitable and indecent controversies.[1]

This is the legacy of the seventeenth century to the eighteenth. Though it did not suit George Whitefield or John Wesley, it was typical of the age. The attitude was a great help towards conformity, but it also helped the dissenters, so long as they carried their religion in a gentlemanly way and did not try to foist it upon anyone. It helped towards that most remarkable of all English compromises, whereby the legislation against dissenters was kept on the statute book for a hundred years but breaches of it were condoned every year by an Indemnity Act. Parliament, like Lord Chesterfield, kept up appearances, but exercised a tutorial discretion towards those who found conformity a little difficult.

We must not, however, over-emphasise religious liberty, especially when it was due more to slightly contemptuous good nature than to conviction. What made eighteenth-century England so satisfied with itself was that, unlike other and, obviously, inferior nations, England had civil liberty. Since people had been talking about liberty, singular or plural, for a hundred years, its connotation was complex. The legalistic interpretation given to liberties under the early Stuarts had by no means disappeared. It had been strengthened in 1641 by the abolition of the Court of Star Chamber and other Privy Council jurisdiction, by the reversal of the *Case of Shipmoney*, and indeed by most of the early legislation of the Long Parliament, which had not been repealed in 1660. It had been strengthened, too, by the Habeas Corpus Act, 1679, which had removed the limitations on the value of the writ of *habeas*

[1] *Letters of Lord Chesterfield*, II, pp. 350-1.

corpus. Meanwhile *Bushell's Case* (1670)[1] had established the independence of juries; and, as James II discovered in the *Seven Bishops' Case* (1688),[2] no English institution was so independent or, if need be, so truculent as a London jury, whose members generally retained some of the dour obstinacy of the old Roundheads.

The Bill of Rights, 1689, was in the main a return to the early Stuart notion of concrete liberties. It may be regarded as the supreme example of English pragmatism; but even if anybody had wanted to start arguments over political philosophy there was no time and this was not the occasion. James II had escaped and William of Orange was in the country with a Dutch army. He was prepared to be reasonable, but he held all the cards and he knew what he wanted. It was therefore necessary to produce a formula for his accession which would find favour with the majority of active political leaders and would also be acceptable to William. There is political theory inherent in its strictly practical terms, but the Bill of Rights is not a declaration of the rights of man. It set out in twelve propositions the manner in which King James and his advisers 'did endeavour to subvert and extirpate the Protestant Religion, and the laws and liberties of this Kingdom'. The Lords and Commons then declared, 'for the vindicating and asserting their ancient Rights and Liberties', that seven actions were illegal or against law and, as to the rest, that something specified ought to be done or not done. These 'oughts' are, in the main, akin to moral obligations or constitutional conventions, but distinctions are drawn only incidentally.

The Act of Settlement, 1701, put all these liberties on a firm foundation by providing for the independence of the judges. The judges of the late seventeenth century were a poor lot because they were Royalist yes-men; but those of the eighteenth century included some of great eminence, like Lord Holt, Lord Mansfield and Lord Camden. This was the great century of the common law, which Blackstone summed up in his *Commentaries*; and though his political theory received some heavy blows from Jeremy Bentham, his common law was on the whole both sound and elegantly expressed. English liberty was not merely a philosophical concept: it was the sum of the liberties of the common law.

[1] 6 St. Tr. 999.   [2] 12 St. Tr. 183.

In this respect it can be pulled apart like an onion. It will then be found that not all the liberties came from the English Revolution; some were fought for after the French Revolution, especially the freedom of the press.

Even so, eighteenth-century liberty—and we change from the plural to the singular—had a wider connotation. The essential contrast between England and most of the other States in Europe was that it had representative government. Though Roman Catholics and dissenters were excluded, the House of Commons was more representative in the reign of Queen Anne than it was at the end of the century. Representation was not based on any rational principle; but the dominant social class, the landed interest, was strongly represented in both Houses with some regard to geography and some to social status, while the mercantile interest had at least the degree of representation warranted by its place in the economy. The people who mattered thus took an active part in the process of government. The Court was still the centre of power; but no legislation could be passed, taxation levied, or standing army maintained in time of peace, except by authority of a representative parliament. Ministers were chosen by the Queen, but they had to behave with reasonable discretion, for they were useless to her if they could not get the support of Parliament for her measures and policy, and they ran the risk of impeachment. Nor had the Queen any power of arbitrary imprisonment, or power to suspend or dispense with the laws. The courts were independent in fact, and on the accession of George I they became independent in law; and anybody whose rights were infringed had a legal remedy. The Houses of Parliament, too, had achieved the fundamental principle of their independence, that of freedom of speech: they could, as Sir Robert Walpole showed, be 'managed' by suitable use of the royal prerogative, but they had to be bought or persuaded.

This is what Lord Chesterfield (for instance) meant by 'liberties' under George II. In this sense England was a free country.[1] Also, there were neither serfs nor slaves, though probably most of the villagers and labourers were no better off than those in villages and towns in

---

[1] See David Hume in Essay XI (1894 ed., p. 50), where he distinguished between civil liberty and absolute government.

Europe under 'despotic' Governments. During the course of the eighteenth century, however, a broader definition of liberty became current, mainly under the influence of Locke. It was assumed that in the state of nature all men were free, though it was generally assumed, with Locke, that they were bound by a law of nature, whose precepts could be worked out because they were necessary for survival. Man enters civil society in order to provide a common authority to decide disputes and punish offenders. The purpose of positive law, therefore, is not to abolish or restrain freedom, but to preserve and enlarge it. This is one version, derived from Locke.[1] The other, given by Blackstone,[2] is that in the state of nature there is natural or savage liberty, and when man enters civil society he gives up some of this natural liberty. Political or civil liberty is therefore 'natural liberty so far restrained by human laws (and no farther) as is necessary and expedient for the general advantage of the public'.

That both versions postulated a state of nature about which there might be a good deal of argument is irrelevant. The idea which got into circulation was that liberty was an objective, if not the objective, of statesmanship. The liberty of the British Constitution was not a happy accident of recent history, good because the British people, or those who mattered, were so much better off than lesser breeds without the law, but a near approach to an ideal which all nations ought to seek to attain. Restrictions on liberty had to justify themselves. To use the lawyers' phrase, they had to be shown to be necessary and expedient. There could be much argument over what was necessary and expedient, for instance in relation to Navigation Acts and Corn Laws, but the presumption was against all laws in restraint of liberty.

In essence this idea has never been lost, even in the reaction to the French Revolution. It is however in conflict with other ideas. It is of course possible to argue that regulation on Sunday trading, the sale of liquor, combinations of working men, hours of labour, wages, and so forth, is necessary and expedient: but most of their protagonists did not start with the presumption that these laws were bad because they

---

[1] *Second Treatise of Civil Government*, §57 (Gough's ed., p. 29).
[2] 1 Bl. Comm. 125.

141

interfered with liberty and then prove to the satisfaction of Parliament that, nevertheless, they were good because they were necessary and expedient. Similarly, nobody has sought to show that laws providing for employers' liability for accidents, compulsory insurance against third-party risks, sickness, unemployment or old age, and compulsory education, though restrictions on liberty, are necessary and expedient restrictions. Moreover, there is plenty of room for argument over the question which the eighteenth century was unable to answer unanimously, of the criteria on which we can decide that a restriction is necessary and expedient.

Adam Smith, whose *Wealth of Nations* was published in 1776, could answer that question. His underlying assumption was that each man sought his own economic advantage. Any restriction on 'natural liberty' which prevented a man from acquiring more wealth was prima facie objectionable, for instance, the poor law 'settlement' which created scarcity of labour in some parishes and excess in another,[1] or Corn laws,[2] or preferential laws in favour of particular industries. According to the system of natural liberty, the sovereign has only three duties, to defend the country, to administer justice, and to erect and maintain certain public works.[3] This does not mean that other legal restrictions, such as those designed to prevent the spread of fire, or to restrict the issue of paper money, may not be desirable.[4] Subject to these qualifications, however, one may say that liberty—that is, freedom to act without legal restraint—is politically desirable because it is economically desirable. This must not be pressed too far. Adam Smith had lectured in Glasgow on theology, ethics and jurisprudence as well as on political economy. In the last field he 'examined those political regulations which are founded, not upon the principle of justice, but that of expediency, and which are calculated to increase the riches, the power and the property of a State'.[5] He was well aware that there were springs of human behaviour besides the desire for wealth; in the *Wealth of Nations* they were not his concern.

It was, however, the *Wealth of Nations* and not his general political

---

[1] Adam Smith, *Wealth of Nations* (1937 ed. by E. Cannan), pp. 140–1.
[2] *Ibid.* p. 650.   [3] *Ibid.* p. 651.   [4] *Ibid.* p. 308.
[5] R. G. Gettell, *History of Political Thought*, p. 272.

philosophy which was so widely read. Its influence was not due only to its merits as a book. Indeed its merits as a book were in large measure due to the author's ability to take ideas from a wide range of material and to apply them to the rapidly changing conditions of his age. To say that he was the prophet of the industrial revolution would be to go too far: but, having lectured in Glasgow and observed things around him, both in Britain and in France, he discussed in this book, in a comprehensive manner, the broader problems with which the new industrial middle class was concerned and drew conclusions which led him to reject the assumptions on which the landed interest had governed England for a century. The part of Britain which interested him was not the static agricultural system of the champion counties, but the dynamic commercial and industrial system of Clydeside and industrial England, which needed to be liberated from a code of laws ill-adapted to the new conditions being created by the industrial revolution. There is nothing new in his concept of liberty; what he did was to justify in a particular sphere the sort of liberty which Locke had already postulated.

There is, however, a great difference between Locke's influence and Adam Smith's influence. Locke defended an existing system and gave it some sort of justification. His ideas were therefore generally accepted among educated men; even the non-jurors accepted most of Locke and denied only the right of revolution—which even tories like Blackstone denied as soon as the Hanoverian title became secure. Adam Smith, on the other hand, was critical of the existing order; his ideas aroused the antagonism of vested interests and were never fully accepted until the middle of the nineteenth century.

All this discussion about the nature of liberty applies only to the ideas prevailing among the small governing class. What the man in the village thought about it we do not know. Nor indeed do we know what views on the subject prevailed in the back streets of the new industrial towns. The little evidence available suggests that neither thought about it. 'Wilkes and Liberty' were supported by the mob in 1769, but there was great social distress which made Wilkes, as an enemy of the Government, the friend of the people. The riots and general discontent after Waterloo, which culminated in Peterloo and the Six Acts of 1819, were due mainly to the collapse of the wartime boom, not to seditious ideas imported from the French Revolution. There was a development of political consciousness among the workers in the last years of the eighteenth century and the early years of the nineteenth, and it produced, first, popular support for the Reform Bill and, subsequently, the Chartist Movement. It was accompanied by a general rise in the standard of living and was clearly due to it, for it was more evident among the artisans than among the labourers.[1] There is no evidence that liberty, as such, had much appeal. The politically conscious workers wanted the vote, annual parliaments and an equal system of representation: and in one of the senses of the eighteenth century this was liberty. But there was also a section of working-class opinion, cutting into but not always coincident with the section seeking political reform, which wanted some form of socialism, that is, some limitation on the liberty of employers in the interest of the workers. These were, however, minorities. The mass of urban workers began to think in political terms in the second half of the nineteenth century and most of the rural workers did not come into the picture until the eighties. There is no doubt that they accepted the liberal opinions which then prevailed in both parties, but there was no special emphasis on liberty as an end in itself. There was more concern with working and living conditions.

It will be convenient to postpone the discussion of individualism and socialism to a later chapter, since this aspect of liberty became confused by nationalism. So far as all aspects of liberty are concerned it is important to recall the warning given in chapter I that an idea which is controversial in one generation ceases to be so in the next, or possibly the next-but-one. It then becomes a *datum*, a premise upon which further argument may be based, not about the premise itself but about its consequences.

2. LIFE, LIBERTY AND PROPERTY

It is unnecessary to say very much about the 'fundamental rights' of life, liberty and property because they were never in issue after the Civil War and they became an accepted part of the Revolution Settle-

[1] M. Dorothy George, *London Life in the Eighteenth Century*, p. 18.

144

ment. It is, however, important that they were established as the most fundamental of the 'liberties' of Englishmen. As we have seen, the generic term 'liberty' included specific and fundamental 'liberties'. A sinister imputation thus attached to anybody who was not prepared to support 'liberty' as the whigs and Liberals defined it: it could be insinuated that he was in favour of arbitrary government, just as, in later times, it could be insinuated that a person opposed to imperialism was unpatriotic and a person opposed to socialism wanted to abolish the social services or to establish unrestricted competition.

The rule that, to quote the Constitution of the United States, no person can be 'deprived of life, liberty or property without due process of law' comes from c. 29 (c. 39 in the 1215 edition) of Magna Carta. The fact that the historians have shown that in 1225 it meant something rather different[1] is irrelevant; for the chapter was progressively interpreted by Acts of Parliament and decided cases during the fourteenth and fifteenth centuries, and no Stuart lawyer denied, or could reasonably have denied, that the correct translation (in modern English) was: 'No man shall be taken into custody, or detained, or deprived of his property, or outlawed, or exiled, or killed or in any way molested, except by due process of law.'[2]

What was in dispute was the meaning of 'due process of law'. The phrase *per legem terre* was wide enough to cover all lawful power. The contention of Coke and the other common lawyers was that 'lawful' meant lawful according to the common law: but the common law was, historically, merely the body of law worked out by the Courts of King's Bench, Common Pleas, and Exchequer (and the Court of Exchequer Chamber). There were, however, many other courts,[3] each of which had its 'law'; and 'law' in this wider sense included the law and custom of Parliament, the jurisdiction of the King in Council and the Court of Star Chamber, the ecclesiastical law of the Court of High Commission and the inferior ecclesiastical courts, the maritime law of the Court of Admiralty, and even the equity of the Court of Chancery.

[1] W. S. McKechnie, *Magna Carta*, pp. 437–59.
[2] 2 Co. Inst. 45–56; *Darnel's Case* (1637), 3 St. Tr. 1 (arguments for both sides, but especially John Selden for Sir Edmund Hampden and Heath, A.G., for the Crown); Faith Thompson, *Magna Carta*, pp. 86–99 and 295–307.
[3] See the Table of Contents of Coke's *Fourth Institutes*.

Since the verdict of the Revolution was in favour of the common law, we are apt to assume that that law was comprehensive. It must therefore be remembered that Coke's *Institutes* deal in detail with only two branches of the law, the law of real property (in Coke *on Littleton*) and those sections of the criminal law (the pleas of the Crown) which were dealt with by the Court of King's Bench and the justices of oyer and terminer and gaol delivery. The other major branches of the law were discussed only incidentally because, in the main, they were within the jurisdiction of courts other than those of the common law.

The common lawyers claimed that the Courts of High Commission, Chancery and Admiralty could be kept within their jurisdiction by prerogative writs, especially habeas corpus and prohibition. Indeed, in *Darnel's Case*[1] it was claimed, unsuccessfully, that habeas corpus, issued out of the King's Bench, could even be used to question a committal by the King in Council. The politicians became involved for four reasons. First, the Court of High Commission was used to enforce uniformity on Puritan clergy and laymen. Secondly, the Council and the Star Chamber were used to enforce the various types of taxation invented (or restored) by King Charles' advisers, including benevolences and forced loans. Thirdly, a grant of monopoly by letters patent often included a grant of power to the monopolist to enforce the patent by imprisonment. Fourthly, pressure was brought upon the civil population by wide powers conferred on courts martial. In these matters the politicians necessarily had the support of the common lawyers: and indeed, as we have seen, up to the Long Parliament the argument was placed almost wholly on a legal basis.

The contest was wholly a lawyers' battle until 1621, when the question of monopolies became important. The conflict over personal liberty became fiercer, however, after *Darnel's Case* in 1627. The five knights were imprisoned for refusing to pay forced loans, and applications for bail on writs of habeas corpus were rejected. On the latter point, certainly, they had a weak case, though Coke and his friends did not think so because they took *lex terre* to mean the common law. In order to get the assent of the House of Lords, however, the Petition of Right, 1628, raised no fundamental issues but merely sought to remedy

[1] (1627) 3 St. Tr. 1. The substantive point was argued on an application for bail.

146

the specific grievances then felt. No man was to be compelled to make or yield any gift, loan, benevolence, tax, or such like charge except by Act of Parliament; no one was to be called before the Privy Council to make answer, or take an unlawful oath, or be confined, or otherwise molested on account of an illegal tax, or for refusal thereof; no freeman was to be imprisoned or detained contrary to Magna Carta, c. 29 (which was recited); the billeting of soldiers and sailors was forbidden; and no commissions of martial law were to be issued.

This by no means covered the ground; nor had the Petition of Right the sort of compulsion which an Act of Parliament would now have: it was far from being the basis for Hampden's case against shipmoney. A large part of the problem was solved when the Court of High Commission, the Court of Star Chamber, and the criminal jurisdiction of the Council, the Council of Wales and the Marches, the Council of the North, etc., were abolished by the Long Parliament. The abolition of the High Commission brought the ecclesiastical courts within the control of the King's Bench by writs of prohibition, and a similar control in respect of Admiralty had already been acquiesced in. Coke's attempt to control Chancery by prohibition had failed; but the principles of equity were gradually settled by the Chancery lawyers, and equity became, in all except the purely formal sense, a branch of the common law. The abolition of the Star Chamber and other criminal courts made the control of the King's Bench over the criminal law complete. Moreover, except where an information was laid by the Attorney-General before the King's Bench,[1] a person could not be tried for a serious offence unless he was presented by a grand jury, though this requirement became gradually of less importance as justices of the peace assumed the responsibility of holding preliminary inquiries. In any case the trial itself was by petty jury.

Since the legislation of the Long Parliament was not reversed at the Restoration, the common law had obtained complete control, except where a person was imprisoned by order of either House of Parliament

---

[1] Only in case of misdemeanour. An information could also be laid by the Master of the Crown Office at the suit of a private person, but only by leave of the Court. A person could be arraigned before a petty jury on a coroner's inquisition, without an indictment. There was no indictment on an impeachment.

in accordance with the *lex et consuetudo parliamenti*. Moreover the defects of the writ of habeas corpus were removed successively by the Petition of Right, the Act abolishing the Star Chamber, 1641, and the Habeas Corpus Act, 1679. Hence the only provisions of the Bill of Rights, 1689, which relate directly to personal liberty are those which forbid excessive bail and seek to provide (not very effectively) for the proper empanelling of juries. John Locke was able to claim the rights to life, liberty and property as fundamental rights by the law of nature,[1] and thence they passed into the fifth amendment to the Constitution of the United States of America.

Curiously enough, too, the jury became one of the bulwarks of liberty. This was purely fortuitous. One of the advantages of the Court of Star Chamber under the Tudors was that it could deal with the powerful men who could control sheriffs and overpower juries. Under the early Stuarts there was greater fear of the power of the Crown; and the Star Chamber was used to enforce the King's unpopular measures. Also, juries were often chosen from the sort of men who favoured liberty, the new urban middle class. It was better to be tried by one's peers[2] than by the King's officials because one's peers shared one's prejudices. It was possible at common law to reverse the verdict of a jury on writ of attaint,[3] but this was denied in *Bushell's Case*.[4] The Star Chamber used the more effective method of punishing jurors who found against the weight of evidence: but the courts of common law were held in *Bushell's Case* not to have the power of fining, even when, as in *R.* v. *William Penn and William Mead*,[5] the jurors had apparently been contumacious. A City of London jury was of course a protection for Quakers, and at the beginning of the nineteenth century it was a protection for Radicals. In later years it became a protection against unconscionable prosecutions only because, being composed of quite ordinary people, it usually applied a modicum of common sense. It was, however, no protection for the eccentric who

---

[1] *Second Treatise of Civil Government*, §§6, 25, etc.
[2] The notion that the *judicium parium* of Magna Carta was trial by jury was, however, not widely held until the eighteenth century.
[3] Sir William Holdsworth, *History of English Law*, I, pp. 337–40.
[4] (1670) 6 St. Tr. 999.
[5] (1670) 6 St. Tr. 951.

148

insisted upon being stupid; and there was no fundamental right to be stupid.

In the American colonies the eighteenth-century tradition remained, and life, liberty and property became fundamental rights protected by the Constitution. Even the grand jury, which became a useless anachronism in nineteenth-century England, is still constitutionally protected in the United States of America. The notion of liberties protected by the law of nature, which passed from Locke and Blackstone to the American colonies, in England did not survive Bentham's assaults. Even in 1885, however, Dicey could formulate a 'Rule of Law' whose first aspect was that 'no man is punishable or can be lawfully made to suffer in body or goods except for a distinct breach of law established in the ordinary legal manner before the ordinary courts of the land'.[1] Dicey was too good a pupil of Bentham to assert the Rule of Law as a fundamental right; but, if he meant only that the Englishman had a prejudice against bureaucratic powers interfering with the fundamental liberties recognised by the common law he was certainly right. The notion that the citizen may do as he pleases so long as he does not offend against the civil or criminal law, or in other words that he will not be 'pushed around' by government officials,[2] is a valuable popular prejudice. It is a prejudice of which tories and whigs, Conservatives, Liberals and Labour, but especially tories, Conservatives and Labour men, have had to take account. Nobody denies, or has since the Revolution denied, the right to personal liberty, but it has been very easy for liberals to argue that those who opposed some other aspect of liberty opposed all aspects and wanted to restore the Star Chamber or import the Inquisition. The very name 'Star Chamber' is a potent political weapon.

3. FREEDOM OF THOUGHT

The fundamental idea of the English common law is that 'every crime is to a greater or less extent a breach of the peace'.[3] To hold an opinion, however reprehensible it may be to others, is not in itself a breach of

---

[1] A. V. Dicey, *Law of the Constitution* (1st ed.), p. 174; (9th ed.), p. 188.

[2] '*Nec super eum mittemus, nec super eum ibimus*': Magna Carta (1225), c. 29.

[3] Sir J. F. Stephen, *History of the Criminal Law*, II, p. 241.

the peace. In some kinds of treason the intention constitutes the crime, but even in those cases the law requires its manifestation by some overt act, such as meeting, conspiring or consulting.[1] Sedition is not a crime, though publication of a document or a statement with a seditious intention is, and so is a seditious conspiracy. In other words, the common law worked on the assumption that 'the thought of man is not triable'. This was not true, however, of the ecclesiastical law of England, which inherited ideas from the canon law of the Church of Rome. Thought was triable in the ecclesiastical courts (and in the Court of Star Chamber) because until 1640 they used the *ex officio* oath, by which the accused was required to swear that the accusation was not true.[2] In practice, no doubt, the average heretic wanted to go forth and preach his heresy: but this merely aggravated what was already an offence. In a small and close society a man's opinions soon became known; he could then be given the *ex officio* oath and be required to swear, for instance, that he believed in the several and collective divinity of the Trinity.[3]

In the days when clerics were rampant there were two ways of ensuring a quiet life. The one was to pay no attention to theology but to go to church regularly and conform with whatever happened to be the prevailing fashion. The other was to be a Roman Catholic under Mary I, a moderate Protestant under Elizabeth I, an Arminian under Charles I, a Presbyterian under the Long Parliament, an Independent under the Lord Protector, and an unbigoted Anglican under Charles II. It is not surprising that by the time of the fourth Earl of Chesterfield the proper thing to do was to carry one's religion like a gentleman. It was this attitude of social conformity, together with quiet and gentlemanly contempt for fanaticism, which made a contemptuous toleration a practicable policy in the eighteenth century. It was, in the main, a whig attitude; a tory would normally be no less irreligious in principle but would be less tolerant of 'snivelling Puritans'.

The close connexion between religion and politics was bad for both,

[1] *R. v. Thistlewood* (1820), 33 St. Tr. 681 at 920.
[2] Sir J. F. Stephen, *op. cit.* I, pp. 338, 342.
[3] An interesting collection of the doctrines in which a man had a duty to believe is in an Act of May 1648: it was probably never put into force because of Pride's Purge, which ousted the Presbyterians: *ibid.* II, p. 465.

but worse for religion. But the distaste for religious enthusiasm also had other roots. The ecclesiastical courts had been censors of morals as well as of religious belief. In two years between 1638 and 1640 the Archdeacon's Court in the diocese of London dealt with about 1800 persons, three-quarters of whom were charged with tippling during divine service, breaking the Sabbath, or not observing saints' days.[1] Many cases dealt with sexual offences, from sodomy and incest to fornication. 'The courts seem to have had authority to punish anything which they regarded as openly immoral or sinful, without reference to any rule or definition whatever.'[2] Drunkenness, swearing, and witchcraft, too, were ecclesiastical offences. Thus, an inferior ecclesiastical court had something of the character of a modern police court, but with the clergy and their lay assistants deciding what the offences were to be. The attitude of the nineteenth century is indicated by Sir James FitzJames Stephen's comment:

It is difficult even to imagine a state of society in which on the bare suggestion of some miserable domestic spy any man or woman whatever might be convened before an archdeacon or his surrogate and put upon his or her oath as to all the most private affairs of life, as to relations between husband and wife, as to relations between either and any woman or man with whom the name of either might be associated by scandal, as to contracts to marry, as to idle words, as to personal habits, and in fact as to anything whatever which happened to strike the ecclesiastical lawyer as immoral or irreligious.[3]

This attitude was, of course, the result of a slow accretion of changing opinions. It would itself be deemed by a Stuart parson both immoral and irreligious. The peak of clerical pretension was passed in 1640, when the Long Parliament abolished the *ex officio* oath. The ecclesiastical courts (other than the Court of High Commission) were restored in 1661, but without the power of putting the oath. Meanwhile the Puritans had rigidly enforced social conformity by other means, and in the reaction of the Restoration the ecclesiastical courts could not re-establish their authority. Even heresy virtually ceased to exist as an enforceable offence, and the writ *de haeretico comburendo* was abolished

[1] *Ibid.* p. 404.   [2] *Ibid.*
[3] *Ibid.* p. 413.

in 1677. The Act of that year saved the jurisdiction of the ecclesiastical courts in cases of 'atheism, blasphemy, heresy or schism, and other damnable doctrines and opinions';[1] but in fact those courts ceased to exercise jurisdiction over laymen.

Toleration was not practicable under Charles II and James II because, on the one side, there was fear of papal supremacy and a reproduction of the oppression of the reign of 'Bloody Mary'; and because, on the other side, Puritanism was associated with regicide, treason, sedition, and the unlovely aspects of Puritan uniformity. Elizabeth's Act of Uniformity of 1559, with the increased penalties of 1581 and 1593, had been enforced with varying degrees of success until 1640. Presbyterian uniformity replaced Anglican uniformity by an ordinance of 1645, but the law was much relaxed as the Independents became powerful in the Commonwealth and the Protectorate. In 1661 Elizabethan uniformity was restored, and the law was strengthened by the Act of Uniformity of 1662. In 1665 the Five Mile Act forbade a dissenting minister to come within five miles of any Parliamentary borough without taking an oath, and the Conventicle Act of 1670 sought to suppress conventicles. The Toleration Act, 1689, was narrow in its scope and did not apply at all to Unitarians. All this legislation applied to Roman Catholics as to other Nonconformists, but there was a separate and more rigorous stream of legislation against papists. In practice, however, the State gave up the attempt to enforce uniformity of religious opinion after 1688, though the penal laws were not repealed until the first half of the nineteenth century. Nonconformists were second-class citizens; they could not hold public office or be elected to Parliament because of the Test and Corporation Acts passed by the Cavalier Parliament. In practice, however, Protestant dissenters were excluded from their operation by occasional conformity (that is, taking the sacrament once a year) and Acts of Indemnity.

A bare recital of legislative amendments gives some impression of changing opinion. There was a rational case for toleration, put by John Milton in the latter part of *Areopagitica* and by John Locke in his

---

[1] The offender could be ordered to recant and, if he did not, would be excommunicated, whereupon he could be imprisoned for six months: Stephen, *op. cit.* p. 468.

Letters concerning Toleration; and the latter had great influence throughout the eighteenth century. But political attitudes are rarely determined purely by rational considerations. Four other factors were important; and, since their influence varied according to social or economic interest and the differential weight of prejudice, toleration gave ample scope for political controversy over religion, which was still fierce in 1832 and, as we have seen, continued until near the end of the nineteenth century. First, there was a feeling, which the new type of 'society' clergyman did his best to strengthen, that the Church of England was one of the pillars of the established order. There was little sentiment about it until the nineteenth century, when the public schools and the colleges of Oxford and Cambridge made the Church one of the institutions whose value was represented by the old school tie. Even in the eighteenth century, however, a good whig, and still more certainly a good tory, would support the Church because it was part, though usually rather a poor relation, of the landed interest. The Land, the Church and the Army went together because, as Lord Melbourne said of the Garter, there was no 'damned merit' about any of them. What really mattered, of course, was the Land; but jobs had to be found for younger sons, who could hardly be expected to enter a competitive profession like the law. This particular factor, it will be seen, operated against toleration. Every gentleman of respectability was expected to support the Church without being too much of an enthusiast.

Secondly, there was a strong anti-papist sentiment which operated against toleration of Roman Catholics. It became less fierce as the danger of a forced reversion to Rome receded, but even in 1780 it was possible to start anti-papist riots, and the battle over Roman Catholic relief split the tories in 1829. In Ireland the religious conflict was also one of class, and many English landowners had Irish estates.

Thirdly, the anti-clericalism which had prevailed in England since Cardinal Wolsey (at the latest) was strengthened by Archbishop Laud's attempt to enforce uniformity, by the attempt of the clergy to enforce their own views of social morality through the ecclesiastical courts, and by the rigours of Puritan morality, whose recollection lingered long. Nor was it weakened either by the evident corruption of so many

153

clergy of the Church or by the theatrical exhibitions of the Methodists.[1] The quiet resignation of the dissenters, the fact that so many of them were doing well in business (though not yet numerous enough to challenge the supremacy of the landed interest), and common objection to clerical pretensions helped towards toleration of Protestant dissent. As late as the Oxford Movement dislike of sacerdotalism, as well as fear of Rome, weakened the Conservative party.

Finally, the clergy themselves, or such of them as gave more than a passing thought to religion, became rationalistic. Too much emphasis can be laid on 'the Age of Reason'; but when theology was taken out of religion differences of dogma became irrelevant and ritual became a matter more of taste than of faith. It was better to use the Tudor Prayer Book in an attractive church; but if the shopkeepers preferred to listen to a boring sermon in a meeting-house it did not seem to matter, provided that nothing disrespectful or seditious was said. Besides, if dissenters had votes, anybody who wanted to retain his interest in a borough had to be courteously condescending to them. Of course they were outside the pale, but one would expect that of shopkeepers, and almost invariably they were appropriately deferential.[2] In fact they were much easier to manage than the mob that dominated the open boroughs; generally they were too rich to be bribed and too interested in their businesses to ask for more than a share in contracts. They did not ask for a share of the patronage which was intended for the support of impecunious relatives of the landed interest.

The electoral aspect became more important as the industrial revolution developed, especially when the first Reform Act strengthened the electoral strength of the dissenting interest. It became necessary to give up the eighteenth-century compromise, whereby the dissenters were left in peace as second-class citizens. Toleration became almost religious equality, though the Church was disestablished only in

---

[1] Blackstone is always a good example of popular prejudices among the more enlightened conservatives. For his anti-clericalism, see 4 Bl. Comm. 47: 'the clergy [under Henry IV] taking advantage from the King's dubious title to demand an increase of their own power.'

[2] As late as 1874 Joseph Chamberlain could speak of 'the decorous timidity of prosperous Dissent': quoted by John F. Glaser, 'Nonconformity and the Decay of Liberalism', *American Historical Review*, LXI, p. 358.

Ireland and (in 1919) in Wales. By that time the churches had rendered unto Caesar everything that Caesar could possibly claim, and (at least according to the High Church party) rather more than God could properly concede.

Within the broad range of toleration thus conceded there was ample room for differences of opinion. Though the active whigs were generally as good—or as bad—churchmen as most of the tories, and the tories were almost as tolerant as the whigs, Oxford and the more exclusively agricultural counties were generally biased for the Church and against an extension of freedom of conscience, while Cambridge and the commercial centres (as well as East Anglia) were biased towards greater freedom of conscience. In the nineteenth century the Church generally went Conservative and the Nonconformists were generally Liberal, until the enfranchisement of the working class made both church and chapel strong minorities. Then both became more nearly impartial, though the Church tended to be passively Conservative and the Nonconformists passively Liberal. Since 1919, however, the 'religious vote' (other than the Roman Catholics and many of the Jews) has gradually become Conservative: and one important element in the balance of parties is the extent to which the religious vote fluctuates in size, though nobody has produced convincing statistics.

4. FREEDOM OF SPEECH

Freedom of speech is a sort of derivative freedom. If a person is falsely imprisoned, he has a writ of habeas corpus to set him free, an action of false imprisonment against the person who imprisons him, and an action of assault against anybody who forcibly arrests him; assault is also a criminal offence. There is, however, no writ or remedy for deprivation of free speech. The right of free speech is simply an example of what Coke called 'that natural faculty which permits every one to do anything he pleases except that which is restrained by law or force'.[1] In other words, it arises because everything is lawful that is not unlawful.

In relation to free speech controversy has usually arisen over heresy, treason, blasphemous and seditious libel, and censorship.

[1] Co. Litt. 116; *ante*, p. 131.

Of heresy not much more need be said, for it arose out of the assumption that every person had to assent to the doctrines of the national church. In fact, however, heresy has not been punishable by burning since 1677, and the last cases were those of Legatt and Wightman in 1612.[1] Even a good tory like Blackstone could rejoice over the abolition of the writ *de haeretico comburendo* by the 29 Car. II, c. 9: 'In one and the same reign, our lands were delivered from the slavery of military tenures; our bodies from arbitrary imprisonment by the Habeas Corpus Act; and our minds from the tyranny of superstitious bigotry, by abolishing this last badge of persecution in the English law.'[2]

Heresy is still a crime by ecclesiastical law, though it is punishable only by excommunication, deprivation, degradation and other ecclesiastical censures, which of course have no effect on a person who has no wish to remain in communion with the Church of England. The crime developed for laymen was not heresy but blasphemous libel. After the Restoration the Court of King's Bench produced a whole series of related crimes, such as perjury, forgery, conspiracy and criminal libel, which had formerly been punished by the Court of Star Chamber and the Court of High Commission. So far as blasphemy was concerned it was assumed that the Christian religion was the foundation of morals and government and was therefore part of the common law of England. This was a reflexion in the minds of hard-headed lawyers of the theory that the law of nature was the law of God. The doctrine was not a matter of serious political controversy until the French Revolution. A unitarian, a deist, an agnostic or an atheist, even if he used language as coarse as that of Thomas Paine, was until the French Revolution less dangerous than a Jacobite. Religion was an affair of the upper classes and the poor were not supposed to be religious. Indeed, the offence of George Whitefield and John Wesley was greater than that of those who merely produced books and pamphlets for the literate classes, since the former brought an emotional religion to vast crowds. They

---

[1] St. Tr. 727; Coke thought the issue of the writ *de haeretico comburendo* to be illegal: 12 Co. Rep. 93.
[2] 4 Bl. Comm. 49 (there were plenty of other badges, but at least nobody could suffer death for not being the right sort of Christian).

did not, however, attempt to subvert the British Constitution as by God and the law established. For this and other reasons, already mentioned, religion dropped out of politics.

The French Revolution brought them back into association, especially after the Terror. That Revolution had attacked both Church and State; and the established order was already threatened by the growth of the towns. The Star Chamber had exercised a wide jurisdiction over libels in the days when the Civil War was, so to speak, stoking up. Elliot, Holles and Valentine were charged with seditious words as well as a seditious conspiracy in Parliament,[1] though the conviction was quashed on writ of error to the House of Lords in 1668; many others, including Prynne, Bastwick and Burton, were dealt with in the Star Chamber. The jurisdiction was taken over by the King's Bench in 1660, but its exercise was necessarily different because the inquisitorial procedure of the Star Chamber could not be used in the King's Bench, where questions of fact had to be left to a jury. The Star Chamber had closely regulated the press,[2] and the system of licensing was established by the ordinance of the Long Parliament of 1644, against which Milton wrote *Areopagitica*. It was reimposed by the Licensing Act, 1662, a temporary Act which remained in force until 1694 and then expired. Nevertheless, there were many cases of seditious libel after the Restoration. The later years of Charles II were, as we have seen, the period in which the technique of political opposition was developing. Such opposition under the earlier Stuarts had led to the Civil War. The notion that there could be an opposition to the King which was not seditious but a normal part of Parliamentary government had not been accepted. What the eighteenth century called a 'formed opposition' could be regarded as a conspiracy to overthrow the King's Government; criticism of the Government could be regarded as seditious speech or writing. Hence whiggism was seditious, and Royalist or tory judges felt strongly about it. In fact they overreached themselves, especially under the notorious Scroggs, C.J., who was impeached for arbitrary and illegal conduct in the exercise of his office.

---

[1] 3 St. Tr. 293. The case was, however, on information in the King's Bench, a similar information in the Star Chamber being withdrawn.

[2] Sir J. F. Stephen, *History of the Criminal Law*, II, p. 309.

157

Nor was his successor (after an interval of two years), the Judge Jeffreys who held the 'Bloody Assize' after the Duke of Monmouth's rebellion (in which, it will be remembered, Lord Shaftesbury was implicated), noted for his judicial impartiality. Since the law was used oppressively and opinion was moving against the King, it was inevitable that political opposition should develop against the law and the judges who administered it.

The *Case of the Seven Bishops* (1688)[1] was a trial for seditious libel. The recent precedents were not followed. It had been consistently held that the question whether words were seditious was one of law for the judge, and not one of fact for the jury. In this case, however, the whole question was left to the jury. It would seem, as a matter of legal principle, that where an accused pleads not guilty the judge should explain the law in his charge to the jury and leave to the jury the question of 'guilty or not guilty?'.[2] The contrary was, however, held by a majority of the King's Bench in *R.* v. *Shipley*,[3] and by the judges in the House of Lords when Fox's Libel Bill was under consideration.[4] Nevertheless, Fox's Bill was carried and became law as 32 Geo. III, c. 60 (1792): it provided, in effect, that the jury should find a verdict of guilty or not guilty.

Fox's Libel Act is of fundamental importance in the history of the freedom of the press. Sir FitzJames Stephen says that, under the law as it stood at the outbreak of the French Revolution, a seditious libel was 'written censure upon public men for their conduct as such, or upon the laws, or upon the institutions of the country'.[5] This did not prevent opposition in Parliament because, by reason of the privilege of Parliament, affirmed by the reversal in 1663 of the conviction of Elliot, Holles and Valentine, and by the Bill of Rights, 1689, anything said in Parliament could not be questioned in any court or place outside. It did, however, hinder the development of party government in the country, because anything said against the Government could be prosecuted as seditious words and any party 'literature' against the Government was

[1] 11 St. Tr. 1339.
[2] See Erskine's speech for the defence in Thomas Erskine, *Speeches*, I, p. 151: but the contrary view has been held by high authority: Sir J. F. Stephen, *History of the Criminal Law*, II, pp. 315–62.
[3] (1784) 4 Doug. 73.   [4] 22 St. Tr. 296.   [5] *Op. cit.* II, p. 348.

a seditious libel. John Wilkes' *North Britain* (no. 45) and the *Letters of Junius*, for instance, were seditious libels.[1] Dr Shipley, whose case led to Fox's Act, was Dean of St Asaph and had published a pamphlet called *The Principles of Government in a Dialogue between a Gentleman and a Farmer, written by Sir William Jones*. It was in substance an argument for Parliamentary reform, though incitement to rebellion might possibly have been read into it as innuendo.[2]

Party controversy had, however, been acute since the Revolution, and had become particularly acute since the loss of the American colonies. Even Burke might have been accused of seditious libel because of his published attacks on Lord North's Government. A great deal was said in public about the liberty of the press. What this meant in law was that (since 1694) anything could be published, without licence, but subject to the law of libel. But 'what the public at large understood by the expression was something altogether different,— namely, the right of unrestricted discussion of public affairs, carrying with it the right of finding fault with public personages of whose conduct the writer might disapprove'.[3]

What in fact had happened was that, in drafting informations or indictments for seditious libel, prosecutors had usually pleaded in-nuendos which showed an intention to subvert the Constitution as by law established. The jury had then to say not merely whether there had been publication, but also whether there were such innuendos. In the Dean of St Asaph's case no innuendos were pleaded and the jury had merely to find publication, which was in fact admitted; and accordingly, as the law then stood, the Dean was undoubtedly guilty. So would Burke have been guilty: and the only justification for saying that there was any liberty to criticise the Government was that Governments, in their wisdom, did not usually prosecute unless they could aver some-thing more than a criticism of the Constitution.

---

[1] Wilkes' case was never brought to trial because he pleaded privilege against arrest as a Member of Parliament and was released on habeas corpus. The *Letters of Junius* were held to be seditious in *R.* v. *Woodfull*, 5 Burr. 2661.

[2] No innuendo was, however, pleaded, and Erskine was able to point out that much stronger language about the right of rebellion was in Locke's *Second Treatise of Civil Government: Speeches*, I, p. 182.

[3] Sir J. F. Stephen, *op. cit.* II, p. 349.

159

Fox's Libel Act did not, on its face, alter the situation. It merely said that on indictment or information for libel 'the jury sworn to try the issue may give a general verdict of guilty or not guilty upon the whole matter put in issue...and shall not be required or directed... to find the defendant...guilty merely upon the proof of publication by such defendant...of the paper charged to be a libel, and of the sense ascribed to the same in such indictment or information'. In practice, however, this was asking the jury to decide whether the defendant had a seditious intention, and a seditious intention has been defined by Stephen as:[1]

An intention to bring into hatred or contempt, or to excite disaffection against the person of Her Majesty, her heirs and successors, or the Government and Constitution of the United Kingdom, as by law established, or either House of Parliament, or the administration of justice, or to excite Her Majesty's subjects to attempt otherwise than by lawful means the alteration of any matter in Church or State by law established, or to raise discontent or disaffection amongst Her Majesty's subjects, or to promote feelings of ill-will and hostility between different classes of Her Majesty's subjects.

An intention to show that Her Majesty has been misled or mistaken in her measures, or to point out errors or defects in the Government or Constitution as by law established, with a view to their reformation, or to excite Her Majesty's subjects to attempt by lawful means the alteration of any matter in Church or State by law established, or to point out, in order to their removal, matters which are producing or have a tendency to produce feelings of hatred and ill-will between different classes of Her Majesty's subjects, is not a seditious intention.

The change in the law came, as so often, long after opinion had changed; in spite of the law of criminal libel there had for a century been effective opposition to the 'Establishment' in Church and State. Indeed, a reaction was about to set in because of the excesses of the French Revolution. The broad-minded landed class, whose architecture and literature breathe calm self-assurance even today, suddenly sensed that the social structure was a complicated edifice, each part of which was in equilibrium only if every other part was in equilibrium. Burke did not put it in those terms because (unlike our generation)

[1] *Digest of the Criminal Law*, p. 56.

he had not been a pupil of Sir Isaac Newton. He expressed himself in the more emotional language of a literary politician who preached the inevitability of conservatism. Since juries were now, under Fox's Act, the judges of what was seditious libel, they were necessarily affected by the environment;[1] and on the whole the law was harsher in the years immediately after 1792 than before.[2] Also, the law both of treason and of sedition was strengthened by the Treason Act, 1795, at the same time as the law relating to seditious assemblies was strengthened by the Seditious Meetings and Assemblies Act, 1795.

This legislation of 1795 was due to panic on the part of Pitt's Government. The police system was ludicrously inefficient; the industrial revolution had created large groups of illiterate working men among whom wild ideas could easily be developed without anybody knowing it; rioting was almost endemic; and the only knowledge of what was going on in the country came from informers who made a living from their reports, true or false. There was among the middle classes a strong movement for Parliamentary reform organised in bodies like the Constitutional Societies; and this movement had spread among the working class in London, who were for this purpose led by the members of the London Corresponding Society. The first part of Thomas Paine's *Rights of Man* had been published in London in 1791 and the second part in 1792. Pitt first showed signs of panic in the spring of 1792, and the Ministers were assured by their private correspondents that something like a rebellion was brewing.[3]

The prosecutions of 1792 were generally favourable to the Government, though Daniel Eaton was acquitted by a friendly jury.[4] In Scotland in 1793 they went well for the Government with the assistance of the notorious Lord Justice Clerk, Braxfield, whom we remember best as 'Weir of Hermiston'; and Robert Burns composed 'Scots, wha hae'

---

[1] The prosecution usually demanded a special jury so as to secure a jury of higher social status than a common jury, and it was easy enough to 'pack' a special jury, at least until 1817: see J. Bentham, 'Elements of the Art of Packing' in *Works*, v, p. 79; and W. H. Wickwar, *The Struggle for the Freedom of the Press*, pp. 43–6.

[2] J. F. Stephen, *History of the Criminal Law*, II, pp. 364–9. The Attorney-General claimed in 1795 that there had been more prosecutions in the past two years than in the previous twenty years: W. H. Wickwar, *op cit.* p. 17.

[3] P. A. Brown, *The French Revolution in English History*, p. 93.

[4] 22 St. Tr. 755.

after hearing the sentence on Thomas Muir.[1] In 1794, however, the Government charged thirteen members of the London societies—seven of the Corresponding Society and six of the Constitutional.[2] The Habeas Corpus Act was suspended; ten of the accused were held in custody and examined by the Privy Council by methods reminiscent of the inquisitorial procedure of the Star Chamber, except that torture was not used when the better educated among the accused stood mute of malice. Nevertheless, Thomas Hardy and John Horne Tooke were both acquitted of treason and the other prisoners were then discharged.[3]

It has been suggested[4] that Pitt was using this agitation as a means for detaching the Duke of Portland from Charles James Fox and thus of strengthening his Government.[5] It is more likely that the Ministers really thought that there was a treasonable conspiracy on foot. Public opinion was becoming hysterical on both sides. Burke's *Reflections on the Revolution in France* was charged with an emotion which seemed to the landed interest to be entirely justified as the excesses of the French Revolution developed. Thomas Paine's *Rights of Man* was equally emotional, and his success in strengthening the American Revolution by his writings[6] was remembered. The industrial areas were wracked by one of the frequent depressions produced by the industrial revolution; and political reform seemed to many to be the remedy. The Constitutional Societies had made the mistake of calling a 'Convention', which in the contemporary atmosphere seemed even more dangerous than a 'Soviet' might have seemed in 1918. Nor can the reform leaders of this period be acquitted of the charge of wild talk. George III had made himself a politician, and it was almost impossible to attack the tories without attacking the King. A great many people must have been guilty of seditious libels, though the Government made the mistake of prosecuting for high treason.

The trials had the effect of stimulating the appeal of the London Corresponding Society, to which Thomas Hardy had belonged, and

---

[1] P. A. Brown, *op. cit.* p. 97. But Burns changed his mind in 1795: H. W. Meikle, *Scotland and the French Revolution*, p. 121.

[2] P. A. Brown, *op. cit.* p. 119.   [3] 24 St. Tr. 199 and 25 St. Tr. 1.

[4] The matter is discussed by P. A. Brown, *op. cit.* ch. VII.

[5] The Duke of Portland entered Pitt's administration in July 1794.

[6] F. J. Gould, *Thomas Paine*, ch. II.

162

in which Francis Place played an active part. The large public meetings, of which Place himself did not approve, provided one of the excuses for the legislation of 1795. Also, King George III was attacked by the mob on his way to and from Parliament in December 1794, and there were riots in other towns. The mob was demanding not Parliamentary reform, nor liberty and equality, but bread: it was nevertheless clear that a rebellious spirit was abroad. Moreover Britain and France had been at war since February 1793; and, in spite of the 'Glorious First of June' (1794), the war was going badly. However, Napoleon and war-time inflation solved the internal problem for the time being. The fear of invasion, which did not disappear until the naval victory at Trafalgar in 1805, justified repressive government. This was successful until the long war, and especially the disorganisation caused by the peace in 1814 and 1815, produced industrial depression. The discontent was led into political channels by the London Radicals.

Old Major Cartwright established the first Hampden Club after the Peace of Paris in 1814 and sent round printed petitions for annual parliaments, equal electoral districts, and votes for all taxpayers.[1] Henry Hunt ('Orator Hunt') and William Cobbett became allies in 1812 and the latter initiated the twopenny *Political Register* ('Two-penny Trash') in November 1816.[2] Their case was that much of the post-war distress had political causes, since a single small class ran the machinery of government in its own interest. They therefore sought so to arouse public opinion as to force a reform of Parliament by constitutional means. There were, however, sporadic riots in many parts of the country, generally due to the fear of the workers that the introduction of machinery would create unemployment, or to the actual unemployment created by the cessation of war contracts and by demobilisation. There was no serious revolutionary movement; indeed, many of the cheap pamphlets with which the country was flooded were not Radical at all.[3] To the oligarchy in power, however, it seemed incredible that the rapid growth of social unrest, coinciding with a rapid growth of periodical publications, was not due to conspiracy; and

---

[1] Graham Wallas, *Francis Place*, pp. 115–16.
[2] G. D. H. Cole, *Life of William Cobbett*, p. 207.
[3] A. Aspinall, *Politics and the Press*, p. 29.

they were helped towards that conclusion by the spies and provocative agents whom Lord Liverpool had inherited from William Pitt. Both Houses of Parliament set up Secret Committees, which reported that there existed a conspiracy to overthrow established institutions and divide up property.[1] In March 1817 the Habeas Corpus Act was suspended and legislation against public meetings and reading rooms was hastily passed.

The good harvest of 1817 and a temporary revival of trade caused the troubles to subside, but there was another cycle of disturbances in 1819, culminating in August of that year in a great reform demonstration in St Peter's Fields, Manchester, which was broken up by the yeomanry with some loss of life. 'Peterloo' was, of course, violently attacked both in the press and in Parliament, and therefore the Government had to defend itself equally violently. Cobbett had escaped to the United States in 1817 and did not return until November 1819— he brought the bones of Thomas Paine with him. Many of the other Radical reformers were, however, arrested.

Meanwhile Richard Carlile was waging a war of his own. He had started publishing in 1817 as a man of straw for W. T. Sherwin, who had begun the *Republican* but feared arrest. Carlile was forthwith arrested for republishing William Hone's parodies, but was released when Hone was acquitted. He then proceeded to republish the works of Thomas Paine but was not prosecuted until early in 1819 nor tried until after Peterloo. The Government had decided not to repeat the mistake of 1794 and charge high treason. Carlile was charged and convicted of blasphemous libel for publishing Paine's *Age of Reason* and Palmer's *Principles of Nature*. He defended himself by reading long extracts from these books, which were thus widely republished in the newspapers and in Carlile's own publication called *The Mock Trial*. Many others, both publishers and newsvendors, were prosecuted and convicted for blasphemous or seditious libel, thus giving publicity all over the country to atheistic, deistic, reform and republican opinion.[2]

Parliament met in November 1819, and the Prince Regent was

[1] G. D. H. Cole, *Life of William Cobbett*, p. 215.
[2] W. H. Wickwar, *The Struggle for the Freedom of the Press*, ch. III.

unwisely advised to include in his speech a paragraph which must have been relished by all who knew the Prince's reputation:

Upon the loyalty of the great body of the people I have the most confident reliance: but it will require your utmost vigilance and exertion to check the dissemination of the doctrines of treason and impiety, and to impress upon the minds of all classes of His Majesty's subjects that it is from the cultivation of the principles of religion, and from a just subordination to lawful authority, that we can alone expect the continuance of that Divine favour and protection which have hitherto been so signally experienced in this Kingdom.[1]

The pamphleteers made the most of their opportunity. As William Hone put it:

> Go and impress, my friends, upon all classes,
> From sleek-faced swindlers down to half-starved asses,
> That from religious principles alone
> (Don't be such d—d fools as to blab your own)—
> Temperance, chasteness, conjugal attention
> With other virtues that I need not mention,. . .
> Can they expect to gain Divine protection
> And save their sinful bodies from dissection.[2]

The reference to the Prince Regent was even plainer in another ballad, illustrated like the one above by George Cruikshank. Fifty editions, or some 100,000 copies, are said to have been produced before the end of 1820:

> THE DANDY OF SIXTY who bows with a grace
> And has *taste* in wigs, collars, cuirasses and lace;
> Who to tricksters and fools leaves the State and its treasure
> And, when Britain's in tears, sails about at his pleasure;
> Who spurned from his presence the Friends of his youth,
> And now has not one who will tell him the Truth. . . .[3]

These libels simply could not be prosecuted because they could not be read in court.

This Parliament passed the 'Six Acts', but against the opposition of the whigs. Lord Grey, for instance, pointed out that whereas only 3000 copies of the *Age of Reason* had been sold, 50,000 copies of

---

[1] *Ibid.* p. 131.   [2] *Ibid.* p. 133.   [3] *Ibid.* p. 142.

Methodist and Evangelical publications were circulated every month. A few months later, however, the whigs were provided with more congenial ammunition by the return of Queen Caroline. The Prince, who had been the friend of Fox but had kept the tories in office, was now George IV; and the 'friends of his youth' gloried in the opportunity of supporting the Queen against him. This silly woman became, quite fortuitously, the leading actress in the struggle for the freedom of the press. The lead was taken by William Cobbett, who was both an Anglican and a monarchist. His attack was not against monarchy, or Christianity, or the British Constitution: it was an attack on 'Old Corruption' in the form of a defence of a virtuous Queen (or, at least, an allegedly virtuous Queen) against a vicious King and a corrupt Government. Though much of what was said in the popular press, and most of what was said in the popular pamphlets, was technically seditious, it was almost impossible to prosecute, both because it was unwise to exhibit the King's reputation and because no jury could be trusted to convict. Moreover, there were tory publications at least as libellous of the King and his tory Government.

There were in fact very few public prosecutions for seditious libel after 1820, though an attempt was made to put down deism and atheism by prosecutions for blasphemous libel. This was, however, the active period of the prosecuting societies, groups of tories, usually well-intentioned but sometimes not, who sought to prevent the growth of what they deemed vicious habits and opinions by securing the enforcement of the law. That law, as we have seen, derived from an age when Christian opinion was uniform and opposition to the Government was treason. It was therefore easy to secure convictions, even when judges were unsympathetic, unless juries ignored the judge's directions on the law. The two prosecuting societies were the Society for the Suppression of Vice and the Encouragement of Religion and Virtue, and the Constitutional Association for Opposing the Progress of Disloyal and Seditious Principles, which we may call the Vice Society and the Constitutional Association respectively.

The Vice Society was a product of the Evangelical Movement in the Church of England. It was founded in 1802 and by the end of 1803 it had obtained nearly seven hundred convictions. Later an older society, called the Proclamation Society, which had been founded by William Wilberforce to carry out George III's Proclamation of 1787 against vice, profanity and immorality,[1] was merged with the Vice Society. That Society accordingly came under the influence of Wilberforce; and Zachary Macaulay and Charles Simeon were members.[2] Sydney Smith's comment on the Society has been thus recorded by Professor Coupland: '"A corporation of informers", he called it, "supported by large contributions" and bent on suppressing not the vices of the rich but the pleasures of the poor, on reducing their life "to its regular standard of decorous gloom", while "the gambling houses of St James'" remain untouched.'[3] The criticism was a little unkind. What the Clapham Sect really wanted was a religious conversion of the pagan masses whose souls were being endangered by the numerous temptations which drink, Sunday amusements, 'wakes' (and other opportunities for boisterous fun), blasphemous and obscene literature, and so forth, put in their way. They therefore tried to enforce the law not on one class but on all classes. The fact that it was easier to suppress the amusements of the poor than those of the rich was an unfortunate incident which enabled the Webbs to say that the object was to reclaim 'the lower orders' to a life of regular and continuous work.[4]

The Constitutional Association was a less reputable body. It was founded in 1820 under the highest tory auspices; among the members were the Duke of Wellington and some twenty other peers, nine bishops and ninety-seven other clergymen, and nearly forty members of the House of Commons.[5] But the active officials may be suspected of doing well out of its activities and there was little evidence of Christian charity in its activities. It was founded on the assumption that there was a weakening of the bonds between the humbler ranks of society and their natural guardians and protectors and a spirit of hostility to the liberty, property and security of all. Among the causes was a licentious press under the direction either of avowed enemies of the

[1] S. and B. Webb, *History of Liquor Licensing*, pp. 140–6.
[2] W. H. Wickwar, *The Struggle for the Freedom of the Press*, p. 36.
[3] R. Coupland, *William Wilberforce*, p. 55.
[4] *History of Liquor Licensing*, p. 147.
[5] W. H. Wickwar, *op. cit.* p. 183.

Constitution or of persons whose sole principle of action was their own private and selfish interest.[1]

In the period after 1820 the Constitutional Association was the more active of the two societies. It found an unexpected obstacle, however, in the obstinacy of grand and petty juries. Since it was essentially a tory body it had whig opinion against it, and that opinion was growing in a generation for whom the French Revolution was grandfather's bogy. Even a hand-picked special jury could not always be trusted to enforce a harsh law in the vindictive manner which the Association desired. Its challenge to Richard Carlile led to its Waterloo. Carlile, his family, his shop assistants and an apparently interminable series of volunteers kept the shop open, used every prosecution as a means of advertisement for his wares—which were undoubtedly blasphemous as the law stood—and gradually exhausted the funds of the Association. Its vindictive proceedings alienated the support of reasonable tories and the sources of its funds dried up. The 'Carlile interest' found support among younger members of the Bar who disliked this political perversion of legal proceedings even more than they disapproved of blasphemy. Judges began to dislike the use of their courts for religious and political propaganda.

The Association died in 1822, but the Vice Society continued the good work. In that same year the Society failed to secure a verdict against an obscene libel published by William Benbow. Even Carlile objected to the publication of this kind of stuff and regretted that it was published by a Radical publisher. It was still possible to get verdicts against blasphemous publications, but even the Vice Society gave up in 1823. The Home Office and the Attorney-General continued for a few months, and there was a last attempt to close Carlile's 'Temple of Reason' in Fleet Street in May 1824. By now it was one of the City's most famous buildings. No less than nine of his shop assistants were brought up at the Old Bailey before the Recorder, who had a reputation for being hard on blasphemy. All were convicted, but the sentences varied according to the nature of the defence, not according to the nature of the offence, and the Home Office gave up. In 1825 Carlile, who had been in gaol for

[1] Wickwar, *op. cit.* p. 181.

168

five years because he refused to pay his fines (indeed, he had no means of paying), was released.

There were later prosecutions for seditious libel; indeed, there were nine under the Whig Government of 1831–3, chiefly because the whigs had to show that they were as tough constitutionalists as the tories. The climate of opinion had, however, changed. The old idea that the Church of England was right, the Nonconformists (other than the unitarians) misguided schismatics, the unitarians wrong, the Roman Catholics dangerous, and the atheists vicious revolutionaries, was disappearing. Even the Roman Catholics had been relieved of most of their disabilities in 1829. All forms of religion were now 'respectable'. Atheism was not, as Charles Bradlaugh showed forty years later; but it was usually dealt with not as blasphemous libel but as conduct tending (if it did so tend) towards a breach of the peace—and such conduct might be charged against a Protestant controversialist who made himself a nuisance to Roman Catholics. Nor was the mere expression of political opinion regarded as seditious, or at least as seditious enough to justify prosecution. After 1830 even the most 'ultra' of tories had to admit that opposition to the Government was meritorious: they recurred to the old idea (on which impeachment had been founded) that the King had been badly advised, and accordingly that it was their duty to turn out the Ministers by peaceful means. 'His Majesty's Opposition' started as a joke in 1806, but it became eminently respectable in 1830. Republicanism never became respectable, but it was tolerated. Indeed, it began to die when George IV died, though it lingered into the twentieth century.

There was indeed a strong literary movement, historically connected with Milton and Locke but taken up by Bentham and the Mills, in favour not merely of freedom of thought but also of freedom of speech. This movement was influential because, after 1832, the fear of the 'mob' rapidly died out. Under William Pitt's scheme revolution had to be nipped in the bud by preventing the development of seditious conspiracies. Spies and informers were therefore used to track down those leaders of opinion who might incite the 'mob' to violence. Sir Robert Peel inherited this system when he became Home Secretary in 1822, but he soon realised how easily it could be abused, and there was a notable decline of public prosecutions based on informers' evidence. In 1829 he established the Metropolitan Police, and by 1850 the whole country was adequately policed. The 'Bobby', standing at the corner of the street, could deal with riots before they started by asking people to 'move on, now'.

Even more important was the rise in the standard of living brought about by the machines which the Luddites had tried to smash. The 'mob' ceased to be a mob and became respectable working men living in back streets. Certainly there were pockets of disturbance, where one tenth or more of the population lived in conditions of appalling squalor and misery: but these relics of the 'mob' were not centres of revolution. Revolutions were made by middle-class 'intellectuals', who for this purpose had to organise themselves into seditious or treasonable associations. Accordingly the danger—if there was a danger—came not from seditious words or writings but from seditious meetings and organisations. In practice, seditious words could be ignored unless they were a direct incentive to crime.

In fact, however, revolution became less and less likely as the standard of living rose and the franchise was extended. The story might have been different had the House of Lords and the King obstructed the Reform Bill of 1832. The fact that the middle classes had the vote prevented the Chartist Movement from being effectively led. In 1868 the potentially dangerous element, the educated working class of the towns, was given the vote and eventually learned how to use it. England had its revolution, but by Act of Parliament.

Yet the law of treason, blasphemy and sedition remains substantially unchanged. Stephen's definition has an important proviso because nobody can conceive of a court holding a statement blasphemous or seditious merely because it would have been so in the eighteenth century. Courts do move with the times, and the law laid down by them varies from age to age. Even so, England has perhaps the most illiberal laws of any free country and at the same time the most effective demonstration of freedom of speech in the world—Speakers' Corner in Hyde Park, London.

Freedom of speech is another social heritage, now owned by all parties except the communists (who in fact make the most use of it).

The concept is nevertheless important in political controversy because it acts as an inhibition when it conflicts with imperialism. The British, like the French and the Americans, are really not very good imperialists, because they encourage freedom and then cannot suppress it. The political controversies in respect of Ireland, South Africa, India, etc., must be mentioned in their proper place: but it must always be remembered that Her Majesty's Opposition is even more prone than Her Majesty's Government to emphasise that liberty is a desirable virtue and oppression, even with the best of motives, a vice.

5. LIBERTY OF ASSOCIATION

Though in many fields it needs modification, Sir Henry Maine's doctrine of the movement from status to contract[1] does apply to association. The idea of association, as we now conceive it, is that of a temporary combination, for particular purposes, of free and equal citizens. It creates a club, a society, a trade union, or something of that kind, whose members, being free and independent citizens, join, subscribe to, and resign from the body concerned. Association of this character clearly depends upon the individualist nature of modern society. Medieval institutions were based mainly on status. Since the English family was never institutionalised (as it was among some of the Aryan-speaking peoples), the typical institutions, from which our law of association developed, were the several branches of the Church; the boroughs, the counties, the hundreds and the vills; the gilds; and charitable foundations, like hospitals, schools, colleges and universities, outside the ecclesiastical organisation. These were institutions of customary law, many of which preceded the development of the common law; and some of them may have preceded the establishment of monarchy. In customary law the idea of free association was to be found almost exclusively in the commendation of feudal law, whereby a man took an oath of fealty to a lord and expected to be protected by him. Apart from this case, and perhaps the orders of knighthood, customary law knew very little of the sort of association which one was free to join or not to join or, having joined, free to leave or not to leave.

[1] Sir Henry Maine, *Ancient Law* (Pollock's ed., 1930), ch. v.

171

The King was initially concerned in two respects. First, if land was vested in an institution it was difficult to secure the performance of feudal services, especially if the land was held by an institution of the Church. Accordingly, the Statutes of Mortmain, which began in the thirteenth century and ended only in 1960, prohibited alienation to religious bodies without a licence in mortmain, and the prohibition was extended in 1391 to alienations to all bodies, religious and secular alike, which had perpetual succession. Secondly, if the institution required a special privilege, such as a right to hold a court or a fair, or to be immune from a tax or the jurisdiction of a court, it required a charter from the Crown conferring that privilege. These requirements seem to have led the courts of common law to assume, in the fifteenth century, that an institution could not acquire rights at all unless it had, in the case of a religious body, a charter from the Pope or, in the case of a secular body, a charter from the Crown,[1] though the existence of such a charter might be inferred from the fact that the institution had exercised such rights for a long period.

Thus, incorporation became a royal prerogative, which was as likely as any other prerogative to be abused under the Stuarts. Moreover the reigns of the Tudors and the Stuarts were the period in which the trading company became important. Such a company needed a charter for two purposes, to be incorporated and to engage in foreign trade. It was thus possible to confer a monopoly upon a company. The later Parliaments of Elizabeth I and the Parliaments of James I made an attack upon monopolies, but Elizabeth was wise enough to leave the question to the courts of common law, which in effect decided that a monopoly by letters patent was valid (a) for a new invention (that is, the modern 'patent'), (b) if granted to a company of merchants for the regulation of trade, or (c) if otherwise in the public interest, for example for the protection of copyright or for the production of saltpetre.[2] In substance, this was accepted by Parliament in the Monopolies Act of 1624.

Incidentally, in the process of these discussions the common law developed a prejudice in favour of the freedom of trade. It was, of

[1] Sir William Holdsworth, *History of English Law*, III, pp. 475–9.
[2] *Ibid.* IV, pp. 350–3.

172

course, a prejudice in favour of the freedom of internal trade, freedom from monopolies, because external trade was under royal control; but when once a theory has been established as dogma its origin is often forgotten, and we shall see how the problem of 'free trade' against 'protection' was helped by lawyers' prejudices.[1] In the present context, however, it is more important that a corporation could be established only by the Crown and that a trading corporation could be given a monopoly. On the other hand, a corporation once established was not under royal control. It could not be given powers inconsistent with the common law; the rights of the corporators inter se could not be varied; and a charter could not be withdrawn except by proceedings in a court of law.[2]

The power of the Crown effectively to control trade, domestic or foreign, was however much limited by the abolition in 1641 of the Star Chamber. Moreover the mercantile community had considerable power in Parliament after the Revolution, particularly because many landowners had interests in foreign trade. The powers of the Crown were placed at their highest in 1684 in East India Company v. Sandys,[3] and thereafter they were whittled down both by the lawyers and by Parliament. The exclusive powers of the East India Company and the Hudson's Bay Company were maintained by Act of Parliament after the Revolution, and remained a source of political controversy for a hundred years, but whig prejudices against monopolies prevented the creation of any new monopolies, even in overseas trade.[4]

Where an association could function without exercising rights the common law imposed no limitations, provided that its purpose was lawful. Most unincorporated associations, however, did want to exercise rights—to hold property, real and personal, to enter into contracts, and to serve in the courts. Among them were all the dissenting churches, including the Church of Rome, none of which could expect to obtain a royal charter. In the world of commerce, too, were unincorporated associations, the most famous of which were the stock

---

[1] Chapter VIII.
[2] Sir William Holdsworth, op. cit. IX, p. 48.
[3] (1684) 10 St. Tr. 371.
[4] Holdsworth, op. cit. VI, pp. 333–5.

173

and commodity exchanges and Lloyd's. At a later stage came the trade unions, the political unions, the mechanics' institutes, the women's colleges, the political parties, and so forth. This development would have been impossible had the common law ruled, since the Government had to be persuaded of the desirability of a project before a charter could be obtained.

The necessary flexibility was obtained through the concept of trust worked out by the Court of Chancery. If a group of Independents wished to erect a meeting-house, they could raise the money among themselves, vest it in a body of trustees, and empower the trustees to purchase land, erect a building, employ a minister and maintain the building. In the nineteenth century an alternative method was provided by the Companies Acts, which applied especially to commercial and industrial companies: but the great network of voluntary associations of all kinds, which is so characteristic of the British Constitution, became possible because of the flexibility of the law of trusts. That flexibility, in turn, gave rise to the notion, never precisely formulated and yet generally accepted, that there was a 'right' of association. No formality whatever was required. If a number of people raised a subscription among themselves for any purpose whatever, religious, political or otherwise, they automatically created a trust whose objects, unless unlawful, could be enforced in the Court of Chancery. The very rigidity of the common law had led to the remarkable flexibility of equity.

This development had the same causes as the development of the other liberal doctrines considered in this chapter. In spite of the pressure towards religious conformity in the seventeenth and early eighteenth centuries, the Reformation had led to the multiplication of sects and it was quite impossible for the law (in the broader sense which includes equity) to assume that they did not exist. The great development of trade in the sixteenth and seventeenth centuries created the opinion that trade should be free of unnecessary restrictions, and the laws against usury, forestalling, ingrossing and regrating had to be ignored, modified or repealed.[1] The one great exception to the liberty of association was to be found in the development of the

[1] Sir J. F. Stephen, *History of the Criminal Law*, III, pp. 196–201.

law relating to conspiracy, especially in its application to trade unions.

Of treasonable and seditious conspiracies not much more need be said. The early law of treasonable conspiracy was liberal because of the survival of feudal ideas. Where the King persistently refused justice to a vassal the latter had a right to defy the King and, after such defiance, to levy war against him.[1] Until Edward III the Kings of England were vassals of France in respect of their French dominions. Edward III claimed the kingdom of France as well as those of England and Ireland and a stricter law became possible. The Statute of Treasons, 1352, still in force, therefore makes it an offence either to compass or imagine the King's death or to levy war against the King. These phrases were capable of a broad interpretation. Though it was held that there had to be some overt act of 'compassing or imagining', a conspiracy designed to lead to the death or deposition of the King was such an overt act; and in any case this kind of treason was enlarged by temporary statutes necessitated by changing political conditions and especially by the fear of Roman Catholic plots from the Reformation to the defeat of Charles Edward Stuart at Culloden in 1746.[2] The term 'levy war' was similarly capable of a wide interpretation and has in fact been so interpreted as to enable the courts to say that any conspiracy to start a riot with a political object—for instance to break down enclosures, to raise wages, to pull down meeting-houses, to destroy machinery, or in other words to compel the legislature to change the law—is treason.[3]

The restrictions on freedom of association, consequent on these broad interpretations of 'constructive treason', thus became substantial. Even the excesses of the French Revolution, however, did not persuade jurymen to convict for so heinous an offence when what was intended was at most a seditious conspiracy. As we have seen, both Thomas Hardy and Horne Tooke were acquitted of high treason in respect of

[1] Pollock and Maitland, *History of English Law*, II, p. 505.
[2] E.g. 21 Ric. 2, c. 3 (1397); 26 Hen. 8, c. 13 (1534); 35 Hen. 8, c. 3 (1543); 1 Edw. 6, c. 12 (1547); 1 Eliz. 1, c. 5 (1558); 13 Eliz. 1, c. 1 (1571); 13 Car. 2, c. 1 (1661); 9 Will. 3, c. 1 (1698); 12 & 13 Will. 3, c. 3 (1701).
[3] *Trial of Lord George Gordon* (1781), 21 St. Tr. 485 at 644. See, on treason generally, Sir J. F. Stephen, *History of the Criminal Law*, II, pp. 241–83.

the activities of the Constitutional Society and the London Corresponding Society.[1] The law was forthwith strengthened in 1795 by the Treason Act, but that Act was repealed by the Treason Felony Act, 1848, except as to compassing the death, destruction, bodily harm or restraint of the Sovereign. Though the Statute of Treasons, 1352, remains law, only genuine rebellion, or adhering to the King's enemies (as in *R. v. Casement*[2] and *William Joyce v. Director of Public Prosecutions*[3]) would now be regarded as worthy of prosecution under that Act. Lesser offences would be brought within the Treason Felony Act, 1848, or the Treachery Act, 1953.

In the same way, the broad definition of seditious conspiracy has been stepped down. A conspiracy is any agreement between two or more persons to do an unlawful act or to do a lawful act by unlawful means.[4] Originally applied to conspiracy to carry on legal proceedings in a vexatious or improper way, it was extended to sedition after the failure of the Crown to secure convictions for treason against Thomas Hardy and Horne Tooke in 1794. Since seditious conspiracy requires a seditious intention similar to that required for seditious libel, it has followed the same path.[5] In effect it has been used—as against 'Orator' Hunt for his part in Peterloo in 1819, Vincent for his speeches in Newport during the Chartist agitation of 1839, and Daniel O'Connell for his part in the Repeal agitation of 1844—to prosecute political agitators who used the instrument of 'mob oratory' to raise discontent and disaffection.

It will be seen that treason and seditious conspiracy were very wide crimes; but their severity was in practice mitigated by political considerations. In the first place, political opposition to the Government in power became not only proper but thoroughly respectable as soon as opposition to the Government ceased to be opposition to the Sovereign. Though relics of the old concept, that the Government was the King's Government, continued until 1841, there was a slow development, retarded by the French Revolution, from Charles James Fox to 1830.

---

[1] 24 St. Tr. 199 (Hardy); 25 St. Tr. 1 (Horne Tooke).
[2] [1917] 1 K.B. 98.   [3] [1946] A.C. 347.
[4] Sir J. F. Stephen, *History of the Criminal Law*, II, p. 227.
[5] *Ante*, pp. 160–71.

176

Though Fox could be accused of being unpatriotic during the French wars and Conservatives still think it unpatriotic to oppose a Government at war or engaged in such operations as those in Suez in 1956, no such accusation could be levied against opposition in time of peace after the tories went into opposition in 1830. The speeches which Opposition politicians could make in the House of Commons could also be made on the hustings and in the great electioneering campaigns which developed after 1860. The agitations of the major politicians could be copied by the minor politicians; and, indeed, any political speech can be made anywhere, over the whole range of politics from fascism to communism, so long as there is no incitement to the use of physical force. Whatever the law says, an association designed to effect changes in the law cannot be a treasonable or seditious conspiracy so long as it seeks to attain its objects by constitutional means, that is, by Act passed by a Parliament lawfully elected.

Secondly, republicanism has ceased to be a political issue of any importance. England had its republic in the seventeenth century—though it was called first a commonwealth and then a protectorate—and did not like it much. George III persuaded most of his American subjects to try a second experiment, and they and their successors have made a success of it. Had the French been equally successful in 1789, the whigs might have become a republican party. The Terror and Napoleon consolidated the party of 'Church and King' and left republicanism to the lunatic fringe. Moreover William Pitt, the insanity of George III, and the incompetence of George IV, gradually created the constitutional monarchy which Queen Victoria inherited and consolidated. Joseph Chamberlain, Sir Charles Dilke, and other Radicals were republicans in principle, and there are still republicans on the left of the Labour party. On the other hand, no practical politician thinks it worth while to argue the point, partly because it would be political lunacy to do so, and partly because the substitution of an elderly politician for a young Queen would have no political effect and not much social effect. Thus, the monarchy has been taken out of politics, except in so far as it continues to be more closely associated with conservative than with radical institutions. On the other hand, the law of treason and sedition was laid down in a monarchical age, when (as in 1688) the remedy for political grievances was to depose the Sovereign and choose another. It is therefore used only in extreme cases.

Thirdly, 'mob oratory' is no longer a political weapon of importance. As we shall see, it is easy for a trained police force to handle a small crowd, and to prosecute for minor offences, without using the sledge-hammers of the old law.

Finally, when seditious movements are particularly dangerous, as in Ireland before 1921 and in Britain during great wars, Parliament creates new and temporary statutory offences. Southern Ireland now has its own republic, whose example has not been contagious in spite of its large export of Irishmen to the United Kingdom. Ulster might want to fight the Battle of the Boyne over again if any attempt were made to end the 'partition' of Ireland; Wales or Scotland might possibly rebel against government from London, or England rebel against government by Welshmen and Scots; but the law of treason and sedition is unimportant because there is no treason or sedition, except among the few eccentrics who add colour to a drab existence and who can if necessary be bound over to keep the peace or sent to prison for 'obstructing a policeman in the execution of his duty'. In fact, if not in law, any person can help to form any association he pleases.

There was, however, one great exception, which is still in political controversy, at least in some of its aspects. Associations of employees, or trade unions, have always been treated differently from other associations, though the motives have varied.

Before the Black Death (1349) most landless men were villeins, or even serfs, tied to the soil and bound to render services to their lords. The Black Death, by halving the working population, remarkably increased the tendency, which had been developing in the fourteenth century, for landowners to employ hired labourers; and, by making labour scarce, the plague tended to put up the level of wages both on the land and in the towns. It was therefore sought, by the Statutes of Labourers of 1349 and 1350, to regulate the employment of hired labour.

The Statutes created a new status, that of wage-earner. Indeed, there were two types of that status, for in some respects a distinction was drawn between the mechanics or artisans and the labourers or servants. That idea of status persisted into the eighteenth century and was given up with great reluctance even when the industrial revolution made it impossible to enforce the law. Nor was the status always disadvantageous to the worker. Free competition would be beneficial to him—if anybody had thought it possible to adopt such an idea— when there was what we now call 'full employment', that is, a surplus of jobs to which he had access. It would be to his detriment when there was a surplus of labour. The Statutes of Labourers did not give the wage-earners security of tenure; but in effect they imposed on employers (especially landowners) a moral obligation to look after their labour force, and many of them did. Wages were fixed either by a landowning Parliament or by landowning justices of the peace; and, naturally, they were not fixed at too generous a level. On the other hand, the Tudor statutes also placed on the justices of the peace the obligation of pro- viding poor relief for those who were poor and unable to work. When in the late eighteenth century their functions in this regard came under criticism, the allegation was not that they were too harsh but that they were too generous.

The efficacy of a law depends, however, on the power of enforce- ment, which in turn depends very largely on the strength of public opinion in favour of the law. Though in many parts of the country the traditional system of agriculture, with the labourer virtually tied to the soil, continued in the eighteenth century, the use of new methods of cultivation, especially through the growing of roots and imported grasses, produced a capitalist agriculture for which it was necessary to inclose the common fields and the waste-lands and in which labour was as much a commodity as corn. Consequently, in many parts of the country there was free trade in labour long before Adam Smith. It was, however, in the towns, and especially among the artisans, that the Statutes of Labourers broke down. By 1750 those Statutes, though still in the books, were for all practical purposes dead. Parliament did not readily give up the idea that wages could be fixed by law. There was legislation both to fix the prices of bread and fuel and to fix wages, even in the eighteenth century.[1] So far as the workers were concerned,

[1] Sir William Holdsworth, *History of English Law*, XI, pp. 469–75.

they were ineffective in raising wages, even if they sometimes kept them down; and from the end of the seventeenth century there were 'combinations' of journeymen, one of whose functions was to maintain, or improve, the rates of wages.

This development arose out of the growth of capitalist industry, for two reasons. First, so long as the artisan could hope, by his skill, to make himself a master-craftsman, he would tend to be an individualist, more concerned with prospects than with wages: but where, as in the luxury trades, capital was necessary for success as a master-craftsman, there were no such prospects and combination became essential to maintain wages. Secondly, combination was practicable only where there were few employers but many employees. Trade unionism (as it was called in the nineteenth century) therefore proceeded apace when the factory system developed, though it had long been practised in other trades, like the felt-makers, the tailors, the weavers, and the printers, in which capital was needed for successful trade. To say that trade unionism was a reaction to capitalism is, of course, to make a generalisation which neither workmen nor masters would have recognised in the eighteenth century. What the employer wanted was to be free to fix wages so that he could compete in the open market in his own trade: he did not think of himself as a member of the capitalist class, though he would recognise that a precedent created in some other trade might be extended to his own. Nor did the employee think of himself as a member of the working class: though he too would recognise a precedent when he saw it.

Hence it was the worker rather than the employer who wanted to continue the old tradition of fixing wages (and prices) by Act of Parliament. The initial purpose of a 'combination' was to petition Parliament; only when this failed was it realised that employees, like employers, had to fend for themselves, and that they could protect themselves against the consequences of capitalist competition, or secure to themselves the benefit of a shortage of labour, only by combining to refuse work. The change occurred in the second half of the eighteenth century. In 1756 the weavers succeeded in getting their wages fixed under an Act of Parliament, but the clothiers protested that they could not meet the competition of Yorkshire if the wages fixed by the justices were paid; and in the following year the Act was repealed. Though Acts were passed for the benefit of the silk weavers in 1777 and the paper trade in 1795 (but only for the fixing of hours of work), the tradition of fixing terms of employment by Act of Parliament was on the way out.[1]

It was consistent with the tradition that combinations of workers to raise wages by strikes should be prohibited: so long as Parliament fixed wages such combinations were clearly seeking to usurp the authority of Parliament. Accordingly, there were from 1720[2] statutes forbidding combinations in various trades. When Parliament accepted the view of the employers that wages should not be regulated by statute, however, it did not at the same time accept the implication that the journeymen must be free to bargain, in combination, with the employers. On the contrary a general prohibition of combinations for the raising of wages, shortening the hours of work or decreasing the hours of work was enacted in the Combination Acts, 1799 and 1800. To enter such a combination, or wilfully and maliciously to endeavour to prevent any person from taking employment or wilfully and maliciously to try to induce any workman from leaving his employment, or to attend any meeting for any such purpose, became an offence. The employers had found a new fundamental liberty; 'the right of every man to employ the capital he inherits, or has acquired, according to his own discretion, without molestation or obstruction, so long as he does not infringe on the rights or property of others, is one of those privileges which the free and happy Constitution of this country has long accustomed every Briton to consider as his birthright'.[3] What is more, when the woollen operatives sought to enforce the old statutes by which wages were fixed, the Acts were first suspended (in 1802) and finally, in 1809, repealed. Further attempts were made by the London operatives to secure the enforcement of the Statute of Apprentices, 1562, and other ancient laws generally; they were unsuccessful because, at least in respect of the fixing of wages by justices of the peace, the powers were

---

[1] S. and B. Webb, *History of Trade Unionism* (1920 ed.), pp. 50–3.
[2] Sir J. F. Stephen, *History of the Criminal Law*, III, p. 206.
[3] *Report of the Committee on the State of the Woollen Manufacture in England*, 1806, p. 12; quoted by S. and B. Webb, *op. cit.* p. 62.

permissive. When in 1813 the operatives petitioned Parliament to make the laws effective, the laws were forthwith repealed.[1] The operatives had lost their statutory protection and were thrown on the open market, but without power of combination.

The Acts of 1799 and 1800 were tory legislation. The comprehensive Bill which formed the basis of the Act of 1799 was suggested by Wilberforce and introduced by William Pitt. It was opposed by Benjamin Hobhouse and Lord Holland.[2] The amending Bill of 1800 was brought in by the tory members for Liverpool, one of the few towns in which members of the working class, being freemen, had votes. It was supported by Sheridan and opposed by Pitt and the Law Officers, and eventually a compromise measure was passed.[3] It must of course be remembered that Britain was still under the shadow of the French Revolution, that Napoleon had just begun his meteoric career, and that every combination of workmen was assumed to be potentially seditious. However, the Combination Acts did not suppress trade unionism. Some employers actually encouraged it. Prosecutions were undertaken only when employers suffered from it. In the main, the Acts were used to resist demands for higher wages and to put down strikes; and they were used more successfully against the unskilled workers than against the craftsmen. Among the latter a rigid discipline developed, which has much to do with the discipline of the modern trade union. Among the former were frequent outbreaks of violence, particularly when new machinery was introduced. Since the workers were refused the remedy of collective bargaining, violence was the only remedy, and it became almost endemic in the later years of the French wars and in the great post-war depression. Another result of these oppressive laws was the development of working-class solidarity, especially in the new industrial towns where depression hit all trades alike and common action against the 'bosses' was thought to be the remedy.

It was, indeed, in the post-war depression that the movement for the repeal of the Combination Acts began. Though the Acts applied to

---

[1] S. and B. Webb, op. cit. p. 60. A few sections of the Act of 1562 remained in operation until 1875.
[2] J. L. and B. Hammond, The Town Labourer, pp. 111–12.
[3] S. and B. Webb, History of Trade Unionism (1920 ed.), pp. 70–1.

employers as well as to employees, combinations of employers to reduce wages were not infrequent, while combinations of workers were ruthlessly suppressed. The high-water mark was reached in 1819, the year of Peterloo and the Six Acts. Francis Place had become interested in the Combination Acts in 1819, when the compositors of *The Times* were prosecuted for a combination and were sentenced by the Common Sergeant, 'Bloody Black Jack':

Prisoners, you have been convicted of a most wicked conspiracy to injure the most vital interests of those very employers who gave you bread, with intent to impede and injure them in their business: and, indeed, as far as in you lay, to effect their ruin. The frequency of such crimes among men of your class of life, and their mischievous and dangerous tendency to ruin the fortunes of those employers which a principle of gratitude and self-interest should induce you to support, demand of the law that a severe example should be made of those persons who shall be convicted of such daring and flagitious combination, in defiance of public justice, and in violation of public order.[1]

Place's active propaganda for the repeal of the Combination Acts began forthwith but he did not succeed in getting a Select Committee until Hume proposed it in 1824. Place's views were those of a good Benthamite: he wanted not to encourage trade unions but to destroy them; and he thought they would be destroyed if the Combination Acts were repealed, because it would no longer be necessary to have combinations to protect employees against the tyranny of the law.[2] The Acts were repealed in 1824, during a trade boom, and at once produced a great extension of trade unionism and strikes. There were widespread protests from employers, and Huskisson followed Hume's example of proposing a Select Committee and packing it, though this time with Government supporters. As a result there was a new Bill, much less favourable to the trade unions. The Act of 1825, commonly known as 'Peel's Act', made trade unions and collective bargaining legal, but created a number of wide and vague offences.[3] In any case,

---

[1] Graham Wallas, *Life of Francis Place* (new ed.), pp. 200–1.
[2] *Ibid.* p. 217.
[3] Sir J. F. Stephen, *History of the Criminal Law*, III, pp. 214–15.

the Act of 1825 coincided with the collapse of the boom; and trade unionism is ineffective in a depression.[1]

The curious feature of these Acts, as we look back upon them, is that they were passed with so little political agitation. It is, however, curious only because we know how controversial trade unionism became after 1867. Among the landowners in Parliament the 'condition of the people' was a matter of much less concern than the divorce of Queen Caroline or Roman Catholic relief. The rates of wages in industry were of no interest to landlords; few masters or men had the vote and hardly any of the masters had electoral influence; Huskisson and Peel were of plebeian origin and knew something about industry, but not many people on either side of the House shared their knowledge. By 1824 the fear of the 'mob', which had been at its highest in 1819, had somewhat subsided. Hence it was possible for a tailor of Charing Cross and a Radical M.P. to persuade a bored Parliament to pass a Bill whose importance few recognised.

The Act of 1825, which repealed the Act of 1824, was not however as important as the operatives thought. Trade unionism could not really be effective until the railway and the penny post made possible stoppages of work on a national scale. Something of this was realised when the trade unions of 1826 failed to do much in the prevailing depression. The abler workers and their middle-class friends, especially in London, turned again towards political action. The 'mob' supported the agitation for Parliamentary reform in 1830–1 and, when it was found that the Reform Act had merely strengthened the employers, helped to produce the Chartist movement. There was also wide support for 'the nonsensical doctrines preached by Robert Owen and others respecting communities and goods in common'.[2]

Meanwhile there had been a revival of trade unionism with the recovery of trade in 1830. This time it took a partly political turn, for it was thought that the workers would be more successful if they could

---

[1] The terms trade union and trades union were not in use until the period 1830–4. Strictly speaking, the former should be used of a union within a trade, the latter of a union in two or more trades. Webb, *op. cit.* p. 113. The convention has not, however, been generally followed.

[2] The *Fabian* socialists' phrase: S. and B. Webb, *History of Trade Unionism* (1920 ed.), p. 156.

form what came to be called 'One Big Union'. This frightened both political parties—they were still only half a century from the French Revolution of 1789 and there was another French Revolution, though a more respectable one, in 1830. It was then found that, notwithstanding the Act of 1825, the law could still be used by employers to repress trade union activity, for three reasons. First, the offences under the Act of 1825 were very wide and could, for instance, be interpreted to include peaceful picketing. Secondly, many unions had an initiation ceremony, probably copied from the freemasons and the Orange lodges, in which an oath played a part. Since this oath could be held contrary to an Act of 1797 and one of the Six Acts of 1819, it was possible for the six Dorchester labourers (the Tolpuddle Martyrs) to be sentenced to transportation in 1834. Thirdly, the common lawyers 'discovered' that a strike was a conspiracy in restraint of trade and therefore unlawful at common law.

The word 'discovered' has to be used because of the legal fiction that when a court invents a new tort or crime it merely declares the law. As FitzJames Stephen pointed out, 'no case has ever been cited in which any person was, for having combined with others for the raising of wages, convicted of a conspiracy in restraint of trade at common law before the year 1825'.[1] This does not mean that the lawyers just invented it out of thin air—after all, there had been no conviction for seditious conspiracy before 1795. There were dicta from the cases on monopolies of the seventeenth century laying down that the common law favoured freedom of trade, and other dicta in later cases. Though dicta are not binding, the task of a lawyer is to make the law consistent, and a consistent legal opinion is good enough. It was therefore perfectly possible for lawyers to 'discover' a common law rule by which trade unionists could be convicted of conspiracy: and many eminent lawyers did so, though other eminent lawyers discovered exactly the opposite. It is unnecessary to decide between them, for Parliament eventually did so; but not before the trade unions had for forty years operated under the threat of prosecution for criminal conspiracy.

We are not yet in the realm of political controversy. Parliament was still dominated by the landed interest, though as the nineteenth century

[1] *History of the Criminal Law*, III, p. 209.

185

advanced many of its members came to be interested in mines, railways, and even manufactures. The urban middle classes, whose incomes came from trade and industry, were also strong. The trade unions waxed and waned according to the state of employment; but, operating under repressive laws, and under the constant fear of prosecution, they emphasised their functions as friendly societies. In the field of industrial relations their members were more concerned to protect their vested interests as craftsmen than to fight the employers on broader issues which would have brought Parliament and the courts of law into action against them. There were exceptions, as with the engineers' lock-out of 1852, a considerable number of small strikes between 1853 and 1859, and the larger strikes caused by the depression which set in during 1873.

During this period, too, began the reign of the professional trade-union official, concerned more with organisation and finance than with militant trade-union action and politics; but in politics he was generally a Radical. Men of this type brought back into trade unionism the idea with which the trade unions had started, that of bringing pressure on Parliament to enact laws favourable to trade unionists. The method adopted involved the trade unions in becoming allies of the Liberal party, though they were not yet very helpful allies because few trade unionists had votes. Moreover the Liberals were by no means sure that they wanted such allies, because so many employers were Liberals. On the other hand Disraeli, with his usual political skill, saw that if most of the 'bosses' were Liberal, working men might become Conservative.

A great change occurred when the household franchise was introduced in the boroughs in 1867, for most trade unionists had the vote; and, though the Liberal party was still dominated by employers, no member for a borough seat, whether Liberal or Conservative, could forget after 1867 that his seat might depend on trade-union, and certainly on working-class, votes. It happened, too, that a favourable climate had been provided by the Royal Commission of 1867–8. Its appointment was due to a series of outrages in Sheffield, for which some of the local trade unions were believed to be responsible. Robert Applegarth, general secretary of the Carpenters' and Joiners' Union, saw that these outrages were bringing the whole trade-union movement into disrepute; and on his suggestion the Royal Commission was appointed. The case for the larger unions was, with the assistance of Frederic Harrison and Thomas Hughes, two of the Commissioners, admirably presented, so as to emphasise the large, efficient and solid unions, like the Engineers' and the Carpenters', as great friendly societies interested in collective bargaining and industrial peace by negotiation. The employers, on the other hand, attacked trade unionism as such and insisted on the individual bargain. They brought evidence to show that the social insurance schemes were unsound, and thus concentrated attention upon them. The outrages were found to be the work of a few local societies, and to have declined since 1861. Four-fifths of the Sheffield societies were not implicated.[1]

The recommendations of the majority of the Commission—Harrison and Hughes wrote a minority report—are less important than the change of opinion which resulted from the enquiry. The Liberal Government was able, in the Trade Unions Act, 1871, to abolish the rule, discovered by the courts, that a combination was an unlawful conspiracy because it was in restraint of trade. At the same time the Criminal Law Amendment Act, 1871, repealed the Combination Act of 1825 and tried to define what kinds of picketing should be unlawful. Neither Act was very successful in effecting what the draftsmen presumably intended; but for our present purposes the main point is that the desirability of trade-union action had been conceded. On the other hand the Liberal Government, in the opinion of the trade unions, had not conceded enough, and the Criminal Law Amendment Act in particular was resented. The Liberal Government was not wholly to blame, because the worst provision, from the trade-union point of view, had been inserted by the Lords and assented to by the Commons against the advice of the Government. Nevertheless, some trade-union votes must have been cast against the Liberals at the general election of 1874; and in 1875 Disraeli's Government replaced the Criminal Law Amendment Act by the Conspiracy and Protection of Property Act, 1875, which seemed to the trade unions—who were not yet sufficiently familiar with the ingenuity of lawyers—to give them more or less what they wanted.

[1] S. and B. Webb, *History of Trade Unionism*, pp. 265–9.

The extreme opinion, that there was something obnoxious about trade unionism, did not at once disappear, though after 1875 trade unions had to be tolerated because neither of the great political parties dared to accept the idea of suppression. Moreover the trade unions did not become really militant until the end of the great depression, which started in 1873 and did not disappear until the late eighties. Then the 'new unionism', which involved great organisations of unskilled workers, began seriously to interfere not only with the profits of employers but also with the convenience of ordinary citizens. Moreover the party alignment had become a class alignment: for after 1886 most of the wealth of the country, including the larger capitalists, was Unionist, while the active trade unionists were Liberals. Indeed, as Parliament took up the problem of the 'condition of the people', the trade unions decided that they needed strong working-class representation in the House of Commons. As we have seen in the second volume, this attitude resulted in the creation of a Labour party dependent primarily on trade-union funds.

Meanwhile the threat of the 'new unionism' had been met by the employers not by recourse to Parliament—for neither party after 1884 could be expected to take legislative action which might lose it working-class votes—but by recourse to the courts. The use of the criminal law had been rendered impossible by Disraeli's Act of 1875, but the piecemeal legislation of the nineteenth century had left open the possibility of taking civil proceedings. The Statutes of Labourers had given a remedy against a person who enticed a servant away from the employment of another. The Statutes had been repealed, but meanwhile there had grown up an action for enticement, to which attention had been called by legal proceedings in 1853.[1] Founding themselves on this action, the Court of Appeal held in 1893,[2] and were followed by the House of Lords in 1901,[3] that a combination to induce persons to break their contracts, or even not to enter into contracts, was actionable as a civil conspiracy. Thus the members of the committee of a trade union could be sued for damages if they 'called out' their men for a strike.

---

[1] *Lumley* v. *Gye* (1853), 2 E. & B. 224.
[2] *Temperton* v. *Russell*, [1893] 1 Q.B. 715.
[3] *Quinn* v. *Leathem*, [1901] A.C. 495.

What is more, the House of Lords held, in the famous Taff Vale case,[1] that a trade union registered under the Act of 1871 could be sued in respect of a tort committed by its officials on its behalf. In other words, whenever an employer suffered damage from a strike called by a trade union, that employer could recover the damage from the trade union.

The Taff Vale decision was the principal cause of the foundation of the Labour party, since even old-fashioned trade unionists, who thought that the trade unions should keep out of politics, now realised that political action was necessary to enable the unions to function. They were unable to secure a change in the law, however, until the Liberals obtained a majority in 1906; and the Conservative party thought it unwise to use the veto of the House of Lords on the Trade Disputes Act, 1906. The law had one last fling in 1910, when in the Osborne case[2] it was held that a trade union could be restrained by injunction from using its funds for political purposes. The Trade Unions Act of 1913 therefore authorised the creation of a separate political fund, though any member could refuse to pay by 'contracting out'. After the General Strike in 1926 the Conservative Government (under pressure from back-benchers) changed this to 'contracting in'; and in 1946 the Labour Government changed it back to 'contracting out'.

One result of all this litigation and legislation is that associations of employees occupy a peculiar position. Any body of citizens can form any kind of association so long as it does not engage in treasonable or seditious or otherwise illegal activities. But the wage-earner (and, we must now add, the salary-earner) has since the fourteenth century been regarded as a peculiar type of citizen. Though he lost his peculiar status during the industrial revolution, he had to be given express legislative authority to form the only kind of association in which he is interested as wage-earner. Parliament had sought to regulate wages, and when Parliament gave up that task (in principle only temporarily) it was thought that there was something nefarious in an association designed to protect wage-earners against the economic power of employers. If we started with a clean slate, we should probably think

[1] *Taff Vale Railway Co.* v. *Amalgamated Society of Railway Servants*, [1901] A.C. 426.
[2] *Amalgamated Society of Railway Servants* v. *Osborne*, [1910] A.C. 87.

of a trade union as an ordinary type of association. We cannot because, in law, it has always been a peculiar type. Hence opinion can vary from a belief that a trade union is subject to restrictive rules which do not, for instance, apply to associations of shopkeepers, to a belief that trade unions have been given special privileges under the law. The conflict is helped by the fact that some of the trade unions provide most of the funds of the Labour party.

6. THE RIGHT OF PUBLIC MEETING

The right of public meeting used to be the duty of public meeting. In the customary law of England the county, the hundred, the manor and the borough were assemblies. 'Of the right of attending the county court we read no word. Of the duty of attending it we read much, and obviously this duty was irksome.'[1] The hundred, the manor, or the borough similarly had its court; and, though the custom varied, there was in every case a body of men who could be summoned to do suit of court. Nor was representation unknown; when the justices in eyre came into the county every vill had to send a reeve and four men and every borough a jury of twelve. Parliament itself is a public assembly to which (before the Representation of the People Acts) the King summoned the archbishops, bishops, abbots, earls and greater barons individually and the counties, cities and boroughs had to send their representatives. To secure representatives, the sheriff summoned a meeting of 'the county' and (sometimes) the mayor or bailiffs summoned a meeting of the 'borough', at which candidates were proposed and seconded and perhaps the candidates themselves spoke.

It is true that in due course the duty to do suit of court became a privilege, a franchise: but the idea that the men of the county should, if they wanted to petition the King, meet 'in full county' continued into the eighteenth century. Indeed, there was something suspicious, perhaps seditious, about a meeting which was not summoned by the Lord-Lieutenant, the sheriff, the mayor, or a magistrate, especially if it was held in secret, for the people concerned might be papists, or Puritans, or Jacobites. The main complaint against the Methodists was

[1] Pollock and Maitland, *History of English Law*, I, p. 537.

that they held assemblies of people of the lower orders and infused into them a dangerous fund of enthusiasm. Radicals like 'Orator' Hunt, who held public meetings, were 'rabble-rousers'; and it was wise to have the yeomanry standing by, as at Peterloo.

On the other hand, it has never been suggested that, if two or three, or even a hundred or so, choose to meet together in, say, the debating hall of the Cambridge Union Society to debate the proposition, ''Tis folly to be wise', or even to meet together on Market Square, peacefully and decorously to celebrate the escape of King James I from the Gunpowder Plot, they are an unlawful assembly. In the sixteenth century an assembly was unlawful if three or more persons met together to commit a riot or a rout and did not in fact commit it:[1] but the Star Chamber took a broader view, and by the beginning of the eighteenth century the assembly was unlawful if reasonable people had reasonable fear that there would be a breach of the peace.[2] Moreover the Riot Act, 1714, which is still in force, dealt with a situation in which 'any persons, to the number of twelve or more, [are] unlawfully, riotously and tumultuously assembled together, to the disturbance of the public peace'.

Until the French Revolution the law so stated was thought to be adequate, because political meetings, except under the quasi-official sponsorship of the magistrates, were rare; and what were to be feared were sporadic outbreaks of violence, like rick-burning, breaking down inclosures, pulling down meeting-houses, breaking up Methodist meetings, and so forth, which could be dealt with either as constructive treason (that is, levying war) or as riotous assemblies. The collection of people in the towns, the spread of revolutionary ideas after 1789, and the spirit of unrest created by the economic difficulties of the French wars, caused apprehension among the governing class, which became even more acute in the period of distress after Waterloo. The Seditious Meetings and Assemblies Act, 1795,[3] imposed severe restrictions on meetings of more than fifty people 'for the purpose or on the pretext of considering of or preparing any petition, complaint, remon-

---

[1] 3 Inst. 176.
[2] Holdsworth, *History of English Law*, VIII, p. 326.
[3] *Ante*, p. 161.

191

strance, or declaration, or other address to the King, or to both Houses or either House of Parliament, for alteration of matters established in Church or State, or for the purpose or on the pretext of deliberating on any grievance in Church or State'. Notice had to be given in a newspaper under the authority of at least seven persons (a copy of which might be demanded by a justice of the peace). The Act also restricted 'lectures and discourses on and concerning supposed public grievances, and matters relating to the laws, constitution, and government of these Kingdoms...' in the Cities of London and Westminster.

The Act remained in force until 1869, but it was supplemented by the Seditious Meetings Act, 1817, which forbade various kinds of public meetings as well as secret societies, and by the Seditious Meetings Act, 1819, one of the 'Six Acts' passed after Peterloo. The courts, too, took a hand by developing the concept of 'reasonable fear'.[1] In fact, however, the regulation of public meetings has become a minor branch of the law. There is no longer fear of the 'mob' because there is no mob.

One factor of great importance is the growth since 1820 of trade unions, co-operative societies, and other voluntary bodies. The great meetings of the nineteenth century were dominated by orators who, in the style of the Methodists, sought to play on the emotions of the crowd. Now it is difficult to get a crowd; and at a conference every member is accustomed to hear argument and weigh it. The 'mass meeting' is used in the trade unions, but to take decisions, not to listen to oratory; anybody can speak, and often the speakers differ from each other. But trade unions, co-operative societies, the political parties, and other bodies also use the committee meeting, and so frequently that a great part of the population knows the rules of debate. The old technique of rabble-rousing, generally by using insulting language so as to start a 'row' and so obtain publicity, has been used by communists, fascists, 'loyalists', and others; but it is necessarily on a small scale and can usually be handled by an unarmed professional police force. Most public meetings have to be in private or civic halls, where the lessees have to obey the rules laid down by the lessors. Public meetings in the

[1] A. V. Dicey, *Law of the Constitution* (8th ed., pp. 497–512); and (9th ed., by E. C. S. Wade), pp. 547–76.

open air, such as in public open spaces, are subject to local by-laws. In any case the police are usually present, can take action before trouble arises, and can prosecute for some such offence as obstructing the police in the execution of their duty or using insulting words.

In principle, the right of public meeting, subject to reasonable restrictions designed to prevent disorder, has been fully accepted by all the main parties for a century. The right is, however, no longer of great importance because, with a literate population reading millions of newspapers a day and holding millions of radio and television licences, the platform is no longer an important instrument of propaganda, though the political parties still use it. What remains of importance is the right of private meeting at which freedom of speech and association can be practised.

CHAPTER V

NATIONALISM

I. NATIONALITY AND NATIONALISM

Between John Brown of Dover and Jean Dupont of Calais are twenty-one miles of water which can be crossed in ninety minutes by sea and ten minutes by air. Politically, however, there is a great gulf between them. John Brown is a British subject, English-speaking, a Protestant, looking towards London for culture and government. Jean Dupont is a French citizen, French-speaking, a Roman Catholic, looking towards Paris for culture and government. Apart from these superficial characteristics, added not by nature but by history and politics, John Brown and Jean Dupont are as alike as two peas from the same pod. If they had been exchanged as babies, nobody would know it. The only difference between them is their nationality, which is the cause of all the other differences. That nationality arises because, by an accident of history, Dover is part of the United Kingdom of Great Britain and Northern Ireland while Calais is part of the French Republic. That, too, is an artificial division. Had the Kings of England remained Dukes of Normandy; had Henry VI not lost his French dominions; had Mary Tudor not lost Calais; had Mary Stuart had a son by Francis II; had the younger Pitt absorbed Picardy into the Kingdom of Great Britain; had Bonaparte freed Britain from its landed aristocracy; had Winston Churchill's project of a union with France proved acceptable to the French; in short, had any one of a hundred or so events happened, the national boundary between the United Kingdom and France would have been shifted, John Brown and Jean Dupont would be fellow-citizens, and most if not all of the artificial distinctions between them would not have existed.

It is necessary to make these rather obvious remarks because, as heirs of history, we tend to assume that nationalist sentiment, within the existing boundaries, was an inevitable development, that there is something fundamental about British nationalism, and that it is more than a socially inherited prejudice. Though we have seen boundaries redrawn

194

and new nations created, the purpose was to convert social groups which called themselves nations into nation-States; we forget that it has still not been settled whether the United Kingdom is a nation-State or a State containing three or four nations, that some people in the geographical entity called India thought that Indians were one nation and others thought that they were two, and generally that the extension of the nation-State is the consequence of the export from Western Europe of the idea or sentiment of nationalism.

The only people in the United Kingdom who have ever called themselves nationalists have always had an adjective. They were or are Irish nationalists, Welsh nationalists or Scottish nationalists because they wished to emphasise that the United Kingdom, as established in 1800, contained not one nation but four nations, the English, the Welsh, the Scots and the Irish. That there was once a kingdom called England and a kingdom called Scotland cannot be doubted, and so the fact that there was once an English nation and a Scottish nation can reasonably be postulated. Whether there ever was a Welsh nation or an Irish nation, or whether some people associated with Wales and Ireland invented the Welsh nation and the Irish nation because there was once an English nation, is a matter on which there might be argument. These difficulties merely illustrate the fact that nationalism is a sentiment, an invented or socially inherited theory or prejudice, strongly impregnated with emotion.

The emotion may be weak or strong. It rises and falls above its minimum; and indeed there may be no minimum, for a man may be so much a citizen of the world as not to be a nationalist at all, or so good a Welsh nationalist as to have no sentiment towards the United Kingdom, or so good a Cornishman as to have no sympathy with Englishmen and other foreigners. Moreover, though we think of nationalism as common to the whole of a nation-State, and as rising and falling as nationalist sentiment waxes and wanes, this is a generalisation, for it affects different people differently. For some the dominant political sentiment may be nationalism, for others, internationalism; for some, association with a church or a religious community, or a linguistic group, which is either smaller or larger than the nation, must take precedence over patriotism if they happen to be in conflict; international finance, professional relationships, the common interests of the proletariat or the aristocracy, are alternative groupings in which common sentiment may develop; and generally it must not be assumed that nationalism is a sentiment shared equally by all members of a nation. It is indeed this variety which makes nationalism relevant to party politics. We shall see that the two most important movements of the past hundred years in the United Kingdom have been, first, the intensification of nationalism, in the variety called 'imperialism',[1] which reached its peak in 1880–1900 (Queen Victoria's Jubilees of 1887 and 1897 provide convenient points of reference), and, secondly, the development of what may be called 'socialism', which probably reached its peak in 1945–50, though we are too near to it to be quite sure. The one was responsible mainly for the predominance of the Conservative party from 1886 to 1906 and the others for the development of the Labour party. On the other hand, we shall also see that there have been Radical and Labour imperialists and Conservative socialists. With us, the party line is not strictly an ideological line; nor is there an ideological consistency in either party. Indeed, nationalism (or even imperialism) and socialism (as interpreted in Britain) are not necessarily in conflict.

[1] 'Imperialism' was first used in England in the late sixties: see A. C. Bodelsen, *Studies in Mid-Victorian Imperialism*, p. 127. It then had no sinister connotation. To be an imperialist was to be one of the small band of enthusiasts, like J. A. Froude, who were interested in the people of the self-governing colonies and were anxious for their closer association with the United Kingdom. It did not become 'party political' until 1872, when Disraeli thought it a good line to buy. It thus became associated with the policy of the Conservative Government of 1874–80. This brought in two other aspects, the 'spirited foreign policy' of that Government, and the 'little wars' of the 'prancing proconsuls', as well as the Proclamation of 1878 by which Queen Victoria became Empress of India. From this it spread in the eighties into the 'scramble for Africa' and in the nineties to Joseph Chamberlain's tenure of the Colonial Office, and the Boer War. By this time it was, in the eyes of left-wing Liberals, thoroughly vicious, though the word did not become really naughty until the Indian nationalists developed their propaganda. That propaganda was founded on J. A. Hobson's *Imperialism* (1902), which in turn inspired V. I. Lenin's *Imperialism: The Highest Stage of Capitalism* (1917).

In this chapter and the next, the word 'imperialism' means, unless the context otherwise requires, heightened or aggravated nationalism. No pejorative comparison is intended. Though 'imperialist' is generally a term of abuse, or at least has been since 1919, it is in these chapters simply a description, implying no judgment of value.

2. ENGLISH NATIONALISM

Before 1948 when (it is believed) the Asian communists invented the term 'colonialism',[1] the enemy of the Asian nationalists was 'British (or French) imperialism'. The French were accused of this naughty practice because there had been, in the nineteenth century (and there were relics in the twentieth), a British imperialism. As we shall see, it was a type of nationalism, a nationalism carried to its logical conclusion: and so the conflict between British imperialism and colonial nationalism was a conflict between British nationalism and colonial nationalism. This colonial nationalism was, however, one of the numerous importations from the United Kingdom. It was as British as the mercantile banks in the main streets of Calcutta, Colombo, Rangoon or Singapore. So far as there was a conflict at all (and by 1948 British nationalism had become a very mild disease), it was a conflict between British nationalism and British-imported nationalism, very like the conflict between the British nationalism of Lord Carson and the British-imported nationalism of that other English Irishman, Charles Stewart Parnell.[2]

French nationalism is usually dated from the campaign of Joan of Arc

[1] Strictly speaking, they perverted it. 'Colonialism' was used in 1902 by J. A. Hobson (*Imperialism*, 1938 ed., p. 4) to mean 'the migration of part of a nation to vacant or sparsely populated foreign lands, the emigrants carrying with them full rights of citizenship in the mother country, or else establishing local self-government in close conformity with her institutions and under her control'. Canada, Australia and New Zealand are (or were) examples of 'colonialism'. Hobson, though he 'adopts the point of view of bourgeois social reformism and pacifism', is high authority for communists because he was quoted by V. I. Lenin in his pamphlet, *Imperialism: The Highest Stage of Capitalism*. By 'imperialism' Hobson meant the acquisition by conquest or annexation of territories occupied by economically backward peoples. The territories so acquired are often called 'colonies', and in fact in the British system if they are made British territory the inhabitants become British subjects, though in other cases (for example 'protectorates') they are merely British protected persons. What the Asian communists meant by 'colonialism' was the maintenance of British, French, Portuguese or Dutch rule in southern and south-eastern Asia. The term was ideologically possible because Lenin had drawn no distinction between 'colonialism' and 'imperialism'; and it was thought desirable, apparently because it enabled the communists to use nationalist sentiment for a policy of subversion, to substitute 'colonialism' for 'imperialism'. 'Imperialism' was being used (even by nationalists) of Russian aggression in Eastern Europe and Indian activity in Kashmir, Junagadh, Hyderabad, and the Naga Hills.

[2] T. P. O'Connor, *The Parnell Movement*, pp. 339–42. Parnell's paternal forebears were English and he was educated in English schools and at Magdalene College, Cambridge. His mother was American.

and the coronation of Charles VII in 1429.[1] In the development of ideas no precise dates can be given; but nationalist ideas began to develop both in England and in France during the Hundred Years War (1336–1451). As the Chatham House Report on *Nationalism* says: 'National feeling can only be said to appear when men from one part of England are regarded throughout the whole of the rest of the country as being kith and kin, in contrast to "foreigners" who dwell in other lands beyond the sea.'[2] That kind of common consciousness would develop more rapidly in the neighbourhood of London (as it did in the neighbourhood of Paris) than in the north and the west. It would develop, too, more rapidly among the statesmen of the Court and the barons and knights of the Army than among the labourers and common soldiers. The change taking place from Edward III onwards was that learned and leading men were ceasing to regard England as the fief or patrimony of the King and were beginning to regard it as a political unit of King and people, a *respublica* or State. Within that State every person would owe allegiance to the King not by reason of an oath of fealty to him as overlord or tenant of his lands but by birth within the realm. England was fruitful soil for this idea for several reasons.

First, the feudalisation of England never had been complete in the sense that every person other than a tenant-in-chief owed allegiance to a mesne lord. There were no great lords in England as there were, in France, the Dukes of Normandy, Aquitaine and Burgundy, exercising a unique jurisdiction (subject to the rights of their own tenants-in-chief) within their fiefs. There were numerous small tenants-in-chief whose rights within their own manors were limited by the rights of the King, large areas were within the King's demesne, and the oath of a tenant of a mesne lord saved the fealty that the tenant owed to the King. The Plantagenet Kings had been able to extend their peace from the boroughs and highways to practically the whole country, so that the King's writ ran everywhere, the King's court exercised jurisdiction in every county, and a general or common law had developed out of the local and feudal customary law. In other words, there was a strong central government reaching into the remotest hamlet through royal officers and even spreading into Wales, Scotland, Ireland and France.

[1] Chatham House Group, *Nationalism*, p. 17. [2] *Ibid.* p. 10.

Secondly, though Latin continued to be the language of the learned until the Reformation, and could still be used by Francis Bacon at the beginning of the seventeenth century, and though Norman French was used in the courts until 1362, English was becoming the language of ordinary speech, so that English was used in Parliament 'parce que la langue française est mal comprise du peuple'.[1] Moreover, though English was still spoken in many dialects, the East Midland variety of the Midland dialect was becoming standard English because of its use by the King's court and the royal officers.[2] Thus, England developed in the fourteenth century one of the strongest features of modern nationalism—so strong that a common language is often held to determine the existence of a separate 'nation'—though in England the common administration and the common law were more important than the common language. What is more, after the invention of printing, and especially under the Tudors, there developed a strong vernacular literature, which was not only pre-eminent but, in the case of Shakespeare (who did not forget to split the ears of the groundlings), strongly nationalist.

Thirdly, the Church of England had rarely been under the close control of Rome. The schism of 1377 further weakened an already weak papacy. From the time of John Wyclif (1324–84) there had been discontent with the corruption of the Church, and though Lollardism went underground after the statute *De Haeretico Comburendo* in 1400, it remained a strong anti-papal influence. The breach with Rome in 1534 gave England a national Church. Moreover education escaped from the control of the Church. Increasing prosperity brought about by inclosures and the development of trade produced a new crop of 'grammar schools', brought pensioners and commoners to the universities, and converted the inns of court into colleges for the study of the indigenous common law. The canon law disappeared as a subject of study in 1535 and active steps had to be taken to maintain some of the prestige of the civil law. The universities ceased to be peripheral members of the republic of learning and developed into indigenous institutions based upon colleges, as Oxford and Cambridge are today.

[1] Chatham House Group, *Nationalism*, p. 14, quoting Froissart.
[2] *Ibid.*

199

Finally, England was provided with a fictitious national history, partly through the printing of historical romances like Sir Thomas Malory's *Morte d'Arthur*, published by Caxton in 1485, but also by the publication of ancient law books which, read in the context of the sixteenth century, seemed to suggest that English institutions like Parliament, the jury and the common law had existed since the Anglo-Saxons if not since the ancient Britons. The Magna Carta of 1225 was printed in Latin in or about 1499 and in English in 1534, and it was known that there were earlier charters. Holinshed's *Chronicles*, giving Matthew Paris' account of the granting of the charter of 1215, was published in 1577. It was assumed by Coke and others that Magna Carta, as interpreted by them, was declaratory of the common law, which came from Anglo-Saxon England. Coke's repugnance to the Norman Conquest is evident from many asides in his *Institutes*. Thus, England had acquired a nationalist history.

Mary Tudor's marriage to Philip of Spain might have brought England into the Habsburg dominions, but she died childless, and Elizabeth Tudor succeeded while Philip II was unable to enforce any claim that he might think himself to possess. Elizabeth's refusal to marry, and Mary Stuart's failure to produce a son by Francis II of France, saved England from the dynastic squabbles of the Continent. The accession of James VI of Scotland, the son of Mary Stuart by Lord Darnley, merely united England and Scotland, without associating the former with either Habsburg or Valois. Thus England kept out of the European family system which had replaced the feudal system and cared as little for 'nations'. England was a small nation-State in constant peril of French, Spanish and papal plots and threats of invasion. There is nothing like a good enemy for strengthening nationalism; England under Elizabeth had plenty of enemies and, what is more, an attempted invasion by the Spanish Armada, broken up in a manner that could go down into history. Even James VI and I had the Gunpowder Plot, still celebrated by schoolboys and freshmen.

England would not have been the prototype of the nation-State had Britain not been an island. Wales had been finally incorporated by Henry VIII and, though there was always danger from Scotland so long as Mary Stuart was alive and free, the divisions among the Scots and the accession of James VI of Scotland as James I of England removed that danger. Thus, so long as England could keep the seas against the other maritime powers of Western Europe, Englishmen could glory in their national independence. In *King Richard II* William Shakespeare celebrated the English 'moat':

> This royal throne of kings, this scepter'd isle,
> This earth of majesty, this seat of Mars,
> This other Eden, demi-paradise,
> This fortress built by Nature for herself
> Against infection and the hand of war,
> This happy breed of men, this little world,
> This precious stone set in the silver sea,
> Which serves it in the office of a wall
> Or as a moat defensive to a house,
> Against the envy of less happier lands,
> This blessed plot, this earth, this realm,
> this England.

'This seat of Mars', it will be noted, exhibited a defensive nationalism, as was inevitable under Elizabeth I. Indeed, after the loss of Calais in 1558 the English Government rarely sought possessions on the continent of Europe, except Gibraltar, an exception which proves the rule. English or British nationalism has seldom been aggressive, mainly because seapower gave access to the wide open spaces and opportunities for trade. In that respect it has not been typical of nationalism. Mainly it has been isolationist, seeking alliances only for defensive purposes against ebullitions of nationalism, or dynastic ambitions, in other countries. To some extent this must be qualified because the accession of William of Orange in 1689 and of the Hanoverians in 1714 brought Great Britain into European conflicts, though as a somewhat reluctant partner, and generally the whigs were antagonistic to this type of foreign adventure.

Three other characteristics of British nationalism must be mentioned. First, it could not be founded on a union of all English-speaking peoples, at least after the American Revolution. In any event, six languages were still spoken in the British Isles.[1] Though the unification

---

[1] English, Welsh, Gaelic, Manx, Erse and Norman French.

of the English language helped towards the establishment of English nationalism, and the spread of that language, not only in the British Isles but also in other British territories, has helped to spread British nationalism, it is not a linguistic nationalism like the German or the Italian. Secondly, the invention of the fiction of 'race' by Gobineau and Houston Stuart Chamberlain came too late to have much influence on British nationalism, except on the 'imperialism' which developed late in the nineteenth century. Obviously the British peoples, however narrowly defined, are not an ethnic group. Even Tennyson, who could be a jingo,[1] said, in welcoming Princess Alexandra of Denmark: 'Saxon and Norman and Dane are we'. Though British people have generally shown more colour prejudice than the French, the Spaniards and the Portuguese, there has been so much miscegenation in the British Isles that a narrowly racial theory has always looked a little ridiculous.[2] This has been helped by the survival of a feudal theory of nationality. Though since 1948 there has been (not for nationalist reasons, but to meet the needs of the other independent countries of the Commonwealth) a status called citizenship of the United Kingdom and Colonies, its practical applications have been few. In the United Kingdom itself the important status is that of British subject, that is, subject of the Queen: and that status has been and is acquired by every person born within the dominions of the Crown and also (since 1948) in every independent country of the Commonwealth. Every British subject has a right of admission to the United Kingdom and nowhere under British rule has there been any prohibition against intermarriage except those of age or relationship.

Thirdly, British nationalists have been inhibited by the whig theory, which both parties have inherited, that there was freedom under British rule. Even in Ireland Cromwell's methods could not be copied; since the Evangelical Movement there has been a prejudice against slavery;

[1] How Tennyson forsook the whiggism which he had acquired in Cambridge and found his true self when he became a tory and an imperialist is explained with a wealth of nationalist sentiment in Esmé Wingfield-Stratford, *History of English Patriotism*, II, pp. 370–83.

[2] But cf. Joseph Chamberlain, 'The Anglo-Saxon race is infallibly destined to be the predominant race in the history and civilization of the world': quoted by the Chatham House Group, *Nationalism*, p. 187. See also the quotation from Dilke, *post*, pp. 246–7.

the fundamental liberties have often been restricted but never completely taken away; and there has been a prejudice in favour of representative government. The swing of the pendulum in British party politics has helped because, when the Government has thought restrictions on liberty necessary and expedient, the Opposition has usually said that they were not.

3. CROMWELLIAN IMPERIALISM

As soon as the Arabs and the Portuguese made oceanic navigation practicable all the peoples of the North Atlantic seaboard stood to benefit. Having ice-free harbours on or near the Atlantic and ships which had traversed the narrow seas, they were able to seize the trade which developed with the Americas, down the west coast of Africa, and across the Indian Ocean to India, Ceylon and Malaya (whence came the trade with China). Moreover the trade of the Mediterranean peoples, especially the Venetians and the Genoese, was declining because of the closing by the Turks of the caravan routes to Asia. The English were in a particularly favourable position because they had twenty major ports and a good river system which enabled goods to be transported into and out of a large part of the country, and because, so long as Shakespeare's 'moat' was held by an adequate navy and the Scots could be kept under control, economic development could proceed without serious risk of devastation by invasion, which helped to destroy the power of Venice and the Hanseatic League.

On the other hand, the English came late into the competition for oceanic trade, in spite of the discovery of North America by the Cabots (who were probably Genoese) from the port of Bristol. 'The Englishman of the Tudor period was not by nature or tradition an explorer or a conquistador. The cult of the map and the flag was unknown to him: he had no desire to search out the distant places of the earth, or to found a new England beyond the seas.'[1] England was a small country with a population under the Tudors of less than three millions. The standard of living was low and internal communications, apart from the network of rivers, were bad. There was under the Tudors rapid

[1] J. B. Black, *The Reign of Elizabeth*, p. 195.

growth in the manufacture of cloth, and a trade in cloth gradually replaced the trade in wool. This export trade provided the means for the importation of luxuries, the use of which was stimulated by Henry VIII's extravagance and the enlargement of the wealthier class. A large part of the trade was, however, in the hands of Venetian and Hansa merchants. There were English ships trading in the narrow seas and even so far afield as Iceland. In the reign of Elizabeth I the era of trading companies began; and in the long run perhaps the most significant event, though it did not so appear at the time, was the grant of a charter to the East India Company at the end of 1599. Meanwhile, however, Spaniards and Portuguese had established themselves in Central and South America and Portuguese were on the coasts of Africa and in India, Ceylon and Malaya. At the accession of James I in 1603 there was no sign of an English Empire beyond the seas, though abortive attempts had been made to find the north-east and north-west passages to India and to establish colonies in North America. These abortive attempts were, however, evidence of the development of an adventurous spirit among the landed and mercantile classes. Even stronger evidence were the voyages of Francis Drake and Thomas Cavendish around the world. These were the leaders in the new company of buccaneers, whose main purpose was to plunder the riches which the Spaniards were bringing back from South America. They could not be called pirates only because they had the Queen's authority.

In the main, however, English policy was directed towards Europe. France, Spain and Portugal were tending to become nation-States; but foreign policy was still primarily a matter of dynastic ambition supported by dynastic wars, marriages and other alliances. Henry VIII had tried to cut a dash in European squabbles and to give effect to the claims of the kings of England to the overlordship of France, though he achieved no notable success. Mary I lost Calais. Elizabeth I was hard put to it to defend Shakespeare's 'moat', though the weather and English seamanship destroyed the Spanish Armada in 1588.

The union of crowns in 1603 began the process whereby England was removed from continental politics and turned her face—if we may use a nationalist formula—towards the mighty ocean. Shakespeare's 'moat' was completed, and the kingdom of Scotland could no longer be played off against the kingdom of England in the game of advancing dynastic pretensions. The imperialist historian[1] will not go so far as to say that the execution of Charles I caused the adoption forthwith of a national (that is, nationalist) policy. Oliver Cromwell was the heir of the earlier Stuarts; the later Stuarts took part in European power politics; and the first two Georges were more concerned to use British power and influence to support their electorate of Hanover than to develop what came to be called the British Empire. Nevertheless, the sentiments and interests of the governing class necessarily had great weight after 1649—which, as it happened, followed the Treaties of Westphalia—and brought external policy clearly within the realm of party politics. In a sense, Oliver Cromwell was the first of the imperialists.

The unification of the three countries of the British Isles into the Commonwealth of England, Scotland and Ireland had no imperialistic motive. Charles II had been proclaimed in Scotland and the Civil War had not been won in Ireland. The conquest of Scotland and Ireland was therefore a necessary corollary of the revolution in England. In some measure, too, the Dutch War of 1652 was another corollary. The Civil War had to be fought at sea as well as on land, for Prince Rupert controlled a Royalist navy in 1648 and held Jersey, the Scilly Isles and the Isle of Man as well as ports in Ireland.[2] Sir Henry Vane therefore reorganised the navy and it was placed by the Parliament under the command of Robert Blake. The *casus belli* was the refusal of the Dutch admiral, Tromp, to lower his flag to Blake in the Straits of Dover; but the fact that war could break out over a point of honour is indicative of a background of rivalry between two militant nationalisms.

The rebellion of the Dutch against the Habsburgs had been completed by the Treaty of Munster in 1648, but meanwhile the Dutch cities had become the great European centres of trade, the Dutch merchant fleets were on every ocean, and the beginnings of a Dutch Empire had been laid. On sentimental grounds, and perhaps on economic grounds too, a union of the peoples of the Netherlands and the British Isles might have been anticipated. The suggestion was indeed

---

[1] J. R. Seeley, *The Growth of British Policy*, II, pp. 1–2.
[2] *Ibid.* II, p. 28.

made by the Dutch in 1585, but Elizabeth I preferred a more cautious policy of alliance.[1] In 1651 the offer of union came from the English Parliament but was rejected by the Dutch. This offer was founded partly on common religious sentiment, but mainly it was an incident in the English Civil War. The infant Prince William of Orange, afterwards William III of England, was the grandson of Charles I. The sudden death of his father, William II of Orange, had strengthened the republican party in the Netherlands, but the House of Orange was popular and was now a branch of the House of Stuart. James Stuart had taken refuge with his sister, the widowed Princess of Orange, and the Netherlands would remain a centre of Royalist intrigue unless, like Scotland and Ireland, they were brought within the Commonwealth.

The failure of these negotiations gave emphasis to the commercial rivalry between the two countries. Under James I and Charles I the foundations of an English Empire had been laid in North America and the West Indies. The English mercantile marine was by no means so powerful as the Dutch fleets, which had captured most of the carrying trade of Northern Europe, including most of the English trade. In 1651 the English Parliament passed the first of the Navigation Acts—though there were narrower precedents from Henry VII and Henry VIII— whereby the produce of Asia, Africa or America could not be brought into England or Ireland or any of the territories of the Commonwealth, except in English ships manned by English sailors, and the produce of Europe could not be brought into any of the territories of the Commonwealth except in English ships or ships of the country of origin of the produce. There were some provisions for the protection of English shipping, but none for the protection of Dutch shipping, and Blake was instructed to exercise a right of search in the Narrow Seas, a claim to the dominion of which had been made, on the basis of records of doubtful validity, by Charles I.[2] Indeed, Tromp's decision to sail within range of the English fleet and to refuse to strike his flag was due to information that a Dutch convoy had been fired on by English ships because the convoying warships refused to strike, and that the seven ships of the convoy were in danger of capture.[3] The States General

[1] J. B. Black, *The Reign of Elizabeth*, pp. 317–18.
[2] T. W. Fulton, *The Sovereignty of the Sea*, ch. IX. [3] *Ibid.* pp. 401–3.

tried to prevent a war, but there was a series of naval battles in 1652 and 1653.

The war strengthened a nationalism which was already characteristic of the English Republic. Loyalty to the nation had to replace loyalty to the King, and England's greatest poet and pamphleteer had already in 1641 thanked God because he had built up 'this Britannic Empire to a glorious and enviable height, with all her daughter islands about her'.[1] The successes of the army in the British Isles were followed by the exploits of the navy. They were not all successful, for Blake had opponents worthy of his own quality. Inevitably, however, there was an increase of chauvinism, shown for example by Marchamont Needham's preface to his translation of John Selden's *Mare Clausum*[2] and Waller's panegyric of 1655 to Oliver Cromwell:

> The sea's our own; and now all nations greet,
> With bending sails, each vessel of our fleet.[3]

National sentiment, commercial ambition, and religious zeal combined to influence whatever there was of public opinion. 'The godly Barebones Parliament of 1653, who looked askance at the Dutch as carnal and worldly politicians, held it necessary that the seas should be secured and preserved as peaceable as the land, in order to prepare for the coming of Christ and the personal reign.'[4]

Though Cromwell was as good an imperialist as any, he had never been very keen on the Dutch war. It involved a conflict between two Protestant republics, the weakening of the army in order to strengthen the navy, a vast expenditure which the Commonwealth could not afford, the possibility of a combination of the Roman Catholic powers, and even the risk of a Royalist counter-revolution. The dismissal of the Long Parliament in April 1653 put Cromwell in charge of the negotiations with the Dutch when they opened in June of that year. Another suggestion for the union of the British Isles and the United Provinces was not well received by the Dutch; nor were the alternatives offered by the new Council of State. When Cromwell became Lord Protector

---

[1] John Milton, 'Of Reformation touching Church Discipline'.
[2] T. W. Fulton, *op. cit.* p. 411.
[3] Sir Charles Firth, *Oliver Cromwell* (World's Classics), p. 372.
[4] T. W. Fulton, *op. cit.* p. 413.

in December, however, he proved to be more flexible, and the treaty signed in April 1654 did not recognise British sovereignty over the Narrow Seas.

The Parliament men were less successful in the Americas than in Europe. From the earlier Stuarts they had inherited Virginia and Maryland; New England (Massachusetts, Plymouth, Connecticut, New Haven and Rhode Island) and Newfoundland; Bermuda; and the Leeward Islands (St Kitts, Nevis, Montserrat, Barbados, and Antigua). The termination of the first Dutch War prevented a projected attack on New Netherlands (now named New York and New Jersey), but Acadia (Nova Scotia) was captured from the French and Jamaica from the Spaniards while a small colony was established in Surinam (Guiana). Nothing was lost, but only because the Commonwealth took steps to enforce its control. Royalist sentiment predominated in Virginia, the Leeward Islands and Bermuda, but all the colonies were anxious to trade with the Dutch, who had most of the carrying trade in their hands. In 1649 Virginia, Maryland and Bermuda repudiated the authority of the Commonwealth, and in the following year Barbados and Antigua followed. The Puritan colonies of New England were by no means Royalist, but they were as little prepared to be governed by the Puritans of England as by Charles I.

The Parliamentary theory of empire must be gathered from the provisions of the Navigation Acts, 1650 and 1651.[1] The latter was enacted 'for the increase of the shipping and the encouragement of the navigation of this nation, which under the protection of God is so great a means of the welfare and safety of this Commonwealth'. Its provisions implied a theory of economics, but fundamentally their purpose was to strengthen the defence of the country by encouraging the building of ships and the employment of English seamen. To that object the English possessions in the Americas were expected to contribute. They were, as the preamble to the Act of 1650 put it, 'planted at the cost and settled by the people, and by authority of this nation', and they 'are and ought to be subordinate to and dependent upon England: and hath been ever since the planting thereof been, and ought to be, subject to such laws, orders and regulations as are or shall be made by

---

[1] J. A. Williamson in *Cambridge History of the British Empire*, I, pp. 215–17.

the Parliament of England'. The Act of 1650 was designed primarily to put down the Royalists in Virginia, Bermuda, Barbados and Antigua, but it also implied, like the Act of 1651, that the plantations must contribute to the safety of the nation. Not too much should be read into the assertion of Parliamentary power, for it is really aimed at the royal prerogative, now temporarily defunct, not at colonial autonomy. The latter became an issue in the next wave of imperialism a century later. The constitutional provisions were aimed at the proprietors and chartered companies empowered by James I and Charles I, not at the assemblies of the American (and West Indian) colonies. What is important for the time being is the assertion of a theory of imperielism, an addendum to the nationalist sentiment which forced the Common-wealth, against Cromwell's judgment, into the first Dutch War. Either the British Isles and the United Provinces (with their respective de-pendencies) must be united, so that the English can share in Dutch maritime prosperity, or the Dutch trade must be suppressed.

Cromwell had not gone so far. With him the dominant sentiment was not imperialism but religion, and he brought the Dutch War to an end before the New Netherlands could be captured. Also, he did his best to conciliate the New England colonies as outposts of Puritanism.[1] His decision to wage war against the Spaniards, however, satisfied both religious and imperialist sentiment. Though the Spaniards claimed the whole of the West Indies to be within their jurisdiction, the Spanish colonies were weakly defended and would provide useful bases for attacks on the Spanish treasure ships. The fleet which sailed under Admiral Penn in December 1654, however, was not very successful. 'The Lord', said Cromwell, 'hath greatly humbled us.'[2] However, the Lord was merciful enough to add Jamaica to the British Empire.

4. CONTINENTAL ADVENTURES

The Restoration did not put an end to Cromwellian imperialism: it accorded too well with sentiment and self-interest. The English had become both a maritime power and a colonial power. Though under the Commonwealth and the Protectorate not much had been added to

---

[1] Firth, *Oliver Cromwell*, p. 388. [2] *Ibid.* p. 395.

English territory—and Acadia (Nova Scotia) was restored to the French under Charles II—the Navigation Act implied a new relation between the plantations and the English Government. Since the Act of 1651 was no longer lawful at the Restoration it was re-enacted in 1660 and extended to exports, though of course it no longer applied to Scotland.[1] The interests of the colonial peoples were by no means ignored. They could, and did, take part in the carrying trade which the Navigation Acts sought to protect. They were given a monopoly in the English tobacco market and an attempt was made to give them a similar monopoly in naval stores. Their protection against the Dutch and the French, and indeed the extension of their territories, was one of the motives of the Navigation Acts. On the other hand, the idea that the colonists were 'flesh of our flesh and blood of our blood' had not yet been invented: and indeed while the Restoration gallants and the Georgian gentlemen might regard the planters of Virginia and Bermuda as younger sons of the best families, nobody of importance would want to claim kinship with the ranting Puritans of New England. The curious idea that the successful tradesman was a brother if he was a colonial, whereas the village shopkeeper belonged to a lower order of society, had not yet arisen.

Because the emphasis was upon trade, interest was devoted mainly to 'sugar and spice and all that's nice' in the tropical colonies and in Asia. Under Charles II, Barbados was 'the principal pearl in His Majesty's Crown',[2] though it suffered severely, with the other Leeward Islands, in the Dutch War of 1665–7. Cromwell's colony, Jamaica, went through a bad period until it became the centre of buccaneering, and thereafter of the logwood business on the mainland. Generally, in spite of the wars, the West Indies prospered with slave labour imported from Africa; the West India interest provided a powerful phalanx in the politics of the eighteenth century.

On the other side of the world the marriage of Charles II to Catherine of Braganza brought Bombay into the King's dominions. It was at first of no great importance except as a naval base; but in that respect it was important because the Dutch captured Malacca in 1641, Colombo in

---

[1] In practice, however, Scottish seamen were treated as English.
[2] Quoted by J. A. Williamson in *Cambridge History of the British Empire*, I, p. 240.

1656, Nagapatam in 1658 and Cochin in 1663. The Portuguese still had Goa, but had lost Hooghly (Calcutta) in 1632. In effect the Dutch had almost wiped out the Portuguese in Asia and had made themselves predominant in the East Indies. The English East India Company could get little of the spice trade, which became virtually a monopoly of the Dutch company. The English company therefore tended to concentrate on direct trade between India and Europe, but in India they competed with the Dutch, who bought Indian goods with silver and sold them for spices in Ceylon and the East Indies. Both companies were interested in trade, not territory; and it is only hindsight which enables us to say that the foundations of the Indian Empire were laid under the later Stuarts. By the end of the century there were small English settlements at Madras and Calcutta, but merchants had flocked to Bombay to secure the protection of the English flag, and it had a population of more than 50,000.[1]

The settlements in Africa were established mainly for slave trading. The Dutch had had almost a monopoly of this lucrative trade under the Commonwealth and the Protectorate, but the third English African Company, chartered in 1662, established itself for a short time. It took a lease of a fort of the East India Company on the Gold Coast (now Ghana) and took over the Dutch stations when they were captured in 1663. It also established itself on the Gambia in 1664. The company failed in 1672; but its successor, the Royal African Company, replaced it in the Gambia and the Gold Coast and established itself on the Slave Coast (now Nigeria).

Finally, in North America Carolina (with the Bahamas) became English by an old-fashioned grant to proprietors in 1663, the year in which New Netherlands (New York and New Jersey) was captured from the Dutch. This enabled New England and Virginia to be connected; and in 1682 William Penn received a grant which covered what are now Delaware and Pennsylvania.

It will be seen that the impetus to colonial expansion given by the Commonwealth and the Protectorate continued after the Restoration. The plantations and the trading corporation were regarded as sources

---

[1] W. H. Moreland and A. C. Chatterjee, *Short History of India* (2nd ed.), p. 261. Bombay had been transferred from the Crown to the East India Company in 1668.

of wealth and were supported not only by the city merchants but also by many landowners and by the Court itself. Charles II was personally not very interested, but James, Duke of York, took an active part,[1] and Lord Chancellor Clarendon was patron of the group which established Carolina. On the other hand, the Restoration had brought England back into the dynastic system of western Europe. Charles II was half a Frenchman by inheritance, and even more French in his outlook. His marriage with Catherine of Braganza put him on the French side, though the main attraction was the dowry, which included Bombay and Tangier as well as a large sum of money.[2] Also he sold Dunkirk to the French, though it had been Spanish territory. Charles' favourite sister Henrietta was married to 'Monsieur', younger brother of Louis XIV of France, and it was through her that the notorious Treaty of Dover of 1670 was negotiated. Moreover Charles II was antagonistic to the republican regime in the United Provinces, not merely because he objected to republics but also because the young Prince William of Orange was his nephew.

Until 1670, or thereabouts, the various interests and prejudices combined to continue the Anglo-Dutch rivalry of the Protectorate, and the second Dutch War of 1665–7 was essentially an imperialist war which began with English attacks on the Dutch possessions in West Africa and North America long before it was formally declared. The Royal Navy was not very successful and the English economy was weakened by the Plague of 1665–6 and the Great Fire of 1666. In 1667 it was decided not to send a fleet to sea, with the result that the Dutch navy was able to make a successful raid up the Thames, a blow to nationalist pride which could not easily be forgotten. On the other hand the war had serious economic effects on the United Provinces, and in 1667 peace was made on the basis that the English kept New Netherlands but surrendered Surinam (Guiana) and amended the Navigation Act in favour of the Dutch.

[1] He was the first governor of the Royal Africa Company; he bought East India stock in 1684; and he succeeded Prince Rupert as governor of the Hudson's Bay company: G. N. Clark, *The Later Stuarts*, p. 59.

[2] Three sights to be seen,
Dunkirk, Tangier, and a barren queen:

quoted by E. Wingfield-Stratford, *History of English Patriotism*, I, p. 401.

Though there was another Dutch War in 1672–4, the Treaty of Breda of 1667 really ended the first phase of English imperialism. There were still sources of conflict; but there was an implicit division of the world into spheres of influence. In North America and West Africa the English were dominant; in the East Indies the Dutch were dominant. 'The Breda Treaty helped the two peoples to keep out of each other's way',[1] but it was not conclusive because there were still possibilities of conflict in the West Indies, Africa and India. The more important developments were the increasing power of the French under Louis XIV, the success of the Counter-Reformation, and the rise of an opposition to the Stuarts after 1670. Though the secret clauses of the Treaty of Dover were not disclosed until 1678, there was a growing fear of Roman Catholic domination. The Dutch were the natural allies of the English, and in any case William of Orange was in control in the United Provinces from 1672.

If party politics were in full blast, one would expect a conflict between those who supported imperialism in the outposts and those who supported adventures in Europe, the blue water school and the dry land school. In fact, however, foreign and colonial affairs were essentially a matter for the royal prerogative until the middle of the eighteenth century. The whigs were concerned primarily with the establishment and the maintenance of a Protestant succession to the throne. They disliked the cost of continental wars. On the other hand, they could not deny the importance of keeping down the pretensions of Louis XIV; nor could they do much more than acquiesce in the continental politics of William III and the first two Georges. The blue water school was unimportant until the time of William Pitt, Earl of Chatham.

5. PITT'S IMPERIALISM

The Augustans who ruled England, and therefore Scotland, under George I and George II were by no means free from nationalist prejudices. In spite of the Act of Union, the Scots were still a bit of a joke, except when they had power in their hands. The elder Pitt could sway senates by his oratory; and oratory rarely appeals to sweet reason.

[1] G. N. Clark, *The Later Stuarts*, p. 67.

213

Dr Samuel Johnson was no impartial observer of his country's fortunes. The Old Pretender could still secure the support of English Jacobites in 1715, though his son failed in 1745; and both Pretenders got some support in the Highlands.

Nevertheless, the earlier part of the Augustan age was, comparatively speaking, one of those periods when the river of nationalism runs shallow. Mr Wingfield-Stratford called it 'The Prose Age';[1] and, since he was a dealer in poetry, he said that its mark was a 'tendency towards a coarse and material outlook upon life'. To describe the outlook of the eighteenth-century gentleman as 'coarse' would seem to be a relic of Victorianism. Manners were certainly coarse; but the literature and the arts of the period show a refinement which the Victorians might have envied. It is true, however, that there were few romantic illusions about politics or politicians. Those who wield power, whether as sovereigns, politicians or military commanders, always have 'public faces' behind which lurk the real human beings. The politicians of the first two Georges were singularly honest with themselves and still more about each other. Dr Plumb's description of Sir Robert Walpole might be a picture of the age:

He loved money; he loved power; he enjoyed adulation and hated criticism. But in everything he did he was richly varied and intensely human. And he was given less to humbug than the majority of this country's statesmen. Vulgar, coarse, ostentatious he might be, yet his aesthetic judgment remains incomparably good—unrivalled, indeed, amongst prime ministers.[2]

Nationalism is not humbug, though like all emotions it can be blarney in the mouths of efficient politicians. The enthusiasms of the seventeenth century were only just beginning to wax again. The whigs ruled Britain, and Walpole ruled the whigs.

Mr Wingfield-Stratford allows[3] that Walpole had a measure of patriotism; but, since the main objects of Walpole's policy were to increase commerce and keep the peace, it was not the more strident sort. His main contribution to nationalism was, however, to convince the tories that patriotism was not the last refuge of a scoundrel, as that good

[1] *History of English Patriotism*, I, p. 472.
[2] J. H. Plumb, *Sir Robert Walpole*, I, p. xi.
[3] *History of English Patriotism*, I, pp. 474-9.

214

tory Dr Johnson put it, but the first refuge of those who wanted to turn the whigs out of office. It is a little difficult to take Viscount Bolingbroke seriously, for both his *Dissertation upon Parties* (1734) and his *Idea of a Patriot King* (1738) were obviously 'party political'. Disraeli took him seriously—though he too was being 'party political':

It was his inspiring pen that made Walpole tremble in the recesses of his Treasury, and in a series of writings, unequalled in our literature for their spirited patriotism, their just and profound views, and the golden eloquence in which they are expressed, eradicated from Toryism all those absurd and odious doctrines which Toryism had adventitiously adopted, clearly developed its essential and permanent character, discarded *jure divino*, demolished passive obedience, threw to the winds the doctrine of non-resistance, placed the abolition of James and the accession of George on their right basis, and in the complete reorganization of the public mind laid the foundation for the future accession of the Tory party to power, and to that popular and triumphant career which must ever await the policy of an administration inspired by the spirit of our free and ancient institutions.[1]

Disraeli was never guilty of the English sin of understatement. To suggest that Bolingbroke produced the long period of tory rule from 1783 to 1830 is to go rather far. There is, however, an apostolic succession from Bolingbroke to Chatham, and thence to the younger Pitt, Lord Liverpool, the Duke of Wellington and (owing to the defection of Sir Robert Peel) Benjamin Disraeli. Bolingbroke did not put the case for the Tory party. He put the case for a fusion of parties on the basis that the Revolution and the accession of the House of Hanover had destroyed the case for party. The 'patriot king' was to govern with the good counsel of wise statesmen. He would not have powers wide enough to interfere with the liberties of his subjects, and Parliament would be independent, not rendered subservient by corruption. The difficulties which his exposition failed to meet were two. First it meant drumming Walpole out of office, and too many, including Walpole himself, believed that this was the purpose of the exercise. Secondly, the only possible patriot king was 'Poor Fred, who was alive and is dead', that is, Frederick, Prince of Wales: and Poor Fred was the darling of the tories only because his father was in the pockets of the whigs.

[1] B. Disraeli, *Whigs and Whiggism*, p. 219.

215

Walpole realised that 'patriotism' was a new name for opposition to Walpole. 'A patriot, sir, why patriots spring up like mushrooms! I could raise fifty of them within four and twenty hours. I have raised many of them in one night. It is but refusing to grant an unreasonable or insolent demand, and up starts a patriot.'[1] Nevertheless, though Walpole was right in thinking that the main qualification for 'patriotism' was opposition to him, the long period of peace and prosperity was creating a tendency towards military adventure. From 1725 to 1734 Bolingbroke's house in Battersea was not merely a centre of opposition to Walpole but also a centre of a new brand of nationalism which eventually forced Walpole into the War of Jenkins's Ear in 1739. From 1726 to 1736 the *Craftsman*, in which Bolingbroke's letters appeared, was the main forum of opposition agitation; and, after 1734, when Bolingbroke went into voluntary exile to write his essays on history and *The Idea of a Patriot King*, the lead was taken by Lord Cobham's 'boy patriots', including Cornet William Pitt—though he was deprived of his cornetcy for a speech against the Crown in 1736.[2]

William Pitt was the grandson of a nabob and by family connexion a whig,[3] though he was sent to the tory university. After a year in Utrecht, where he evidently learned a good deal more than at Oxford, he became a cornet in the King's Own Regiment of Horse, then generally known as Cobham's Horse and afterwards as the 1st Dragoon Guards.[4] He took his military duties seriously, but they were by no means incompatible with a political career and in 1735 he entered Parliament. As an officer of a regiment connected with the Court and a relation of whig peers, he might have been expected to support Walpole; but Walpole was the leader of what in our day would be called the 'old gang'; and most of the bright young men wanted something more exciting than sound finance and government by 'loaves and fishes'. Hence Pitt became one, and very soon the leader, of the 'boy patriots'. Though a careful student of Locke, and therefore fully accepting the Revolution Settlement, he reacted against the sweet

---

[1] Lord Rosebery, *Walpole*, p. 228. This was in the debate on Jenkins's Ear in 1739.
[2] Basil Williams, *The Whig Supremacy*, pp. 194–5.
[3] His father was a tory, perhaps because his grandfather was not.
[4] B. Williams, *Life of William Pitt*, I, p. 40.

reason of the older whigs and developed an emotional nationalism. 'He disciplined himself to an intense, almost passionate, belief in England's greatness, to a knowledge and love of her ancient traditions and her happy Constitution, and to that overmastering sense of duty which ranks him with Cromwell alone among our statesmen.'[1]

His first great speech was on 8 March 1739, when he made a violent attack on the Government for the agreement with Spain over Jenkins's Ear. 'Is this any longer a nation? or what is an English Parliament if, with more ships in your harbours than in all the navies of Europe, with above two millions of people in your American colonies, you will bear to hear of the expediency of receiving from Spain an insecure, unsatisfactory, dishonourable convention?'[2] In this short passage we see not merely an aggressive nationalism but early evidence of the tory belief in the virtues of 'Our Navy' and 'Our Empire'.[3] He had picked a

[1] *Ibid.* p. 59.　　　　　　　　　　　　[2] *Ibid.* p. 77.

[3] The use of 'we' to express the idea that the people of England (or Britain) are a continuing entity with perpetual succession came into poetic use in the seventeenth century. Shakespeare had made 'England' a person, though it was still neuter, not a female. It was John Milton who made 'this Britannic Empire' and 'this great and warlike nation' into a somewhat obstreperous female (E. Wingfield-Stratford, *History of English Patriotism*, I, pp. 354–5). 'Britannia' came in with Dryden (*Britannica Rediviva*, 1688), though her portly form is Georgian and *Rule, Britannia!* was in the *Masque of Alfred*, which James Thomson wrote in 1740.

Meanwhile 'she' had also become 'we'. *The Interpreter*, an anonymous pamphlet, in verse, of the time of James I, spoke of 'our honour', 'our ships', 'the narrow seas, where we are masters', etc. (E. Wingfield-Stratford, *op. cit.* I, p. 298). Dryden said of Oliver Cromwell:

> 'He made us freemen of the Continent
> Whom nature did like captives treat before.'

(E. Wingfield-Stratford, *op. cit.* I, p. 371); and Waller, in his panegyric to Cromwell in 1655, spoke of 'our sea' and 'our fleet' (Firth, *Oliver Cromwell*, p. 372). By the Earl of Chatham's time it was possible to use 'us' retrospectively in ordinary speech. As he said in 1755, 'It was our Navy that pioneered the restoration of the Barrier and Flanders in the last war [1747] by making us masters of Cape Breton' (B. Williams, *Life of William Pitt*, I, p. 269). By the nineteenth century 'we' could take the responsibility for all the virtues and vices, victories and defeats, of everybody who had ruled 'us' since Oliver Cromwell: 'Much has been said of the wicked waste of which we were guilty, when we interfered in a Spanish question [the Spanish Succession, 1701–13] with which we had no concern' (J. R. Seeley, *Expansion of England*, p. 32). It is significant that Mr Wingfield-Stratford first uses this corporate 'we' in relation to a naval battle, 'our first great naval triumph off Dover, under the staunch Hubert de Burgh' (that is, in 1217): *History of English Patriotism*, I, p. 55. This was when 'England was beginning to feel her soul': *ibid.*

217

popular line and, though Walpole secured a majority, the Government was forced into war. Pitt was, however, over-optimistic about the navy, which was badly equipped, feebly manned, and badly handled. This gave ample scope to the Opposition, and there was as yet no theory—because it was developed by the tories when they waged war incompetently—that a patriotic Opposition should support a wartime Government for the sake of the men in the ships. The Opposition was, however, almost as divided as the naval commanders, and Pitt's invective could not bring down the Government. What weakened Walpole was the general election of 1741, which was not well managed for the Government because of the apathy of the Duke of Newcastle: and the Government was defeated not on the failure at Cartagena but on the Chippenham election petition—a fitting end for the most astute of the politicians of 'Old Corruption'.

If the invective of the Patriots had been due even in part to anxiety for office—and in defending himself against 'the atrocious crime of being a young man' Pitt had admitted that he might perhaps have some ambition[1]—they were disappointed. Nor did they succeed in getting Walpole impeached. In fact, Pitt himself admitted, ten years later, that in some respects (though not all) he had misjudged Walpole.[2] This does not mean that Pitt's patriotic fervour was 'party political'. He was well aware that jingoism was popular in the country, but there is no reason to suppose that he was putting on an act, or even that he convinced himself by the exuberance of his own oratory. He was 'our first great imperialist statesman'[3] because he honestly felt the emotions for which his oratory was so well suited. What is interesting is that this aggressive nationalism was a reaction by the young men against a lengthy period of comparative peace and prosperity. To be fully effective it needed the imaginative genius of Pitt, for it is at least as difficult to put genuine emotion into politics as it is to put it into poetry. But neither the objects nor the methods of Walpole could enthuse the young men. They wanted honour and glory, waving flags and martial

[1] B. Williams, *Life of William Pitt*, I, p. 85.
[2] *Ibid.* pp. 92–3.
[3] E. Wingfield-Stratford, *History of English Patriotism*, I, p. 551—perhaps a little hard on Oliver Cromwell.

music. There is nothing poetic about the reduction of the National Debt. The imperialists of our fathers' time said that the age of Walpole was 'materialist',[1] though in fact Pitt's ultimate objective, as imperialist statesman—apart from honour and glory—was to free and expand British trade. His most loyal supporters came from the City of London, the East India Company, and the West India interest. On the other hand, the economic motivation must not be pressed too far. The immediate objective was the limitation of the power of the House of Bourbon, which was thought to be dangerous both to British people and to the people of George II's electorate of Hanover; and Pitt's technique was to use seapower to attack the Bourbon empire at its outposts in America, Africa and Asia. He therefore drove the French Government out of North America and, in substance, out of India. To accuse 'Britain' or 'England' of aggressive imperialism for the sake of profit is itself an exercise in nationalism, since it assumes that there is an entity called 'Britain' or 'England' which profits. This is, of course, a nationalist fiction. The only entities are British Governments and British people. The Governments suffered a considerable increase in the National Debt; and among British people, both of Pitt's time and in the future, some gained and some lost. It is impossible to draw a balance sheet. Nor did Pitt or any of the Patriots produce an estimate. They thought, or assumed, that it was in the interest of the British people—and Pitt was very conscious that they included the people of the American colonies—that the power of the Bourbons should be clipped. Others doubted the value of these military and naval adventures. There were, however, strong emotional factors on both sides of the political fence.

Actually, the initial conflict was not over objectives but over methods. The traditional method was to send troops into Germany and to pay heavy subsidies for German mercenaries. This method was followed by Walpole in 1741 and was continued by Carteret, though with greater vigour because he really believed in the necessity to halt French pretensions. Though Pitt fiercely attacked Carteret, he in fact used the same method when he became Secretary of State in 1756. Nor had his predecessors neglected to fight in the outposts of Empire. What

[1] E. Wingfield-Stratford, *History of English Patriotism*, I, chs. IV and V *passim*.

Cromwell attempted we have already seen. The Spanish monopoly of West India trade was destroyed in 1670, and from 1674 there had been a tacit understanding that the English and the Dutch would keep out of each other's way. It is true that the war of 1689–97 produced few changes of territory, but colonial questions were thought by William III to be extremely important when he was negotiating the secret treaties of 1698 and 1700 with Louis XIV.[1] It is true, too, that during the War of the Spanish Succession the Duke of Marlborough concentrated on defeating Louis XIV in Europe and was not anxious to send troops to America; but the effect of the war was to cripple the French seapower and to leave the Royal Navy in command of the sea; and by the Treaty of Utrecht, 1712, Britain obtained Gibraltar and Minorca in the Mediterranean, most of Nova Scotia, the French part of Newfoundland, and the French territories in the Hudson Bay.

Pitt's nationalism could be more aggressive because Walpole had, for the time being, solved most of the major problems. These were, to keep out the Stuarts and to put public finance on a sound footing after the bursting of the South Sea Bubble. Even before Culloden there was not much hope for Charles Edward Stuart, and after the Treaty of Aix-la-Chapelle in 1748 there was none. Pitt could enormously expand the National Debt because there was faith in the public credit. He could not solve the problems of Hanover, a mill-stone around all British necks until 1760, but the Triple Alliance of 1717 had prevented the outbreak of general war for sixteen difficult years, during twelve of which Walpole was first Minister. That peace was too precious to be broken by adventures in America or India. Nor, as Pitt himself discovered, was it practicable to start such adventures without risking war in Europe. Walpole was forced into the War of Jenkins's Ear in 1739, but that colonial war got lost in the major War of the Austrian Succession, which continued without satisfaction to anybody until the Treaty of Aix-la-Chapelle in 1748. The seven years of peace which followed was merely a truce. Even if the Pelhams kept the peace (and Henry Pelham 'fled to Heaven' in March 1754, leaving his brother the Duke of Newcastle in sole charge), it was unlikely that Frederick of Prussia would.

[1] *Cambridge History of the British Empire*, I, pp. 322–4.

In fact, however, desultory war was being waged in the outposts. In particular, the French were spreading from Canada down the Ohio valley into territory claimed by the colony of Virginia, and in 1754 there was a battle on the border which led to George Washington's surrender of Fort Necessity. Both sides sent reinforcements, but some of the Canadian ships were attacked by the Royal Navy and there were more skirmishes on the contested border in 1755, in which the French were generally victorious. In view of the impending war, Newcastle tried to revive the 'old system' by subsidies for Russian and Hessian troops, but feared that he could not get them through Parliament. After much hesitation, he decided not to bring Pitt into the Cabinet, but Pitt then made his great speech of 13 November 1755.[1] Pitt was dismissed from the Pay Office, which he had held since 1746, but without any control over policy. He was now free to wage war in the House of Commons, where he 'could do with the House what he liked, except obtain votes'.[2] The loss of Minorca, the capture of Oswego, and the collapse of the 'old system' through Frederick's invasion of Saxony, did not move the obstinate Newcastle; but Murray's insistence on becoming Lord Chief Justice and Henry Fox's resignation compelled Newcastle at last to resign. Pitt was commissioned as Secretary of State in December 1756 and made the cleanest sweep of Ministers since 1714, to the great disgust of the whig families.[3]

Pitt's policy was easier to formulate than to put into practice. The 'old system' of making continental alliances and fighting battles with mercenary troops stiffened by small British contingents was to be given up. The war would be fought in the interests of British trade, and therefore in regions where victories would benefit that trade—in the Mediterranean, the Atlantic, the West Indies, America, and India. The Hanoverian troops would be sent home and Britain would be defended by a reformed militia officered by the country gentlemen. The Royal Navy would have to be strengthened so that it could sweep the French navy off the seas. The American colonists would be provided with troops and equipment so that the French aggression could be halted and pushed back. In India the East India Company would be supported by the Royal Navy, and if need be by the secondment of regular troops.

[1] Williams, *Life of William Pitt*, I, pp. 268–70.   [2] *Ibid.* p. 272.   [3] *Ibid.* p. 285.

Pitt had no party support: he disliked the system of 'connexions' long before George III came to the throne. The whigs were against him, though there was no 'formed opposition' and Newcastle was not likely to join with Henry Fox. Pitt had to rely on the independent country gentlemen, commonly called 'tories', and the mercantile interest, which was wider than the City of London because it included those who had estates in the West Indies and America and those who held stock in the great trading companies. It was an insecure foundation upon which to rest a Government, since it excluded many of the most active of the professional politicians. Moreover Pitt could expect nothing more than armed neutrality from the King, who in fact decided in April 1757 that he could take the risk of dismissing Pitt. It was, however, not easy to find a new Ministry, and Pitt on his side realised that he could not govern without help from the whig connexions. In June 1757, therefore, the Pitt–Newcastle Ministry was formed with Pitt as Secretary of State and Newcastle at the Treasury and with the support of the Grenville and Bedford connexions. It was one of the strongest administrations for many years, and it lasted until 1761, by which time George III had come to the throne with ideas of his own.

Already in his short Ministry of 1756–7 Pitt had sent back the Hanoverians and the Hessians, raised additional regular troops (including two Highland regiments from the clans which had followed Charles Edward in the '45), and reformed the militia. He also started a building programme for the Royal Navy, which in four years trebled the fleets. A strong force was organised for America and an appeal was made to the colonists. An addition was made to the fleet in Indian waters. On the other hand, he had to change his ideas about Germany, for the Crown was bound by treaty to provide troops and in any case it would be useful to keep the French engaged in Europe while operations were conducted in America.[1] Hessians and Prussians were employed for this purpose, while the Electorate provided (and paid) the Hanoverians. After he returned to office he was even convinced of the necessity of sending British troops to Germany.

[1] 'America', said Pitt in 1761, 'has been conquered in Germany': B. Williams, *Life of Pitt*, II, p. 131.

The first conquests were the French factories in West Africa, and they destroyed the French slave trade. Then, in July 1758, came the surrender of the islands of Cape Breton and St Jean (that is, part of Nova Scotia and Prince Edward Island); then came the forts of Oswego and Frontenac on Lake Ontario, and finally Fort Duquesne (renamed Pittsburg), which swept the French out of the Ohio valley. Goree, off the west coast of Africa, was captured at the end of 1758. The year 1759 was called *annus mirabilis*. The attack on Martinique failed, but Guadeloupe was captured and so was Marie Galante. In September Quebec fell to General Wolfe and meanwhile Clive was winning victories in India. By 1760 all Canada was in British hands and the power of the French East India Company had virtually been destroyed. In 1761, while peace negotiations were in progress, Dominica and Pondicherry were captured. In the following year, after Pitt had resigned and war had broken out with Spain, the territories captured were Martinique, Grenada, St Vincent and St Lucia in the French West Indies (which left the French with nothing more than half of San Domingo), and Havana and Manila among the Spanish territories. By the Treaty of Paris of 1763 some territory was returned or exchanged, but the whole of the French territory in North America, except Louisiana and the islands of St Pierre and Miguelon, became British, and so did the Spanish colony of Florida (the French ceded Louisiana to the Spaniards). In the West Indies St Vincent, Tobago, Dominica and the Grenadines became British colonies. In Africa Senegal was retained but Goree returned to the French. In India the whole of Bengal was free of French jurisdiction, and elsewhere the French had only the factories which they owned before 1749. Finally, Minorca was returned to the British Crown in exchange for Belleisle, captured before Pitt resigned.

These terms were much more favourable to the French than those which Pitt had offered before his resignation in 1761. He had, however, shot his bolt. There can be no doubt of the popularity of his victories, nor of those of the King of Prussia to which he contributed. Indeed, victories are always popular. He was, however, an imperious commander, and he was almost as imperious towards his colleagues as towards his subordinates: but whereas his subordinates were chosen by him for their zeal and efficiency and welcomed his clear, imaginative, and well-founded directives, his colleagues were the great whig lords like Newcastle, Bedford and the Grenvilles, who were not accustomed to taking orders. However popular he might be in the country, they provided him with much of his parliamentary majority. Unlike him, too, they were great landowners, who watched with distaste the growth of the taxation and the heavy load of debt required not only for his imperialist adventures in the outposts but also for the maintenance of a large army, partly British and partly subsidised, in Europe.

Much of the antagonism to Pitt was personal. He was born to rule in an environment which did not favour dictators, even dictators who founded their rule on popular support. The whig lords would not abdicate and there was a new and ambitious king. Whether George III wanted to make himself a 'Patriot King' may be doubted;[1] but certainly he did not intend to be King Pitt's rubber stamp: nor did the imperious Pitt find it easy to be friendly with Lord Bute (or indeed, with anybody else). There was, too, a case against him, which was not well put in his day, though the Duke of Bedford almost formulated it.[2] If it be assumed that nationalism is not a British monopoly, there must either be perpetual war, interrupted from time to time by truces, or there must be a *modus vivendi* among the nationalist Governments. Even if the proper purpose of a British Government is to advance British interests—a purpose which some would controvert (especially in such a simple issue as that of the slave trade)—and accordingly aggressive nationalism or imperialism can be justified, it is still necessary to draw up some sort of balance sheet, so that the disadvantages of war may be balanced against its advantages. Similarly—and this was fundamentally the point in issue in 1761—where there is war, the immediate advantages of onerous peace terms imposed upon an enemy must be balanced against the disadvantages of giving a justification for the renewal of the war.

In fact, of course, when nationalism is rampant it is idle to talk of balance sheets, because nationalist conflicts cannot be settled by cool calculation. The real question is whether there is enough war-weariness and economic distress to offset nationalist ambitions.

---

[1] See Romney Sedgwick in *Letters from George III to Lord Bute.*
[2] For example, *Bedford Correspondence*, III, p. 16.

6. THE AMERICAN REVOLUTION

The fact that a great and highly self-conscious nation has grown out of the thirteen American colonies must not be taken to imply that the American Revolution was a conflict between British and American nationalism; at that time neither was very strong. Common ideas began to develop in North America as migrants moved from New England towards the south. They were helped, too, by common danger from the French during the Seven Years War and by the elder Pitt's efforts to secure the collaboration of the colonies. But the several colonies had very different characteristics, and their relations with each other were less close than their relations with Great Britain. American nationalism was more the consequence of the War of Independence than its cause. Those who actively supported the Revolution were comparatively few, and probably they were not much more numerous than those loyalists who opposed it.

On the other hand, many of the colonists were not very loyal subjects of George III either. There was no particular reason why they should be. Many of them were descendants of settlers who had left England in order to practise their religion in their own way. Among them were Presbyterians, Independents, Roman Catholics and Quakers who would still have been under disabilities if they had remained in England. There were, too, Scots, Irishmen, Dutchmen and Germans, many of whom had never seriously considered themselves to be subjects of George III. Nor was nationalism strongly developed among all the Englishmen who had migrated. As we have seen, nationalism is a conventional phenomenon which was never very strong among all sections of the English people until the nineteenth century. Nor had the colonists been treated, except by the elder Pitt, as 'kith and kin'. The colonies were sources of profit. They were thought of in Great Britain as being owned by the collective entity usually known as England. The term 'empire' was now in use—the elder Pitt sometimes used it in his speeches—but it was often in the form of 'our empire'. The colonies were 'our colonies'. The colonists were sometimes thought of as 'our fellow-citizens', entitled to the same rights as other British subjects: but this did not mean that a colony was a junior partner in the firm.

That idea was another development of the nineteenth century, expressed poetically in Kipling's

> Daughter am I in my mother's house,
> But mistress in my own.[1]

Many of the colonists reciprocated; they clamoured for their rights but were unconcerned about their duties[2]—at least in part because the idea of duty to the community was not much developed even in Britain. Among many there was personal loyalty to George III, which impelled support for the British forces and led, after the rebellion proved successful, to the migration of loyalists to New Brunswick and Ontario.

Opinion was similarly divided in Great Britain. The initial steps were not matters of high politics. The successful termination of the Seven Years War implied some reconstruction in North America, since British territory had been enormously expanded, generally to the advantage of the colonists. The United Kingdom Government expected to withdraw most of the regular forces and to leave the initial defence against the Indians and the French (if the latter returned) to local forces. Experience had shown how difficult it was to obtain adequate forces by requisition on the provinces. It was therefore proposed that there should be a standing army in North America, the cost of which, at least in part, should be borne by the colonies. Even Edmund Burke and Benjamin Franklin thought this to be reasonable, and the opposition to the proposal, when made in 1763, had been silenced by Pitt.[3] Nor was there much opposition in Parliament to the measures proposed by Grenville for raising the money—the suppression of smuggling, the alteration of customs duties, and the imposition of a stamp duty. The Stamp Act, 1765, was passed by 205 votes to 49 after a languid debate, most of the opposition coming from the West India interest.[4]

The dismissal of Grenville in 1765 had nothing to do with his American policy, though George III had not approved of it. Opposition to the Revenue Act, 1764, and the Stamp Act, 1765, was however

---

[1] But Thomas Pownall, writing in 1764, had a vision of a 'grand marine dominion... united into one Empire': *Cambridge History of the British Empire*, I, p. 650.

[2] C. H. Van Tyne, *The Causes of the War of Independence*, p. 73.

[3] *Cambridge History of the British Empire*, I, p. 637.

[4] *Ibid.* p. 646.

growing in Great Britain because the colonial boycott was affecting British trade. Though Grenville and the Duke of Bedford argued vehemently against concession,[1] Pitt thundered on the other side. It was he who suggested that the Stamp Act should be repealed but that the power of Parliament should be asserted, though the Declaratory Act, 1766, went rather further than he intended. On the other hand, his view of the law was not accepted by most of the lawyers, including Lord Mansfield; and George III as well as some of the politicians thought it impolitic to give way to the colonial agitation. Pitt himself came into office in 1766, but he was ill when Charles Townshend, as Chancellor of the Exchequer, proposed increased import duties on glass, paper, painters' colours and tea and decided upon a more efficient system for the prevention of smuggling.

American affairs were now in the centre of political controversy. The King, Grenville and the Duke of Bedford were for coercing the colonists. The Rockingham whigs and the Earl of Shelburne were against it; and so, presumably, the Earl of Chatham would have been had he been able to attend to business. Townshend died suddenly in September 1767 and the Bedford whigs joined the Government. Shortly afterwards Shelburne resigned and soon afterwards he was followed by Chatham himself. When Parliament met in 1768 the Cabinet under the Duke of Grafton was divided. Eventually it was decided to repeal the new duties, but by a majority of one. The tea duty was retained not for the raising of a revenue but for the maintenance of the principle. The decision was not carried out, however, until Lord North became Prime Minister in 1770.

The actions of the American extremists did not make friends in Parliament. Nor were their quasi-legal arguments convincing as the British Constitution then stood. The real question, however, was not what the law was but whether it was politic to enforce a principle which the active men in the colonies were prepared to resist. The country gentlemen were for the most part in favour of strong measures, while the merchants were generally for conciliation.[2] Even the Rockingham whigs were divided. Chatham objected to violence on both sides. In

[1] Ibid. p. 659.
[2] B. Williams, Life of William Pitt, II, p. 296.

1774 he suggested that the only way of dealing with the Americans was to 'proceed like a kind and affectionate parent over a child whom he tenderly loves; and, instead of these harsh and severe proceedings, pass an amnesty on all their youthful errors'.[1] His broad conception of nationalism came out more strongly, however, in his speech of January 1775:

I contend not for indulgence but justice to America. Resistance to your acts was necessary as it was just. The Americans are a brave, generous and united people, with arms in their hands and courage in their hearts: three millions of them, the genuine descendants of a valiant and pious ancestry, driven to those deserts by the narrow maxims of a superstitious tyranny. Of the spirit of independence animating the *nation* of America, I have the most authentic information.[2]

Chatham was speaking in the House of Lords with no party or connexion behind him, no organisation to propagate his views, no whips to give notice of his intentions or to bring supporters to vote for him or even to give him a cheer. It was magnificent, but it was not politics. Even more magnificent was Burke's great speech of March 1775 on *Conciliation with the Colonies*, surely the ablest of his political pamphlets and the least cheapened by 'party political' arguments. But Burke, too, had no catholic view of empire. For him as for Chatham the colonies were territories subordinate to Britain and useful for British trade, though he was for conciliation based upon the recognition of colonial liberties:

My hold of the colonies is in the close affection which grows from common names, from kindred blood, from similar privileges, and equal protection. These are ties which, though light as air, are as strong as links of iron. Let the colonies always keep the idea of their civil rights associated with your government:—they will cling and grapple to you; and no force under heaven will be of power to tear them from your allegiance. But let it be once understood, that your government may be one thing, and their privileges another: that these things may exist without any mutual relation; the cement is gone; the cohesion is loosened; and everything hastens to decay and dissolution. As long as you have the wisdom to keep the sovereign authority of this country as the sanctuary of liberty, the sacred temple consecrated to our common faith, wherever the chosen race and sons of

---

[1] B. Williams, *Life of William Pitt*, II, p. 299.   [2] *Ibid.* p. 305.

England worship freedom, they will turn their faces towards you. The more they multiply, the more friends you will have; the more ardently they love liberty, the more perfect will be their obedience.... Deny them this participation of freedom, and you break that sole bond, which originally made, and must still preserve, the unity of the empire.[1]

This was very like the Conservative theory of empire which developed in the twentieth century, though it was based on the assumptions of mercantilism. Adam Smith's attack on that system was not published until 1776 and did not prove convincing until the nineteenth century. Adam Smith himself said that 'to propose that Great Britain should voluntarily give up all authority over her colonies, and leave them to elect their own magistrates, to enact their own laws, and to make peace and war as they might think proper, would be to propose such a measure as never was, and never will be adopted, by any nation in the world'.[2] Even if advantageous from the point of view of expense, such sacrifices are 'mortifying to the pride' and contrary to the private interest of the governing class. If it were done, however, Great Britain would not only be freed from expense but would also be enabled to enter into an advantageous commercial treaty.

By thus parting good friends, the natural affection of the colonies to the mother country, which, perhaps, our late dissensions have well nigh extinguished, would quickly revive. It might dispose them not only to respect, for whole centuries together, that treaty of commerce which they had concluded with us at parting, but to favour us in war as well as in trade, and, instead of turbulent and factious subjects, to become our most faithful, affectionate, and generous allies; and the same sort of parental affection on the one side, and filial respect on the other, might revive between Great Britain and her colonies, which used to subsist between those of ancient Greece and the mother city from which they descended.[3]

These were powerful voices, though they did not tell the same story; nor did they carry many votes. For the majority in both Houses of Parliament the American colonies were juvenile delinquents who

---

[1] Edmund Burke, *Works* (1834 ed.), I, p. 203.

[2] Adam Smith, *Wealth of Nations* (Cannan's ed., 1937), pp. 581–2. On the other hand, Fox said on the Quebec Bill of 1791: 'I am convinced that the only method of retaining distant colonies with advantage is to enable them to govern themselves': Lord Stanhope, *Life of Pitt*, II, p. 90.

[3] A. Smith, *op. cit.* p. 582.

needed a good spanking. The 'Boston tea-party' of December 1773 had silenced the Opposition; and coercive measures, which the Government was incapable of enforcing, were passed in the Parliament of 1774. Parliament was dissolved in the autumn and the Opposition became 'a demoralised remnant of seventy-three members'.[1] It was in this Parliament that Chatham and Burke made their great speeches, but they were baying at the moon. In November 1775 the Duke of Grafton resigned and the office of Secretary for the Colonies was transferred from Lord Dartmouth to Lord George Germain, 'whose competence for administration was apparently inferred from his proved incapacity for military command'.[2] The defeat in March 1776 of Grafton's motion to enlarge the powers of the Peace Commissioners was the signal for civil war, and the Declaration of Independence was issued on the 4th of July, 1776. The Rockingham whigs virtually seceded from Parliament and Chatham was unable to lead the Opposition because of another attack of the gout. Only Charles James Fox, with a handful of followers, supported the doctrine that liberty implies liberty for the other fellow, as well as for oneself.

7. THE ROMANTIC MOVEMENT

Emotionalism in politics is no new phenomenon. The largest political organisation in the world, the Church of Rome, has lived on it for centuries. Emotionalism nevertheless waxes and wanes; and we see from the quotations that with Chatham, Burke and Fox it is waxing once more. The first signs of the Romantic Movement were John Wesley and the Methodist Movement, which discovered that it could use the raw and unfettered emotions of uneducated working people to effect what was called religious conversion. It was, however, beginning in poetry also with James Thomson, Thomas Gray and Cowper, though it did not flower until the age of Byron, Wordsworth, Coleridge, Keats and Shelley. Politics, unless entirely corrupt, is always emotional: but the degree of emotionalism fluctuates. Moreover the idea which is emotionalised may change. Religion, liberty, the nation, the Empire, the 'race', the people, the slaves, and so forth, are all capable of being

[1] *Cambridge Modern History*, VI, p. 446.   [2] *Ibid.* p. 447.

romanticised. The results, too, may be rather odd. Oliver Cromwell, the Earl of Chatham, Edmund Burke, Charles James Fox, William Wilberforce, Lord Palmerston, W. E. Gladstone, Benjamin Disraeli, and Ramsay MacDonald (in his prime) were the greater British romantics.

The particular Romantic Movement with which we are now concerned was the reaction to the rationalism, materialism, commercialism, neo-classicism—call it what you will—of the eighteenth century. It will be seen from the names given above that it showed itself both in conservatism and in liberalism and that eventually it became the foundation of socialism. The quarrel of Burke and Fox was a conflict of romantics. Burke saw in the French Revolution the destruction of his romantic scale of values, an ancient religion, a proud aristocracy, a noble monarchy, a great tradition. Fox saw in the Revolution, until it degenerated, the triumph of his romantic scale of values, not only liberty, equality and fraternity but also nationalism. Fox was accused by Canning of being a friend of every country save his own: but he had the same idealism as Lord Palmerston. Britain was the country of the free; any nation which freed itself from tyranny should be a friend of Britain; and it was wrong for Britain to ally itself with a parcel of tyrants in the hope of restoring Bourbon tyranny in France. He was therefore as romantic as Burke, but his romanticism led him to different conclusions. He was, in fact, a better nationalist than the younger Pitt. But Pitt, too, though usually a cold and calculating politician, had carried off from Cambridge some elements of the romanticism of Cromwell and Milton, of Spenser and Thomas Gray, of Byron, Wordsworth and Coleridge. He was a 'sensible' politician, who gave Britain, after the *débâcle* of the War of American Independence, ten years of efficient administration, during which the Government was able so to build up its power as to come triumphantly through the Revolutionary wars charged with the responsibility for the second British Empire. Pitt was no romantic imperialist, and the second British Empire was a by-product of the war: but his association with the Clapham Sect and his support of the agitation against the slave trade—which even Burke had defended—shows that he, too, had a streak of romanticism.

With the younger Pitt, indeed, British nationalism descends to a lower key. The shock of the American War was profound, not so much because of the loss of the American colonies as because of the incompetence shown not only in America but also on the high seas. To be saved from invasion only by the equal incompetence of the French and Spanish navies was indeed galling. Braggart nationalism was impossible in such conditions. The younger Pitt was by no means free from nationalist motives, but he could not afford his father's heroics. Moreover the French Revolution placed Pitt on the side of the vested interests; and even Burke's hysterical emotionalism could not hide the fact that the governing class was not only saving the country, after its own fashion, but also preserving its necks. The more generous emotions were those of Charles James Fox and the young Wordsworth, not to mention the thousands of lesser men who saw in the French Revolution the end of dynastic tyranny. Romanticism was thus on the side of the Revolution. The spirit of the eighteenth century prevailed in Britain even during the meteoric rise and fall of Napoleon Bonaparte.[1]

There was, it is true, a change when war was resumed in 1803, after the Treaty of Amiens. The earlier war could be represented as a war to restore Bourbon tyranny; the later war could be thought of as a war to put down Napoleonic tyranny. The moat was in danger, and nothing rouses the English more than a threat of invasion. Even Fox was on the side of the militant angels and the Royal Navy developed its evangelist (not always careful of all the Ten Commandments) in Admiral Lord Nelson. This was the period when Wordsworth and Coleridge became nationalists and Sir Walter Scott was becoming a best-seller.

The word liberty [says Mr Hough of Wordsworth],[2] becomes gradually emptied of its former content, and is identified with English national security: a proper object of solicitude indeed: but it must be confessed that the exhortation to

> Save this honoured land from every lord
> But British reason and the British sword

falls somewhat tamely on the ear after the ardours of *The Prelude*.

[1] For the mud-slinging nationalism of the *Anti-Jacobin*, see Esmé Wingfield-Stratford, *History of English Patriotism*, II, pp. 96–100. Its best number was its last, in which Canning had the poem including:

> 'A steady patriot of the world alone,
> A friend of every country but his own.'

[2] Graham Hough, *The Romantic Poets* (1958 ed.), p. 53.

232

Wordsworth's patriotic poetry of this period in fact contains more patriotism than poetry; and, though Coleridge was writing his best verse, his imagination was stunted when he touched on politics. Other poets, too, were inspired by danger. Thus, Mrs Iliff wrote:

> Let Buonaparte his legions boast,
> We tremble not with coward fears.
> Our tars shall keep the sea, our coast
> Be guarded by our volunteers.[1]

This was, in fact, rather a high level of attainment for anti-Napoleonic jingoism. Generally, not only prose and verse, but also the newer products of 'Grub Street', the political cartoons, even in the hands of a man like Gillray, were crude and vulgar.

Nor were there politicians whose oratory could rise above this very pedestrian level. Jingoism was undoubtedly a popular phenomenon. It did not suit Pitt and Fox, both of whom died in 1806. Erskine was more of an advocate than a politician. Addington, Grenville, Perceval and Jenkinson (Lord Liverpool) could hardly be described as orators. Only Canning had his tongue tipped with gold. It will be noted, too, that jingoism and liberty were associated. True, there was nothing much in liberty except freedom from Napoleonic rule: it was the Foxite liberty deprived of its essence, the attack on privilege in Britain. Nevertheless, anti-Napoleonic nationalism was primarily defensive, and a strong reaction set in after Waterloo. Meanwhile, more territory had been acquired in the outposts of empire: but the nationalism of this period can hardly be described as imperialist.

[1] E. Wingfield-Stratford, *History of English Patriotism*, II, p. 121.

CHAPTER VI

IMPERIALISM

I. RADICAL IMPERIALISM

The scattered territories remaining to the British Empire after the American Revolution were increased during the French Wars and, with few exceptions, remained in that Empire for the hundred years after Waterloo. After 1815 extensions came mainly not from new conquests, but through expansion in North America, India, Africa and Australasia from existing plantations and colonies. The fundamental idea of those who lost the American colonies, that colonies were sources of commercial wealth for the mother country, did not immediately disappear. The gradual acceptance of Adam Smith's arguments, however, led to the view that the prosperity of the mother country was assured not by attempts to create monopolies, but by maintaining law and order and providing efficient and honest administration. The whig theory that this could be done by extending British institutions to the colonies was, however, thought to be applicable only to the colonies formed by European migration, that is, those in North America and Australasia and Cape Colony. A modification was adopted in Bengal under Lord Cornwallis. The revenue was fixed and the *zamindari* treated as whig landowners, though without representation in an assembly; and English courts were established to administer English law. Elsewhere, including other parts of India but excluding the older colonies in the West Indies, the Crown Colony system was established. With the weakening and, by 1850, the disappearance of the trading monopoly, Burke's conception of a trust for the inhabitants could be developed. The maintenance and encouragement of trade were by no means inconsistent with a trust; for (as the experience of the American colonies had amply demonstrated) trade enriched the local inhabitants and provided the revenues from which roads, bridges, railways, irrigation works, schools and hospitals could be financed.

Within the range of these concepts there was ample room for differences of political opinion. In fact, however, the British Empire tended

234

to drop out of politics. The strength of the West India interest gradually declined, and it was finally destroyed by the emancipation of the slaves in 1833—though it had already been much weakened by the abolition of the nomination boroughs. India had been at the centre of political controversy between 1782 and 1784, and was in the public eye during the long proceedings against Warren Hastings from 1786 to 1795; but as a political problem it ceased to be important between Pitt's legislation of 1784–6 and the Indian Mutiny of 1857. In 1813 the India (but not the China) trade was opened to private traders,[1] and the Charter Act of 1833 ordered the East India Company to close its commercial business with all convenient speed. There had been a responsible Minister, the President of the Board of Control, since 1784, and after 1812 he was always in the Cabinet. Even so, imperialism as a political phenomenon was dormant from 1784.

The controversies about India in 1782–4 related mainly to patronage, and much of the argument was 'party political'. George III had been able to keep Lord North in power between 1770 and 1782, it was thought, because of the judicious exercise of patronage. The Rockingham Ministry of 1782 made a frontal assault on patronage and electoral corruption, but it could do nothing about India because of the opposition of the Earl of Shelburne.[2] The Shelburne Ministry which followed the death of the Marquis of Rockingham was defeated by the coalition of Fox and North before it could produce its India Bill, which was very like that subsequently produced and passed by Pitt.[3] Fox's India Bill of 1783 was apparently drafted on Burke's instructions.[4] It would have vested the patronage in a body of named Commissioners; and it was assumed by the opponents of the Coalition that this was an attempt to keep it in the hands of Fox and North even when they were out of office. It was therefore easy for George III to stimulate the House of Lords to reject the Bill and thus to turn out a Government which he disliked. Since this put Burke out of office it must be assumed that his

---

[1] 'In 1813, Parliament briefly discussed and then dismissed Indian affairs for another twenty years': C. H. Philips, *The East India Company, 1784–1834*, p. 299.
[2] Lucy S. Sutherland, *The East India Company in Eighteenth Century Politics* pp. 382–6.
[3] *Ibid.* p. 392.
[4] *Ibid.* p. 397.

opposition to Pitt's Bill of 1784 and his persistent attack on Warren Hastings were in part 'party political'.

On the other hand, there was more behind the impeachment of Warren Hastings than a mere politician's manoeuvre. The sense of moral responsibility which Chatham and Burke had exhibited in the dispute with the American colonies was not an isolated phenomenon, based on the assumption that the Americans were 'flesh of our flesh and blood of our blood'. It was part of a general extension of a sense of moral obligation. The Methodism which the Wesleys had taken from Oxford to the working class was, as we have seen, mainly a religion without a morality because it was based on a psychological conversion rather than on moral persuasion: but the Nonconformist Conscience was developing among the dissenting sects. The Baptist Missionary Society was founded in 1792 and William Carey sailed for India in the same year. The London Missionary Society, founded in 1795, was theoretically unsectarian but in practice Congregationalist. Also, the evangelicalism which was taken from Cambridge to the Clapham Sect was, in part, based upon the sense of dignity of the ordinary human being, slave or free. In relation to Indian affairs it was a little obtuse, perhaps because two members of the Clapham Sect had connexions with the East India Company. The main object of the evangelicals was to secure authority for the sending of Christian missionaries to India. The evangelicals collaborated in the work of the London Missionary Society, though most of the Anglican missionary activity was done by the Church Missionary Society, founded by Vernon and Charles Simeon in 1799. These missionaries, of all denominations, helped to create a humanitarian public opinion both in India and in Britain. Burke was concerned with an entirely different aspect of the government of India, the harm which the East India Company might be presumed to have done by its wars and its methods of raising revenue. He had mastered all the papers by an impressive devotion to parliamentary duty—not wholly without malice aforethought—and he saw that these methods, wherever adopted, would do harm to the people. 'Fraud, injustice, oppression, peculation', he said in 1785 in his speech on the Nabob of Arcot's debts,[1] 'engendered in

---

[1] Edmund Burke, *Works* (1834 ed.), I, p. 318.

236

India are crimes of the same blood, family and cast, with those that are born and bred in England.' The enrichment of the English 'nabobs', who were alleged to have helped George III and Pitt to win the general election of 1784, was, of course, an important question of party politics to a member of the Opposition: but Burke realised that the people who suffered from these transactions were, in the long run, the people of India.[1] Though he had never been there, he was able to imagine, and to put into his most passionate prose, the misery which Hyder Ali Khan must have caused in the Carnatic:

I was going to awake your justice towards this unhappy part of our (Indian) fellow citizens, by bringing before you some of the circumstances of this plague of hunger...but I find myself unable to manage it with decorum; these details are of a species of horrour so nauseous and disgusting; they are so degrading to the sufferers and to the hearers; they are so humiliating to human nature itself, that, on better thoughts, I find it more advisable to throw a pall over this hideous object....

There follows a description of the Carnatic, taken wholly from maps and papers, which those of us who have been there can recognise even today. But this was a new idea, to treat the Tamil and the Telugu as real people and to insist that it was the duty of the Government to restore 'a land desolated by fire, sword, and famine'.[2]

The change which occurred in the next generation was not, however, due primarily to a change of politics. The slave trade was forbidden to British subjects and British ships in 1807 and efforts were made to secure its extinction by international agreement—in the case of Spain and Portugal at the expense of the British taxpayer. After other efforts proved unsuccessful, slavery was abolished in the British dominions, at the expense of the British taxpayer, between 1833 and 1838. The East India Company was deprived of its trading activities in 1833, but its territories were not taken over by the Crown until 1858. Generally, however, the changed attitude resulted not from a new imperialism among the politicians but from its absence. The defeat of Napoleon had put the colonies almost out of mind. From 1801 to 1854 they were theoretically under the control of the Secretary of State for War because the Colonial Office was not an important office. The

[1] *Ibid.* p. 329.   [2] *Ibid.* p. 334.

237

President of the Board of Control was one of the least important members of the Cabinet.

During this period the Empire overseas was governed by a band of devoted public servants. Sir James Stephen (1789–1859) was 'Mr Mother Country'[1]—he was also called 'Mr Over-Secretary'—for a long period ending in 1847. He was a Cambridge evangelical,[2] son of the James Stephen, Master in Chancery, who was a member of the Clapham Sect. He was therefore in principle a tory whose actions were dictated by a strong, and indeed an overpowering, religious belief with all the characteristics of evangelicalism;[3] he had a profound distaste for slavery, and he thought of the colonies not as a source of profit but as an onerous responsibility. It was the duty of the trustee to administer them for the benefit of their inhabitants, but he thought that Canada and Australia would soon become independent states, though (as he hoped) gradually and in a friendly fashion.[4] He was therefore opposed to the extension of colonial territories. His was the 'official policy' which E. G. Wakefield had to fight in his efforts to colonise Australia and New Zealand.

India, too, was expected to become independent in due course. Sir Thomas Munro, Governor of Madras from 1820 to 1827, wrote in 1824 that:

we should look upon India, not as a temporary possession but as one which is to be maintained permanently, until the natives shall in some future age have abandoned most of their superstitions and prejudices, and become sufficiently enlightened, to frame a regular government for themselves, and to conduct and preserve it. Whenever such a time shall arrive, it will probably be best for both countries that the British control shall be withdrawn.[5]

---

[1] So called by Charles Buller in a pamphlet originally published in 1840: 'In some back room—whether in the attic, or in what story we know not—you will find all the Mother Country which really exercises supremacy, and really maintains connection with the vast and widely-scattered colonies of Britain': E. M. Wrong, *Charles Buller and Responsible Government*, p. 146.

[2] Mr E. L. Woodward, *The Age of Reform*, p. 352, says that he was educated at Trinity College, but this is a mistake: he was a pensioner at Trinity Hall. His mother was Wilberforce's sister.

[3] See *Life of the First Sir James Stephen*, privately printed.

[4] E. L. Woodward, *The Age of Reform*, p. 352. As we shall see, this idea was developed by the Manchester School, *post*, pp. 255–8.

[5] *Ibid.* p. 389.

T. B. Macaulay, another scion of the Clapham Sect,[1] expressed the same idea in a famous passage of his speech on the Charter Bill in 1833:

It may be that the public mind of India may expand under our system till it has outgrown that system; that by good government we may educate our subjects into a capacity for better government; that, having become instructed in European knowledge, they may, in some future age, demand European institutions. Whether such a day will ever come I know not. But never will I attempt to avert or retard it. Whenever it comes, it will be the proudest day in English history. To have found a great people sunk in the lowest depths of slavery and superstition, to have so ruled them as to have made them desirous and capable of all the privileges of citizens, would indeed be a title to glory all our own. The sceptre may pass from us. Unforeseen accidents may derange our most profound schemes of policy. Victory may be inconstant to our arms. But there are triumphs which are followed by no reverses. There is an empire exempt from all natural causes of decay. Those triumphs are the pacific triumphs of reason over barbarism; that empire is the imperishable empire of our arts and our morals, our literature and our laws.[2]

This idea was worked out by Macaulay's brother-in-law, Charles Trevelyan, in his pamphlet on *The Education of the People of India*.[3] He said that the connexion between England and India could not be permanent, and no effort of policy could prevent the Indians from regaining their independence. There were, however, two methods. One was revolution, which would put India back where it had been. The other was a gradual development of European knowledge and institutions.

[1] He was the son of Zachary Macaulay, whose antagonism to the slave trade began in Jamaica, and who was Governor of Sierra Leone between 1793 and 1799, that is, before it became a colony. Zachary married a pupil of Hannah More's, and they took a house in High Street, Clapham, where Tom Macaulay was brought up until he went to Little Shelford, near Cambridge: See G. O. Trevelyan, *Life and Letters of Lord Macaulay*, ch. 1.

[2] Lord Macaulay, *Complete Works*, XI, pp. 585–6, quoted by Eric Stokes, *The English Utilitarians and India*, p. 45.

[3] Charles Trevelyan, who married Macaulay's sister, Hannah More Macaulay, was an employee of the East India Company. Macaulay's description, before his marriage, was: 'He has no small talk. His mind is full of schemes of moral and political improvement. His topics, even in courtship, are steam navigation, the education of the natives, the equalisation of the sugar duties, the substitution of the Roman for the Arabic alphabet in the Oriental Languages': G. O. Trevelyan, *op. cit.* I, p. 393.

Trained by us to happiness and independence, and endowed with our learning and political institutions, India will remain the proudest monument of British benevolence; and we shall long continue to reap, in the affectionate attachment of the people, and in a great commercial intercourse with their splendid country, the fruit of that liberal and enlightened policy which suggested to us this line of conduct.[1]

Macaulay himself was able to put India on the road to independence by means of his famous Minute on Education as Law Member of the Council of India. It has a bad reputation in India because of its criticism of the classical languages of India as media of modern instruction. It is, however, plain in retrospect that, if an independent Indian nation was an ultimate goal, there had to be a lengthy period of development, during which English was the medium of instruction. Macaulay's Minute of 1835 induced the Company to begin subsidising English education in India. Probably that development would have occurred had the Minute never been written; but it is not much of an exaggeration to say that among the consequences of Macaulay's Minute were Mahatma Gandhi, Jawaharlal Nehru, and Mohamed Ali Jinnah.

Macaulay and Charles Trevelyan, however, carry us over from the evangelicals to the Radicals. Strangely enough, there were common elements in their ideas. To the evangelicals religion was fundamental: hence the fact that the peoples of India and the neighbouring territories were Hindus, Muslims and Buddhists implied that they were steeped in superstitions which had to be removed before India (or Ceylon or Burma or the East Indies) could be put on the way towards independence. The fundamental trust imposed on Britain, therefore, was to bring Christianity to the people. Possibly, however, the Radicals had more influence in India. James Mill entered the service of the East India Company in 1819 and became chief executive officer in 1830. He was thus able to influence policy in the direction laid down in his *History of India* in 1818, a policy based narrowly on the principle of utility as elaborated by Jeremy Bentham. Mill knew even less of India than Sir James Stephen knew of the colonies, and it was a much more difficult country to know: but he would have regarded such a criticism as irrelevant, because the principle of utility, like Christianity (or, for

[1] Eric Stokes, *The English Utilitarians and India*, pp. 46–7.

that matter, Islam or Hinduism or Buddhism), was either true or false; and if it was true it could apply to India as to other countries. Hence the Radicals, like the evangelicals, had a dogma to teach, and a dogma which implied contempt for Indian ideas and institutions. In this respect there was a deterioration in the relations between the United Kingdom and India. The nabobs had enriched themselves at the expense of Indians and had brought great hardships to many; but some of the Company's servants had been interested in Sanskrit, Persian and Arabic and, not being very good Christians, they had been tolerant of the Indian religions. The evangelicals and the Radicals, though holding themselves bound by a trust which the nabobs had never even thought of, and though correctly diagnosing that the future of India depended upon an infusion of western ideas and institutions, concluded from their *a priori* assumptions that there was nothing in India worth preserving. In practice, of course, the application of dogma was much modified by the Company's servants. They did bring law, order and justice to Indians for the first time in their long and tortuous history— for it can hardly be contended, except in nationalist histories, that the Emperor Asoka did so. Most of them rendered distinguished service which Indian history will in due course record. But they made a great many mistakes, because so many were psychologically remote from Indian ideas. They handled villagers and tribesmen better than learned brahmins and moulvis. Nevertheless, this nineteenth-century imperialism was very different from that of the nabobs. It was founded on a sense of duty.

Elsewhere, too, the Radicals were influential. Jeremy Bentham had, by a process of over-simplification, drawn from Adam Smith the conclusion that colonies were useless, though he was not averse from drafting a code for India.[1] James Mill, in the fifth edition of the *Encyclopaedia Britannica*, had found one use for colonies, to take the surplus population from the mother country.[2] Edward Gibbon Wakefield put this theory into practice by colonising South Australia and New Zealand by joint stock companies. The advantage of the colonisation company was that it supplied both colonists and capital, and the

[1] E. Halévy, *The Growth of Philosophic Radicalism*, p. 114.
[2] *Ibid.* pp. 362–3.

plan was said to have been devised by Bentham.[1] This was in a period when the official policy, laid down by Sir James Stephen and accepted by successive Secretaries of State, was against colonial expansion.[2]

Here, too, Radicals and evangelicals were associated. The principal link was John Robert Godley, an evangelical tory whose name is almost forgotten, but who was described by Gladstone as having 'a master mind'.[3] In 1847 Godley began an association with E. G. Wakefield, with the idea of forming a Church of England province in New Zealand. Godley brought in Charles Adderley (afterwards Lord Norton) and George, fourth Lord Lyttelton, both evangelical Conservatives. Godley went to Canterbury, New Zealand; Lyttelton was chairman of the Canterbury Association in England; and Adderley spoke for the new province in the House of Commons.[4] Adderley, indeed, broadened his interests and fought against the whigs' attempt to transport convicts to Cape Town.[5] The Colonial Reform Society was formed in 1849 to support 'responsible government of the colonies by themselves under the banner of imperial unity and fellowship'.[6] Gladstone was asked to become chairman, but refused, and both Peel and Disraeli refused to become members. Thus the Society was in large part Radical, with Wakefield, Sir William Molesworth and Cobden as leading members. The Society was not very influential, but it played a part in the movement, initiated in the early fifties, for the conferment of responsible government on the Australasian colonies.

Benthamism was also active in Ceylon. The reforms of 1833, on which the government of the island was based until the rise of Ceylonese nationalism compelled changes in 1910, were based on reports made by W. M. G. Colebrooke and C. H. Cameron. The latter was a Benthamite: and, though the former is not known to have had Benthamite connexions, his reports show that in large measure he had absorbed Benthamite ideas, perhaps with rather more than a touch of

[1] Halévy, *op. cit.* pp. 510–11.
[2] B. Fitzpatrick, *The British Empire in Australia*, p. 41; *ante*, p. 238.
[3] *Life of Lord Norton*, p. 58. His *Letters from America*, published in 1844, was recommended by the American Minister as 'the soundest and most original work on America': *ibid.* p. 33.
[4] *Ibid.* pp. 69–70.
[5] Adderley Street, Cape Town, is named after him: *ibid.* p. 76.
[6] *Ibid.* p. 79.

evangelicalism. These reports, though as usual excessively contemptuous of local ideas, which in this case included the Buddhist religion, were on the whole sensible because they were based less on *a priori* assumptions and more on local investigation.[1] The fundamental idea, however, was that of Macaulay, that the progress of the country depended on an infusion of western ideas and institutions by way of the English language.

The great triumph of the Radicals was the Durham Report on Canada. This was not entirely outside party politics, for the troubles in Canada in 1837 might have led to a combination of Conservatives and Radicals which could have destroyed Lord Melbourne's Government. 'The final separation of those colonies (in North America)', wrote Melbourne, 'might possibly not be of material detriment to the interests of the mother-country, but it is clear that it would be a serious blow to the honour of Great Britain, and certainly would be fatal to the character and existence of the Administration under which it took place.'[2] 'Radical Jack', Lord Durham, was invited to investigate for two reasons. First, it was a way of keeping him out of mischief; secondly, though he could hardly be described as the leader of the heterogeneous Radical group in Parliament, which was incapable of being led, at least his mission would not be regarded as a cause for their voting against the whigs. Durham at first refused; but after further outbreaks in Canada in 1838 he consented. He took with him two Benthamites, Charles Buller and E. G. Wakefield. Afterwards it was alleged that they wrote the Report; but research has now established that the greater part of it was in fact written by Lord Durham himself.[3]

Though the Durham Report is the greatest of our State papers, it has considerable faults.[4] The material for the descriptive chapters had to be collected in eight months. Lord Durham did not himself visit the Maritime Provinces and he did not spend much time in Upper Canada (Ontario). His analysis of the communal problem in Lower Canada (Quebec) is unconvincing to those who know what has happened to the French-Canadians or have seen communalism else-

[1] G. C. Mendis, *The Colebrooke-Cameron Papers*, I, p. xxxiii.
[2] R. Coupland, *The Durham Report*, p. xxix; cf. Adam Smith's remark, *ante*, p. 229.
[3] C. H. New, *Lord Durham*, pp. 565–76.
[4] R. Coupland, *op. cit.* pp. xlvii–xlix.

where. The chapter on Lands and Emigration was written by E. G. Wakefield and is concerned mainly with his policy of 'systematic colonization'. The value of the Report lies in two characteristics. First, it assumes the importance of 'the well-being of our colonial fellow-countrymen and the integrity of the British Empire'. Secondly, it recommends that Upper and Lower Canada be united and be given responsible government. The two ideas are closely connected. The Canadians had 'a strong feeling of attachment to the Crown and Empire', but this feeling could not be relied upon if the development of the colonies were cramped. The solution to this problem was constitutional—and here Radical Jack came into his own—the strengthening of the influence of the people on its Government and limiting the interference of the imperial authorities in the details of colonial affairs. The Crown must 'submit to the necessary consequences of representative institutions; and if it has to carry on the Government in unison with a representative body, it must consent to carry it on by means of those in whom that representative body has confidence'.[1]

Though the two Canadas were united in 1840, the recommendation for responsible government was not accepted until 1846. The system was then worked out by Durham's son-in-law, Lord Elgin, Governor of United Canada from 1847 to 1854. It was extended to the other colonies in North America, which were federated in the Dominion of Canada in 1867. It had already been extended to the colonies of Australia and New Zealand, and the Australian colonies federated into the Commonwealth of Australia in 1900. It was applied to Cape Colony in 1872 and to the Union of South Africa in 1909. Since 1947 it has been extended to India, Pakistan, Ceylon, Ghana, Nigeria, Sierra Leone and the Federation of Malaya. Meanwhile Lord Durham's idea has been developed and extended.

The changes made in the character of the British Empire between 1784 and 1858, in the later period under Radical inspiration, were in large measure outside party politics. One explanation, which must be discussed in a later chapter, is that Adam Smith's ideas were gradually accepted and that the political conflict concentrated not on the Navigation Acts but on the Corn Laws. This was a consequence of the inde-

[1] R. Coupland, *op. cit.* p. 141.

244

pendence of the United States and the vast extension of British trade, based upon the coal and iron of the United Kingdom and the fertility of invention of its manufacturers. The mercantile community did not need the Navigation Acts but the agricultural interest thought that it did need the Corn Laws. The problem of the colonies was therefore freed from the complications of economics and vested interests. Another explanation, however, and perhaps the more important, is that the emotional temperature had been lowered by the loss of the American colonies and the removal of foreign colonial competition. Except in the Newfoundland fisheries, the French had no footing in Canada. Most of the Spanish and Portuguese territories in America had become independent countries. Most of the West Indies were either independent or British. In Africa there was as yet no colonial competition. In Asia the Dutch had the East Indies but Singapore, Malacca and Penang were doing well from the Dutch trade as open ports. There was a vast British Empire, but it was no longer in danger, its trade was not particularly valuable—nothing like as valuable as foreign trade—and it was thought that much of it, perhaps most of it, would follow the American example. Mr Mother Country, both in the Colonial Office and in the Board of Control, could go his own way subject to such control as the comparatively insignificant and frequently changing Ministers in charge chose to exercise—though we must note that Charles Buller exaggerated his autocracy.

Even so, the progress of the overseas territories was considerable because they benefited from British trade and the influx of British capital. There was an entity called the British Empire around which sentiment could gather. It is not surprising that initially this sentiment was mainly Radical, though we have already pointed out that it was also infused by evangelical ideas. The Durham Report, Wakefield's enterprises in Australia and New Zealand, Adderley's battle against the sending of convicts to Cape Colony, Gladstone's interest in colonial problems after his periods of office under Sir Robert Peel,[1] the agitation for responsible government in Australia and New Zealand after 1846, all helped to create an imperialist sentiment. It was, for the time being, in a minor key. The opinion prevailing, especially after the repeal of

[1] Paul Knaplund, *Gladstone and Britain's Imperial Policy*, chs. II and III.

the Corn Law and the Navigation Acts, was that the Anglo-Saxon colonies were destined to become independent countries, but that the break should be effected in a friendly fashion. Even in this formulation of the opinion, however, there are evident traces of nationalism and even racialism. The colonists were 'our own people' destined to become new Anglo-Saxon States. At least the young men of the sixties could become mild imperialists.

Sir Charles Dilke was an able young man who came up to Trinity Hall in 1862. His tutor was Leslie Stephen, son of the Sir James Stephen who was called Mr Mother Country, and another young don in residence was Henry Fawcett, the blind economist. Both Stephen and Fawcett were Radicals. George Otto Trevelyan, the son of Charles Trevelyan by his wife Hannah More Macaulay, was in residence next door at Trinity College and was prominent at the Union, of which Dilke became President. Dilke, Fawcett and Trevelyan were elected to the Parliament of 1868, and frequently acted in consort with two other Cambridge men, William Harcourt and Lord Edward Fitzmaurice. Before being elected, however, Dilke had made a tour of the English-speaking countries—the United States, Canada, New Zealand, Australia, Ceylon and India—and had published a substantial work in two volumes entitled *Greater Britain*. In the main it was a description of peoples and places little known to Dilke's contemporaries, and it is significant of the period—1866 and 1867—that a young man like Dilke should choose this new type of Grand Tour. It was possible because of the railway and the steamship, though it was still necessary to cross America by coach. Dilke's object was not, however, merely to see strange sights and meet strange people. He had already decided to make politics his career, and his book contains a great deal of observation on political problems, always surprisingly mature in so young a man, but frequently erroneous in its forecasts of development. His imperialism is indicated by the preface:

In 1866 and 1867 I followed England round the world: everywhere I was in English-speaking, or the English-governed lands. If I remarked that climate, soil, manners of life, that mixture with other peoples had modified the blood, I saw, too, that in essentials the race was always one.

The idea which in all the length of my travels has been at once my fellow and my guide...is a conception, however imperfect, of the grandeur of our race, already girdling the earth, which it is destined, perhaps, eventually to overspread.

In America, the peoples of the world are being fused together, but they are run into an English mould: Alfred's laws and Chaucer's tongue are theirs whether they would or no. There are men who say that Britain in her age will claim the glory of having planted greater Englands across the seas. They fail to see that she has done more than formed plantations of her own—that she has imposed her institutions upon the offshoots of Germany, of Ireland, of Scandinavia, and of Spain. Through America, England is speaking to the world.

Sketches of Saxondom may be of interest even upon humbler grounds: the development of the England of Elizabeth is to be found, not in the Britain of Victoria, but in half the habitable globe. If two small islands are by courtesy styled 'Great', America, Australia, India, must form a Greater Britain.

The book went into three English editions, and had an enormous sale in the United States, though in pirated editions.[1] It did much to popularise the fiction of the English 'race'. What Dilke clearly had in mind were language, institutions and ideas, and we must remember the superiority of British and American institutions, governmental and non-governmental, in the sixties of the last century: but, since Dilke evidently assumed that this superiority would be perpetuated and British or American influence expanded, for instance to China, it was easy for other imperialists to assume that it was a matter of biological inheritance. Nor was his 'Greater Britain' an imperialist conception, as we now understand that term. It included the United States, which in his view ought to absorb Canada; he foresaw that the leadership of 'Saxondom' would be assumed by the United States; and in short his 'Greater Britain' was an entity in which 'Saxon' ideas and institutions would hold sway, not a British Empire. Indeed, he could find no justification for the continuance of the government of colonies—by which he meant territories like the United States, Canada, Australia and New Zealand, populated by British emigrants—from London unless the colonials themselves wished it, and then only if they were prepared to accept the obligations involved, for instance in respect of defence.

[1] Stephen Gwynn and Gertrude M. Tuckwell, *Life of Sir Charles Dilke*, I, p. 69.

On the other hand, he saw no objection to the continuance or even extension of British rule over dependencies, by which he meant India and the Crown colonies, inhabited by backward peoples who could not govern themselves. British rule was advantageous both to Britain and to the dependent peoples, provided that Britain's function was that of trustee for those peoples. He was critical of the manner in which that rule was actually carried out, and in particular of the insolence of the local English inhabitants towards the 'natives'—a point on which John Stuart Mill commented favourably;[1] but the alternative he believed to involve anarchy.

It must be remembered that Dilke was a young man just down from Cambridge. Many of his judgments were hasty and have not stood the test of time; and indeed twenty years later he was embarrassed that the book was still in demand.[2] Nevertheless, it had a very wide influence. It helped to build up the Conservative imperialism of the late nineteenth century, presently to be discussed. Dilke was, in respect of defence and external affairs, Joseph Chamberlain's political mentor, though their ways parted in 1886. The imperialism which could be read into *Greater Britain* had more body than Disraeli's vague flourishes: his Greater Britain contained real people, whereas Conservative imperialism has always been a little surprised to find that 'our flesh and blood' really had flesh and blood, especially when this implied that they also had minds of their own. The historian of English nationalism says that

it was Charles Dilke's *Greater Britain* that first gave the ordinary reading public some conception of what the empire really was. Not only did it contain disquisitions upon all sorts of colonial problems about which the ordinary man had understood nothing and cared less, but it was throughout inspired by a spirit definitely imperialist, that condemned a narrow nationalism on the one hand and cosmopolitanism on the other.[3]

This, however, is the Conservative imperialist interpretation of Dilke's own brand, which was highly personal.

On the other hand, Dilke gave Radical imperialism, to which the

---

[1] Gwynn and Tuckwell, *op. cit.* p. 71.
[2] Sir Charles Dilke, *Problems of Greater Britain* (1890), p. vii.
[3] Esmé Wingfield-Stratford, *History of English Patriotism*, II, p. 571.

Benthamites and, in a small measure, the Manchester School[1] had already contributed, a new twist. This Radical imperialism could take pride in the extension of English ideas and institutions without implying that it was the destiny of the British people to rule half the world, nor denying that people in other countries who had taken with them, or adopted, English ideas would want to govern themselves. Dilke was at first an Under-Secretary and then a Cabinet Minister (from 1882) in Gladstone's second administration, but he had no direct concern with the colonies; and his immediate political influence was ended by the divorce proceedings of 1886, in which he was co-respondent.[2] Meanwhile he had helped to educate Joseph Chamberlain, though the partnership broke up over Home Rule (and the divorce suit). Dilke was out of politics from 1886 to 1892, though he wrote *The Present Position of European Politics* (1887), *The British Army* (1888), and *Problems of Greater Britain* (1890). By 1890 his imperialist views had matured. He argued no longer for the break-up of the British Empire nor for the absorption of Canada in the United States. He still doubted whether 'trade follows the flag', though he pointed out that British territories were able to secure capital cheaply because of the security which British rule offered. He thought, too, that the British Empire was advantageous both to the Britons at home and to those overseas. It stimulated the energy of the people at home and prevented the growth of 'a hopeless provincialism' in the colonies. He discussed at length the project of Imperial Federation, pronounced it futile because of local nationalism, and suggested that the Imperial tie should be strengthened by co-operation in matters of common interest like defence, communications, naturalisation, legislation and the administration of justice. He was, in fact, moving towards the conception of the modern Commonwealth.[3]

Dilke was again elected to Parliament in 1892 and sat there, as a respected back-bench Radical, until his death in 1911. Though not a Labour member, he represented a mining constituency and gave great assistance to the nascent Labour party. In matters of foreign and

[1] *Post*, pp. 255–8.
[2] Roy Jenkins, *Sir Charles Dilke*, chs. XII–XVI.
[3] C. A. Bodelsen, *Studies in Mid-Victorian Imperialism*, pp. 73–5.

colonial policy, and of defence, he was often the mentor of the Labour members and taught them some of the facts of life, of which many of them were profoundly ignorant in these particular fields. He therefore had something to do with the ideas which the Labour Government of 1945 put into practice in 1947–8.

2. VICTORIAN IMPERIALISM

Eighteenth-century imperialism was carried into the nineteenth by George Canning. Since it was highly emotional in its content, it was necessarily affected by his early demise, and only Lord Palmerston carried on the Canningite tradition, though no doubt Benjamin Disraeli was influenced by it. In any case the times were not propitious. In the period after Waterloo British politicians, whether they were relics of the old whigs like Lord Grey and Lord Melbourne or manufacturers' sons like Sir Robert Peel and W. E. Gladstone, were inevitably concerned with the solution of the political and economic problems posed by the Industrial Revolution. Moreover the solutions adopted involved the break-up of the Conservative party. The Canningites joined the whigs and helped them to pass the first Reform Bill. The Irish famine in the hungry forties compelled the repeal of the Corn Law in 1846; and the Navigation Acts slipped quietly into limbo in 1849. Though in an imperialist age whigs, liberals and socialists are all infected with imperialist sentiment, it is more commonly found among Conservatives. It could not be expected to revive, therefore, until Disraeli had nursed the country gentlemen out of their psychological depression, a process much helped by the discovery that the repeal of the Corn Law did not destroy British agriculture and that even under free trade landowners had surplus revenues which they could put into profitable investments. By 1880 the country gentlemen were interested in urban rents and stocks and shares, and by 1886 'money' was Conservative.

Though he was a schoolboy when the nineteenth century began, Lord Palmerston seems to straddle the centuries. This is because he carried into the second half of the nineteenth century the Foxite tradition that in every country the British Government was the friend of liberty and, potentially, the enemy of despotism. The principle was by no means uniformly applied, for Palmerston was good at quick improvisations to meet what seemed to him to be needs of the moment, and he rarely discussed generalities. In so far as it was applied, however, it was a recognition of the theory of nationalism. Nations consist of people, not royal families: *les nations n'ont pas de cousins*.[1] On the other hand he was no friend of democracy. Though he was a member of the Reform Ministry which carried the first Reform Act he was never very keen on it, and there was no question of a further extension of the franchise so long as he was alive. The Reform Act of 1867 followed quickly upon his death in 1865. Ideologically, however, the periods which he straddled were the pre-Victorian and the Victorian. He was First Lord of the Admiralty in 1807 and he died as Prime Minister in 1865. He was Foreign Secretary for fifteen years and Prime Minister for nine years, with three years in between as Home Secretary.

Palmerston was not an imperialist in the sense that he was much concerned with the expansion of British dominion beyond the seas. As Foreign Secretary he was responsible for the capitulations in China and the acquisition of Hong Kong: but this was an application of the principle in the famous Don Pacifico case, that anybody who interfered with a British subject must pay for the privilege. He had no particular concern with the extension of British rule in Australasia, India or South Africa.[2] Nor, indeed, was he a supporter of the form of aggressive nationalism of which Napoleon, Bismarck, Mussolini and Hitler were the great examples. He was, however, largely responsible for what may be called the 'Great Power' concept. This meant that British influence should be used in any (or almost any) conflict which might occur in any part of the world, whether or not any British interest was directly involved. There was, of course, almost invariably an indirect interest. Even if none of the widespread British possessions was directly involved, there was the risk of an alteration in the balance of power in Europe, or of an extension of the conflict in such manner that British interests might be affected. On the other hand, the com-

---

[1] E. L. Woodward, *The Age of Reform*, p. 214.
[2] He did, however, support the extension of British rule in India to the Khyber Pass, in order to protect India against the Russians: E. Ashley, *Life of Viscount Palmerston*, I, pp. 23–5.

plaint of Lord Derby in 1864, that the policy of the Government in relation to the Schleswig-Holstein controversy was one of 'meddle and muddle',[1] might be extended to other controversies. The 'Great Power' concept was not criticised in itself, save by the Radicals of the 'Manchester School'. It was assumed that the influence of the British Government (that is, 'England' or the 'United Kingdom' in nationalist language) should everywhere be powerful because it was founded on economic power, the strength of the Royal Navy, and even the prestige of the British Army (though not much of that was left after the incredible inefficiency of the Crimean war). What was thought by nationalists of the other school was that this influence should be exercised with dignity and restraint: it should, so to speak, be the influence of a prefect, not that of a fourth-form bully.

On the other hand, Palmerston's blustering policy had the support of public opinion. He was, said G. M. Trevelyan, 'the Foreign Minister before the footlights, detested by our own and other Courts, feared by his colleagues, but loved by the hearty, pugnacious, despot-hating Englishmen of that period'.[2] When in 1850 he ordered a blockade of the Greek coast in support of a number of private claims, including a claim by Don Pacifico, a Portuguese Jew born in Gibraltar, for damages for the pillaging of his home in Athens, he was severely criticised in the House of Commons, but carried the House and the country with him by the famous speech which ended with the question 'whether, as the Roman in days of old held himself free from indignity when he could say, *Civis Romanus sum*, so also a British subject, in whatever land he may be, shall feel confident that the watchful eye and the strong arm of England will protect him against injustice and wrong'.[3] His support for the Russell Government of 1847–51 was so essential that Queen Victoria and the Prime Minister were forced to keep him at the Foreign Office; and when he was 'dismissed' in 1851 the Government was so weakened that he soon had his 'tit-for-tat'.[4] When the Crimean war was being mismanaged in 1855 and the Government was defeated,

---

[1] E. L. Woodward, *op. cit.* p. 311.
[2] *Life of John Bright*, pp. 187–8.
[3] E. Ashley, *Life of Viscount Palmerston*, I, p. 223.
[4] *Ibid.* p. 334.

Lord Derby considered it impracticable to form a Government unless Lord Palmerston took office, which he declined to do; Lord John Russell was supported by Palmerston but could not persuade the Peelites and others to take office under him, whereupon the Queen had no alternative but to invite Palmerston to form a Government. 'The country', said Lord John, 'wanted Lord Palmerston either as War Minister or as Prime Minister.'[1] He was out of office in 1858-9, but with that exception he governed Britain, virtually with the support of all parties except the Radicals, until his death in 1865.

It may seem surprising that while the Liberal party was gathering its strength for its triumphs under Gladstone there should be such agreement on an aggressive foreign policy. The explanation is in part that Nonconformity was still not as strong as it became between the second and third Reform Acts, and that the combination which gave the Conservative party predominance from 1886 to 1905 was being formed across party lines. As a critic of imperialism has put it:

The keystone of our foreign policy was a balance of Powers conceived as essentially hostile to one another; the conduct of that policy was in the hands of an aristocratic caste governed by dynastic traditions and working by secret diplomatic methods wholly divorced from popular influence and interests. Cobden saw how easy it was for an ambitious or bellicose statesman to appeal to the fighting spirit of our people by the pursuit of a spirited policy directed, now against the aggressive intentions imputed to our traditional enemy France, now against the rising menace of Russia, and again for the punishment of some injury or insult imputed to some weaker State— Turkey, Greece, China, or Japan. His parliamentary career virtually coincided with the Palmerstonian era, in which began to sprout the seeds of the modern imperialism, distinguished from the earlier processes of territorial aggrandizement by the plainer and more conscious action of commercial and financial interests handling the levers of State policy.[2]

There are tendentious statements in this quotation, which is taken from a book published in 1918 by a man who had been the propagandist of the 'little England' wing of the Liberal party at the end of the nineteenth century. Palmerston did not in fact engage in more 'secret diplomacy' than anybody else; he said little in his confidential despatches

[1] *Letters of Queen Victoria*, 1st ser. III, p. 119.
[2] J. A. Hobson, *Richard Cobden, The International Man*, p. 10.

that he did not say in public, and indeed the contemporary criticism was that he said too much in public. The last sentence of the quotation refers to the thesis which Mr Hobson had already developed, and failed to prove, in his book on *Imperialism* (1902). Nevertheless, the quotation does give an impression of the way in which opinion was developing. Mr Wingfield-Stratford refers to the views of Palmerston, Peel, Gladstone and Cobden, as expressed in the Don Pacifico debate, as different versions of a middle-class philosophy: 'In Palmerston it is active and militant; in Peel it is passive, seeking only to leave and to be left alone; in Cobden it rises to the ideal, the frock-coated perfection of the nineteenth-century industrial apprentice, brought up on the teachings of Samuel Smiles.'[1] Allowing for the sneer inevitable in a devotee of Benjamin Disraeli, who had also spoken in the debate, there is something in this also. Palmerston was living up to his reputation as the Victorian John Bull. But later in the century even John Bull put on a frock-coat when he went to call on his stockbroker, and Disraeli's genius was best exhibited by the way in which he lined up the frock-coats as well as the hunting-jackets behind the Conservative party. The distinction between urban and rural was, so far as the wealthier classes were concerned, breaking down. Prosperity was making wealthier Englishmen proud and truculent, and indeed Palmerstonian. At the same time the expansion of education, under the competition of Church and Chapel, was creating a reading public for the newspapers. The new literate classes could hardly be expected to show much knowledge of the arts of diplomacy, but they liked a politician who converted foreign affairs into a sporting contest. The Conservative party eventually profited from this association between wealth and the working class, though not until after Disraeli had 'dished the whigs'.

Moreover, Palmerston had behind him not merely the growing imperialist sentiment of the new Conservatism, but also the Foxite tradition that it was the duty of the British Government to encourage liberal institutions and to combat despotism. For instance, the Crimean war (for which Palmerston was not responsible, though eventually he

---

[1] E. Wingfield-Stratford, *History of English Patriotism*, II, p. 284. (It would be surprising if Cobden had read *Self-Help* ten years before its publication.)

was called on to see it through) could be represented as a war against Russian despotism, though in fact it was fought on behalf of a worse despotism, that of the Turks, and in alliance with Louis Napoleon. Nor did the war do anything whatever to forward liberal institutions.

There was developing a school which was in substance anti-imperialist, though that term was not yet known. Since it was led by Richard Cobden and John Bright, it was generally known as the 'Manchester School'. As we shall see, free trade was not just a question of a proposition in economics. It had its romantic side. Commerce dealt with men who went down to the sea in ships, ships that pass in the night, people rocked in the cradle of the deep, and so forth. Much of this was romantic nationalism associated with the 'little old red duster' (the red ensign of the British mercantile marine): but there was also a romance of commerce not necessarily associated with British ports or British bottoms. Sugar and spice and all that's nice need not come from the British Empire, and dark-skinned maidens might wear the calico of Manchester and Rochdale without being taught any version of 'God Save the Queen'. The proposition in economics did imply, however, that Lancashire lassies ate American wheat and Argentine beef because Lancashire calico was fashionable in Tahiti. 'The cotton trade, which [Cobden] entered as a clerk when fifteen years old, was doubly rooted in internationalism, drawing its materials entirely from foreign soil, and dependent, as it soon became, for its prosperity and profits upon the expansion of its world markets.'[1]

It was alleged by Lord Morley that Cobden's ideas were founded not on emotional sympathy but on a 'positive and scientific feeling for good order and right government'.[2] But a political doctrine must be founded on some principle adopted *a priori* and therefore irrational. Professor Thorold Rogers, whose analyses are not always to be trusted, says that the Manchester School 'affirmed that freedom was the natural condition of the individual, and that restraint must always be justified in order to be defended'.[3] If that is so, Cobden shared that sentiment with his inveterate political enemy, Lord Palmerston, though they

[1] J. A. Hobson, *Richard Cobden: the International Man*, p. 23.
[2] J. Morley, *Life of Cobden* (1883 ed.), p. 65.
[3] James E. Thorold Rogers, *Cobden and Public Opinion*, p. x.

applied it differently. Cobden was something of a nationalist: he could not fail to be so in his environment: but he did not express his nationalism in terms of military success or colonial expansion. Nor did he think that what was good for the English was not good for the French or the Russians. On the contrary, he thought that if they ceased interfering in each other's affairs and devoted their resources to 'improvement', they would all benefit. Even this is, of course, a theory of nationalism, a *laissez faire* nationalism; but it verges upon internationalism.

Cobden was not, however, the sole representative of the Manchester School. Behind John Bright's opposition to Palmerston's foreign policy was the Quaker objection to all war: but he did not put his opposition on that ground because he doubted whether he could, in all circumstances, maintain the extreme non-resistance principle.[1] Hence his speeches received wide support from the rising tide of Nonconformist opinion. At the outbreak of the Crimean war this was a small minority opinion: forty years of peace and Palmerston's nationalist bluster gave popular support to the war-mongers:

Because their two names [Cobden and Bright] had become a national synonym for plentiful bread, they were now once more joined for the nation's curse that is the lot of the peace-lover in time of war. They were the 'traitors', they were the 'Russians'; Bright was burnt in effigy; he and his friend were caricatured and vilified in the newspapers that had so often praised them, they were abused in the halls of meeting that had resounded with the thunder of their [Anti-Corn Law] League. The Tory papers joined in the hue and cry, and their old enemies rejoiced to witness the humiliation of the calico-printer and the cotton-spinner who had dictated terms to the gentlemen of England.[2]

Nevertheless, Cobden and Bright expressed opinions which in due course became dominant, at least so far as concerned European wars. Bright expressed that opinion best in his speech of 31 March 1854 on the Crimean war:

The past events of our history have taught me that the intervention of this country in European wars is not only unnecessary but calamitous; that we

[1] G. M. Trevelyan, *Life of John Bright*, p. 218.
[2] *Ibid.* pp. 215–16.

256

have rarely come out of such intervention having succeeded in the objects we fought for; that a debt of £800,000,000 has been incurred by the policy which the noble Lord [Palmerston] approves, apparently for no other reason than that it dates from the time of William III; and that, not debt alone has been incurred, but that we have left Europe at least as much in chains as before a single effort was made by us to rescue her from tyranny. I believe, if this country, seventy years ago, had adopted the principle of non-intervention in every case where her interests were not directly and obviously assailed, that she would have been saved from much of the pauperism and brutal crimes by which our Government and people have alike been disgraced. This country might have been a garden, every dwelling might have been of marble, and every person who treads its soil might have been sufficiently educated. We should indeed have had less of military glory. We might have had neither Trafalgar nor Waterloo, but we should have set the high example of a Christian nation, free in its institutions, courteous and just in its conduct towards all foreign States and resting its policy on the unchangeable foundations of Christian morality.[1]

Britain did not intervene in another European war until 1914.

Victorian imperialism, in fact, was more concerned with the outposts of Empire—for Disraeli's acquisition of Cyprus and the control of the Suez Canal were intended for the defence of communications to India. Here, too, Bright set the anti-imperialist tone before Disraeli had come into his own. In one of his first speeches to Radical, Nonconformist, Birmingham in 1858 (a young man named Joseph Chamberlain was in the audience), John Bright said:

I believe there is no permanent greatness to a nation except it be based upon morality. I do not care for military greatness or military renown. I care for the condition of the people among whom I live. There is no man in England who is less likely to speak irreverently of the Crown and Monarchy of England than I am; but crowns, coronets, mitres, military display, the pomp of war, wide colonies, and a huge Empire, are, in my opinion, trifles light as air, and not worth considering, unless with them you can have a fair share of comfort, contentment and happiness among the great body of the people. Palaces, baronial castles, great halls, stately mansions, do not make a nation. The nation in every country dwells in the cottage; and unless the light of your constitution can shine there, unless the beauty of your legislation and

---

[1] James E. Thorold Rogers, *Speeches of John Bright* (1883 ed.), p. 239.

the excellence of your statesmanship are impressed there on the feelings and conditions of the people, rely on it, you have yet to learn the duties of government.[1]

This was not, however, an issue that the Manchester School had to face, except in India and there only to a limited degree. Bright made speeches about India in the fifties, both before and after the Mutiny, which can now be read with pleasure by Englishmen and Indians alike.[2] It was also his view that the Canadians should determine the destiny of their country, whether it were continuance as a colony, independence, or absorption in the United States.[3] But Palmerston was not an imperialist in the sense in which Joseph Chamberlain was after 1886. The Manchester School disappeared with Palmerston, for Cobden died in 1864 and Palmerston in 1865. The leadership of the Liberals then fell to Gladstone who, up to 1880 or thereabouts, sensed the direction which Nonconformist opinion was taking—though he was himself far from Nonconformist—and thus went to the left while Bright, getting older, moved to the right. In any case, Bright was not a statesman but an orator with a few simple ideas, the ideas of the lower middle class of his time. Though he became a Cabinet Minister he was neither a good administrator nor very helpful in council. The high reputation and indeed popularity which he obtained, after the revulsion against the stupidities of the Crimean war, were helpful to the Liberal party: but Gladstone was, after 1865, the Liberal party.

With the death of Palmerston the story has to revert to the outposts of Empire. There was increasing tension in Europe, due to the rise of Prussia and German nationalism, but after the defeat of the French in the Franco-Prussian War of 1870 it was witnessed mainly by a scramble for colonies. The growth of British imperialism was in part a reaction to the competition for territory in which the British, French and German (and eventually Italian) Governments were concerned. It was, however, partly indigenous also. It began very modestly as a piece of sentiment. Gladstone pointed out, in a speech in 1855,[4] that in 1815

[1] G. M. Trevelyan, *Life of John Bright*, pp. 274–5.
[2] James E. Thorold Rogers, *Speeches by John Bright* (1883 ed.), pp. 1–63.
[3] *Ibid.* pp. 81–4.
[4] Paul Knaplund, *Gladstone and British Imperial Policy*, p. 185.

the number of emigrants from the United Kingdom was 2000, while in 1852 it was 368,000. This latter figure was misleading because most of the migration was from Ireland. In the decennium 1871–81 the net loss by migration was 164,000 from England and Wales, 93,000 from Scotland, and 661,000 from Ireland. In the depression of the eighties, however, the figures increased to 601,000 from England and Wales, 217,000 from Scotland, and 738,000 from Ireland.[1] The Irish must be distinguished from the English and the Scots because a great many of them went to the United States not as ambassadors of Britain but as opponents, if not enemies, of the Queen. Nor did all the English, Welsh and Scots go to the British dominions beyond the seas. Nevertheless, a great many loyal subjects of Queen Victoria went to the outposts of Empire and became even more loyal to the Queen and even more affectionate towards 'the old country' and 'home' than they would have been if they had stayed in London, Manchester or Glasgow. The number of emigrants implied a closer relation between the British peoples at home and abroad. Family ties were not broken until the third generation; and, even if there had been no other reasons for the development of racialism and imperialism, migration would probably have produced them. There was now something in the idea of 'kith and kin' and 'hands across the sea'. Indeed Gladstone himself (in 1878) wrote an article on 'Kin beyond Sea', opening with the lines:

> When Love unites, wide space divides in vain
> And hands may clasp across the spreading main.[2]

It was easy to generalise from real kin to fictitious kin, from family to 'race'; and Sir Charles Dilke, who was now in harness with Joseph Chamberlain on the Opposition side, had given what was thought to be a lead.

Moreover the self-governing colonies were no longer scattered plantations. Canada had been federated in 1867. In 1871 it had 3,700,000 inhabitants, produced field crops worth $111,000,000, and had exports of $58,000,000 and imports of $84,000,000. Even far-off Australia had in 1870 a population of 1,600,000. In the seventies some thing like one-eighth of the 'European' subjects of Queen Victoria

[1] Statistical Abstract for the United Kingdom, 1934, p. 8.
[2] W. E. Gladstone, Gleanings of Past Years, p. 203.

were in her dominions beyond the seas. That population, too, was growing rapidly; and optimists forecast that by 1950 the populations of the self-governing colonies would exceed that of the United Kingdom.[1] Communication was now easier. Steamships had enabled Charles Dilke to take a new sort of Grand Tour in 1866–7, and the Suez Canal was opened in 1869. The Atlantic cable was completed in 1866 and that to Australia in 1872.[2]

Emphasis is, for the moment, given to the self-governing colonies because it was in relation to them that Victorian imperialism began. They were the colonies which might, the imperialists feared, go the way of the United States. Though the argument never reached political level, except in an occasional aside, there was a body of opinion which thought not only that the self-governing colonies would become independent, but that they ought to be forced to be free because they were a burden on the mother country. It has already been mentioned that Bentham, misinterpreting Adam Smith, held the view that colonies were valueless. The movement for freedom of trade, too, became mixed up with a movement for 'retrenchment', or the reduction of taxation. Many duties, besides the duties on corn, were removed after 1846, but taxation was still, in Victorian opinion, heavy and therefore an unnecessary burden on productive industry. The Crimean war and Palmerston's foreign policy added to this burden in spite of Gladstone. The most easily attacked expenditure was that on defence, and especially on the navy, which had to be converted from sail to steam and from 'hearts of oak' to ironclads. It was argued by some that the main purpose of the navy was to protect the colonies, whose contribution to British prosperity was small because trade with the United States was far more valuable than trade with the colonies, and trade with the colonies would be equally valuable if they became independent countries and taxed themselves for their own defence. This argument, put forward especially by Goldwin Smith, was met by a series of counter-arguments designed to show how valuable the colonies were to Britain and how important it was to maintain the imperial connexion.[3]

---

[1] C. A. Bodelsen, *Studies in Mid-Victorian Imperialism*, p. 83.
[2] *Ibid.* p. 84.
[3] See generally *ibid.* ch. 1.

This was a war of books, pamphlets and periodicals, waged mainly by the Radicals on the one side and on the other by the clubmen of Pall Mall, forgotten worthies whose only memorials are the libraries of their clubs. Imperialism did not become a political issue until Disraeli made it so. No Government either would or could take such a broad decision as that the colonies should be encouraged to break away from the mother country. The Gladstonian Liberal party was, however, a composite body. In 1868 Lord Clarendon, who was a Palmerstonian if not a Canningite, was at the Foreign Office. Lord Granville, a whig, was at the Colonial Office, but on colonial matters he was in the hands of his officials, who carried on the tradition of Sir James Stephen that colonies were a bit of a nuisance. The Manchester School, or what was left of it, was represented at the Board of Trade by John Bright. The older group of Radicals was not represented in the Cabinet until 1870, when W. E. Forster was promoted. Where Gladstone himself stood on colonial matters was not at all clear. In 1855 he had coolly weighed the advantages and disadvantages of colonies:

I do not think them desirable simply to puff up our reputation.... It is plain that they are not to be desired for revenue, because they do not yield it. It is plain that they are not to be desired for trading monopoly, because that we have entirely abandoned. It is plain that they are not to be desired for patronage, properly so called, within their limits, because they will not allow us to exercise patronage, and I am bound to say, I do not think the public men of this country have any desire so to exercise it. With respect to territory, it is perfectly plain that mere extension of territory is not a legitimate object of ambition, unless you are qualified to make use of that territory for the purposes for which God gave the earth to man. Why then are colonies desirable? In my opinion...they are desirable both for the material and for the moral and social results which a wise system of colonisation is calculated to produce. As to the first, the effect of colonisation [i.e. by emigrants] undoubtedly is to increase the trade and employment of the mother country ...[The moral and social benefit is that we create 'so many happy Englands' living under good laws and institutions]. If it please Providence to create openings for us upon the broad fields of distant continents we should avail ourselves in reason and moderation of those openings to reproduce the copy of those laws and institutions, which have made England so famous as she is.[1]

[1] Paul Knaplund, *Gladstone and Britain's Imperial Policy*, pp. 198–203.

This is not the emotional imperialism of the Queen's Jubilee, and Gladstone went on to approve the system of the independent colonies of Greece and to say how much better it would have been if the American colonies had remained as friendly colonies or even had separated by a friendly arrangement. He condemned the government of colonies from Downing Street and praised the work of the Radicals who were interested in colonial reform. But the colonies would not wish to separate if they were governed 'upon a principle of freedom': 'Defend them against aggression from without—regulate their foreign relations (these things belong to the colonial connexion, but of the duration of that connexion let them be the judges)—and I predict that if you leave them that freedom of judgment it is hard to say when the day will come when they will wish to separate from the great name of England.'[1]

But since then Gladstone had been Chancellor of the Exchequer; and it fell to his first Government to complete the implementation of the unanimous resolution of the House of Commons in 1862 that the colonies should provide for their own internal defence. There had been a gradual withdrawal of British troops from the self-governing colonies under Lord Palmerston, and the process had been continued under the Conservative Government of 1866. The Gladstone Government, against strong protests from the colonists, decided to withdraw troops from New Zealand in spite of fears of a Maori rising, and also refused a loan for defence purposes. There were other events, such as a proposal to cede Gambia to the French, which seemed to suggest not merely lack of interest in the Empire, but even antagonism to it.

These incidents would not have been important if there had not been a rising tide of opinion which Disraeli was quick to notice. Disraeli's own position had been as ambiguous as Gladstone's. Though always inclined to sentimentalise over the 'greatness of England', and so forth, he was too astute a politician to make much of a principle unless he saw some party advantage in it. He had, from time to time, thrown out vague ideas about an 'Imperial Union'.[2] But he had also (in

---

[1] Knaplund, op. cit. p. 225.

[2] For example, in 1847: Life of Disraeli, I, p. 840; in 1850: ibid. p. 1069; in a confidential letter to Lord Derby in 1851: ibid. p. 1149; and in 1859: ibid. p. 1631.

private) spoken about 'these wretched colonies' which were 'a mill-stone round our necks', and 'these colonial deadweights which we do not govern'; and, according to Sir William Gregory, his expressions about the colonies 'were always those of contempt and a contented impression that we should sooner or later be rid of them'.[1]

In 1872 Gladstone's Government was in difficulties. The dispute over the disestablishment of the Irish Church in 1869 had weakened the Church vote, and the dispute over the Education Act of 1870 had weakened the Chapel vote. The Radical opinion which, a little later, Joseph Chamberlain was to lead, was reacting against the dominance of the whigs. The decision to submit to arbitration the dispute with the United States over the *Alabama* and other ships was galling to a public opinion which had become accustomed to Palmerstonian ways. In the circumstances Disraeli decided to 'take the field' (to use Lord Morley's phrase), in the belief that the opportunity for a Conservative victory was at last coming to him. He therefore made two major speeches, in Manchester in April 1872, and in the Crystal Palace in June of the same year. The former was, in the main, an exposition of Conservative policy in relation to constitutional matters, including Ireland; and it was in this speech that he made his famous reference to 'exhausted volcanoes'.[2] The second speech was devoted mainly to imperial matters:

If you look to the history of this country since the advent of Liberalism—forty years ago—you will find that there has been no effort so continuous, so subtle, supported by so much energy, and carried on with so much ability and acumen, as the attempts of Liberalism to effect the disintegration of the Empire of England....Statesmen of the highest character, writers of the most distinguished ability, the most organized and efficient means, have been employed in this endeavour. It has been proved to all of us that we have lost money by our colonies. It has been shown with precise, with mathematical demonstration, that there never was a jewel in the Crown of England that was so truly costly as the possession of India. How often has it been suggested to us that we should at once emancipate ourselves from this incubus! Well, that result was nearly accomplished. When those subtle views were adopted by this country under the plausible plea of granting self-government to the colonies, I confess that I myself thought that the tie

[1] C. A. Bodelsen, *op. cit.* pp. 122–3.   [2] Volume I, p. 130.

was broken. Not that I for one moment object to self-government, I cannot conceive how our distant colonies can have their affairs administered except by self-government.

But self-government, when it was conceded, ought to have been conceded as part of a great policy of Imperial consolidation. It ought to have been accompanied by an Imperial tariff, by securities for the people of England for the enjoyment of the unappropriated lands which belonged to the Sovereign as their trustee, and by a military code which should have precisely defined the means and the responsibilities by which the colonies should be defended, and by which, if necessary, this country should call for aid from the colonies themselves. It ought, further, to have been accompanied by the institution of some representative council in the metropolis, which would have brought the colonies into constant and continuous relations with the Home Government. All this, however, was omitted because those who advised that policy...looked upon the colonies of England, looked even upon our connections with India, as a burden upon this country; viewing everything in a financial aspect, and totally passing by those moral and political considerations which made nations great, and by the influence of which alone men are distinguished from animals.[1]

Disraeli's biographer, writing in 1920, calls this 'the famous declaration from which the modern conception of the British Empire largely takes its rise'.[2] That is, of course, plain nonsense. There is not and never has been an Imperial tariff, any effective control over waste lands in the Crown's dominions overseas, any military code by which Britain could call for assistance, or any central council. This was in fact a 'party political' speech, one of the opening moves in an electioneering campaign. What Disraeli alleged to be Liberal policy never was Liberal policy: but it is an old political tactic to take the views of a section of opinion, preferably the extremist section, in the Government and to attribute them to the whole Government. Disraeli simply imputed to Gladstone's Government what he took to be the views of the Manchester School, which had already been under attack in the pamphlet war. J. A. Froude, for instance, had already said all that Disraeli said, and

---

[1] *Life of Benjamin Disraeli*, II, pp. 534–5.
[2] *Ibid.* p. 535. Mr Wingfield-Stratford went even further. Apart from the reference to Crown lands, which he thought to be a defect, 'the speech will hold, in relation to the Imperial faith, a similar position to that of the Apostles' Creed in the Christian theology': *History of English Patriotism*, II, p. 565. But that was written in 1913, while imperialist sentiment, though in decline, was still very much alive.

264

a good deal more. Though in 1870 he merely attacked the Manchester School for seeking to destroy the greatness of 'England' by assuming that all that 'she' had to do was to produce calico and hardware, in 1871 he blamed the Liberal politicians for adopting the views of the Manchester School and keeping themselves in power by 'humouring the so-called interests of the capitalists and manufacturers'. 'The universal impression which they have created throughout the Empire outweighs their own feebly uttered and stammering denials.... Whatever Ministers may think now, it is certain that they did contemplate, and did most ardently desire, that at least Canada should declare herself independent.' This was good stuff both for the country gentlemen and for the workers enfranchised by the Reform Act of 1867: and it is surprising not that Disraeli picked it up but that he did not make more of it.

The Liberal policy which was adopted, that of granting self-government without strings, in so friendly a fashion that the self-governing colonies would remain voluntarily in close association with the United Kingdom, in due course became Conservative policy also. Nevertheless, the importance of the speech cannot be denied. In those days people not only listened to speeches, they read them in the newspapers, where they were (in the case of a Disraeli) printed almost in full. They were commented on in the weeklies, and discussed at length in the quarterlies. They were therefore fully thought out and carefully phrased. Disraeli had sensed the rise of imperialist sentiment and had decided to annex it. By so doing he helped to increase imperialist sentiment, for every Conservative politician became an imperialist propagandist. In turn they influenced others, from parsons to poets. Tennyson's jingoist verses, for instance, began in 1872, though there is evidence that he was becoming infected in 1870.[2] This development, like Disraeli's speech, was an indication of the movement of opinion; for Mr Dooley might have remarked of Tennyson (though he did not) that he kept his eye on his publishers' returns. So long as Palmerston was dominant Tennyson was Palmerstonian;[3] when imperialism became

[1] C. A. Bodelsen, *Studies in Mid-Victorian Imperialism*, pp. 106–12. The quotations are from J. A. Froude, 'England's War', *Short Studies on Great Subjects*, III, pp. 279, 280.
[2] C. A. Bodelsen, *op. cit.* pp. 124–6.
[3] Esmé Wingfield-Stratford, *History of English Patriotism*, II, pp. 371–2.

265

the vogue in the best circles, he became imperialist. This was probably quite unconscious on his part: he was the poet of the cultured middle class and his ideas simply moved with those of his public. Since a new volume from Tennyson was always the 'book of the month', he became, in the circles in which poetry was read, a most efficient imperialist propagandist.

How far imperialist sentiment affected the result of the general election of 1874 cannot be determined. The Church felt itself in danger of disestablishment; Nonconformity was sore over the Education Act; Joseph Chamberlain and his 'caucus' probably lost more whig votes than they gained Radical votes; and, as always, there was Ireland. At all events Disraeli's Government of 1874–80 made no attempt whatever to put into effect his very tentative 'programme' of 1872. It annexed Fiji and established a protectorate in Malaya. It annexed the Transvaal and got dragged into the Kaffir Wars of 1877 and 1878[1] and the Zulu war of 1879. It acquired Cyprus and the Suez Canal shares and joined with the French in taking control of Egypt. It engaged in an Afghan war in 1878 and extended the frontier of India to the Khyber Pass. This list makes the Government seem more pugnacious than it really was. The wars in Africa and Asia were primarily due to 'prancing proconsuls'; but the proconsuls were prancing because of the movement of opinion and because they felt that the Government would support them. All proconsuls like Empire-building; and the contrast between the law and order of their own territories and the anarchy outside was a standing invitation to extend boundaries by 'little wars'. The extent to which their ambitions could be put into execution, however, depended upon public opinion and the character of the Government at home.

The results of Disraeli's imperialism had no connexion with the policy expressed in his Crystal Palace speech. He was really less of an imperialist, in the strict etymological sense, than a follower of Palmer-

---

[1] Lord Beaconsfield's lively private secretary claimed to be speaking for his chief when he said that the troubles began with Lord Carnarvon (Secretary of State for the Colonies, 1874–8) who sent out Mr J. A. Froude, 'a desultory and theoretical *littérateur*, who wrote more rot on the reign of Elizabeth than Gibbon required for all the *Decline and Fall*'. Froude's task was 'to reform the Cape, which ended naturally in a Kaffir War': *Life of Disraeli*, II, p. 1292.

ston. The British Empire, as he saw it, made a small nation of 33 million people a 'Great Power'. As Gladstone realised, and emphasised in his Midlothian speeches, this concept implied that the more British responsibilities were increased by extending the outposts of Empire, the heavier the burdens laid upon the 33 million people, the less it became capable of intervening, if it wanted or had to, in the continent of Europe, and the 'greater' it became as a 'Great Power'. This intrinsic contradiction was of course masked by the almost continuous rise in British national production. J. A. Hobson was able to allege in 1902 that the acquisition of territory was due to the anxiety of manufacturers and traders for the acquisition of raw materials and markets at the expense of the British taxpayer. He did not, however, prove his case and, indeed, he almost proved the opposite, that the burdens of Empire were heavier than the profits. British trade with the United States and South America was far more important than British trade with the self-governing colonies; British trade with the self-governing colonies was more important than British trade with the dependencies, other than India; and the extension of British rule in India to the Khyber Pass had no appreciable effect on British trade. It is of course true that, from the point of view of British trade, it was better to have a dependency under the British flag than under the French or the German flag, because under the British flag it remained a free trade area, whereas under the French or German flag it became part of the protectionist system of the metropolitan country. There is, however, no evidence that this was more than an incidental advantage of the Conservative imperialism of the late nineteenth century, and it was more than offset by the heavy expenditure on all the 'little wars' that were fought between 1877 and 1902. It would be difficult to draw up a balance sheet, but it is plain enough that Conservative imperialism was in large measure emotional, and indeed the emotions were shared by many in the Liberal party. It was, however, good Liberal tactics to suggest that there was something sinister about it, and that the British taxpayer was being called upon to subsidise Conservative traders and manufacturers.

The Conservative tradition treats Disraeli as a great political philosopher. This, however, is to mistake the character of his genius.

Nothing that he said or wrote brings him into the same class as Burke, though he was a master of phrases and many of them have slipped into the English language. He was, however, a very great party politician. Some would say that he had remarkable political intuition, but it was rather more than that. His mind was always on party and politics, and he had a great capacity for seeing how people were reacting and would react. Even so, he often threw out an idea just to see if it caught on.[1] He had a remarkable command of language and he dressed up that idea in his best and most careful prose. If the idea did not catch on, he dropped it; and the idea in his Crystal Palace speech did not, except in a small section of Conservative opinion. It was Palmerston's 'Great Power' concept which did prove popular; indeed it is still popular today; and Disraeli played it up. He used it, for instance, in his last great speech as Prime Minister, that at Guildhall in November 1879:

If there be a country...one of the most extensive and wealthiest of empires in the world—if that country, from a perverse interpretation of its insular geographical position, turns an indifferent ear to the feelings and fortunes of Continental Europe, such a course would, I believe, only end in its becoming an object of general plunder. So long as the power and advice of England are felt in the councils of Europe, peace, I believe, will be maintained, and maintained for a long period. Without their presence, war, as has happened of late [no doubt the Franco-Prussian War of 1870 and the Russo-Turkish War of 1878], seems to me to be inevitable. I speak on this subject with confidence to the citizens of London, because I know that they are not ashamed of the noblest of human sentiments, now decried by philosophers [that is, Liberals]—the sentiment of patriotism; because I know that they will not be beguiled into believing that in maintaining their Empire they may forfeit their liberties. One of the greatest of Romans, when asked what were his politics, replied, *Imperium et Libertas.* That would not make a bad programme for a British Ministry. It is one from which Her Majesty's advisers do not shrink.[2]

The citizens of London who partook of the Lord Mayor's turtle soup and Disraeli's oratory probably understood as little of this 'policy' as the images of Gog and Magog who looked down upon the banquet. After-dinner speeches, like oysters, ought not to be dissected.

[1] For example, in his younger days, the leadership of the aristocracy.
[2] *Life of Benjamin Disraeli,* II, pp. 1366–7.

Mr Wingfield-Stratford's comment on Disraeli's use of the word 'race' might apply equally to *Imperium et Libertas*: 'He is probably wise not to enclose an idea so vast and complex within the prison of a definition, but it is to be regretted that he never gave a doctrine so fundamental, and withal so clear in his own mind, the advantage of a more formal and detailed exposition.'[1] This vast and complex idea was not enough to win the general election of 1880. The 'little wars', Gladstone's fire and brimstone in Midlothian, a depression in agriculture due to cheap American corn and low freight rates, the beginning of a depression in industry, the return to the Liberals of the Nonconformist Conscience, and the swing of the pendulum, gave the Liberals victory.

Gladstone's Midlothian campaign had put opposition to aggressive nationalism on a high moral plane. It was *wrong* to wage war against Kaffirs, Zulus and Afghans: it was *wrong* to do a deal with the Turks in which Cyprus was the *quid pro quo* and to buy Suez Canal shares from a profligate Khedive. He was not of the school of Cobden and Bright. He could make speeches which pleased the imperialists:

I believe that we are all united—indeed, it would be most unnatural if we were not, in a fond attachment, perhaps in something of a proud attachment, to the great country to which we belong—to this great Empire, which has committed to it a trust and a function given from Providence, as special and as remarkable as ever was entrusted, to any portion of the family of man. Gentlemen, when I speak of that trust and that function I feel that words fail me: I cannot tell you what I think of the nobleness of the inheritance that has descended upon us, of the sacredness of the duty of maintaining it. I will not condescend to make it a part of controversial politics. It is a part of my being, of my flesh and blood, of my heart and soul. For these ends I have laboured through my youth and manhood till my hairs are grey. In that faith and practice I have lived; in that faith and practice I will die.[2]

Since this was said in Midlothian it may be regarded as electioneering, and certainly it would not have been said if the flood of imperialist propaganda had not made it worth while. Even so, Gladstone obviously believed his own statement: he, too, was affected by the emotions of the time. But he disagreed fundamentally with Disraeli's approach. His own was influenced by his mystical Christianity. 'England', the

[1] *History of English Patriotism*, II, p. 545.
[2] Quoted by Esmé Wingfield-Stratford, II, pp. 440–1.

269

Great Power, was a Christian entity and 'her' actions had to be justified by Christian morality. He was probably not unaware that this approach suited the Nonconformist conscience, but there is no doubt that, making allowances for the extravagances of electioneering, he believed in his own case.

He confided to his diary that the Almighty led him on;[1] and since it was also leading Paul Kruger,[2] there was reason to hope that a collision in the Transvaal would be avoided. Agreement was in fact reached without a war, though, owing to the usual incompetence of the man on the spot, not before the battle of Majuba Hill. The battle was only a skirmish, but it was not very consistent with the concept of a Great Power that a British detachment should be ignominiously defeated by a handful of Boer farmers. Nor was Gladstone's experience happier in Egypt. The bombardment of Alexandria and the occupation of Egypt were Disraelian, but the sending of General Gordon to Khartoum was a blunder for which the Liberals paid dearly. Gordon's assassination by the forces of the Mahdi was his own fault and the failure to relieve the garrison can be defended. But Conservative propaganda made the most of the opportunity and, probably, strongly influenced the election of 1885 (though the 'deal' between the Conservatives and Parnell helped). The result of the election induced Gladstone to decide for Home Rule, thus splitting the Liberal party and giving the Conservatives twenty years of power, broken only by the short and ignominious Liberal Governments of 1893-5.

It is at first sight a curious coincidence that British imperialism should reach its apogee soon after the third Reform Act established (or, strictly speaking, almost established) the principle of one man, one vote, one value. It is, however, not a coincidence. Disraeli had been right in his belief, when he 'dished the whigs', that enough working men would vote Conservative to give his party a majority. They accepted the Victorian social hierarchy and voted for the men from the new or reformed public schools. There were signs of a break in the tradition—the Dock Strike of 1889, for instance—but the social pyramid was only very slowly undermined. The first products of the board schools voted for the first time in 1885; by 1906 they were a

[1] *Life of Gladstone*, III, p. 1.   [2] *Ibid.* p. 29.

majority of the electors. 'Our masters' had learned their letters; but the public school and university men still had a majority of the seats in Parliament, filled all the administrative posts in the civil service, provided all the officers of the armed forces, held all the benefices in the Church of England, and ruled India and the colonial dependencies. In short, they ruled the whole Empire except the self-governing colonies. Imperialism was part of the common stock of ideas of this small but active class. The arch-imperialist, Joseph Chamberlain, was not one of them, but he had all the enthusiasm of the convert. John Bright in 1882 accused him of making a speech the tone and argument of which were 'exactly of the stuff on which the foreign policy of Lord Palmerston, and I may almost say of Lord Beaconsfield, was defended'.[1] Since he did not belong to the 'old boy' network he rebelled against Gladstone, who did; and henceforth his career had to lie in the Conservative party. Given the prevailing ideas, he had to be a better imperialist than the products of Jowett's Balliol. He very properly sent his abler son, the one who was expected to succeed in politics, to Rugby and Cambridge;[2] the less able, who was expected to succeed in business, went to Owen's College.

Collecting colonies was not quite like collecting postage stamps or old silver, though there was something of the collectors' delight in it. The abler educationalists of the Victorian era, of whom Benjamin Jowett, Master of Balliol, was the most successful, fired their pupils with both ambition and a zeal for the public service. The new evangelism was anxious less to convert the heathen than to rule them in a Christian spirit. They were to receive all the benefits of civilisation, including Christianity, education, honest and efficient administration, the rule of law, trade and commerce, roads and railways, scientific agriculture, a good medical service and even—though in the fullness of time—self-government. This was 'England's' privilege and duty, the Englishman's burden.[3] The belief of Gladstone and some of

[1] G. M. Trevelyan, *Life of John Bright*, p. 435.
[2] Austen Chamberlain was sent to Cambridge because J. R. Seeley, author of *The Expansion of England*, was Professor of Modern History: *Life of Joseph Chamberlain*, I, p. 494.
[3] As A. G. Gardiner said, the white man was an Englishman: *Life of Sir William Harcourt*, II, p. 467.

the other politicians of the older generation, that 'England' was accepting too many responsibilities, left large tracts of Africa, Asia and the Pacific outside the benefits of British rule. When imperialism swept France and Germany (and later Italy and Japan) there was competition and conflict. The Victorian Englishman did not believe that it was a good idea to allow the French and the Germans to have colonies. Obviously British rule was *summum bonum*, but it was necessary to avoid a European war. This competition, too, prevented the extension of British rule to the Arabs of Turkey, to Persia, to Siam, and to China. Some of the areas thus omitted came into British control, subject to mandates, by the peace treaties of 1919–20; but by that time Victorian imperialism was almost dead.

There were, of course, other points of view. One, pregnant with future developments, was that of the 'native'. There can be little doubt that the ordinary Asian or African peasant, who accepted the social hierarchy as his forebears always had done, was happier under British rule than his forebears had been for many centuries, subject to the qualification that sometimes the avenues for profitable employment of the kind he preferred, on the land or elsewhere, did not always keep pace with the rapid rise of population due to medical services and the elimination of famine. On the other hand, the attitude of superiority—it might often be described as arrogance—implicit in the Englishman's sense of his civilising mission, was galling to the educated Asian, especially if he were educated in England.[1] Moreover the English trader or planter, who was increasingly the salaried employee of a limited company, often had the arrogance without the sense of duty towards the country in which he served. These attitudes helped considerably towards the development of Indian and colonial nationalism, though it would have developed in any case.

Further, though imperialism affected the Liberal party as well as the Conservative party, the Radical tradition did not die. Sir William Harcourt, John Morley and Sir Henry Campbell-Bannerman kept it going, even during the Boer War; and young Lloyd George provided

---

[1] See, for example, Mahatma Gandhi, *My Autobiography*; Jawaharlal Nehru, *An Autobiography*; Sir John Kotelawala, *An Asian Prime Minister's Story*. Gandhi was called to the English Bar: Nehru and Kotelawala were at Cambridge.

powerful support. This involved, however, a battle within the Liberal party between Rosebery and Harcourt, Asquith and Lloyd George. In the course of this controversy the theory that imperialism was a capitalists' conspiracy was developed. It was stimulated particularly by the activities of Cecil Rhodes in South and Central Africa. It was, no doubt, to him that Harcourt referred when he spoke of the British Empire being 'committed to land speculators, to mining syndicates'.[1] The theory was not fully elaborated, however, until 1902, when J. A. Hobson published his *Imperialism*.

The new Jingo version of imperialism[2] had difficulty with the self-governing colonies. They were not ignored. Queen Victoria herself was made to say in the Queen's Speech of September 1886 that 'There is on all sides a growing desire to make closer in every practicable way the bonds which unite the various portions of the Empire'.[3] A host of well-meaning and often ignorant busy-bodies, now forgotten except by specialist historians, considered how the colonies could be brought to share in Britain's imperial magnificence, especially after Canada committed the deadly sin of going protectionist.[4] Most of the English writers were quite unaware of the strength of colonial nationalism and thought that the colonials were merely Englishmen beyond the seas who, because of distance and frontier conditions, could not share in the active political and intellectual life of Britain: so rude and barbarous were their conditions that they had not even learned Cobden's proposition in economics. Accordingly, some form of closer union was suggested. Until after 1887, when the first Colonial Conference was held, this was not thought of as a union of equals. It was thought of as the

---

[1] *Life of Sir William Harcourt*, II, p. 497.
[2] Jingoism was the name invented in 1878 for the policy of those who favoured intervention by the United Kingdom in the Russo-Turkish War. It derived from a popular music-hall song by W. Hunt, of which the chorus was:

> 'We don't want to fight, but by Jingo! if we do
> We've got the ships, we've got the men, and got
> the money too.'

It was then extended to all who advocated a bellicose or 'forward' policy.
[3] *Life of Joseph Chamberlain*, II, p. 269.
[4] C. A. Bodelsen, *Studies in Mid-Victorian Imperialism*, pp. 130–45. The first tariff was levied in 1859, but Canada went really protectionist in 1879.

grant of a privilege by the mother country to the Englishmen overseas, so that they could share some of the privileges of the Englishmen at home, such as taking a part in foreign affairs and helping to defend the Empire, though most of the writers hedged on the subject of imperial taxation for defence purposes. There was no agreement among the authors about the machinery. Even the Imperial Federation League, established in 1884 when opinion was becoming more mature, had to dissolve itself in 1893 because it could not agree about objectives.[1] Some still thought along the lines of Disraeli's speech of 1872: the grant of self-government was doubtless necessary (and the word 'doubtless' in this context means that there was doubt), but it should have been accompanied by some reservation relating to tariffs, Crown lands, and perhaps defence.

Two writers must, however, be mentioned separately because of the extent of their influence. The more important was J. R. Seeley, whose *Expansion of England* was published in 1883 and at once obtained a very wide circulation. It consisted of the text of two courses of lectures delivered in Cambridge, where Seeley was Charles Kingsley's successor as Professor of Modern History.[2] Seeley was no Jingo, and if he had been he would not have thought it proper to introduce Jingoism into his lectures. He believed, however, that the history of England 'ought to end with something that might be called a moral'.[3] Since it is the history of England it must be the history of the English State: and the most important factor in the history of the English State is 'the simple obvious fact of the extension of the English name into other countries of the globe, the foundation of Greater Britain'.[4] 'We' have in fact founded two Empires; the one 'we' lost is now a State, English in race and character, larger than any State in Europe except Russia; nevertheless, 'we' have created another, and the question now is whether 'we' shall lose that also or whether 'we' shall be able to do what the United States does so easily, that is, hold together in a federal union countries remote from each other. If 'England' does the latter

---

[1] Bodelsen, *op. cit.* pp. 205–14.
[2] Charles Kingsley's predecessor was 'Mr Oversecretary Stephen'. The historical library at Cambridge is named after Seeley, who was at Caius.
[3] *Expansion of England*, p. 1.   [4] *Ibid.* p. 8.

it will rank with Russia and the United States in the first rank of States, measured by population and area, and in a higher rank than the States of the continent.[1]

We—and this 'we' means the readers of this book and not Seeley's phantom 'England' or 'British Empire'—are not concerned with either his theory of history or the fascinating manner in which he worked it out. The great influence of the book was due in large measure to its merits as a work of art. It was, however, also due to the acceptance by its readers of the *a priori* assumptions of its author. Seeley was not one of the lunatic fringe, as Froude was. He was an able and judicious historian, calmly lecturing to undergraduates on the basis of assumptions which he shared with them.[2] The more modern reader, who has seen nationalism turn to filth in Adolf Hitler, may find these assumptions less easy to accept. Especially will this be so if he has a nationalism of his own, Scots, Welsh, Irish, Canadian, Australian, Indian, Ghanaian, and so forth. The old lady of the sea, 'England', is more amorphous than she was. We are not quite certain that it was 'we' who 'conquered and peopled half the world in a fit of absence of mind'.[3] The undergraduate from Hoxton, who has come up to hear one of Professor Seeley's successors give a very different version of modern history, may wonder at what point in his short but, no doubt, distinguished career he helped to conquer and settle half the world. Clearly there is an assumption which needs to be proved, namely that when a person who was called 'English' (though he probably called himself 'Irish') crossed the Atlantic to join the police force in Boston, Massachusetts, he did something on behalf of 'England' and implicated all the so-called English for all time. If 'we' settled America 'we' also joined the Boston police force, opened a saloon in Medicine Hat, married a Zulu in Pietermaritzburg, and committed suicide when we failed to make a strike in Kalgoorlie. If we settled New South Wales by being transported to Botany Bay for picking pockets in Piccadilly, we were also hanged for highway robbery on Hounslow Heath.

Seeley added a qualification to the nationalist assumption that there

[1] *Ibid.* p. 16.
[2] For his influence on Joseph Chamberlain, see *Life of Joseph Chamberlain*, I, p. 494.
[3] *Ibid.* p. 8.

was an entity—called 'England' by people who called themselves English and 'Britain' by people who called themselves Scots—which won the battle of Waterloo and occupied Vancouver Island and is therefore a Great Power. The qualification was that the bill-boards on the Pacific Highway, announcing that Vancouver Island is 'a little bit of old England', state the literal truth and not advertisers' blarney. Vancouver Island is a bit of England beyond the seas because 'we' settled it; and it does not matter that since 'we' did that lots of people from lots of odd places have built their frame-houses on that delectable island. Indeed, Trois Rivières, in spite of its name, is also a little bit of old England. On the other hand, India is not, apparently because though 'we' conquered it, we ruled it with an Indian Army.

Seeley did not justify these assumptions nor even state them: they are simply implicit in his disquisition. Nor did he invent them. They had grown up over a century or more and were the common currency of academic and political discussion. Seeley's audience would have been surprised and disgusted had he challenged them—though probably he did not even think of it. What the *Expansion of England* did, therefore, was to apply current prejudices to the new situation developing through the industrialisation of France and Germany, the increasing activity of the Russian Government, and the growth of the population of the United States. The claim of 'England' to be the greatest of the Great Powers was being challenged, and Seeley was able to prove from his assumptions that 'England' would still occupy her proud position provided that she brought England beyond the seas back into the English State.[1]

J. A. Froude, the Oxford historian, cannot be pinned down so easily. He was a friend and disciple of Thomas Carlyle and therefore

[1] As we shall see, the assumptions also led to the conclusion that the most dastardly act that any politician could propose was the dissection of 'England' by granting Home Rule to the Irish. Hence Seeley was a vigorous opponent of Home Rule: Sir J. R. Seeley, *The Growth of British Policy*, I, p. xx. On the other hand, the Home Rulers could point out that 'Ireland' was not part of 'England'. The former was a nation in her or its own right, with the same sort of perpetual succession. She or it had masses of grievances against 'England' which justified the Irish in asking for Home Rule or even independence. Professor Dicey, another Unionist, had therefore to protest against 'this delusion of personification': A. V. Dicey, *England's Case against Home Rule*, pp. 10–11; and *post*, pp. 330–2.

276

had prejudices besides those of imperialism. When Lord Carnarvon, to Disraeli's unconcealed disgust, sent Froude to South Africa in 1874 as his emissary, Froude found himself in sympathy with the Boer way of life and concluded that all the British Government needed was a naval base and a coaling station at the Cape. This attitude differed from that adopted in his earlier writings, which were strongly imperialist. Later, with *Oceana*, which was published in 1886 and therefore three years after Seeley's *Expansion of England*, he came back to imperialism. *Oceana* might be described in modern terminology as the log of a journey by a V.I.P. in Australia and New Zealand. Its model was Dilke's *Greater Britain*, but it was a very inferior production and would not be worth mentioning were it not that 75,000 copies were sold within a year. Whether this popularity was due to the anxiety of people to learn about these remote colonies, or to the interest aroused by Froude's views on imperial policy, cannot now be ascertained. Probably the popularity was due to the strength of imperialist sentiment, which was now at its peak. In respect of politics the book repeats the usual criticism of the Manchester School and the hoary story about the secret intention of the Liberals to get rid of the colonies. The colonies are, however, useful because they enable the people to leave the slums for the wide open spaces. There is also the old story that a great nation cannot remain great if it relies on underselling its neighbours in calicoes and iron-ware; and there is the rather newer story that 'England's' competitors are catching up. Only the colonies can save England from being reduced to a minor State like Holland. So far, the book is nothing more than an inferior attempt to make the imperialist case look rational. It goes on to argue about various devices for attaching the colonies more closely to the mother country and concludes that the strongest bonds of union are the spiritual bonds, by which he means loyalist sentiment on the one side and imperialist sentiment on the other.

Obviously there is not much of novelty in this: nor was there much in the sequel, *The English in the West Indies*, published in 1888, except a general impression that in the West Indies English civilisation was receding before a revival of barbarism. It is, however, difficult to assert that much of novelty could have been said. The argument of

Empire was getting worn out. Imperialism was at its peak and was kept high by the Queen's Jubilees, the Colonial Conferences, Cecil Rhodes, the Boer War, and the Tariff Reform controversy. It can now be seen, however, that it was slowly declining, partly because the rise of German power recalled public attention to Europe, and partly because Conservative imperialism was so much involved in the conflict over Home Rule.

The last of the apostles, Joseph Chamberlain, learned his imperialism from Sir Charles Dilke,[1] but he was an apt pupil because he was by nature pugnacious and because he was a manufacturer of screws. The fact that there was nothing about the British Empire in the *Radical Programme* suggests that, in 1885, he thought it could not be used to catch votes, at least by the Liberal party. But the views expressed by him on foreign and imperial questions in the Cabinets of 1880–5 and 1886 made it easy for him to follow the imperialist line when he became an ally of the Conservative party. As a Liberal, he had not favoured the permanent occupation of Egypt, but he changed his mind when he visited Sir Evelyn Baring (afterwards Lord Cromer) in Egypt in 1889. Nor was there any inconsistency in this particular change. Baring was himself a Liberal, and was offered (but refused) the Foreign Office by Campbell-Bannerman in 1905. He wrote the Liberal proconsul's creed, from which some lines may be quoted:

> Is there no profit when the slave
>   Who groaned beneath the tyrant's ban,
> Crushed from the cradle to the grave,
>   Has learnt the dignity of man?
> Is there no profit when the flood
>   Is poured upon the fruitful soil
> To cheer the peasant's sullen mood,
>   And yield a recompense to toil?
> Is it no gain that wisdom's light—
>   The child of Science and of God—
> Should pierce the black Egyptian night
>   Spread where the Sultan's horse has trod?

---

[1] *Life of Sir Charles Dilke*, II, pp. 94 *et seq.*; *Life of Joseph Chamberlain*, I, pp. 494–6.

> Is it no gain to stem disease,
> To let the humble joy in life,
> To grant the peasant rustic ease,
> Where all erstwhile was fear and strife?[1]

This came from a greater than Chamberlain, and it never became Chamberlain's brand of imperialism; but it was not inconsistent with the *Radical Programme* nor inappropriate for the pupil of Sir Charles Dilke. If it were permissible to interpolate four inferior lines the whole might be the policy of both parties in the middle of the twentieth century:

> Is it no gain to teach the way
> To rule by motion, speech and vote,
> Obey the rules of Erskine May,
> Study the books that Bagehot wrote?

That, as it happened, was not what Cromer taught nor Chamberlain learned.

Nor did Chamberlain raise the imperial cry at the general election of 1892. He had made a few flights of fancy. In 1887, at Toronto, he had annexed the United States. 'They are our flesh and blood.... Our past is theirs. You cannot if you would break the invisible bond which binds us together. Their forefathers are our forefathers. They worshipped at our shrines. They sleep in our churchyards. They helped to make our institutions, our literature and our laws. These things are their heritage as much as ours....'[2] The Irish Americans on the other side of Lake Superior must have loved it. In 1889, while expressing doubts about the practicability of Imperial Federation, he desired 'to draw closer the ties which unite us with kindred races and with the nations that own our rule'.[3] But at the general election he fixed on two main lines of argument. 'First, the Ulster question and the appeal to Nonconformists. Second, the social question and the appeal to the working classes.'[4] His task was to win the Midlands; his allies the Conservatives could win the imperialist vote. At the general election of 1895 he was already Colonial Secretary.

[1] Marquess of Zetland, *Lord Cromer*, p. 17.
[2] *Life of Joseph Chamberlain*, II, p. 334. [3] *Ibid.* p. 468.
[4] *Ibid.* II, p. 540.

279

Chamberlain asked for the Colonial Office 'in the hope of furthering closer union between [the colonies] and the United Kingdom'.[1] He had long seen the possibilities of the office, and his choice bears witness to the strength of imperialist sentiment in the Unionist parties. He gave that sentiment so much rope that, like Judas, it went and hanged itself. We have seen how Disraeli's imperialism encouraged the pro-consuls to go prancing, to the great embarrassment of his Government. Chamberlain's imperialism similarly encouraged the 'Colossus', Cecil Rhodes. Though Chamberlain was not in the conspiracy which led to the Jameson Raid and tried to stop it as soon as he heard about it, it probably would not have happened had there been a Liberal Government in power. The stationing of Jameson's force on the Transvaal border was Rhodes' act, but it was intended to support an Uitlander rising in Johannesburg, not a foolish attempt to start a rebellion by invasion. Even so, there were enough grounds for suspicion to put the Colonial Office upon enquiry. Rhodes relied upon the acceptance of a *fait accompli* by the British Government and by public opinion in England.

Public opinion was indeed Jingoist, especially after the Kaiser's telegram to President Kruger. Sir William Harcourt's Radical bio-grapher has said: 'On the one side was all the wealth and fashion of the day, inspired by the double motive of imperialism and gain; on the other was the remnant of the Liberal party which, in the tide of specula-tion and Jingoism which was sweeping over the country, remained attached to the traditions of Cobden, Bright and Gladstone.'[2] But the two sides were not of equal weight, and the one side contained far more than 'wealth and fashion'. Harcourt's own phrase was 'stock-jobbing imperialism'.[3] There were a great many imperialists and not many stock-jobbers; but Rhodes was an unscrupulous capitalist adventurer as well as an imperialist, and there was a nasty odour of foul frontier politics about the Jameson Raid which became evident through the proceedings of the Select Committee. It would have been even stronger if the attempt to blackmail Chamberlain into suppressing the enquiry had been known.[4] Chamberlain himself asked (privately) what there was in South Africa which made blackguards of all who got involved in

[1] *Life of Joseph Chamberlain*, III, p. 5. [2] *Life of Sir William Harcourt*, II, p. 388.
[3] *Ibid.* p. 389. [4] *Life of Joseph Chamberlain*, III, pp. 108–16.

its politics;[1] and though many of the facts were not publicly known, a growing body of opinion in Britain began to associate imperialism with shady financial deals and corrupt capitalist politics.

On the other extreme was the right wing of the Conservative party— called by Chamberlain himself the Jingo party—which even in 1896 wanted war with the Transvaal.[2] At this stage, however, nearly everybody was more or less of a Jingo, to an extent which many of their children and most of their grandchildren found nauseating. 'It is not easy, perhaps it is not possible', said Chamberlain's biographer of Queen Victoria's Diamond Jubilee in 1897, 'for living recollection to suggest even faintly to a later age what depth of reverential emotion, what breadth of political vision [?imagination] entered into those days of changing pageantry; nor what were the alternating pulses of affection and pride; nor what was the imaginative power of historic association....'[3] This, however, underestimates the historical imagination of the ensuing generations. They did not understand Victorian imperialism, but they knew how their fathers and grandfathers felt, for Jingoism had become a period piece; and they disliked it almost as much as they disliked Victorian silver and architecture.

Jingoism was not, however, a British monopoly. In West Africa the French had already cut off the Gambia and Sierra Leone from their hinterland and were threatening to do the same for the Gold Coast, Lagos, and the Niger Colony. Had they not been impeded there would never have been a Ghana or a Nigeria. In East Africa Kitchener defeated the Mahdi at Omdurman and then found that the French had established themselves on the White Nile at Fashoda. That problem was eventually settled by their withdrawal, thus giving the present Republic of Sudan its southern provinces. Nor were the Germans backward. In West Africa they were pressing for the expansion of Togoland into the hinterland of the Gold Coast. In East Africa they obtained what is now called Tanganyika. In China they seized Kiao-Chau. Simultaneously the Russians obtained Port Arthur on lease.

---

[1] *Ibid.* p. 114.   [2] *Ibid.* p. 138.

[3] *Ibid.* p. 195. Nevertheless, the Victorians knew how to make a good thing out of a good thing. Mrs Chamberlain wanted a large house for one night for a grand reception: she was offered one for 3000 guineas: *ibid.* p. 197.

Since Britain obtained nothing in compensation, the Government was attacked in Parliament by its own back-benchers. Even the United States declared war on Spain and liberated Cuba, an event which enabled Chamberlain, in his speeches, to revert to the 'racial' theme of Sir Charles Dilke and extol 'Anglo-Saxondom'.

It was, however, in South Africa that Victorian imperialism came under test. The Jameson Raid deprived Rhodes of his Afrikaner support, and he lost his dominating position as Prime Minister of Cape Colony, but Alfred Milner was sent out as High Commissioner. Milner was one of Jowett's young men. The accusation made against the promising young literary men produced by Cambridge in Tennyson's generation, that they just fell short of greatness,[1] might also be addressed to the young politicians and administrators produced by Oxford in the nineteenth century. Milner's is perhaps a special case, for he was born in Germany of a German-born father, though since his paternal grandfather was British he also had British nationality;[2] and his mother was English. Though he was sometimes accused of having Teutonic characteristics, it was probably his imperialism which made him blind to the strength of the case for the Boers of the Transvaal. It is now permissible to conclude, from a study of the available documents, especially those in the *Milner Papers* and the *Life of Joseph Chamberlain*, that the Boer War need never have happened.

Political controversy is however based not on what did happen but on what was known or suspected to have happened. Whether 'suzerainty' was or was not a correct description of the relation between the United Kingdom and the South African Republic does not, for our purposes, matter. With few exceptions British opinion was not prepared to concede what President Kruger really wanted, the status of an independent South African Republic. The word suzerainty itself was unfortunate: but when once it was used—and Kruger was the first to use it—there was no question of any concession. This was one of the consequences of Victorian imperialism. The Uitlanders had grievances, but British opinion did not really consider whether these were serious enough to justify a war; nor did it realise to what extent the Transvaal

---

[1] Esmé Wingfield-Stratford, *History of English Patriotism*, II, p. 371.
[2] The law was changed in 1914.

Government was prepared to make concessions in order to avoid a war. Milner, after the first twelve months, believed that the grievances could not be remedied except by force, and his published dispatches were coloured by that belief. Nor was British opinion prepared for large concessions to Boer opinion which would have 'let down' the Uitlanders: many of them were British subjects, and the Palmerstonian tradition was stronger than ever. On the other hand, British opinion did not want war; neither did the British Government nor even Chamberlain. Nor is it true that Chamberlain deliberately led British opinion to favour war: the most that can be said is that, realising that war might be necessary, he did his best to educate public opinion towards so believing. It was not 'Chamberlain's war', though it might be described as 'Milner's war': if a peaceful solution was possible through Kruger's concessions—there was no question of compromise —Chamberlain did not want war, and therefore he counselled patience.[1] If he avoided war he would probably have had trouble with his Jingo party, but he could carry opinion in the House of Commons and in the constituencies. On the other hand, if it came to war he wanted to carry public opinion into the war.

Liberal opinion was unanimous in distrusting Chamberlain. His great weakness as a politician was that he was always a partisan: he could never 'speak for England' even when England was imperialist. He was a political 'bruiser', as well as a Radical renegade, and he never pulled his punches. His speeches roused the enthusiasm of his supporters but the ire of his opponents. Though the Liberal imperialists supported the war, they never supported Chamberlain; and, because neither Lord Salisbury as Prime Minister nor Lord Lansdowne as Secretary of State for War could make warlike speeches, and because both were in the House of Lords, Chamberlain seemed to be running the war. The attitude of the Liberal imperialists was, however, determined by Paul Kruger. The Boers were not as recalcitrant as they were depicted. The Transvaal Government, advised by Jan Christian Smuts, had tried hard to reach a compromise.[2] Smuts, though a young man,

---

[1] He instructed Milner to continue the Bloemfontein Conference, but Milner had already terminated it without instructions.

[2] S. G. Millin, *General Smuts*, I, chs. XI–XIII.

283

had a broader approach than his colleagues, partly at least because he was educated in England. When these efforts failed and it became obvious that there would be a war, the Republican Government decided to declare it before British reinforcements reached South Africa; and the Boer ultimatum was so framed not only that the Unionist Government was bound to reject it, but also that Liberals who did not feel able to go behind the ultimatum had to support the Government.

The Boer War was a 'little war' in the sense that the success of the Boers would not have involved the stability of the United Kingdom. Had the British people not been prepared to find the money and the troops, or been able to provide the equipment, South Africa might have been lost to the British Empire. This in turn would seriously have diminished what nationalists call 'British prestige', especially when it was seen that everywhere in Europe sympathy was given to the Boers. Thus, Radical opinion had not to face the dilemma of 1914 or Fox's dilemma during the French wars. Radicals could continue to attack the Government, and the renegade Chamberlain in particular, for the policy which led to the war. On the other hand, the Liberals who had been infected by imperialist sentiment could both support the war and criticise Chamberlain. There was thus a split in the Liberal party between the Liberal imperialists and the 'Little Englanders' or 'Pro-Boers'.[1] On the one side were Rosebery, Asquith and Haldane; on the other were Harcourt and Lloyd George, with Campbell-Bannerman occupying an intermediate position.

There is no doubt that public opinion strongly favoured the Government, especially after the initial successes of the Boers in Natal and Cape Colony. This was especially so among the wealthier classes, whose sons volunteered in large numbers for service on the veld, and whose daughters went out to Cape Town to be one of Milner's most difficult problems. Jingoism was dominant; and the popular rejoicing at the relief of Mafeking added the naughty word 'mafficking' to the English language.

On the other hand, the Pro-Boers kept going a stream of anti-war,

[1] A phrase derived, however, from Chamberlain's electioneering at the general election of 1900: 'Every vote given against the Government is a vote given to the Boers': *Life of Joseph Chamberlain*, III, pp. 599, 600.

and therefore anti-imperialist, propaganda. They were helped by the publication in London of *A Century of Wrong*, written in Dutch by J. C. Smuts and translated into English by his wife. It was an emotional piece of war propaganda of which Smuts was afterwards ashamed:[1] but to the discerning reader it brought out the inevitable conflict between British imperialism and Boer nationalism. It was possible to depict the Uitlanders as British subjects who stood up against Boer oppression, as British subjects ought; but it was also possible to depict them as greedy gold-diggers who brought in the British Empire to increase their profits. The gallant young men who marched in column to be mown down by Boer sharpshooters carefully hidden in trenches and on kopjes were good war propaganda; but the generals who led them into these manoeuvres, and the heroism of the Boers themselves, convinced a few that the whole thing was very stupid. Lord Roberts and General Kitchener were sent out, relieved the besieged garrisons, and occupied Pretoria; but Lord Roberts had first to decimate the senior officers of the British Army and their staffs. The 24,000 volunteers from the self-governing colonies who joined the United Kingdom volunteers in South Africa were an advertisement for the British Empire; and Joseph Chamberlain and the other imperialists made the most of it; but they were also an advertisement for self-government.

On 1 September, 1900, Lord Roberts annexed the Transvaal in the Queen's name, and on 17 September the Queen dissolved Parliament. The 'khaki election' was defended on the ground that the Government needed a 'popular mandate' for the settlement;[2] it would also enable the Conservative party to 'cash in' on the war fever before it cooled; and even some Conservatives thought it was 'not cricket'. For the Unionists to win it was necessary that they should attack the Liberal imperialists as well as the Pro-Boers, and that the Liberals of all kinds should increase their attacks on Chamberlain. The fierce emotions of war were turned to the party battle. The quantity of mud thrown on either side has not been estimated.[3] Though the Liberal mud was stickier the Conservative mud was harder, and the Liberals were

---

[1] S. G. Millin, *General Smuts*, I, pp. 113–14.
[2] *Life of Joseph Chamberlain*, III, p. 585. It could not even wait for a new register.
[3] A few stones were thrown, too: *Life of Joseph Chamberlain*, III, p. 602.

knocked out. When the Boer War became an unpleasant memory it was 'Chamberlain's war', a war fought to fill capitalists' pockets,[1] an oppressive war against those 'good sportsmen',[2] Generals Botha and de Wet, a war in which our gallant soldiers were let down by their generals, who were of course supporters of the Conservative party, though their portraits had not been placed on Conservative posters, as those of their successors, Lord Roberts and Lord Kitchener, were.[3]

Moreover, though the Government had a large majority, it was smaller than in 1895. The Liberals (with Labour) won ten more seats in England and four more in Wales, but they lost five in Scotland. Of the total votes cast (ignoring the Nationalists) the Conservatives had only 52·4 per cent, a slight increase over the percentage of 1895. Had the Parliament of 1895 been allowed to run the normal six sessions, in fact, the Liberals might have won.[4] The war was by no means over. The Boer commandos took to the veld and the hills. Kitchener could deal with them only by farm-burning and concentration camps. This went on until the Treaty of Vereeniging of May 1902. Meanwhile the war hysteria had died and imperialist sentiment generally was running down. Queen Victoria was dead and the war profiteers were making merry in Mayfair. The war of the employers against the trade unions had its greatest success in the Taff Vale judgment, and the Government refused to reverse it.

One reason for the gradual running down of imperialist sentiment was that a long guerrilla war was necessarily boring to readers of newspapers who had other things to get excited about. The middle classes began to count the cost of Empire when the income tax was raised to the intolerable figure of fourteen pence in the pound, and there seemed to be no end to the operations for which they had to pay. The working classes, on the whole, were no longer interested in the war, and their opinions were beginning to count because, as the rise of the Labour party and the increasing strength of the trade unions showed, they were becoming conscious of their political power. The Liberals were still divided at first, and indeed the division became more acute as the

---

[1] Including, according to the Liberals, Chamberlain pockets: 'The more the Empire expands, the more the Chamberlains contract': *Life of Joseph Chamberlain*, III, p. 613.
[2] *Life of Sir Henry Campbell-Bannerman*, II, p. 8.   [3] *Ibid.* I, p. 291.
[4] Lord Milner thought so: *Life of Joseph Chamberlain*, III, p. 621.

Pro-Boers became more active. Campbell-Bannerman in effect joined them and spoke of 'methods of barbarism', while the Liberal imperialists attacked Chamberlain and Milner but defended Kitchener.

The Peace of Vereeniging helped to reunite the Liberals and brought politics round to the old domestic issues—religious education, Ireland and free trade. The issue of Protection was raised by Chamberlain, as his biographer goes as near to admitting as a loyal biographer should,[1] to provide the Unionist parties with a policy which would stave off their gradual decline. The expansion of social services along the lines of the *Radical Programme*, brought up to date, would have been more attractive: but there was no question of being able to persuade the Conservative party. On the other hand there had been for some twenty years a strong protectionist group in that party;[2] the Boer War had cost some £220,000,000 and heavy expenditure was needed to keep the strength of the Royal Navy ahead of that of the German Navy; and, above all, 'tariff reform' could be hitched to imperialist sentiment— whose gradual decline was not so obvious then as it is from this distance of time—by including in it a system of preferences in favour of colonial products. As Chamberlain put it in his speech at Glasgow in October 1903—and it became one of the standard texts for the Tariff Reform League:[3]

Our object is the realisation of the greatest ideal which has ever inspired statesmen in any country or in any age, the creation of an Empire such as the world has never seen. We have to cement the Union of the States beyond the seas; we have to consolidate the British race: we have to meet the clash of competition, fortified and strengthened and buttressed by all those of our kinsmen who speak our common tongue and glory in our common flag.

Imperial federation and other schemes of closer union were making no headway, but the self-governing colonies would welcome tariffs on foreign imports which competed with their own produce, and would no doubt be willing to negotiate about preferences on goods manufactured in the United Kingdom.

The story of the Tariff Reform movement belongs to another chapter.

[1] *Life of Joseph Chamberlain*, IV, p. 390.
[2] Benjamin H. Brown, *The Tariff Reform Movement in Great Britain, 1881–1895*.
[3] *Speakers' Handbook of the Tariff Reform League* (6th ed., 1910), p. 257.

Its vigour and failure had, however, some effect on imperialist sentiment. Tariff Reform united the Liberals on a policy of free trade, represented most effectively and persuasively by 'cheap bread' or the 'big loaf'. J. A. Hobson had produced in his *Imperialism* in 1902 a persuasive demonstration that imperialism was a device of the wealthier classes to line their pockets and find jobs for their sons. The Tariff Reform movement was inevitably represented as another device of the landowners and the manufacturers to increase their rents and profits at the expense of the standard of living of the working classes, who would contribute to those rents and profits through the 'dear loaf' or the 'small loaf', increased prices for textiles, and so forth. Imperialism was thus represented as a money-making device of the profiteer, and 'imperialist' became more and more a term of abuse. Even in 1904 Campbell-Bannerman was able to describe the Unionists as those who 'when in doubt played the Empire'.[1] According to Lloyd George, who was of course biased, the agitation for conscription in 1914–16 aroused antagonism because it was conducted by persons who 'were associated in the public mind with extreme Jingoism'.[2] After 1918 even 'Empire' was a dangerous word, and it was gradually superseded by 'Commonwealth'.

There was, however, a kind of afterglow of the Boer War imperialism, a rather cold and academic light radiating from Oxford. To assist him in the rehabilitation of South Africa the arch-imperialist, Lord Milner, recruited a band of young Oxford men called, inevitably, the Kindergarten. They included Lionel Curtis, R. H. Brand (afterwards Lord Brand), Philip Kerr (afterwards Marquis of Lothian), John Dove, Patrick Duncan, Richard Feetham, Lionel Hichens, Dougal Malcolm, J. F. Perry, Geoffrey Robinson (afterwards Dawson) and Hugh Wyndham (afterwards Lord Leconfield).[3] They were all liberal Conserva-

---

[1] *Life of Sir Henry Campbell-Bannerman*, II, p. 160.
[2] *War Memoirs of David Lloyd George*, II, pp. 712–13.
[3] J. R. M. Butler, *Lord Lothian*, pp. 14–15. In the photograph in J. E. Wrench, *Geoffrey Dawson and his Times*, facing p. 80 (Sir) Herbert Baker is included. Dougal Malcolm was not recruited by Milner; he went to South Africa as Lord Selborne's private secretary. Cecil Headlam (*Milner Papers*, II, pp. 381–3) includes three others, John Buchan (afterwards Viscount Tweedsmuir), Basil Williams, and Lord Basil Blackwood. Several of the group came from the College of which Milner had been Scholar and Fellow, New College.

288

tives, educated as imperialists, and enthusiastic supporters of Milner's brand of imperialism. They did a variety of jobs with energy and enthusiasm, though not always with the judgment which one would have expected from older men not so emotionally committed. They came together, after Milner's recall, in a house designed by Herbert Baker and built by Feetham.[1] Feetham, Wyndham, Brand and two others lived there, but it was called the *Moot House* and was used for meetings by members of the Kindergarten. It was there that the *Selborne Memorandum* was written by Lionel Curtis in consultation with the Kindergarten. The purpose of the Memorandum, which was submitted to the Secretary of State by the High Commissioner, Lord Selborne, and published, was to demonstrate that self-government for the four South African colonies implied some form of closer union, probably a federal union.

The problem which the Kindergarten had in mind, however, was not merely closer union in South Africa but closer union in the British Empire. British South Africa—and the adjective must be emphasised— was to take its place as a self-governing unit in the wider unit of the Empire, which would also include the United Kingdom, Canada, Australia and New Zealand. Their point of departure was Lord Milner's farewell speech at Johannesburg on 31 March 1905:

The words 'Empire' and 'Imperial' are perhaps in some respects unfortunate. They seem to suggest domination, ascendancy, the rule of a superior State over vassal States: but, as they are the only words available, we must just make the best of them, and try to raise them in the scale of language by giving them a new significance. When we who call ourselves Imperialists talk of the British Empire, we think of a group of States, all independent in their own local concerns, but all united for the defence of their own common interests and the development of a common civilization; united, not in alliance—for alliances can be made and unmade, and are never more than nominally lasting—but in a permanent organic union. Of such a union the dominions of our Sovereign as they exist today, are, we frankly admit, only the raw material. Our ideal is still distant, but we deny that it is either visionary or unattainable. And see how such a consummation would solve, and, indeed, can alone solve, the most difficult and the most persistent of the

---

[1] J. E. Wrench, *op. cit.* p. 54; but Sir James Butler (*op. cit.* p. 14) says it was owned by Wyndham.

problems of South Africa; how it would unite its white races as nothing else can. The Dutch [i.e. the Afrikaners] can never own a perfect allegiance merely to Great Britain. The British can never, without moral injury, accept allegiance to any body politic which excludes their motherland. But British and Dutch alike could, without loss of integrity, without any sacrifice of their several traditions, unite in loyal devotion to an Empire-State, in which Great Britain and South Africa would be partners.[1]

When the Kindergarten broke up, those members who returned to the United Kingdom, and those who remained in South Africa, retained this ideal. As under Lords Milner and Selborne, the hub of the new imperialism was Lionel Curtis, whose home became All Souls College, Oxford; a charming home, essentially Conservative (though some of its Fellows could be liberal or even Liberal), closely involved in the series of relationships which is sometimes called the 'Establishment'.[2] The *Moot* of Johannesburg was transferred to Oxford. The rump of the Kindergarten, strengthened by the inclusion of Lord Milner, Lord Selborne and L. S. Amery, was further strengthened by the addition of (Sir) Reginald Coupland, Edward Grigg (afterwards Lord Altrincham), F. S. Oliver, and Lord Robert Cecil.[3] It had close connexions with *The Times* through Amery, Grigg and Robinson (Dawson). Its close connexion with the Conservative party—or perhaps it should be said with the more academic side of that party, not the Bonar Laws, the Beaverbrooks or even the Balfours—was obvious from the names. Its influence was extended by the foundation in 1910 of the *Round Table*, of which Philip Kerr (Lord Lothian) was editor from 1910 to 1916. Through Kerr it was connected with Lord and Lady Astor, whose home, Cliveden, provided a meeting place for the 'Moot' and, in the thirties, gave a name to the sinister 'Cliveden Set', which was alleged, quite wrongly, to be doing a deal with Hitler.

The members of the Moot were not, however, entirely agreed. Lionel Curtis thought always in terms of a federal Empire or Commonwealth—and indeed he invented the latter name.[4] For Curtis the

[1] C. Headlam, *Milner Papers*, II, p. 547. [2] Volume I, pp. 236–40.
[3] J. R. M. Butler, *Lord Lothian*, pp. 35–6.
[4] W. E. Forster, one of the Radical imperialists, said in 1876 that colonists were the founders of a Commonwealth: 227 Hans. Deb., 3rd ser., 1726, quoted by A. P. Thornton, *The Imperial Idea*, p. 46. Lord Rosebery, in a speech at Adelaide in 1884, said that there was no need for any nation to leave the Empire 'because the Empire is a commonwealth

problem was 'whether the Dominions are to become independent republics, or whether this world-wide Commonwealth is destined to stand more closely united as the noblest of all political achievements'.[1] Philip Kerr, who knew more about opinion in the Dominions, thought that the strength of Dominion nationalism made any kind of organic union impracticable,[2] and he strove for world federation. In the short term, at least, the ideas of the Moot had no future. They influenced some sections of opinion in the Conservative party, whose second-line politicians, not actively engaged in running the party, have never quite given up the idea that somehow the Commonwealth can be converted into an entity, a 'Great Power'. The emotional strands left by nineteenth-century imperialism have therefore persisted but, though they have been shared by many in Canada, Australia, New Zealand and South Africa, the emotion has never been strong enough to suggest that the Commonwealth could have any kind of corporate existence. Meanwhile, too, emphasis had shifted to those under British rule in Asia and Africa.

Lord Milner in South Africa and Lord Curzon in India were the last of the great proconsuls. Lord Curzon's royal progresses in Asia appeared a little ridiculous to sceptical Liberals, especially when their magnificence, and the competitive magnificence of the Maharajahs, were contrasted with the poverty of the peasant and the rising nationalism of the Indian National Congress. Superficially the Royal Durbar of 1911 was a great imperial triumph, but it represented an Indian Empire that was passing away. In South Africa the Boer War had ceased to be a glorious enterprise. A Royal Commission had conducted a post-mortem and had condemned the Government's inefficiency. The Rand millionaires—as the Uitlanders were now called—had refused to pay their share of the cost of reconstruction, and there was a widespread opinion that the war had been fought to enable them and war profiteers at home—among whom family connexions of the Chamberlains were

of nations'. Lionel Curtis did not know of these precedents, but he used the word in a series of 'eggs' drafted by him for consideration by his friends. This particular 'egg' was hatched in 1916 in a study called *The Problem of the Commonwealth* which was incorporated in a larger work on *The Commonwealth of Nations*.

[1] *The Problem of the Commonwealth*, p. xi.
[2] J. R. M. Butler, *Lord Lothian*, pp. 52, 57.

included—to line their pockets. To this disillusionment was added the disgust felt by so many in the United Kingdom at the importation of Chinese labourers under conditions which could be described, with the usual political exaggeration, as akin to slavery.

At the general election of 1906 Balfour accused the Liberals of being 'apostles of imperial disintegration';[1] but this old fable had been told to the younger electors' grandfathers. Its revival showed the straits to which the Conservative leaders were put in an election dominated not by imperialism, as Joseph Chamberlain had intended, but by labour questions, free trade, Church schools, 'Chinese slavery', and the weakness of a Government which had shed Chamberlain on the one side and Winston Churchill on the other. The increasing tension in the international situation through the ambitions of Kaiser Wilhelm kept a strong nationalism—it can hardly be called imperialism any longer—alive. The war of 1914–18 began as something of an adventure. Except on the extreme left, the German invasion of Belgium and the discovery that the Foreign Office had virtually pledged the United Kingdom Government to assist the French in the event of German aggression, consolidated opinion in favour of war. The Conservatives had been in favour of war even before the invasion of Belgium occurred. Their references to the staff discussions were a rationalisation. The growth of German power by land and sea had necessarily appeared both offensive and dangerous to those whose first article of faith was that 'England' was and ought to be the greatest of the 'great powers', especially on the sea. Though this Conservative opinion would never have supported an aggressive war against the German Emperor, it was not averse from teaching him a lesson once he had started a war.

Though war was in fact declared by a Liberal Government, and Liberals like Lloyd George and Winston Churchill became jingoes almost overnight, Conservative opinion made the running. What was now wanted was ultra-patriotic fervour to support a recruiting campaign, since the Liberals could not be expected to introduce conscription for the armed forces forthwith. As at the beginning of the Boer War, the adventurous and the patriotic rushed to join the Army as

[1] *Life of Sir Henry Campbell-Bannerman*, II, p. 211.

volunteers; the old men from the clubs and the Society ladies—always the old guard of the Conservative party—rushed to help the movement with speeches, autumn flowers and white feathers. The popular song of the moment, *Tipperary*, happened to be a good marching song:

> Good-bye, Piccadilly; farewell, Leicester Square.
> It's a long, long way to Tipperary,
> But my heart's right there.

In fact, the enthusiasm of the right wing suggests, in retrospect, that there were some by whom the first line of the refrain of the satirical song of the later stages of the war:

> Oh! Oh! Oh! it's a lovely war

could have been sung without satire in 1914.

As a matter of fact, the war was more unlovely than ever. After the usual retreat of the British Army, and the usual errors of the German generals, the Army was stuck in the mud of France and Flanders— except, of course, those millions who were buried there or were transported to the Dardanelles, Mesopotamia and Salonika—for nearly four years. Those who survived tended to believe, not only that 'war was too serious a matter to be left to generals and admirals', but also that there were elements of lunacy in nationalist politics. This was, of course, not a universal conclusion. Nationalist sentiment could still be whipped up, as the array of 'hard-faced men' on the Coalition benches of the House of Commons in 1918 showed very clearly. Lloyd George's 'khaki election' of 1918 was, like Chamberlain's in 1900, a great success in the short run, though in the slightly longer run even Lloyd George began to sigh for a little more liberalism. As in the early years of the century, there was a rapid decline in nationalist feeling after 1918. It was evidenced not only by the rise of the Labour party, but also by the increasing concern of politicians of all kinds with the 'League of Nations vote'.

Imperialism did not die without a struggle. As we have seen, Lionel Curtis and most of the *Round Table* group were arguing in favour of a federal Commonwealth even in 1916, and Curtis himself never gave up the idea. The word 'Commonwealth' was certainly acceptable,[1] but to the politicians of the self-governing Dominions of the twenties it meant nothing more than a collection—or perhaps a community—of independent nations owing allegiance to the Crown. The idea of a common policy in defence and foreign affairs, determined by the politicians of the United Kingdom after consultation with the Dominion politicians, was for a time maintained after it became clear that there was no hope of federal, confederate or quasi-federal institutions, but it clearly broke down in the Chanak incident of 1922 and the Locarno Treaty of 1925. Consultation, or at least the communication of proposals and decisions, was continued and still continues, though each of the Commonwealth nations follows its own line. There was, too, Conservative resistance to the idea that India should, in the near future, become a member of the 'club' with the same status as Canada or

[1] At the Imperial War Conference of 1917, Sir Robert Borden (Canada) used the phrase 'Imperial Commonwealth of United Nations' (W. K. Hancock, *Survey of British Commonwealth Affairs*, I, p. 53) and the Report of the Conference referred to 'autonomous nations of Imperial Commonwealth' (Dawson, *The Development of Dominion Status*, p. 175). Shortly afterwards General Smuts made a speech in which he spoke at length about 'the British Commonwealth of Nations' and said that the name 'British Empire' was misleading (Millin, *General Smuts*, II, pp. 43–7). This speech was printed as a White Paper and given a wide circulation as part of British war propaganda. Its theme, that the German Empire was an empire but the British Empire was a commonwealth or community of free nations, was repeated in countless speeches. In official documents, including the Covenant of the League of Nations, 'British Empire' continued in use until the Imperial Conference of 1926, when it did not suit General Hertzog (South Africa) except in a context which took away its nasty flavour. 'We are prepared to co-operate to the fullest extent in laying as solidly as possible the foundations of our Commonwealth of Nations...and here I wish to say a few words as to South Africa's attitude in regard to the Empire or British Community of Nations' (Dawson, *op. cit.* p. 329). Lord Balfour's neat drafting at the same Conference satisfied both the imperialists and the anti-imperialists '...autonomous Communities within the British Empire ...freely associated as members of the British Commonwealth of Nations'.

From 1926 the British Empire disappeared, except among the die-hards. Mr Winston Churchill sought a compromise in his Mansion House speech of June 1943: '...our world-wide Commonwealth and Empire. Some people like the word Commonwealth; others, and I am one of them, are not at all ashamed of the word Empire. But why should we not have both?' (Sir Edward Grigg, *The British Commonwealth*, p. 170). The obvious criticism, that the Commonwealth consisted of the countries peopled by Europeans and the Empire consisted of the countries peopled by Asians and Africans, lost much of its force when India, Pakistan and Ceylon became independent countries within the Commonwealth in 1947–8; but 'Commonwealth and Empire' has generally been regarded as a fad of the Churchillian wing of the Conservative party, an innocuous relic of Victorian imperialism.

Australia. The Government of India Act, 1935, was a Conservative compromise which gave too little according to the Indian politicians and too much according to the right wing of the Conservative party, led from the back-benches by Winston Churchill.

There was no jingoism about the war of 1939–45. The antagonism to Hitler had in fact been far stronger in the Labour party than in the Conservative party, a few sections of which were prepared to ignore *Mein Kampf* and the foul character of National Socialism in the hope of pacifying German nationalism and providing a barrier to the spread of communism. Hitler himself destroyed this section of opinion in 1938–9, and war was declared by a Conservative Government, with the support of the Opposition parties, not as an exercise in nationalism but as an unfortunate necessity. In 1940, in fact, the Conservative party virtually repudiated the Conservative politicians who had sought to pacify Hitler, and the war was conducted under Winston Churchill's leadership with impressive unanimity. The conditions of 1914–18 were not repeated and, though Churchill tried a 'khaki election' it was a complete failure. The Labour party at last achieved power and proceeded to establish independent nations in India, Pakistan, Burma and Ceylon. Nothing was left of the organic Commonwealth except the unity of the Crown, a rather vague Commonwealth sentiment (shared very unequally), and very active co-operation in many important fields, usually non-political. From 1950 even the unity of the Crown disappeared, and successive Conservative Governments have created new Commonwealth nations. 'Imperialism' has disappeared even from communist propaganda, perhaps because the only politicians engaged in empire-building are those of the Soviet Union. The naughty word of the second half of this century is 'colonialism'.

CHAPTER VII

JOHN BULL'S OTHER ISLAND

I. THE KINGDOM OF IRELAND

Nationalism in Ireland, as elsewhere, has its fictitious history. Darrell Figgis, writing in 1921, explained why the Irish Free State would become an entirely different member of the 'Commonwealth of Nations' (he dropped the 'British') from the other members. Ireland was an ancient nation and a mother country in her own right:

...it was she who, when in the eighth and ninth centuries Europe fell into decay after the barbarian in-roads, re-established and rebuilt European civilisation, sending her scholars with her books into every part of the continent of ruin. It was her missionaries indeed, who first brought Christianity to England, and her scholars who taught the first English poet his letters. Before the name of England was heard, the name of Ireland was known and respected. She possessed an intricate, if uncomplicated national polity when the neighbouring island was peopled by distinct and scattered populations of conquerors. By virtue of these ancient dignities she was accorded international rank long after England had risen to nationhood, and when invasion had brought her national polity to ruin and silenced the voice of poet and scholar.[1]

This piece of nationalist fiction has, of course, a foundation of fact. Though Ireland was not part of the Roman Empire, Christianity seems to have reached Ireland in the fifth century; and, in spite of the invasions of the Ostmen, Latin culture never completely died out, though in the seventh and eighth centuries it was confined to a few monastic centres. In the ninth century there were distinguished Irish scholars: but, as an American authority puts it:

Obviously it is unjustifiable (though it has been done) to regard the scholarship of gifted Irishmen who lived on the Continent in the ninth century... as evidence of scholarship in Ireland in the sixth, seventh or eighth century. We do not know where these later men obtained their knowledge; there is little reason to suppose that they got it in Ireland.[2]

[1] Darrell Figgis, *The Irish Constitution*, pp. 7–8.
[2] H. O. Taylor, *The Mediaeval Mind*, I, p. 180.

296

Except for the purpose of getting the record straight, nobody but an Irish nationalist cares whether they did or did not. To suggest that there was in the ninth century an Irish nation which sent 'her' scholars to civilise Europe is as unhistorical as to suggest that in the twelfth century there was an English nation which sent 'her' Norman administrators to put some order into Irish anarchy.

Darrell Figgis slipped easily from 'nation' to 'race'.[1] Others speak of the 'native Gaelic race' which was blended with the Anglo-Normans and some later settlers (for example, the Scots) to form, in the sixteenth century, an Irish nation.[2] That there was an Irish nation in the sixteenth century may be capable of argument; but if the formula 'native Gaelic race' means anything every one of those three words must be peculiarly defined. What in fact was done by the Irish nationalists, as in other parts of the British Isles, was to take a particular period, in this case the middle of the twelfth century, and to assume that the people then living in Ireland were 'native Irish'. All earlier migrations and conquests, including those of the Celts, the Danes and the Norsemen, contributed to make the 'native Irish'; all subsequent migrations and conquests, including those of the Normans, the English and the Scots, were intrusions upon the native Irish. This has the peculiar consequence that whereas in England the Normans became 'English', in Ireland they did not become 'Irish', or at least 'native Irish'. Nor did the Scots who migrated to Antrim, though earlier migrants from Britain, who were probably of more or less the same racial stock as the Scots, did become Irish. One explanation is that, though the Normans spoke French and the Scots probably spoke Gaelic, their descendants were settled mainly on the east and south coasts of Ireland, where English became the local language more quickly than elsewhere in Ireland. As in Wales and Scotland, English gradually pushed out the Celtic language; and the nationalists assume that Gaelic (or Irish) is the 'national' language of the 'native' Irish, though in fact the Gaelic-speaking peoples were originally migrants or invaders. In other words, Gaelic pushed out the indigenous languages and became 'indigenous' or 'native'; English pushed out Gaelic but remained 'foreign', at least for the Irish nationalists.

---

[1] *The Irish Constitution*, p. 9.
[2] E. Curtis and R. B. McDowell, *Irish Historical Documents*, p. 9.

Another reason for this peculiar convention is that from the eleventh century the records are much more numerous, the process of history becomes more obvious, and those who develop emotion over such a conflict as that over Home Rule read history in the light of their emotions. It is possible that Daniel O'Connell was 'native Irish' in the nationalist sense, though he had English as well as Irish forebears;[1] it is certain that Isaac Butt, C. S. Parnell and Eamonn de Valera were not. If we talk in 'racial' terms (that is, biological inheritance) Oliver Cromwell was probably more of a Celt than Eamonn de Valera is. Nevertheless, the political conflict between many of the English and many of the Irish in the nineteenth century was a 'national' conflict, and so it became necessary to have nationalist history. That history could be traced back to 1155 and not much further. Hence the Irish of 1155 were 'native Irish'.

The conflict could be traced back so far because of differences in the histories of Ireland and England. England under the Normans probably had a population of less than two millions,[2] among whom the Normans were proportionately few. The Normans were able to spread throughout England and into the richer parts of Wales and Scotland. They were not above empire-building in Ireland, but they had to estimate (collectively or individually) whether it was worth while to transport knights, men-at-arms and bowmen across the Irish Sea to seize land from the Irish kings when there was still land in Britain. Nobody in fact did so until 1169. Robert FitzStephen then went with a handful of knights because Dermot MacMurrough had obtained Henry II's promise of Norman help to recapture his kingdom of Leinster from Rory O'Connor. Richard FitzGilbert, Earl of Pembroke, commonly called Strongbow, followed because MacMurrough's ambitions grew with his initial successes: and Henry II followed Strongbow because he feared that the latter was becoming too mighty. Incidentally

[1] Among O'Connell's ancestors were persons named Richard Barrett, Christopher Segrave and Christopher Conway: see the Synopsis of the O'Connells of Kerry attached to John O'Connell, *Life and Speeches of Daniel O'Connell*, vol. II. Assuming these and their ancestors to be 'English' while the others and their ancestors (except as specified) were 'Irish', the Liberator was 7/32 of an Englishman. However, as the nationalists used to say in 'John Bull's other Ireland' (Ceylon), the mother-tongue descends on the father's side. Cf. E. L. Woodward, *The Age of Reform*, p. 325.

[2] A. L. Poole, *From Domesday Book to Magna Carta* (2nd ed.), p. 36.

the absurdity of the racial theory is shown by the fact that FitzStephen had a Welsh mother and that Strongbow's subsequent claim to Leinster came through his marriage to MacMurrough's daughter.

Pope Adrian IV had vested the lordship of Ireland in Henry II by a Bull of 1155[1] because the Popes assumed the right to give orders in temporal matters to all Christendom. The only condition in the 'grant' was the payment of Peter's pence, an obligation applying to England also. Henry II received the submission of most of the kings of Ireland when he visited that country in 1171–2. He vested the lordship in his younger son John; and when John became King of England it became annexed to the kingdom of England. By an Act of the Parliament of Ireland in 1541, however, Henry VIII assumed the title of King of Ireland;[2] and Ireland remained a separate kingdom, annexed to the Crown of England or (from 1701) Great Britain until 1800.

In practice, however, Norman or English rule extended, until the Stuarts, only over the eastern and south-eastern coastal strip. The bounds of this Anglo-Norman colony were imprecise, since they depended upon the balance of power between land-grabbing Anglo-Norman barons and predatory Irish kings. By the Treaty of Windsor, 1175, Henry II recognised Rory O'Connor as high-king of the territories not occupied by the Normans, and in that capacity as a liege of the English king. The treaty was unworkable because O'Connor could not make good his claim. In practice the treaty was ignored, and after the death of O'Connor there was no pretence of a high-king or any other single authority outside the colony. On the other hand, the colony was feudalised during the reign of King John and covered two-thirds of the land of Ireland. Indeed, the colony prospered under Norman rule and was known as the 'land of peace', whereas the rest of the country was the 'land of war'.[3]

It must not be thought that there were fixed boundaries. The Acts of the Parliament of 1297 give the impression of a sort of no-man's-land, the marches, in which the Norman barons were supposed to keep the peace, so far as they were able, by private war. Nor was the population

[1] E. Curtis and R. B. McDowell, *Irish Historical Documents*, p. 17.
[2] *Ibid.* pp. 17–18.
[3] A. L. Poole, *From Domesday Book to Magna Carta* (2nd ed.), p. 317.

of the colony exclusively Anglo-Norman. The Irish peasants were usually not expropriated; they exchanged Irish kings and chieftains for Norman lords. In other words, only the aristocracy was Anglo-Norman.

The fact that English rule did not extend over the whole of Ireland was the original cause of the political problem of Ireland. Though in the Celtic period the Irish had enjoyed a high standard of civilisation, the Danish and Norse invasions and internecine strife, and particularly the fact that the Irish churches were cut off from Rome, made Ireland in 1066 more backward than the southern counties of England. It was therefore easier for the Normans and the English to fuse than it was for the Normans and the Irish to fuse. Moreover the Anglo-Norman colony was founded a hundred years after the Norman conquest of England; and during that hundred years Norman efficiency had done much to raise English standards. The differences between Anglo-Norman and Irish standards were therefore so considerable as to make for what was almost a caste distinction. The process of assimilation eventually did occur, though there was a long transitional period in which a distinction could be drawn between the Anglo-Irish and the 'mere Irish' or 'native Irish'. What made it so difficult in Ireland was not only the considerable gulf between the Anglo-Normans and the Irish but also the existence of the 'wild Irishry' outside the King's peace, the 'Irish felons', as the Statutes of 1297 had called them.[1]

The Irish, whether within or without the King's peace, were governed by their own customary laws, though the King's writ ran in the colony[2] and the right to be regulated by English law was often granted as a franchise to Irishmen.[3] This distinction of laws, combined with the existence of 'Irish felons' outside the King's peace, made it necessary to distinguish between 'English' and 'Irish', just as in England immediately after the Conquest it was necessary to distinguish between 'Norman' and 'English'.[4] In both cases there was an element of superiority or even contempt in the distinction; but the distinction lasted much longer in Ireland than in England because, until the Stuarts,

---

[1] E. Curtis and R. B. McDowell, *Irish Historical Documents*, p. 33. 'Wild Irishry' was used in instructions to a new Viceroy in 1530: *ibid.* p. 79.

[2] *Ibid.* p. 31.

[3] F. M. Powicke, *The Thirteenth Century*, pp. 562–3.

[4] Pollock and Maitland, *History of English Law*, I, pp. 90–1.

English jurisdiction did not extend beyond the Pale; and unfortunately it was expressed in matters of record which could be quoted by Irish nationalists of the nineteenth century who, in the nationalist tradition which we have seen operating in England, assimilated themselves to the 'Irish' of the fourteenth century and regarded the English of the nineteenth as responsible for the 'English' in Ireland in the fourteenth century. The fact that some members of the Irish Nationalist party certainly had, and most of them probably had, Anglo-Irish ancestors was, of course, irrelevant. In the Irish nationalist indictment the English are alleged to have shown 'their' contempt for the Irish by 'their' language in the Statutes of 1297 and the Statutes of Kilkenny in 1366. The English nationalist would of course reply that, though it would perhaps have been wiser if these observations had been kept off the record, the documents show how remarkably the Irish have progressed since 'we' annexed Ireland. The debate continues.

However the Statutes of Kilkenny be interpreted, the fundamental cause was the decline of the Anglo-Irish colony since the Scottish invasion of Ireland under Edmund Bruce (and later his brother Robert) in 1315. This was in retaliation for Edward I's invasions of Scotland, and a large part of the country was laid waste before the Scots were defeated in 1318. The effect of this and subsequent events was that by 1341 one-third of the colony ceased to be under English rule. The process was not one of Irish encroachment. The English landowners in Connaught threw off their allegiance and, except in racial terms, became Irish. The Statutes of Kilkenny were an attempt by Lionel, Duke of Clarence, who was Lieutenant for his father, Edward III, to prevent the further decay of the colony. The effort was unsuccessful. Richard II made another attempt, but he was compelled to return to England to defend his throne against Henry of Lancaster, and there was further decline during the Wars of the Roses. Effectively English rule extended only to Meath, Louth, Kildare and Dublin, the area called the Pale after the great ditch was dug in 1454. Since there was weak government within the Pale and something like tribal warfare outside, the condition of the Irish people continued to deteriorate.

Weak government within the Pale and the failure of the English kings to look after their Irish patrimony led to a gradual estrangement between the Anglo-Irish and the English Government. The two pretenders to the English throne, Lambert Simnel and Perkin Warbeck, both received some support in Ireland. Henry VII had too much trouble at home to spare much thought for Ireland, but in 1494 he sent Sir Edward Poynings to put matters straight. Parliaments had been summoned in Ireland since the thirteenth century. In practice they were Anglo-Irish because, as in England, they were Parliaments of landowners. 'Anglo-Irish' in the fifteenth century does not mean 'English' in any racial sense. Since Strongbow married Dermot Mac-Murrough's daughter there had been constant inter-marriage, as the Statutes of Kilkenny testify. In spite of migration from Britain, a separate Anglo-Irish community, with ideas more Irish than English, had developed. In 1460, indeed, the Parliament of Ireland had passed legislation establishing Richard, Duke of York, as Lieutenant of Ireland, though he had been attainted in England.[1] This was, of course, an incident in the conflict between York and Lancaster; but it indicates, as does the support given to the pretenders under Henry VII, that an ambitious viceroy could use the Parliament of Ireland for his own purpose.

Poynings therefore secured the passing in 1495 of Acts, commonly called Poynings' Laws, to the effect that no Parliament could be summoned except by authority of the King in Council, and that the Bills to be passed should require the same authority.[2] This was enacted by the Parliament of Ireland in order to limit the authority of 'Dublin Castle', that is, the Lieutenant's deputy, but the Act could be suspended or repealed. It was sometimes suspended for particular Parliaments, though the Parliament of Ireland was reluctant to increase the deputy's power. In practice under the Tudors Bills sent from Ireland were sometimes altered in London and other Bills sent over for enactment. This practice was ratified by an Act of 1557.[3] In effect, therefore, Bills introduced into the Parliament of Ireland had to have previous sanction in London.

[1] E. Curtis and R. B. McDowell, *Irish Historical Documents*, pp. 72–6.
[2] *Ibid.* p. 83. There were many other 'Poynings' Laws', passed by the same Parliament, for the more efficient government of the Pale and its environs: J. D. Mackie, *The Earlier Tudors*, pp. 128–31.
[3] E. Curtis and R. B. McDowell, *op. cit.* p. 85.

Though Henry VIII was advised to conquer the whole of Ireland and plant it with loyal Englishmen, he could not afford to divert men and money from his continental adventures. The difficulty which all the Tudors had to face was that the revenues of Ireland were insufficient to support an army and they could not afford, or did not want to afford, the expense of maintaining such an army from English revenues. The Irish chieftains, on the other hand, could call out their clans. Hence the only solution was to play off one against another. Both Mary I and Elizabeth I sent over small bodies of troops, and both tried the planting of English settlers. In fact, however, Ireland suffered severely from war and pestilence while England was progressing remarkably.

Moreover a new problem had been created by the Reformation. The legislation of the Reformation Parliament was passed by the Parliament of Ireland, though reluctantly, and Henry VIII became Head of the Church of Ireland. This legislation had no effect outside the Pale and the great chieftains were indifferent. When the Counter-Reformation was extended to Ireland, therefore, it achieved considerable success, even in the Pale. In December 1605 more than two hundred leading gentlemen of the Pale petitioned against the exclusion of Jesuits and seminary priests.[1]

The flight of the Earls of Tyrone and Tyrconnell in 1607 enabled James I to undertake a new experiment in planting. Their lands in Ulster were deemed to have been forfeited to the Crown. A plan for their settlement was drawn up, but was never fully carried out. It did result, however, in the settlement of a considerable number of presbyterians in Ulster and so created another problem for Ireland. It had the effect, too, of drawing the Anglo-Irish Roman Catholics more closely to the 'Irish'.[2]

Indeed Sir Thomas Wentworth, afterwards Earl of Strafford, who became lord deputy in 1633, did his best to unite all classes against the Crown. He forced the English canons on the Church of Ireland, tried to force the Ulster Scots to repudiate the Covenant, and partially expropriated a great many landowners. He did, however, produce an efficient army and pacify the country, so that for the first time the whole

[1] R. Dunlop, *History of Ireland*, p. 87.
[2] *Ibid.* p. 91.

303

of Ireland was efficiently ruled. On the other hand, he created a whole host of grievances which became evident, not only in the Parliament of 1640, which was mainly Anglo-Irish (though the Roman Catholics and the Protestants were almost balanced), but also in the rebellion of 1641, which started in the Pale but became eventually a sort of peasants' revolt. The massacres which followed created a sensation in the English Parliament and inflamed the hatred of popery which had developed since the reign of Mary I. The Roman Catholic gentry eventually controlled the situation and formed a 'confederation' at Kilkenny in May 1642.

Though some sort of government was retained in the Pale throughout the Civil War, and the Irish were by no means united, the council established by the confederation was in fact a revolutionary junto. Since it could hope for nothing from the English Parliament, its main purpose was to secure from Charles I sufficient guarantees, including an Act declaring that 'the Parliament of Ireland is a free Parliament of itself, independent of, and not subordinate to, the Parliament of England'.[1] Had the confederation remained in control and made peace with King Charles, it is possible that after the execution of the King Ireland would have become an independent country. In 1645, however, a papal nuncio, Giovanni Battista Rinuccini, arrived in Ireland. His purpose was not only to secure the predominance of the Church of Rome in Ireland but also to restore the English Church to that faith. He succeeded in preventing agreement with the King; and when he led an army against Dublin in July 1647 the King's representative (the Marquess of Ormond), realising that he could not defend the city, surrendered it to the representative of the English Parliament, Colonel Michael Jones.

Colonel Jones completely altered the situation and was soon on the offensive. Since there was a Royalist reaction in Britain, the Confederates did not give up hope, but sent for Ormond, and at last, in January 1649, made a treaty with the King, though against the opposition of Rinuccini, who left the country. The Royalists were strengthened by the execution of the King, but Jones had been reinforced from England, and in August 1649 proceeded, at first under Cromwell and

[1] E. Curtis and R. B. McDowell, *Irish Historical Documents*, p. 154.

then under other generals, to mop up the Irish garrisons and raiding parties, a process which lasted until terms of surrender were accepted in 1652.

Fighting of sorts had thus gone on for ten years, and the Irish inhabitants suffered severely. They may have suffered even more severely from the settlement, which involved the expropriation of all the lands of the Irish leaders, two-thirds of those of the subordinate leaders, and one-third of the lands of those who had not shown 'constant good affection' to the English Parliament. As a result, it is said that two-thirds of the land of Ireland changed hands.[1] The new landowners were, for the most part, English Protestants. Within a couple of generations the smaller landowners inter-married with the Irish, became Irish themselves, and very often Roman Catholics. The larger landowners were often absentees; but those who remained in Ireland became a Protestant caste. Sir William Petty estimated in 1672 that the total population of 1,100,000 was made up of 800,000 Roman Catholics, 200,000 English, and 100,000 Scots; but an estimate made seven years later suggested that more than half of the substantial houses were occupied by Protestants while only one-tenth of the cottages were so occupied.[2] In other words the division of religious belief was also a class division. Moreover the Protestants were not equally dispersed. Ulster became predominantly Presbyterian, inhabited by successors of the stern Covenanters for whom the Church of Rome was the Scarlet Woman.

Nor was the fighting over. Dick Talbot, Earl of Tyrconnell, a Roman Catholic and a personal friend of James II, was Lord Lieutenant of Ireland when James II left England in 1688. There was no revolution in Ireland, but the gates of Londonderry were closed against an Irish regiment, and other towns of Ulster followed Derry's example. Soon afterwards, James II landed in Ireland. It cannot be said, however, that he had much influence on events. After the relief of Derry and the defeat of an Irish army near Enniskillin, both armies adopted a policy of masterly inactivity until William III took command of the Protestant army and won the Battle of the Boyne on 12 July 1690. It was a famous

---

[1] G. Davies, *The Early Stuarts*, p. 162.
[2] D. Ogg, *England in the Reign of Charles II*, ii, p. 392.

victory, for it is celebrated by the Orange Lodges of Ulster every year. Nevertheless, it did not end the war. James II escaped to France, but the Irish (with French assistance) went on fighting until the treaties of Limerick in October 1691. Under the military treaty 12,000 Irishmen left Ireland for France. The civil treaty, which was generous to Roman Catholics, was never completely ratified by the Parliament of Ireland, and not even partially until 1697.

The Protestants who dominated that Parliament had suffered severely under Tyrconnell, and generosity is not a characteristic of Irish politics on either side. The Protestants did not intend to share their supremacy. 'To effect their object they were even prepared to barter some of their rights to the English Parliament, or, as Grattan expressed it, to kneel to England on the necks of their Catholic countrymen.'[1] But this begs the question. Which was the country of the Protestants, England or Ireland: and were the Ulstermen fellow-countrymen of the Roman Catholics of the south?

2. THE UNION WITH ENGLAND

Only nationalist politicians and their propagandists can, at this stage, put these problems in nationalist terms. The dominant sentiment in England was not an exclusive nationalism but fear of the restoration of popery through an invasion or an insurrection on behalf of James Stuart or the Old Pretender. The prospective allies of the papist Stuarts were the Roman Catholics of Ireland and the Scottish Highlanders; and the people who feared most from the former were the Ulstermen and the Protestants of southern Ireland. The Irish Jacobites actually gave less trouble than those of England and Scotland: but this may have been because the Roman Catholics were reduced to a state of subjection by the penal laws. Those laws were not strictly enforced. 'Though sometimes driven to concealment and always liable to minor hardships, a body of more than a thousand priests carried on its work in spite of the letter of the law. There were more than four thousand monks and nuns.'[2] While Protestants were still burned in France and Spain, no

[1] R. Dunlop, *History of Ireland*, p. 129.
[2] G. N. Clark, *The Later Stuarts*, p. 299.

306

Irish Roman Catholic suffered death for his religion. Even so, the penal laws built up a tradition of grievance which was felt all the more seriously because they were not in practice oppressive enough to produce leaders and stimulate rebellion. The Roman Catholic Irish were not slaves but second-class citizens. In the liberal Constitution which Englishmen extolled the Irish Roman Catholics played no part. Many of the best of them emigrated.

Fear of popery was not, however, the only reason. Most of the penal laws were passed by the Irish Parliament, and William III, at least, tried to tone them down. They were class legislation by the economically dominant faction. Moreover the worst of the laws were passed while the tories were in office under Queen Anne; they applied to dissenters as well as to Roman Catholics and therefore to the Scots of Ulster. The Church of Ireland thus tried to do by law what it had failed to do by persuasion, to secure a position of dominance. It completely failed, and the Roman Church progressed in Ireland throughout the eighteenth century.

Primarily these were problems of Irish politics; but after the Union the Roman Catholic politicians could regard the Irish Protestants as the 'English' and the Roman Catholics as the 'Irish'. In other words, the penal laws were oppression by 'England' of 'Ireland'. This could be made plausible by the fact that under Poynings' Laws the Crown had a veto. William III and his successors had to exercise their powers with discretion, for there was still a 'king across the water' and it would have been unwise to protect their enemies at the expense of their friends. On the other hand, the economic disabilities from which the Irish suffered—all the Irish—may have been made worse by English legislation. English policy was heavily protectionist in the first half of the eighteenth century, and Irish trade was directed into channels which benefited English producers and merchants. How serious this was cannot be estimated. On the one hand the linen industry prospered; on the other hand the woollen industry suffered: but the woollen industry would probably have suffered if there had been no legislation, for the woollen industry of the west of England and North Wales was suffering from Yorkshire competition, and was eventually wiped out, in much the same way. However, this economic legislation, too, was one of the grievances which 'Ireland' built up against 'England'. Even if the Irish had prospered under Protestant rule there would have been the same sense of grievance: for we now have enough examples from Asia and Africa to be able to assert the generalisation that the more prosperous a colony becomes under British rule the more serious political disabilities seem to the colonial people; and Ireland was treated as a colony.

The economic conditions of Ireland were, however, often very bad in the first half of the eighteenth century. The population was dependent on the harvest, which failed when the weather was bad, and there were severe famines from 1726 to 1729 and in 1740–1. Whether they would have been less severe if English legislation had encouraged the development of the wool trade may be arguable; but inevitably they increased the sense of grievance. After 1748 there was a modest prosperity, but as the industrial revolution developed in England, the lowlands of Scotland, and Ulster the disparity between the standards of Protestant and Roman Catholic became more marked. The most severe of all the famines came in the next century, in the hungry forties, and by that time the Irish Roman Catholics had politicians with a sense of mission fortified by a powerful sense of grievance. Their case was exaggerated, as is the way of politics: for politics deals with what is thought to be happening, not with what is happening: and, however interpreted, Irish history could hardly be held to favour British rule.

On the political plane there had developed at the end of the seventeenth century an argument about the power of the English Parliament to legislate for Ireland. It was not a nationalist argument, for it could lead to the conclusion that there ought to be a union between Great Britain and Ireland. In 1703, in fact, the Irish House of Commons, after reciting Irish economic grievances, petitioned for either the full enjoyment of the constitution or union.[1] This had no effect in England, for the Parliament of Ireland, unlike the Parliament of Scotland, was under control, and there was no threat to the Protestant Succession from Ireland as there was from Scotland. Scotland therefore got the economic benefits of union in return for a guarantee of the Hanoverian Succession: Ireland could offer no *quid pro quo*. It was a convenient

[1] G. N. Clark, *op. cit.* p. 308.

dependency in which jobs were found for good whig boys, lay and ecclesiastical, and which was for the most part governed by more or less docile lords justices.

In consequence of a decision of the Irish House of Lords, sitting in its judicial capacity,[1] the Parliament of Great Britain in 1719 passed the Declaratory Act declaring that the kingdom of Ireland was subordinate to the Crown of Great Britain and that the King in Parliament of Great Britain 'had, hath, and of right ought to have full power and authority to make laws and statutes of sufficient force and validity to bind the kingdom and the people of Ireland'. There was, however, no real conflict between the Parliament of Great Britain and the Parliament of Ireland. The system of control through 'loaves and fishes' which Walpole developed in Great Britain he extended to Ireland, with the great difference that there were no whig 'connexions' competing for power. Not until the reign of George III was there any real opposition to Dublin Castle. Then a small group of 'Patriots' developed in the Irish House of Commons. They were helped by the American War, which not only injured the economy of Ireland but produced a good deal of Irish sympathy for the Americans. After the British Parliament had refused to relax the restrictions on trade, a boycott, and the development of the Volunteer movement (designed to protect Ireland against the French, but capable of being used against Dublin Castle), proved convincing; and in 1779 the restrictions on trade were removed.

By now Henry Grattan had taken the lead, and he began at once to press for legislative independence. The Rockingham whigs being in office after the resignation of Lord North, the request was conceded by Acts of 1782 and 1783 which not only repealed the Declaratory Act of 1719, but also bound the Parliament of Great Britain not to legislate for Ireland.

The removal of commercial restrictions did not improve the economy of Ireland; nor did the removal of the restrictions on the powers of the Irish Parliament solve the problem of the constitutional relations between Great Britain and Ireland. The Irish Government was still controlled from London and, with William Pitt in power, it became increasingly tory while Grattan had more sympathy with the

[1] *Sherlock* v. *Annesley.*

309

whigs. Moreover the French Revolution had considerable influence in Ireland, particularly in Ulster, where the dissenting interest began to unite with the Roman Catholics. A pamphlet, written by Wolfe Tone, advocating unity, received wide support; and in 1791 the first Society of United Irishmen was founded in Belfast.[1] There had already been, in 1771, 1774, 1778, and 1782, some relaxation of the penal laws, and opinion in London was by no means averse from the conferment of the franchise on Roman Catholics. This was done by an Irish Act of 1793; but the Irish Parliament, in spite of Grattan's advocacy, refused to concede the right to sit in Parliament.

The alliance between the presbyterians of Ulster and the Roman Catholics did not last. Who started the private fights, the Peep o'Day boys who became the Orangemen or the Defenders who later joined the United Irishmen, is disputed by historians and does not matter. The Peep o'Day boys, who decided to turn the Roman Catholics out of Ulster under the slogan 'Hell or Connaught', were the more successful. The United Irishmen, now almost exclusively Roman Catholic, became a treasonable conspiracy. War between Britain and France having broken out in 1794, Wolfe Tone secured French assistance, but the French attempts failed and Wolfe Tone was captured and condemned to death; he committed suicide before he could be executed.

Pitt had never liked the whig legislation of 1782–3, and in principle he was right because it went either too far or not far enough. His solution was an Act of Union with complete Catholic emancipation but with a subordinate Irish legislature (that is, what was later called 'Home Rule'). The Act of 1793, enfranchising the Roman Catholics, was in accordance with that plan. The scheme eventually proposed did not, however, involve an Irish Parliament, though it did involve complete Roman Catholic emancipation, which would be unobjectionable because in a United Parliament the Roman Catholics would be in a small minority. The scheme of union went through the Irish Parliament only after much direct bribery, on both sides, though the Government had more money. Also, the Government had other advantages, in the way of peerages, places and pensions, which it did not hesitate to use. This

[1] R. Dunlop, *History of Ireland*, p. 147.

became another Irish grievance, though in fact the people bribed and honoured were Protestants, and the division of opinion, even without corruption, was not a division between Protestant and Roman Catholic or a division between enemies of the people and the Irish Roman Catholics. The undoubted grievance of the Roman Catholics was that, owing to the obstinacy of George III, Pitt was unable to propose Roman Catholic emancipation, and resigned.

3. HOME RULE

The Irish problem was an element in British politics from the American War until 1921, though only in a minor sort of fashion until 1830. Pitt was more liberal than most of his Cabinet colleagues, who were concerned much less with the prosperity of Ireland than with the dangers thought to be implicit in the enfranchisement of the Roman Catholics by the Act of 1793, which threatened the Protestant supremacy in Ireland. Charles James Fox took an even more liberal line, though what line he took was not very clear. The fact that George III rejected Catholic emancipation was, of course, one good reason why the whigs should support it; but they were very weak until the reaction against the effects of the French wars set in.

Roman Catholic relief was not, however, a party question. There were tories who favoured it and whigs who did not. The case against it was indeed very weak once the franchise had been conceded to Roman Catholics. Apart from the general prejudice against popery, which the Ulstermen felt even more strongly than the English Protestants, the only effective argument was that the Roman Catholic members of Parliament would be controlled by the clergy of the Church of Rome. The Parliament of the United Kingdom might have given way in 1812 if a veto on the appointment of Irish bishops had been conceded by the Church. The papal authorities were indeed willing to have their lists censored, but the Irish bishops would not consent. What compelled the Tory party to give way, however, was the discovery that Daniel O'Connell and his henchmen could capture every county constituency in which the majority of the forty-shilling freeholders was Roman Catholic. His method was highly organised 'mob oratory'. It was copied by the Anti-Corn Law League and the political parties, and its relics are still with us. His organisation was, however, more effective than that of any of his imitators because he could use the authority of the Roman Catholic priests to enforce political conformity. Usually the Church of Rome, while not in principle averse from engaging in politics, exercises its powers with some discretion, chiefly because, at least on issues which are not regarded as fundamental, Roman Catholic laymen may properly differ. In Ireland the political conflict was between Roman Catholics and Protestants (in County Clare, between O'Connell and a Vesey Fitzgerald). The objective, too, was to secure a Roman Catholic footing in a Protestant Parliament. Moreover the Irish priests were themselves sons of Irish peasants, as profoundly impressed with the wrongs of 'Ireland' as O'Connell himself.

Among Roman Catholic electors the combination of priests and politicians was irresistible. Those Roman Catholics who wanted to vote for a Vesey Fitzgerald—who was, after all, a better landlord than Daniel O'Connell—had to do it openly on the hustings, with the parish priest and his parishioners looking on. Clearly, too, this method of persuasion could be used in every Roman Catholic county in Ireland. Either the Roman Catholics had to be disfranchised, or they had to be allowed to sit in Parliament. Wellington and Peel decided for the latter, though they partially accepted the former also by raising the franchise from forty shillings to ten pounds, thereby virtually disfranchising the peasants, Protestant and Roman Catholic alike. The Tory party nevertheless split, and in 1830 the Reformers took office. Meanwhile the Irish Roman Catholics had ceased to be second-class citizens.

If the problem of Ireland be considered rationally—as, of course, it never was—Gladstone in 1868 came nearest to a solution. He put it in terms of the disestablishment of the Church in Ireland and of land reform. Disestablishment was necessary in order to get rid of the tithe, an onerous and unnecessary burden on the land because, even if the subsidisation of a church could be justified at all—and most of his Nonconformist supporters thought not—it was clearly not the United Church of England and Ireland, whose bishops and parsons had what were little better than sinecures. There were of course strong emotional elements in the arguments for and against Irish disestablishment, especially because of the 'thin end of the wedge' argument: but in rational terms the Irish Establishment could not be defended. The fundamental problem was, however, the low standard of living of the peasant, who was dependent on a potato crop which sometimes failed because of weather, blight and the impoverishment of the soil. Nothing could be done except by a vast measure of agrarian reform and the expenditure of large sums of public money, most of which would have to come from the taxpayers of Great Britain.

The Parliament of the United Kingdom was not unaware of the problem. Economic distress and the turbulent state of Ireland since the French Revolution produced violence and intimidation by secret societies. Between 1810 and 1833 there were 114 commissions and sixty select committees investigating matters relating to Ireland.[1] This was in a period when economic conditions were comparatively good in the aggregate, because until 1845 there had not been a severe famine affecting the whole country for three generations.[2] The absence of famine had, however, allowed the population to grow beyond the resources of the country. From about six millions in 1815 it rose to eight and a half millions in 1845.[3] It could not be expected, however, that the Parliament of the United Kingdom, or even a Parliament of Ireland, would take the necessary measures. The first step towards agrarian reform would be the wholesale expropriation of landlords: and though later in the nineteenth century this became a practicable proposition, it was simply impossible in the years after Waterloo. The fundamental right of property was, as we have seen, the basis of the Whig Constitution. Its maintenance was the essential purpose of that Constitution. Even to take away the proprietary boroughs was considered, at least by the tories, to be a gross infringement of fundamental rights: and in Ireland in 1800 the borough proprietors had been bought out. The Reform Parliament did emancipate the slaves, but only after fifty years of propaganda had convinced a majority of the House of Commons that slave-owning was morally wrong; and even then the owners of slaves had to be bought out. There was nothing

[1] E. L. Woodward, *The Age of Reform*, p. 321.
[2] *Ibid.* p. 316. [3] *Ibid.* p. 315.

313

morally wrong about landed property, not even in being an absentee landlord. On the contrary, property in land provided, according to the ideas of the time, the very structure of society. It was simply incredible that anybody should want to expropriate the landlords in order to provide temporary relief for their tenants—it would be temporary because (though here the argument became a little weak, especially where the landlords were absentees) the economy would break down. It was certainly true that in England the conscientious squire maintained the economy of the village, provided a cushion against a bad harvest, and managed the system of good husbandry. Conscientious squires were fewer in Ireland, but it could not be anticipated that the natural rights of the conscientious squire should be taken away merely because some of the Irish landlords ignored the duties which God had imposed upon them by vesting property rights in them.

Nor could it be expected that the British taxpayer should provide money for land reclamation and development, the establishment of industries, and generally for what is now called planned economic development. The movement of opinion was towards *laissez-faire*, and in the next two or three generations only the lunatic fringe was prepared to assert that the State had a responsibility. What a landowning parliament could do was to impose duties on foreign corn in order to keep up rents, prices and wages; to impose duties on other foreign imports so as to protect British industry; and to require that British goods be carried in British ships in order to protect British commerce. The Union brought Ireland within the scope of these laws. Indeed, the ten per cent duty imposed on manufactured goods (including those from Great Britain) imported into Ireland before the Union, was maintained until 1824, while Irish corn became free of duty in Great Britain.[1] On the other hand, the system of taxation imposed on Ireland at the Union operated harshly because of the heavy increase in taxation and borrowing necessitated by the French wars. On the whole the Irish economy gained little or nothing from the Union: but in any case what was really wanted in Ireland, a considerable public expenditure on projects of development, was quite inconceivable in the early part of the nineteenth century. This was the period of Huskisson, Peel and

[1] E. L. Woodward, *op. cit.* p. 323.

Spring Rice. The task of a Chancellor of the Exchequer was not to find new avenues for profitable public expenditure but to free land and manufactures from the burden of taxation—always remembering that the Corn laws were the safeguard of British agriculture.

O'Connell was himself a landowner, not a harsh one but, in terms of good husbandry, a bad one. He was, too, not an economist but a lawyer and a politician; and, like everybody of his age, except the Manchester School, he thought in political terms. His remedy for the wrongs of Ireland was therefore the repeal of the Union. This would presumably mean—for he never said specifically what it did mean— the rule of Great Britain by the English and Scottish landowners and the rule of Ireland by the Irish landowners, Roman Catholic and Protestant alike. Whether an Irish Parliament would do better for Ireland than a United Kingdom Parliament was at least arguable: but nobody did in fact argue that point because the political question was whether the Protestant minority should be governed by the Roman Catholic majority, or, to put it into Protestant terms, whether the Protestant minority should be governed by O'Connell and the priests. The Protestant majority in the Parliament of the United Kingdom never had any doubt about the answer until 1885.

Home Rule was not O'Connell's formula: it was in fact invented by Isaac Butt, a sound Ulster lawyer who saw that the solution must be a quasi-federal relationship such as that which exists between Northern Ireland and the United Kingdom today. O'Connell's solution was repeal of the Union, and that could not be obtained without a revolution because, even if Parliament gave way, the Orangemen would fight. In fact, however, Parliament was unlikely to give way because of anti-papist sentiment, because too many vested interests were involved, and because agrarian outrage would produce, not an anxiety to get rid of this troublesome country, but pressure for more effective 'coercion' —a word which dominates the history of Ireland in the nineteenth century.

The British parties gradually took up an alignment which is familiar even today, though the Irish problem is off the agenda and 'coercion' elsewhere has become 'the maintenance of law and order'. In principle, the Conservatives wanted firm and resolute government, that is,

315

coercion, followed by concession when order had been restored and the concession could not be represented as a surrender to land-grabbers. The whigs or Liberals, when not in office, thought that coercion was unnecessary, or at least would be unnecessary if adequate and proper concessions were made: when in office, they usually disagreed on the question whether coercion should precede concession or concession precede coercion, and compromised on the basis of coercion and concession coming together, with the result that the one destroyed the effect of the other.[1] Exactly why the antithesis arose is difficult to explain because it goes to the root of the party conflict. Order, regularity and discipline are, of course, essential military virtues because they are means to an end, the disposition of large bodies of persons by a commander: and to persons of the appropriate cast of mind, to whom the military life would especially appeal, they become virtues in themselves. Both conservatism and rebellion are, however, romantic; and the effect of the French Revolution was to divide the romantics, with Burke on the one side and the romantic poets on the other; though eventually most of the poets went over to Burke. It is therefore not surprising that there was a good deal of intellectual confusion in the age of reform. In the nineteenth century nearly everybody went romantic, and the romantics divided into the romantic imperialists who produced the mysticism of the last years of Queen Victoria's reign, and the romantic idealists who looked to the next general election as the first step towards the new Jerusalem.

There were, however, many complicating factors. The agrarian outrages in Ireland were deliberate attacks on the divine right of landed property, a right which became more mundane as industry developed, and disappeared altogether in the eighties, when for the first time Home Rule became practical politics. The romantic humanitarianism which began with the attack on the slave trade developed into the concept of the dignity of the human being, and even the Irish tenant was thought to be human. Imperialism rose to a gigantic crescendo at the end of the century. The officers of the Brigade of Guards at the one end of London and the frock-coated bankers and stockbrokers at the other (London

[1] 'The alternation of kicks and kindness': E. L. Woodward, *The Age of Reform*, p. 331.

316

ended at Liverpool Street) became the symbols of respectability; and nobody could say that the 'moonlighters' or 'whiteboys' were respectable. 'The mob' ceased to be a mob once London was properly policed, but it seemed that Ireland never was adequately policed. Religion became an affair of sects and, like sport, professionalised. What is more the professionals found their social status, at the tail of the professions. The fact that an Irishman paid more attention to his priest than a stockbroker paid to his parson was, no doubt, very odd; but also it was ceasing to be important.

Daniel O'Connell was by temperament a Radical, and so were most of the Home Rulers of the next generation. Though some, like O'Connell, were landowners, they represented the submerged, if not the oppressed, among the Irish. They went through the appalling misery of the famine which started in 1845, a spectre which haunts the Irish of North America and Australia even today, because those who got away (and many thousands did not) handed it down as a family tradition. It was therefore inevitable that the repealers and the Home Rulers should, in English politics, sit to the left of the Liberals. On the other hand, the repealers were never very important in British politics. In 1832 they numbered thirty-eight, a comparatively small (and divided) group in the vast body of Reformers. By 1841 they were down to eighteen.[1] This was largely because O'Connell's initial enthusiasm had flagged. It was one thing to unite the Roman Catholics on the basis of Catholic emancipation. It was another to persuade the Irish as a whole, Protestant and Roman Catholic alike, to a nationalist policy. This was a period in which nationalism was generally weak throughout the United Kingdom, which was still in the reaction after the French wars. Even in Ireland there were people who agreed with the Benthamites that nationalism was a 'vulgar superstition'.[2] After 1841 O'Connell sought to stage a revival, but some of his young men favoured physical force, and O'Connell himself was never powerful after his trial for seditious conspiracy in 1843-4. The young men were nationalists who borrowed from Mazzini's 'Young Italy' the designation of 'Young Ireland'.[3]

---

[1] R. B. McDowell, *Public Opinion and Government Policy in Ireland*, pp. 134-5.
[2] *Ibid.* p. 232.   [3] E. L. Woodward, *The Age of Reform*, p. 335.

Irish nationalism was not, however, purely sentimental. It was not even founded on political repression. Essentially its foundation was economic. The ghastly famine of 1845–6 would inevitably have left bitter memories; for though Peel made gallant efforts to produce remedies, there was no machinery for the purpose and what was improvised was often not only defective but dishonest. On the other hand, the famine and the subsequent migrations eased the pressure of population. It also destroyed most of the old landowners, whose estates were heavily mortgaged. The purchasers under the Encumbered Estates Act, 1849, were mostly Irish, but they were as harsh over evictions as their predecessors; the machinery of the law was still regarded as inimical to the tenants, and the only remedy available was the secret society. On the other hand the Fenian brotherhood, which was established in the United States in 1858 and was active in Ireland between 1865 and 1867, was unable to raise a rebellion.

Gladstone's Government disestablished the Irish Church in 1869, though that Church kept most of its endowments. His Irish Land Act of 1870 was unsuccessful because it did not go far enough, could be evaded, and was rendered almost useless by the fall of agricultural prices after 1875. Meanwhile a new agitation for Home Rule had started, and there were nearly sixty Home Rulers in the Parliament of 1874. Under Isaac Butt the Parliamentary agitation was constitutional and conciliatory, but it completely failed to convince opinion in Great Britain. In 1878 Butt was replaced by Charles Stewart Parnell. Already in 1877 Parnell had led a group which set out to prove by deliberate obstruction that the business of Parliament could not be carried on unless Ireland was given Home Rule. In 1879, too, Parnell joined forces with the Clan-na-Gael, the American branch of the Irish Republican Brotherhood. 'Thenceforward the concerted deployment of Irish revolutionary forces on two fronts—at Westminster and over the Irish countryside—confronted British statesmanship with an unparalleled challenge.'[1] In 1880 the Home Rulers had 65 seats at Westminster though the Liberals had a majority without them.

The Liberals as a body still believed, with Gladstone, that the Irish problem could be met by agrarian reform; and the Irish Land Act of

[1] R. C. K. Ensor, *England, 1870–1914*, p. 57.

1881 went a long way to meet the ancient grievances of the Irish tenants. It also had the political effect, though perhaps it was not foreseen, of killing the vestiges of the theory that Irish constituencies could be carried by 'influence'. Moreover the Reform Act of 1884 vested political power in Southern Ireland in the occupiers of cottages. In effect the two reforms together gave the Irish Nationalist party eighty to eighty-five safe seats. It followed that, at some time or other, and perhaps sooner rather than later, Parnell would hold the balance of power at Westminster. In the Parliament of 1880 the Liberals did not need Nationalist support and in any case they could rely on Conservative support against the Irish: but what would happen if they had no majority? Could they rely on the Irish to support them against the Conservatives and on the Conservatives to support them against the Irish?

As was to be expected, the first of the Liberal leaders to realise that somehow they must compromise over Home Rule was Joseph Chamberlain. In 1879 Chamberlain had written to Morley: 'I have an idea in my head about a modified form of Home Rule which I think is practicable.'[1] What the idea was he did not disclose: but it was probably the germ of the scheme for a 'central board' or 'national board' or 'national council' which he explained at the end of 1884 in conversation with Captain O'Shea. The captain, as Chamberlain probably knew, was the husband of Parnell's mistress; but both the Captain and Mrs O'Shea were dependent on the bounty of an old lady before whom it was necessary to keep up appearances. Friendly relations had therefore to be maintained between Parnell and the captain: and when Chamberlain began negotiations with O'Shea he thought he was negotiating with Parnell. So he was: but he was negotiating through an untrustworthy intermediary who suppressed some of Parnell's letters because he thought himself clever enough to resolve the differences of opinion between Chamberlain and Parnell.

The difficulty was that nobody had defined 'Home Rule'[2] and that both Chamberlain and Parnell made too many public speeches.

[1] *Life of Joseph Chamberlain*, I, p. 318.
[2] Cf. the remark of Chamberlain himself in December, 1884: *Life of Joseph Chamberlain*, I, p. 579.

Parnell's 'Home Rule' started from Grattan's Parliament, and nobody knew how far he was willing to compromise or what relation there would be under Home Rule between the Parliament of Ireland and the Parliament of the United Kingdom. Chamberlain was against 'Home Rule' if it involved an Irish Parliament; but he was willing not only to extend to Ireland the system of elected county councils which Dilke was preparing for England, but also to have a 'central board' or 'national council', if need be separately elected, with powers of taxation and legislation 'on matters not affecting the interests of the Empire as a whole'.[1] The Parliament of the United Kingdom 'would continue to regulate for the common good the national policy of the three Kingdoms'. If this was not Home Rule it went very far: and in fact the Home Rule Bill of 1886, which Chamberlain opposed, did not go very much further.

Chamberlain hoped for a compromise on these lines while recognising that he could not bind Parnell not to press for more.[2] Parnell did not, at this stage at least, want a compromise. He was willing to accept a large measure of local government and even a central board or national council: but, since he intended to press for wider powers (what powers he did not specify, though in public he spoke of Grattan's Parliament and national independence) he did not want the board or council to have legislative powers. This attitude O'Shea never explained to Chamberlain, though Chamberlain must have read Parnell's speeches;[3] and he might at least have been made suspicious by the extreme moderation of the proposal which O'Shea called 'Parnell's scheme'.[4]

Chamberlain had kept Gladstone informed of these negotiations, and the latter, who had done some thinking on his own, favoured 'some plan for a central board of local government in Ireland on something of an elective basis' as 'the only hopeful means of securing Crown and State from an ignominious surrender in the next Parliament after a mis-

---

[1] J. Chamberlain, *A Political Memoir*, pp. 137 and 145; *Life of Joseph Chamberlain*, I, pp. 579–80.

[2] J. Chamberlain, *A Political Memoir*, pp. 151–2. This was, however, six months later, in July 1885.

[3] Cf. the editor's note: *ibid.* p. 139.

[4] *Life of Joseph Chamberlain*, I, pp. 582–3.

chievous and painful struggle'.[1] On the other hand, his concept of a central board was not that of a legislature: it would be primarily administrative, but would make bye-laws, raise funds and pledge the public credit; it would not be directly elected.[2] It is plain that Gladstone recognised the necessity for concession to Irish opinion and thought that, if no concession was now made, larger concessions would soon have to be made. The Cabinet was, however, divided, all the commoners except Lord Hartington being for a central board and all the peers against. Gladstone's subsequent comment is given in two versions, but both mean the same thing, that within six years they would repent the decision to do nothing.

Meanwhile another astute politician was contemplating the next Parliament. When, in May 1885, it was announced that the Liberal Government would propose the partial continuation of the Crimes Act, which was about to expire, Lord Randolph Churchill publicly expressed his concern that the condition of Ireland was so bad under Liberal rule. The Conservative party ought to be careful not to be committed to a policy which would wound the sentiments of their Irish brothers. There was no bargain with the Irish, but Churchill had more than one conversation with Parnell and made it plain that he could not, if he were a member of a Conservative Government, consent to renew the Crimes Act. 'In that case', replied Parnell, 'You will have the Irish vote at the elections.'[3] There was more to it than that, for the Nationalists joined with the Conservatives to defeat the Liberal Government on the Budget; and the divided Liberals were only too glad to resign.

These events led Gladstone to assume that there was some sort of a compact between the Conservatives and the Irish. Nor did the behaviour of Lord Salisbury's 'Caretaker Government' remove the suspicion. The Crimes Act was not renewed and it was plain that in the House of Commons the Government was doing its best not to annoy the Irish, while the Irish were making the path of the Government very easy. Moreover, Lord Carnarvon was made Lord-Lieutenant of Ireland.

---

[1] *Life of Gladstone*, III, p. 191.
[2] *Ibid.* p. 193; *Letters of Queen Victoria*, 2nd ser. II, pp. 652–5.
[3] *Life of Lord Randolph Churchill*, I, p. 395.

He had carried confederation in Canada and tried to persuade the four South African territories to federate; he was therefore familiar with subordinate legislatures. The new Government's declaration of Irish policy had been made not by Lord Salisbury but by Lord Carnarvon: and very soon there were rumours about negotiations between the Viceroy and Parnell. Nor were they without substance. As early as February 1885 Lord Carnarvon had suggested to Lord Salisbury a scheme of Home Rule devised by Sir Charles Gavan Duffy, a colonial statesman of Irish origin.[1] Gladstone's legislation, by getting rid of the landlords and enfranchising the peasantry, had made it impossible to govern Ireland except by force. Nor was this opinion changed when Lord Carnarvon moved to Dublin Castle, where he came under the influence of Sir Robert Hamilton, a civil servant who had already reached the conclusion that Home Rule was the only solution. Carnarvon had discussions with Justin McCarthy and secured Salisbury's consent to an interview with Parnell. It was intended to be exploratory, but it allowed Parnell to persuade himself that if the Conservative party won the election they would produce a measure of Home Rule. This famous meeting took place on 1 August 1885, and it was in that month that Gladstone's conversion to Home Rule was completed.[2]

The Liberals, or at least Chamberlain, did not believe that Parnell would hold the balance of power in the next Parliament. The franchise had been extended to the householders of the counties and Chamberlain's *Radical Programme* was thought, at least by Chamberlain, to be so full of juicy carrots that the working-class electors, both in the boroughs and in the counties, would give the Liberal party a majority. Even so, if 'Dublin Castle' was now convinced that coercion was impracticable, and if the Conservatives decided for Home Rule, it was politically impossible for the Liberals to offer less. On the other hand, if Gladstone decided publicly for Home Rule the Conservatives would probably decide against it. Gladstone therefore kept his ideas to a very narrow circle; and even to them he expressed himself cautiously.[3]

---

[1] *Life of Lord Carnarvon*, III, pp. 151–5; *Life of Robert, Marquis of Salisbury*, III, pp. 151–2.

[2] *Life of Lord Granville*, II, pp. 461–2.   [3] *Life of Gladstone*, III, pp. 215–16.

Parnell, on the other hand, had hopes that the Liberal victory would not be overwhelming. For two years the Irish vote in Great Britain had been organised by the Irish National League with the intention of swaying the marginal constituencies.[1] Lord Randolph Churchill, as we have seen, had already had a contingent promise that it would go Conservative. Both he and Lord Salisbury made conciliatory speeches, without promising Home Rule. Chamberlain, on the other hand, had given an emphatic negative to Parnell's demand for legislative independence. Even so, Chamberlain was not the Liberal party; and on 30 October Mrs O'Shea sent to Gladstone a scheme of moderate Home Rule. Gladstone did not reply, but on 9 November he made a speech of studied vagueness, which could be read as a statement that a Liberal Government would consider Home Rule but also that it wanted a majority free of the Irish vote in Parliament.[2] Nevertheless, Parnell's decision to order the Irish in Britain to vote against Liberal candidates, with few exceptions, was not affected. At the latest possible moment (so as to avoid anti-Irish reaction), the Irish voters received their instructions; and, as events turned out, they may have given twenty-five to forty seats to the Conservatives. In the new Parliament the Liberals had a majority of eighty-four seats over the Conservatives, and the Irish had eighty-six seats.

One consequence became clear immediately. An alliance between the Conservatives and the Irish on a policy of Home Rule would not do. Even if the whole Conservative party would follow a lead in that direction—and it was almost incredible that it would—the Government would not have a working majority. It could get that majority only by splitting the Liberals and coalescing with the whigs. Lord Randolph Churchill's agile mind jumped to that solution before all the results were in: both coercion and anything in the nature of an Irish Parliament were impossible, but there would have to be concessions.[3] Lord Salisbury, in reply, doubted whether the whigs would join, but agreed that, in making the Queen's speech, 'our leaning must be to the

---

[1] T. P. O'Connor, *The Parnell Movement*, p. 512.
[2] R. C. K. Ensor, *England, 1870–1914*, pp. 93–4; T. P. O'Connor, *op. cit.* p. 511.
[3] *Life of Lord Randolph Churchill*, II, 8–14.

Moderate Liberals and that we can have nothing to do with any advances towards the Home Rulers. The latter of course would be contrary to our convictions and our pledges, and would be quite fatal to the cohesion of our party.'[1] Lord Carnarvon was, however, convinced that there had to be either coercion or Home Rule, and he could not, consistently with his public pledges, support the former: hence it had to be Home Rule or his resignation. The Cabinet decided to meet Parliament and not to support Home Rule. Lord Carnarvon wished to resign, but he was 'very strongly pressed to remain for the sake of the peace of Ireland'.[2] In fact, however, he resigned before Parliament met.

Gladstone's view of the general election results was quite different. He was convinced that there was a compact between the Conservatives and Parnell for a measure of Home Rule on lines suggested by Lord Carnarvon—Gladstone, unlike Churchill, knew what had taken place at the meeting on 1 August. If, as he believed, Home Rule was inevitable, he preferred that the Conservatives produce the scheme. He had in mind that in 1829 they had produced Roman Catholic relief, in 1846 they had repealed the Corn Law, and in 1867 they had introduced household franchise, in each case with the assistance of the whigs.[3] Lord Salisbury knew those precedents, though for him they wore a different complexion.[4] However, Gladstone thought that Salisbury might create a fourth precedent and had some reason for thinking so.[5] He therefore informed Salisbury, through A. J. Balfour, that if the Government brought in a measure of Home Rule he would support it.[6] Though he did not know it, the Cabinet had already decided against Home Rule, and Lord Salisbury politely stood on the constitutional principle that he must not disclose the contents of the Queen's speech (which, as it happens, he did not himself know).

Presumably it was Gladstone's intention to keep his conversion secret. It was, however, disclosed to the world by Herbert Gladstone,

---

[1] *Life of Lord Randolph Churchill*, p. 14.
[2] *Letters of Queen Victoria*, 2nd ser. III, p. 711.
[3] R. C. K. Ensor, *England, 1870–1914*, p. 560.
[4] *Life of Robert, Marquis of Salisbury*, III, p. 281.
[5] R. C. K. Ensor, *op. cit.* p. 561.
[6] Lord Gladstone, *After Thirty Years*, pp. 396–8.

in such circumstances that the authenticity of the disclosure could be doubted and that those who did not doubt could believe that Gladstone had been converted by studying the election returns. Lord Hartington at once wrote, for publication, that he stood by his election speeches against Home Rule. Chamberlain, who had also made speeches against Home Rule, thought he had been betrayed and dashed down to Birmingham to speak for the maintenance of the Union, though very soon he was writing to Labouchere about what came to be called 'Home Rule all round', that is, a federal Constitution.[1] Gladstone meanwhile went on hoping that the Conservatives, with their Nationalist allies, would take the plunge, while recognising that they must be turned out if the alliance was dissolved.[2]

The issue was determined by the decision of the Conservatives, announced on 26 January 1886, to introduce a Coercion Bill. Forthwith an amendment to the Address, in the name of Jesse Collings, regretting the omission of measures for the benefit of the agricultural labourer, was moved and put to the vote. There voted for it 257 Liberals and seventy-four Irish; against were 234 Conservatives and eighteen Liberals; the Government was defeated by seventy-nine votes and resigned. Gladstone became Prime Minister and produced a formula which the whigs were unable to accept but which Chamberlain accepted with reluctance. Chamberlain and Trevelyan did not, however, last long when principles of the Home Rule Bill were discussed. According to Lord Morley, Chamberlain made four points: two were eventually conceded, one was a question of drafting, and the fourth was not enough to break up a party.[3] Chamberlain's own comment was:

The disposition of Mr Gladstone and his friends was sometimes conciliatory, sometimes the reverse, and it varied in the ratio of their hopes and fears for the success of the Bill on the second reading. It seems likely that they were misled by their whips as to the state of things in the House of Commons and by Schnadhorst [secretary of the National Liberal Federation, then still 'Joe's Caucus'] as to the position in the country. Every time that they obtained a favourable report of possibilities they retreated from their offers and raised their terms, and at the very last moment an arrangement which had been promised was repudiated and the fate of the Bill thereby sealed.[4]

[1] *Life of Henry Labouchere*, p. 272.   [2] *Life of Gladstone*, III, pp. 270–2.
[3] *Ibid.* p. 302.   [4] J. Chamberlain, *A Political Memoir*, p. 209.

The debate on the second reading of the Bill was one of those rare occasions on which debate is something more than electioneering; every speech helped to sway votes, and nobody knew what the result would be. The political world of those days was, apart from the Irish and a few Radicals, a narrow circle in which one could, in a morning, call on most of one's friends and opponents. Very soon it became clear that among the Liberals the cleavage was, Chamberlain apart, mainly one of rank or class. Most of the commoners were for the Bill, most of the peers against; Gladstone had the greatest difficulty in producing a suitable party for Prince Albert Victor on the Queen's birthday.[1] How many Liberals voted against Home Rule because Lady A turned her back at a ball or Lady B studied the sky in the Park can never be known. All the non-political clubs of Pall Mall became political, and it was embarrassing to visit the Reform Club. Nor was this social pressure upon Liberals offset by adequate pressure from the constituencies. There everybody was thoroughly confused because the Conservatives who had said that coercion was unnecessary now said that it was necessary, while Liberals who had been against Home Rule were for it, and Liberals who had been for a legislative national council were against a national legislature. The tergiversations had been too rapid to allow public opinion to adapt itself. Besides, the gentlemen of the press were as acutely divided as the politicians, and professors were becoming gentlemen of the press.

This welter of argument and prejudice had to produce a conclusion. When the division was taken there voted for the Bill 313 and against it 343, among the latter being ninety-three Liberals. Of these ninety-three Liberals, forty-six were 'Chamberlain's battalion': 'In the sight of the rank and file of Unionists he was the hero of the occasion; in the sight of others he was the enemy for ever, pursued by a spirit of vengeance to his last hour and after.'[2] For the Irish he was 'Judas'.

No summary can do justice to such a controversy as that of Home Rule. Enough has been said, however, to demonstrate that there was initially no great conflict of principle. Until Parnell became leader of the Irish party in 1878 no politician in Great Britain took Home Rule

---

[1] *A Political Memoir*, p. 322.
[2] *Life of Joseph Chamberlain*, II, p. 250.

seriously. Three factors then became important; the realisation that, when the franchise was extended, neither of the great parties would be able to win a single Irish seat outside Ulster, and that Parnell might hold the balance of power; the difficulty of operating the Parliamentary machine with eighty or more Irishmen ready and eager to obstruct; and, above all, the dislike in all parties of the subversion of the principles of British justice implicit in the process of 'coercion' or 'firm and resolute government'.

The difficulty was that 'coercion' was becoming endemic and yet was proving unsuccessful, as 'Dublin Castle' itself admitted privately. Lord Spencer, Lord-Lieutenant from 1882 to 1885, had done his very best to make 'coercion' a success, but it was evident to everybody that he had failed. This was not a party question. The first man to suggest a compromise which might involve an elected legislative body in Ireland was Joseph Chamberlain; and his proposal was defeated in the Liberal Cabinet by a narrow majority. Gladstone was too good a politician not to realise that, that compromise having been defeated, the next Parliament would have to enact a greater concession to Irish opinion. By the end of 1884 he was thinking in terms of Home Rule, and by August 1885 he was sure that it was inevitable. The first leading politician actually to suggest Home Rule, however, was the Conservative Viceroy, Lord Carnarvon; and the proposal was defeated, by a majority, in a Conservative Cabinet before it was carried, by a majority, in a Liberal Cabinet. Meanwhile Lord Randolph Churchill had publicly condemned Liberal coercion; and, until Herbert Gladstone disclosed his father's conversion, no Conservative leader had publicly pledged himself against Home Rule. The situation was such that, even after that disclosure, Gladstone could believe in the possibility of a Conservative Home Rule Bill. On the Liberal side both Lord Hartington and Chamberlain had publicly condemned Home Rule. Hartington was an old whig whose prejudices had to be removed slowly, and he was not given time. Chamberlain went very far towards Home Rule in the Liberal Cabinet of 1886, and he might have accepted the Bill if Gladstone had been more conciliatory. As he said in the debate on the second reading, he would willingly vote for some form of Home Rule, but the term might mean anything from Grattan's

Parliament to his own national council. All turned upon the more or less.[1]

In all this there was, of course, a good deal of electioneering, some jockeying for place and power, and some personal antagonism. What politicians say while election fever is in their veins ought not to be brought up in evidence against them, though it always is. The *Radical Programme* had some harsh words to say about the Government of Ireland and did not positively condemn Home Rule, though it did say that 'Grattan's Parliament, with its separate House of Lords, would be a white elephant'. Its positive recommendation was a national council, the prompt concession of which would probably result in a 'cessation of further agitation'. What the *Radical Programme* said could, *ex hypothesi*, not be said by anybody else: but, since the Conservatives were in 1885 hoping for the Irish vote, they took care to ignore the last pages of the *Radical Programme*, and even Parnell's demand for an independent Ireland under the Crown. The whigs had no such inhibitions and by their speeches pledged themselves even against the sort of formula which Gladstone eventually produced for the Liberal Cabinet of 1886. Gladstone tried to perform the remarkable feat of satisfying both the whigs and the Radicals, but his purpose was frustrated by the stream of more or less accurate information which Labouchere was supplying Chamberlain about doings in Hawarden. Chamberlain's view of his position, first as a Liberal Cabinet Minister and then as one of the Liberal opposition, was that he could publicly agitate any question on which there had not been a specific Cabinet decision, but that he must be consulted by Gladstone about any tentative ideas that the latter might have in his mind; in other words, there was something like collective responsibility for Gladstone's ideas but not for Chamberlain's. Lord Salisbury also had his Chamberlain: but the Fourth Party had no unauthorised programme and Salisbury could toss his ideas about in the 'Hotel Cecil' without having a Labouchere telling tales to Lord Randolph Churchill. Even so, Salisbury had to keep in mind the possibility of Churchill emulating the Disraeli of 1846.

What sort of party images these manoeuvres produced can only be guessed at. Gladstone had done little electioneering in 1885, even in

[1] *Life of Joseph Chamberlain*, II, p. 247.

Midlothian, and Chamberlain was the Liberal leader in the headlines, though few of them related to Ireland. The Nonconformist Conscience was less important in 1885 than it had been in 1880, and Ulster had not realised that it might have to accept a papist Government of Ireland. The party machines, so far as they existed, were at sixes and sevens. It is generally assumed that 'three acres and a cow' attracted the counties and that General Gordon was the hero of the towns: but nobody really knows.

If this is even an approximation to the atmosphere in which Home Rule was produced and rejected as Conservative policy but also produced and accepted as Liberal policy, why was there so much excitement about it? There was, of course, the temporary excitement of the long debate, inside and outside Parliament, from the day in December 1885 when Herbert Gladstone flew the 'Hawarden kite' to the day in June 1886 when the Home Rule Bill was defeated on second reading. During that period every opinion counted because every Liberal 'renegade' reduced Gladstone's majority by two. This period of excitement was preceded by a general election and followed by a general election, and both elections were open. In those days elections were still the great events of the years in which they occurred, in spite of the Ballot Act and the Corrupt and Illegal Practices Act, for the newspapers had not yet discovered women, crime and sport.

In 1886 Gladstone repeated his 'pilgrimages of passion', but this time he had a worthy opponent, though of a very different type. Chamberlain's weapon was savage invective, and he was the more savage because, for many Liberals, as well as for the Irish, he was 'Judas'. People were not interested in his Irish policy; it is doubtful if many understood wherein his brand of Home Rule differed from Gladstone's. He had to give them fire and brimstone. The Liberals lost 137 seats, giving the Unionists a majority of 118, of which seventy-eight were Liberal Unionists. These figures are, however, misleading. Many Liberal Unionists withdrew in favour of Conservatives, many Conservatives withdrew in favour of Liberal Unionists, and the Gladstonian Liberals often had no time or organisation to prevent a seat going Unionist for lack of opposition. In terms of votes cast the Unionists and the Home Rulers were almost equally divided.

There were, however, other reasons for the display of passion which characterised politics between 1886 and 1895. Professor Dicey, writing as an oldish man in 1913, mentioned some of them.[1] The faith of Gladstonian Home Rulers was coloured by Gladstone's nature. 'He was a born enthusiast, he was an orator and a statesman of extraordinary gifts and influence: but his power over his followers, and even over his opponents, mainly depended on the ease with which he first convinced himself, and then convinced many of his hearers, that any cause which he had in hand was the cause of truth and of righteousness.' That was undoubtedly one of the characteristics of Gladstone's oratory, made memorable by Labouchere's remark about God having put the ace of trumps up Gladstone's sleeve: but it was not difficult to produce this sort of sentiment by reciting the wrongs of Irish history. Dicey in 1886 very sensibly criticised the nationalist fiction which gave perpetual succession to 'England' and 'Ireland':

To this delusion of personification is due the notion that Englishmen of today ought to make compensation and feel personal shame for the cruelties of Cromwell, or for Pitt's corruption of Irish patriots; that we are in some way liable and should feel compunction for crimes committed by (possibly) the ancestors of the very men to whom we are now supposed to owe reparation. To the same cause is to be attributed the absurd demand that the Irish Catholics should put on sack-cloth and ashes for the massacres of 1641. To this cause is due the ridiculous claim that living Irishmen should be grateful for the well-meant though most unsuccessful efforts made by the Parliament of the United Kingdom to govern one-third of the United Kingdom on sound principles of justice.[2]

That is undoubtedly true: and to the same cause is to be attributed the ridiculous idea, put forward by Dicey in 1913,[3] that the Phoenix Park murders by a band of assassins in 1882, the boycotting of those who rented land from which the tenants had been evicted and the maiming of cattle during the reign of the Land League, were relevant to the Home Rule debates of 1912–14. This tradition of what Dicey called 'nationality' and is now called nationalism, was indeed pervasive in 1886, on both sides of the Irish Sea. On the one side it was mainly

[1] A. V. Dicey, *A Fool's Paradise*, pp. xx–xxvii.
[2] *England's Case against Home Rule* (2nd ed.), p. 11.
[3] *A Fool's Paradise*, p. xxii.

responsible for the demand for Home Rule, because all the grievances of which the Irish complained could be remedied without it, and were in fact progressively remedied from Gladstone's initial efforts in 1870 to Balfour's comparatively benign administration up to 1905.[1] On the other side it was responsible for the growth of the imperialism discussed in the last chapter. Lord Salisbury himself said that Gladstone, in struggling for Home Rule, 'awakened the slumbering genius of imperialism', though he ought perhaps to have added that there was an efficient band of knockers-up.[2] Even Dicey was not immune from the contagion, though the great prophet of imperialism was a professor not at Oxford but at the other place, Professor J. R. Seeley. What the Home Rulers were proposing to do was, to quote Dicey, to destroy 'that unity of the State which is essential to the authority of England and to the maintenance of the Empire'.[3] The 'delusion of personification' applied to both sides; but one personified 'Ireland' and the other personified 'England' (that is, the United Kingdom) and 'the Empire'. It was a conflict of nationalist emotions and therefore a fierce conflict because both were irrational.

Professor Dicey rightly called attention to the way in which the case for Home Rule was raised to a high moral plane. The wrongs done to 'Ireland' demanded retribution by 'England'. As he said, 'Every claim of the Irish Nationalists became, with the converted Gladstone, transmuted into the demand of "Justice to Ireland"'.[4] The Unionists were not so good at this kind of thing: it was difficult to regard either Joseph Chamberlain or Lord Randolph Churchill as missionaries for the moral law, at least until imperialism became so dominant that the British Empire could be regarded as a special creation of Providence. The Unionists were, however, the maintainers of law, order and justice against political assassination, boycotting, cattle-maiming. What is more, was it right that the loyal Ulstermen should be put under the heels of Catholic priests, moonlighters, whiteboys, boycotters and assassins?

[1] The benignity is best illustrated by George A. Birmingham's humorous novels.
[2] *Life of Lord Randolph Churchill*, II, p. 117.
[3] *England's Case against Home Rule* (2nd ed.), p. 283.
[4] *A Fool's Paradise*, p. xxii.

331

Dicey himself, in all three of his books against Home Rule, tried to remain cool, calm, collected and rational. He had, of course, to make some large assumptions in order to produce a rational case. He assumed, first, the unity of the United Kingdom, where a population of 44,000,000 included an Irish population of 4,000,000, of whom 1,000,000 were in Ulster. He assumed, secondly, the principle of the greatest happiness of the greatest number; and the greatest number were the people of Great Britain. Why one should take the United Kingdom as a unit and not Europe or Ireland was not explained. If Ireland was the unit, as the nationalists contended, the fact that the southern Irish were 3,000,000 and the Ulstermen 1,000,000 at once became significant.

The case was, in fact, irrational on both sides. Nationalist emotion and moral judgments were on both sides. That alone made the conflict fierce. There were, however, other factors. Anti-papist sentiment was no longer very strong in Great Britain; but the anti-clericalism which had developed in the eighteenth century and was maintained by the pretensions of the Anglo-Catholics was still of some importance; and the Irish Roman Catholic priest was usually assumed to be a bit of a Jesuit and therefore an undesirable person. In Ulster 'no-popery' was the slogan of the Orangeman and anti-papist sentiment remained extremely strong. To put Ulster under the control of moonlighters and cattle-maimers was bad enough: to give the priests control of Ulster was something which no good Conservative churchman could contemplate.

The allegations could be made personal. Gladstone was said to have split the Liberal party by suddenly adopting Home Rule, after the election of 1885, in order to get himself into office. Alternatively, Chamberlain had sold himself to the Conservative party because Gladstone would not accept his peculiar, and unintelligible, brand of Home Rule. He was the renegade, the 'Judas' who, having betrayed his master, used all his powers of vituperation against the Grand Old Man. The Conservatives had done a deal with Parnell and then broke the compact when Gladstone had over-trumped them.

The advantage of an emotional conflict is that it cannot last long. Already in 1892 the 'damnable iterations' of the Home Rule debate

332

were becoming a little boring. When Captain O'Shea at last brought his suit for divorce, Parnell could no longer be a Liberal hero, and the Irish party split. Gladstone was nevertheless a man of one idea and had to continue with Home Rule, though when the House of Lords rejected his second Bill in 1893 only a few dogs barked, and most Liberals were glad to be rid of the subject. Chamberlain, with his usual sense of the movement of opinion, looked for new fields to conquer, and found them in South Africa. While he was conquering them the trade unions began their major battle with the employers. The Liberal victory of 1906 had nothing to do with Home Rule; but the Conservatives, with Chamberlain no longer in active politics, were stupid enough to obstruct social legislation by means of their huge majority in the House of Lords and forced the Liberals into a premature dissolution which made them dependent on the Irish vote once more. The battle of 1909–14 was again fierce, partly because more was at stake than the Union, and partly because the Orangemen decided to fight. Kaiser Wilhelm then provided a diversion, and in 1921 a Government with a Liberal Prime Minister and a Conservative majority agreed to convert southern Ireland into a Dominion by the name of the Irish Free State. What good came out of this long battle only President de Valera could tell: and the telling would take a long time because he would begin with Strongbow, in the true nationalist tradition.

CHAPTER VIII

FREE TRADE AND PROTECTION

I. ECONOMICS AND POLITICS

'The main issue before us in politics', said a Conservative Cabinet Minister in 1923, 'is the issue between conflicting schools of economic thought.'[1] There were three such schools, individualism, socialism and nationalism, corresponding to the three parties, Liberal, Labour and Conservative. The Conservative or nationalist school of economic thought was, as usual, capable of expressing itself only in mystical terms:

The historical, national and Imperial conception of economics is essentially part of the whole Unionist, Conservative, or to use a good old time-honoured name, Tory political creed. That creed is based not on the abstract political or economic rights of individuals or of classes, but on England and Englishmen, living realities with their history, their institutions, their character, their possibilities, set in the wider framework of the British Empire.[2]

The quotation is a little unfair, for it does appear from the subsequent discussion that, even in the time-honoured Tory creed, Englishmen also had stomachs. Nevertheless, the quotation exhibits the common confusion between economics and politics.

Mr Amery would have denied that 'confusion' was the right word. His view was that classical economics was based on individualistic assumptions, which were essentially political. His own assumptions were nationalist and imperialist, and therefore he supplied his own brand of 'National and Imperial Economics'. How far this 'confusion', if this is the right word, exists in modern economics is a question on which a constitutional lawyer dare not pronounce. Questions of economic policy are, however, inevitably questions of politics, since they depend upon objectives. Adam Smith himself recognised other motives than the economic advantage of the individual, such as defence, law and order, and nationalist pride, particularly in relation to colonies.

[1] L. S. Amery, *National and Imperial Economics* (2nd ed.), p. 10.
[2] *Ibid.* pp. 11–12.

334

Given the political objective, the economist ought to be able to advise about methods. Economists are not always content with this advisory function. They want to formulate political decisions as well: and there is no reason why they should not, but in that case they are like the rest of us, acting as citizens and not as experts.

The example which aroused Mr Amery's antagonism was the famous pronouncement against Protection issued by fourteen professors and lecturers of economics in 1904:[1]

A return to protection would, we hold, be detrimental to the material prosperity of this country....The evil would probably be a lasting one since experience shows that protection...is likely to extend beyond the limits first assigned to it and is very difficult to extirpate. There are also to be apprehended those evils, other than material, which protection brings in its train, the loss of purity in politics, the unfair advantage given to those who wield the powers of jobbery and corruption, unjust distribution of wealth, and the growth of sinister interests. Secondly, we apprehend that the suggested arrangements, far from promoting amity, may engender irritating controversies between the different members of the Empire....

The judgments about 'those evils, other than material' were presumably derived from the professors' study of politics in countries in which protectionist policies had been adopted; so was experience about the expansion of protectionism in such countries. There were, however, deeper judgments. One, very obvious, was about the 'unjust distribution of wealth': what is a just distribution of wealth? The assertion that a reduction in 'the material prosperity of this country' would be an 'evil' is almost as clearly a judgment about values—a judgment which, for instance, Mahatma Gandhi might not be willing to sustain. What is hidden is the assumption that the forty million people of the United Kingdom could be treated as a unit, 'this country', whose 'material prosperity', even if one knew exactly what that meant, was an advantage however that prosperity was distributed among them. In fact, as the reference to 'unjust distribution of wealth' shows, the assumption was the individualist assumption of Adam

[1] *The Times*, 15 August 1904; the preamble is quoted in L. S. Amery, *My Political Life*, I, p. 243, and the propositions in economics in Free Trade Union, *ABC Fiscal Handbook*, p. 173.

Smith, that if each person was allowed to pursue his material prosperity without interference by constitutional authority, other than for the maintenance of the basic minimum of law and order, the result would be just.

This political preamble was followed by six propositions not open to such criticism, though they were tendentious in the sense that the selection of the propositions was designed to prove the political premises. The initial problem was to get those premises accepted, a proper problem for the Liberal party to solve. A Conservative might start from very different premises, for example, the imperialist premises of the professors' severest critic:

The starting point of all my political thinking . . . had been the British Empire or Commonwealth conceived as a unit and as the final object of patriotic emotion and action. That conception naturally involved the desire, not only to maintain such unity as it possessed, but to make that unity more effective. More concerned with securing that unity through free co-operation than through some definite constitutional scheme, I regarded it as inconceivable that economic co-operation could be excluded from the picture. A union based on foreign policy and defence could have no meaning if it were not supported by co-operation for mutual welfare in peace and for the development of the economic resources of the whole. For without that development the Commonwealth could not hope to hold its own in the world of greater units of power which was obviously coming into being . . . .[1]

If this objective was accepted, the task of the economists was so to advise the politicians about the methods for developing the resources of the Empire that that Empire would be a great unit of power. They would have to ask a great many questions, and there were different politicians to give answers; but it was not for the gallant fourteen to reason why.

Even in a narrower field, however, the economists faced the difficulty of the nature of party policies. They are inevitably broad generalisations, especially when they are expressed in formulae or slogans. Every Liberal Government has imposed or maintained tariffs, and some have increased them. Many Conservative Governments have reduced tariffs. Neither Conservative nor Liberal Governments have

[1] L. S. Amery, *My Political Life*, I, p. 253.

336

objected to the 'nationalisation' of some services, and no Labour Government has proposed the 'nationalisation' of all services. Nor is 'free enterprise' the inevitable alternative to 'nationalisation'. On the contrary, most of the restrictions on 'free enterprise' have been imposed under Conservative Governments. It would be absurd to ask an economist to advise on 'tariff reform' or 'nationalisation'. He would properly ask what reforms, or nationalisation of what, and how.

Moreover the economic consequences of a proposed 'economic policy' are not the only consequences anticipated. Neither Joseph Chamberlain nor L. S. Amery had narrowly economic objectives. They were imperialists who sought to use tariffs to strengthen and unite the British Empire, and to maintain little 'England' as a 'great power'. They got mixed up in arguments about economic consequences because the Liberals (and others) alleged that their proposals involved a lowering of the standard of living of English workers. Whether as a matter of analysis this was true or false (and the proposals were so vague that no economist who was not an amateur politician could answer positively either way), this was a good political point, which had to be answered. Thus, the Tariff Reform League said that taxes on food would not raise the cost of living because there were already taxes on food, namely, tea, sugar, coffee, chicory, cocoa and dried fruits, and so one could take taxes off tea and sugar, and put taxes on wheat, meat and dairy produce.[1] Joseph Chamberlain said that nothing in his proposals 'need increase in the slightest degree the cost of living of any family in this country'.[2] It was a neat formula. Presumably a good Conservative housewife would say: 'Yes, Johnny, you may have another piece of bread and butter. It costs your daddy a little more, but that is to help the little boys in Canada and New Zealand; and our good Mr Chamberlain has reduced the cost of the nice sweet tea that mummy has when she's tired in the morning.' Even a Liberal housewife might help: 'No, Johnny, you can't have another piece of bread and butter. That naughty man Chamberlain has made it cost too much. But you may have an extra spoonful of sugar in your porridge.'

[1] Tariff Reform League, *Handbook for Speakers* (1910 ed.), pp. 9–10.
[2] *Ibid.* p. 10.

The economists got dragged into this, sometimes upside-down.[1] They have influenced party politics since Adam Smith, but the conflict over economic policy is much older than the economists. Exactly how old it is depends upon the meaning of 'economic policy'.

The primary purpose of a fiscal law is to raise money for the Crown. Until the Civil War the Crown was not an abstraction but a real person, so that it was impossible to distinguish between the King's private income and the public revenues of the Crown. 'Economic policy' was therefore a policy which enriched the King. An economical king, like Henry VII, would not only husband his resources, but also stimulate trade so as to make more profit from it. An extravagant monarch, like Henry VIII, was prepared to sell Crown lands, debase the currency, and pile up debts. A 'national' policy was hardly possible until the Parliament men won the Civil War, and then it was far from a purely economic policy, partly because the Government was perpetually short of money and had to raise it where it could, and partly because trade was merely an aspect of foreign and colonial relations. The dominant factor in all policy was the threat from Charles Stuart and his supporters, English and foreign. With his restoration in 1660 there was a new factor, the influence of Parliament on policy, ending in complete control of revenue and almost complete control of expenditure. Fiscal legislation inevitably became a battleground for vested interests. To talk of policy in such circumstances is unrealistic, and the 'mercantile system' was never a system. In any case, the most frequent reason for a change in fiscal policy, as we in our generation know only too well, is that a war has to be financed by increased taxation. Since taxation and public expenditure produce new vested interests, such

---

[1] Cf. Amery's remark that 'underpaying' workmen was contrary to the public interest because the workmen would purchase less as customers and be able to pay less taxes: L. S. Amery, *op. cit.* p. 12. It followed that the employer who 'overpaid' his workmen was a benefactor even if in consequence he had smaller profits to spend and paid lower taxes. The only purpose of this exercise was to indicate that it was not the policy of the Conservative party to encourage a reduction in wages, but it was put as a proposition in economics. For a similar use of 'economic history', cf. Cobden's remark that 'a free import trade was the undoubted constitutional policy of England for six hundred years after the Conquest': R. Cobden, *The Constitutional Right to a Revision of the Land Tax*, quoted in J. Noble, *Fiscal Legislation, 1842–1865*, p. 2. This was, of course, an argument for the removal of the import duty on corn.

338

a change becomes permanent: and this is no new phenomenon because it happened with the Long Parliament's excise of 1643. Further, there was throughout the eighteenth century the problem of patronage. Though Blackstone and Dr Johnson condemned the excise because it was levied by 'hired wretches', the real case against it was that the excise-men could be used to influence elections. A similar problem arose through the financing of short-term debt and other loans by the Bank of England and other whiggish institutions in the City of London. The East India Company and other great trading companies were other useful sources of patronage. In short, politics dominated economics until Adam Smith convinced a whole generation that economics ought not to be a governmental matter at all, and that the liberty to make money (if not to spend it) was the most important of the liberties of the people. This involved the repeal of a host of restrictive laws.

2. THE MERCANTILE SYSTEM

The most famous of the restrictive laws, because they provided a great political controversy in the nineteenth century and split the Conservative party, were the Corn Laws. On them Adam Smith allowed himself one of his touches of sarcasm:

The laws concerning corn may everywhere be compared to the laws concerning religion. The people feel themselves so much interested in what relates either to their subsistence in this life, or to their happiness in a life to come, that government must yield to their prejudices, and, in order to preserve the public tranquillity, establish that system which they approve of. It is upon this account, perhaps, that we so seldom find a reasonable system established with regard to either of those two capital objects.[1]

The earliest of the Corn Laws, which began in 1361, were prohibitions or restrictions on export, designed to prevent famine and keep down the price of corn.[2] For the same reason attempts were made, especially under the later Tudors and the earlier Stuarts, to prevent building and the conversion of arable land to pasture. There were, however, other motives. Exports were thought to be necessary to

[1] *Wealth of Nations* (Cannan's ed., 1937), p. 507.
[2] E. Lipson, *Economic History of England*, II, pp. 451-2.

maintain the 'wealth' of the country; but foreign countries might place an embargo on the export of cloth and therefore it was wise to encourage the production of corn, any surplus of which could be exported. Nor were the landowners averse from having the higher prices which the export trade helped to produce. The mixture of motives is shown by a contemporary note justifying the Acts 39 Eliz. I, cc. 1 and 2 (1597), the former of which restricted building and the second the conversion of arable land to pasture:

The great decay of people. The ingrossing wealth into few hands. Setting people to work in husbandry, whereby idleness, drunkenness and vice are avoided. Swarms of poor loose and wandering people bred by those decays, miserable to themselves, dangerous to the State. Subjecting the realm to the discretion of foreign States either to help us with corn in time of dearth or to hinder us by embargos on our cloths, if we stand too much on that commodity. Danger of famine. Some remedy expected in the country....[1]

Since the motives were mixed, the laws were apt to be changed according as one or another of the motives was dominant. Generally the objective was the stability of prices, so as to protect the producer when there was a good harvest and the consumer when there was a bad one. Hence the laws varied from absolute prohibition of exports to bounties on exports. The Act of 1673, for instance, provided bounties for all corn shipped on English ships above the prices there specified.[2]

On the other hand, in bad seasons corn might have to be imported. This was one of the reasons for hindering the conversion of arable to pasture. As the Act 39 Eliz. I, c. 2, put it:

Whereas the said husbandice and tillage [i.e. by the plough] is a cause that the Realme does more stand upon itselfe, withowt dependinge upon forraine cuntries either for bringing in of corne in tyme of scarsetye, or for vente and utterance of our owne commodities beinge in over great abundance....[3]

But, when there was scarcity, foreign corn had to be admitted free of duty, and when there was a glut and prices were low it had to be completely prohibited. After the Restoration, Parliament adopted the

---

[1] R. H. Tawney and E. Power, *Tudor Economic Documents*, I, p. 89.
[2] E. Lipson, *Economic History of England*, II, p. 453.
[3] R. H. Tawney and E. Power, *op. cit.* I, p. 84.

principle which governed policy down to 1773, and which was revived in 1815, namely, that there should be high import duties when the prices of corn fell below certain limits, and low duties when prices rose above those limits.[1] Because of the low prices of corn for the hundred years after the third of the Restoration Corn Laws, that of 1670, the law gave the producers almost complete protection. The policy of the law was not without its critics, even under the later Stuarts, but it was generally acceptable to the landed interest since it helped to keep up agricultural prices and therefore rents.

There was a similar mixture of motives in the Navigation Acts. The original purpose was defensive. The only way to repel an invasion or to transport knights and bowmen to France or Ireland was to requisition ships, which could be done under the royal prerogative. Hence it was essential for purposes of defence and for the dynastic ambitions of the English kings that there should be a substantial trade carried on in English ships. Laws requiring the use of English ships were in force from 1381, though they were seldom effectively enforced. The earlier Tudors took up the policy with their usual efficiency; but they also had in mind the strengthening of trade[2] and the diversion of its profits from foreign to English merchants.[3] In the reign of Elizabeth I English ships were roaming the seven seas, looking for the profits either of trade or of plunder, though Elizabeth and the earlier Stuarts were more concerned with fisheries in the narrow seas than with marine shipping. Indeed, because of retaliation by the Spanish king, Elizabeth repealed the restrictive provisions, providing instead that goods brought in foreign ships, other than masts, pitch, tar and corn, should pay heavier customs duties. Even this restriction produced Spanish retaliation, but other restrictions were nevertheless imposed. James I and Charles I tried to enforce the laws, and they were extended to the North American plantations; but they were not easily enforced.

The first great Navigation Act, that of 1651, was, however, retaliation against the Dutch. The English Council of State had sent the Lord Chief Justice, Oliver St John, with an imposing retinue, to the

---

[1] E. Lipson, *Economic History of England*, II, p. 462.
[2] J. D. Mackie, *The Earlier Tudors*, p. 220.
[3] *Ibid.* p. 474.

Hague to negotiate a treaty of union which would protect the Commonwealth against its Royalist enemies or, if that was not possible, a treaty of alliance. The Dutch were more anxious to remove English pretensions to the sovereignty of the narrow seas, and the English offer was spurned. Forthwith the Bill which became the Navigation Act was presented to Parliament and passed.[1] It was not, however, rigidly enforced, especially during the war with Spain, when English goods were often carried in Dutch ships to evade Spanish privateers.[2] Nevertheless, the Act was re-enacted in 1660 with amendments designed to stop the loopholes which experience had shown to exist.

This Act was a temporary expedient, designed to remove the dislocation in English trade caused by the Civil War, but became permanent. Its economic effects have generally been held to be bad,[3] but the Navigation Acts were defended even by Adam Smith on the political ground, that they provided the ships and the seamen necessary for the defence of the country. Moreover the economic effects were not well understood. It was assumed that higher freights paid to English shippers were better than lower freights paid to foreign shippers. Above all, the Navigation Acts were favoured by the rising spirit of nationalism. 'England' might, and perhaps would, have become a 'great sea power' even if the standard of living had not been lowered by the Navigation Acts: but in any case the nationalist, like High Heaven (according to Wordsworth), rejects the lore of nicely calculated less or more. Nor did the various groups of merchants, who took the 'more', hesitate to play the nationalist tune. The elder Pitt had no firmer supporters than the merchants of the City of London.

The history of the wool trade in the seventeenth and eighteenth centuries is interesting constitutionally because it seems to be the only case in which the landed interest failed to get its way. Since in most parts of the country the growing of wool was more profitable than the growing of corn, the legislation of Elizabeth I was unable to prevent the conversion of arable land to sheep farming. English wool, being of high quality, was much in demand; and high prices could be obtained

[1] T. W. Fulton, *The Sovereignty of the Sea*, p. 391.
[2] E. Lipson, *Economic History of England*, III, p. 123.
[3] *Ibid.* pp. 130–6.

342

when it was freely exportable. Nevertheless, the cloth manufacturers were able to secure legislation prohibiting the export of wool and thus keeping down its price. This remarkable phenomenon seems never to have been adequately explained.[1] Possibly the members of Parliament representing the manufacturing towns—which were strongly represented until the factory system developed—found this to be the one case in which they had to pay more attention to the interests of their constituents than to those of their landowning patrons. It has been suggested[2] that it was more profitable to the revenue to export cloth than to export wool; and certainly it was in accord with the economic ideas of protectionists, then as now, that manufactured goods rather than raw materials should be exported, since manufacture at home was and is alleged to 'create employment'. On the other hand, the prohibition led to much smuggling because of the considerable difference between the price of English wool in England and in France and Flanders;[3] and from this smuggling the revenue gained nothing except, of course, from duties on imports paid for by smuggled wool. There was, too, a strong element of nationalism in the legislation. The progress of the cloth industry in France and Holland was regarded with dismay, as enriching the competitors of 'England'; and accordingly an attempt was made to prevent their receiving English wool. Even so, these do not seem to be adequate explanations for the failure of the landed interest to prevent legislation which tended to reduce rents.

The position was much the same in respect of leather, though here perhaps the interest of the landowners was not so direct. Indeed, the tanners sided with the landed interest, since the hides would normally be exported tanned and the prohibition of the export reduced the price. The combination was in fact successful, since in 1685 the Act of 1668 permitting the export of leather was revived.[4]

The trade in cloth, too, produced a conflict, though between the

---

[1] It should, however, be noted that the landed interest was less protectionist under George III than it afterwards became. So long as internal communications were bad it had assured markets, and British agricultural production was comparatively efficient: E. Halévy, *History of the English People in the XIXth Century*, I, p. 233 (which refers, however, to the Corn Law of 1773).

[2] Cf. E. Lipson, *Economic History of England*, III, pp. 22–3.

[3] *Ibid.* pp. 23–8. [4] *Ibid.* p. 36.

cloth makers and the East India Company, which imported silks and calicoes; but the only result of prohibition was the development of calico-printing in England, which compelled Parliament in 1721 to forbid the use of printed calicoes, though in 1736 it excluded printed fustian, a mixture of cotton and linen.[1] The cotton industry therefore continued to develop, particularly when inventions made for easier production. In fact, after Arkwright invented the spinning roller and Hargreaves the jenny it became possible to avoid the use of linen as warp; and in 1774 the sale of fine cotton cloth was made legal.

Though all this regulation and restriction was part of what Adam Smith called the mercantile system, it would be wrong to regard it as a system. There was no single theory, or coherent series of theories, behind it. The only common assumption seems to have been that the enrichment of a section of the people enriched the State, or the 'country' or 'England', without much appreciation of the fact that in the process other sections of the people might be impoverished.[2] Where there were obviously several interests involved, like the agricultural interest, the moneyed interest (the large body of bankers discounting bills and issuing notes), the West India interest, the East India interest, and a collection of other mercantile interests, there was no theoretical means, until Adam Smith, of resolving the conflict. Moreover the matter was complicated by the fact that the interests were not exclusive. In practice it was simply a question of political power, which cannot now be sorted because it was extremely complex.

On the other hand, the vested interests cannot be classified with any precision. Even before the personification of 'England' introduced the notion that if some Englishmen became richer *ipso facto* all Englishmen became richer, it was recognised that increased trade increased land values and therefore benefited some at least of the landowners. Such landowners, especially those who had urban land, or mining royalties, were not averse from using the power of Parliament to increase trade. Nor was there a clear distinction between the 'landed interest' and the 'mercantile interest'. The West India interest was drawn largely from the landed interest. Landowners bought stock in the great trading

[1] Lipson, *op. cit.* pp. 39–44.
[2] L. Stephen, *English Thought in the Eighteenth Century*, II, p. 287.

companies. On the other hand, what was wanted was not trade but advantageous trade. It was thought by many that bullion was wealth and that a surplus of imports over exports was paid in bullion and therefore increased the 'wealth of the country'. Hence most of the duties on exports were taken off by Walpole, and bounties were given for exports and drawbacks for re-exports, in the belief that the 'country' was thereby enriched.

Economic nationalism was one of the easiest forms of nationalism to develop, since it was to the advantage of traders to give the impression that what profited them *ipso facto* profited 'England'. The forms of the law encouraged it. It was the king's prerogative to issue the coinage, and for this purpose he had the right to the produce of all gold and silver mines. 'Treasure' in the hands of private persons was obviously not in the hands of the king: but there was a sort of impression that somehow 'England' gained by having more bullion, even if the wealthy alderman buried it in his cellar or put it around his wife's ample neck.[1] Foreign trade, too, was a matter of royal prerogative which the kings fostered by royal charters and by regulating imports and exports. Trade was a matter not so much of competition between English and foreign merchants as of competition between the king of England and his foreign rivals. His function was to make 'England' richer and therefore, by definition, other countries poorer. The ultimate objective was to import nothing—often called 'national self-sufficiency'[2] —and to export as much as possible. The king 'protected' foreign merchants in England and English merchants abroad; and that word 'protection' had a strong emotional content, though it seems not to have become a common expression for preventing competition until the early part of the nineteenth century. Adam Smith preferred 'monopoly', which had an equally tendentious emotional appeal, though in the opposite direction because it had been one of the issues of the conflict with the Stuarts.

---

[1] John Locke helped to popularise this idea: cf. *Works* (1824 ed.), IV, pp. 12–19; and L. Stephen, *English Thought in the Eighteenth Century*, II, pp. 289–92. There is a tendency to minimise the prevalence of the fallacy: cf. E. Lipson, *The Growth of English Society*, pp. 153–5; but Locke's works were widely read by *politicians*, and Adam Smith thought the 'balance of trade' theory important enough to argue against it.

[2] The term seems to have been used since the Commonwealth.

3. FREER TRADE BEFORE THE REFORM ACT

'The year 1776', said Leslie Stephen, 'is marked in political history by the Declaration of Independence; in the history of thought by the appearance of Adam Smith's *Wealth of Nations*.'[1] No less significant, perhaps, was the appearance in the same year of Jeremy Bentham's *Fragment on Government*. Also, it was probably the year in which Arkwright began to produce the machines which he had patented in 1775; and he was able to make use of them because the Act of 1774 had made it lawful to weave fine cotton cloth without a linen warp.[2] These events marked the beginning of the end of the mercantile 'system', though like Charles II it was an unconscionable time a-dying.

Free trade, as a comprehensive doctrine urging that in principle trade should be free from legislative interference, was new with Adam Smith; but every aspect of the mercantile system which he chose for criticism had already been criticised by somebody. Roger Coke's *Treatise* had criticised most aspects in 1671 and 1675. Sir Dudley North's *Discourses upon Trade* (1691) had even gone so far as to generalise: 'Thus we may labour to hedge in the cuckoo but in vain, for no people ever yet grew rich by policies; but it is peace, industry and freedom that brings trade and wealth, and nothing else.'[3] Leslie Stephen quotes from an anonymous pamphlet, *Considerations on the East India Trade*, published in 1701, and attributed by McCulloch to Henry Martyn.[4] David Hume had, in various of his essays, talked a good deal of sense about economics, as he had talked a good deal of sense about nearly everything. Even the 'nation of shopkeepers' (actually, 'shopkeeping nation') had been invented by a tory parson, Joseph Tucker, of whom Leslie Stephen says that 'Nature had designed him for a shrewd tradesman; fate had converted him into a clergyman'.[5]

Until Adam Smith, however, the nation of shopkeepers had many accountants, who could point to a gain here and a loss there, but no

[1] *English Thought in the Eighteenth Century*, II, p. 283.
[2] W. Cunningham, *Growth of English Industry and Commerce*, pp. 345–6.
[3] Quoted by E. Lipson, *Economic History of England*, III, p. 5.
[4] L. Stephen, *English Thought in the Eighteenth Century*, II, pp. 296–9.
[5] *Ibid.* p. 301.

philosophy of political economy. Adam Smith was able to fill the void not only because he was an acute observer and a learned compiler of relevant facts—itself a rare quality, because it is necessary to determine what facts are relevant and what are merely accidental—but also because he had a definite philosophy:

Smith's philosophy of life...is substantially a corollary from the principles which he shared with the French philosophers generally. Its main propositions may perhaps be thus stated. There is a certain natural order in society. The final cause of this order is the happiness of mankind. The main condition for securing its natural fruits is the liberty of each man to follow his natural instincts. So long as those instincts do not bring men into collision, the artificial interference of government is unjust, because it disregards the natural instincts of mankind, and impolitic because it hinders the natural development of the agencies by which men's wants are supplied. The sympathetic instincts are valuable as suppressing the tendency of each man to invade his neighbour's equal rights to life, liberty, and enjoyment. Where they are not sufficiently strong, there and there only, government may rightfully interfere.[1]

This theory is not explicit in the *Wealth of Nations*. Had it been explicit the book might have been less successful, for it would have been controverted by many. The 'natural order', as the country gentry saw it, was an order based upon a hierarchy of property: even Adam Smith, when he was not discussing trade, seemed to recognise it.[2] The arguments for the Corn Laws, which seemed so amusing to the later Victorians,[3] were based on an assumption which those Victorians did not understand, that in the English manor, where there was a proper hierarchy of rights and duties, every man was happy in performing the duties of his station. This was natural because it was based on the soil and on the order of society which it had pleased God to establish. There was nothing natural about industry based upon the 'spirit of trade', the anxiety of the gambler to make profit. Nor were the later Victorians themselves very sure that there was anything natural about a system which enabled capitalists to 'exploit' labour in times of

---

[1] *Ibid.* pp. 321-2.
[2] *Wealth of Nations* (Cannan's 1937 ed.), pp. 670-2.
[3] For example, J. Noble, *Fiscal Legislation, 1842-1865*, pp. 33-4.

347

industrial expansion and throw it back on the poor law, that is, the country gentry, in time of trade depression.

In fact, however, the conflict over free trade was not a conflict of theories or *a priori* assumptions. Politicians are practical men who absorb their theories through their pores. Essentially the conflict was one of vested interests. But Adam Smith dealt with practical issues which politicians understood. Certainly they understood when he explained them, for he had a remarkable power of analysis and synthesis, and a vast knowledge which enabled him to choose apt illustrations. Even today the comment which the reader of the *Wealth of Nations* must make is: 'this is plain common sense'. But in many respects it was the reverse of what many people understood to be common sense in 1776, and only gradually were they induced to give up their current prejudices and accept those of Adam Smith.

Moreover the theory of individualism expressed in Leslie Stephen's reformulation was in 1776 a philosophy of revolution.[1] It implied vast social and political changes (which would, within the next century, entirely subvert the dominance of the landed interest). Within a few years it was revolutionary in a double sense: for these individualist theories were, fundamentally, the ideas of the French Revolution of 1789. The Crown, the Church and the landed interest did not realise that they were fighting an idea; they were defending themselves against the subversion of institutions in whose rights they believed, and whose justification they did not need to prove. Their 'philosopher' was Burke, who produced not a philosophy but another assumption, that of evolution. The monarchy had a right to exist because it existed; the Church had rights because it was established; the landed interest had rights by

---

[1] Professor Elie Halévy says exactly the opposite: '...the *Wealth of Nations* should be considered neither as an Utopian nor as a revolutionary book. Contemporaneous with the Declaration of American Independence, the book was hardly a few years in advance of the average opinions of any supporter of the reforms which were both necessary and possible in the England of the eighteenth century': Halévy, *The Growth of Philosophic Radicalism*, p. 107. But Professor Halévy was writing in the intellectual plane. It is one thing to persuade the intellectuals and another to persuade the politicians, even when politicians have no patrons. When the London merchants petitioned for free trade in 1819–20, Ricardo regretted that it had taken so long from the publication of the *Wealth of Nations* for these ideas to become acceptable. The Corn Laws were repealed after seventy years and the Navigation Acts after seventy-three years.

prescription. These were institutions established by the wisdom of our ancestors, whose justification was not logic but experience. Changes could occur by the process of evolution, but they were produced by adding experience to inherited institutions and ideas. This, fundamentally, was Conservatism, while the individualism of Adam Smith was the foundation of Liberalism.

We must not, however, think of political controversies as clashes of philosophies, or even of principles of economics. Philosophies and principles find their way eventually into political prejudices; but prejudices derive from a man's environment, education and experience as a whole. The conflict occurs within the ring provided by common experience. One man calls himself Conservative and another Liberal; but both have read Locke, Blackstone, Adam Smith and Burke, or inherited ideas from others who have: and so there is no Liberal who is not a little conservative, and no Conservative who is not a little liberal. Moreover a politician has to consider not only his own prejudices but also those of the people whom he represents or leads. No man can lead unless he is followed, and followers are apt to look where they are going. On the other hand, if nobody follows anybody in country as treacherous as politics they will all find themselves in different ditches. Nor can leaders choose forks in the roads without considering the prejudices of patrons and constituents. It took a long time for Peel to repeal the Corn Law, and he might never have done it but for a potato famine: and, what is even more significant, repeal was not whig policy either. That was seventy years after the publication of the *Wealth of Nations*. These matters, as Adam Smith said of retaliatory tariffs, have to be judged by the 'skill of that insidious and crafty animal, vulgarly called a statesman or politician, whose councils are directed by the momentary fluctuations of affairs'.[1]

Nevertheless, the ideas of the *Wealth of Nations* gradually found their way into public policy. The younger Pitt, 'Adam Smith's first and greatest disciple',[2] could do little, partly because of the inevitable opposition of vested interests, and partly because Pitt's main task was to raise the money for a long war, which he did partly by increasing

---

[1] *Wealth of Nations* (Cannan's 1937 ed.), p. 435.
[2] C. R. Fay, *Great Britain from Adam Smith to the Present Day*, p. 16.

taxation (especially by enforcing an income tax), partly by heavy borrowing, and partly by inflating the currency by relieving the Bank of England of its obligation to exchange gold for its notes. Something was done under Lord Liverpool because he himself had liberal views and was prepared to support liberal reforms so long as they did not antagonise the agricultural interest.[1] In 1820, indeed, he enunciated the essential free trade doctrine, in its political aspect, 'I firmly believe that on all commercial subjects the fewer laws the better'.[2]

Since questions of economic policy are, however, questions of politics, and politics is a composite art, it is wise to remember that the gradual liberalising of British economic policy between 1815 and the Reform Act did not stand alone. The end of a long and successful war is always a signal for the stepping down of nationalism; and, although the Napoleonic Wars were not accompanied by the ballyhoo of war propaganda, which now produces so rapid a reaction, the final defeat of Napoleon necessarily reduced the nationalist temperature. Moreover the cessation of war contracts, the return to unemployment of the soldiers and sailors, and the means which had to be taken to meet the enormous charges on the National Debt, gave first place to the economic problem.[3] On the other hand, it was thought of not only as an economic problem but also as a problem of public order. The governing class had seen the French republic turn into an aggressive imperialist dictatorship, but could not forget that it began as an uprising of the 'rabble' against the forces of order and stability, the Church, the Crown, the aristocracy, and the landed interest. There was, too, plenty of seditious literature in circulation. For the period immediately after 1815, therefore, reaction was dominant. In the field of economics the landed interest had become accustomed to high agricultural prices and expected them to be maintained, while the manufacturers and merchants wished to maintain the virtual monopoly of foreign markets which they had obtained through the blockade of Europe, the failure of Napoleon's 'continental system', and the freedom of Great Britain from the

---

[1] *Life of Lord Liverpool*, II, p. 139.
[2] *Ibid.* III, p. 8.
[3] Even Roman Catholic relief might be a problem of economic politics. Writing to Canning in 1827 Lord Liverpool said that 'those who vote on either side of the Catholic question will be *thinking* about corn': *Life of Lord Liverpool*, III, pp. 452–3.

invasions and rebellions which had ravaged so much of the rest of Europe.

Though the Corn Law had theoretically been in force during the wars, there had in fact been free trade in corn, because prices had been far above the price (66s. in the Act of 1804)[1] at which corn could be imported free of duty. In 1815 the statutory price was raised to 80s., which was fully protective because the market-price was falling rapidly. There was, however, a sudden rise of price in 1816, which coincided with industrial depression, and there were riots in many parts of the country. The market-price was down again in 1817, but rose to 80s. in 1818, and there was further distress. Popular agitation in the towns necessarily found a scapegoat in the landed interest, which monopolised Parliament and kept up the price of bread. Manufacturers and workmen could therefore combine in a demand for Parliamentary reform and the repeal of the Corn Law. The combination ended with Peterloo and the Six Acts of 1819.

There was, however, a rapid recovery in industry and employment, corresponding with a rapid fall in the price of corn. It was the turn of the agricultural interest to protest, and the protest was directed mainly at the burden of taxation, which was alleged to favour the manufacturer at the expense of the land. There was also argument over the Corn Law. Though the importation of corn was absolutely forbidden because the price was low, the agriculturalists criticised the rule which allowed free importation as soon as the price rose to 80s., and asked for a sliding scale above that price. They objected, too, to the practice whereby the importer could store his corn in bond until the price rose to 80s., and then release it without paying duty, since the knowledge that there was corn in bond tended to keep down its price. They also asked for a bounty on the export of corn when the home market was glutted.[2]

This conflict between the landed interest and the manufacturing interest was not a conflict between tory and whig, since both groups were divided, more or less according to private or constituency interest. Finally, the Government gave way and admitted the principle of the sliding scale. Under the Act of 1822 it was provided that the duty

---

[1] The figure relates to wheat: there were different figures for other varieties of corn.
[2] E. Halévy, *History of the English People in the XIXth Century*, II, pp. 112–13.

351

should be 12s. when the price was 70s., 5s. when the price was 80s., and 1s. when the price exceeded 85s.; but the Act was not to come into force until the price rose to 80s., and importation was to cease when the price fell to 70s. In fact, the price never rose to 80s. and therefore the Act (apart from one clause relating to colonial corn) never came into effect. In 1827 Canning tried to liberalise the law by a new sliding scale. Foreign corn would be admitted, with a duty of 20s., when the price rose to 60s., and would be free at 70s. If, however, the price fell below 60s., extra duty would be payable. The Bill passed the Commons but it was so amended in the Lords (after Canning had become Prime Minister) that it was dropped. It was replaced (under the Duke of Wellington) by a more protectionist Bill which continued in force until Peel's Bill of 1841.

The landed interest was on the defensive because, as soon as the price of corn rose, everybody tended to blame the law. On the other hand, the landed interest criticised high taxation, much of which they blamed on the protection of industry: and here the economists and the merchants joined with the landed interest. Again it was not a 'party political' question, though among the tories the free trade group tended to be found among the followers of Canning, whose ideas of economics were provided by William Huskisson.

The campaign for freer trade opened in 1819 with a petition from eighty London merchants, asking Parliament to take the difficulties of trade and industry into consideration. Since this was ineffective, a second petition, with many more signatures, was presented in 1820. Ministers had encouraged, if not invited, these petitions, and they were naturally received cordially; committees of inquiry were appointed by both Houses. The first result, carried against the opposition of the shipowners, was a vast consolidation and liberalisation of the Navigation Acts. They had become so complex that only the expert knew what they contained; and they were out of date because the American colonies were now the United States of America, most of the Spanish colonies were independent countries, the Royal Navy no longer fought with merchant ships, the British mercantile marine was the largest in the world, and the Dutch were no longer serious competitors. It was politically impossible completely to repeal the Navigation Acts, for old ideas never die, they only fade away; but Thomas Wallace and William Huskisson at the Board of Trade severely pruned the restrictions between 1822 and 1825, and the Acts faded out, gently and decorously, in 1849.

Between 1822 and 1825 trade was prosperous. It was therefore possible for the Chancellor of the Exchequer to reduce taxation in spite of the fact that in 1816 the House of Commons had insisted on repealing the income tax and had never replaced the £15,000,000 thus lost to the revenue.[1] Not all the remissions of taxation related to trade policy, but conditions were such that Huskisson, who was President of the Board of Trade from 1823 to 1827, was able to make

a clean sweep of prohibitions and prohibitive duties, substituting moderately protective rates and setting 30 per cent as the upper limit beyond which protection would be thwarted by smuggling. Silks, hitherto protected by prohibition, were allowed the full 30 per cent; linens, threatened with the loss of their old bounty, 20 per cent; woollens, 15 per cent; cottons, the strongest of the textiles, 10 per cent, which was no more than an offset to the duty on raw cotton. To strengthen the manufacturer against foreign competition the duties on many raw materials of the textile and metal industries were lowered. In line with these reductions on imports, the remaining export prohibitions and bounties on export were withdrawn.[2]

These changes enabled the Customs laws to be codified in a single statute for the whole of the United Kingdom, over a thousand Customs Acts being repealed.[3] 'The age of chivalry', said Canning, quoting Burke, 'is gone: and an age of economists and calculators has succeeded'.[4]

These economic changes have to be mentioned in isolation, but they were not in fact isolated. Canning was applying a liberal policy at the Foreign Office; Peel at the Home Office was reforming the penal laws and the prison administration; F. J. Robinson (afterwards Lord Goderich) was reducing the assessed duties on the landowners as well as making trade freer; Lord Liverpool, nearing the end of his life, was showing himself to be liberal. David Ricardo, Adam Smith's

---

[1] C. R. Fay, *Great Britain from Adam Smith to the Present Day*, p. 56.
[2] *Ibid.* p. 57. See also E. Halévy, *History of the English People in the XIXth Century*, II, p. 199, where other figures, relating especially to metals, are given.
[3] C. R. Fay, *op. cit.* p. 58.
[4] E. Halévy, *op. cit.* p. 175.

successor and a Benthamite, died in 1823, but his theories lived after him and were propagated by the Benthamites; and the young men of that group were organised by John Stuart Mill, a youth of seventeen years of age, into the 'Utilitarians'. In 1824 Bentham founded the *Westminster Review*; and in 1825 the Benthamites, with Lord Brougham, founded University College, London, where young Mill attended lectures on political economy and jurisprudence. In Parliament Joseph Hume led the Radicals on economic matters and Lord Brougham on legal and constitutional matters. Hume's great triumph was the repeal of the Combination Acts in 1824, though he and the other Radicals completely misunderstood the probable effects and a new Combination Act had to be passed in 1825.[1]

In respect of some matters the Radicals and the Canningite tories were fundamentally opposed; but there was enough common ground to enable much liberal legislation to be passed. Nor were party lines so clear that such legislation had to be regarded as 'party political'. Indeed, the majority of members of the House of Commons attended only when something of particular interest was under discussion. It happened that, for the first time since 1815, high prices for agricultural products coincided with a trade boom. So long as this situation prevailed neither the landed interest nor the mercantile interest had any special grievance. Even the workers were enjoying something like full employment and were thinking in terms of raising wages by combination rather than in terms of machinery-smashing and Parliamentary reform. Hence Parliament could be left to 'professionals' like Canning, Peel and Huskisson and the 'economists and calculators' on the Opposition benches.

There was a sudden economic collapse in 1825, due apparently to over-investment. There was, however, no demand for the reversal of economic policy. On the contrary, the liberals claimed that the collapse was due not to the policy of freer trade, but to the fact that it had not gone far enough. The workers, too, renewed their demand for the repeal of the Corn Law, with the result that for a short period foreign corn had to be admitted. The Government's main reaction, however, was to reform the banking laws in such manner that the private banks began

[1] *Ante*, pp. 183–4.

354

to be replaced, as in Scotland, by joint-stock banks. As we have seen,[1] a proposal for a more liberal Corn Law passed the House of Commons but was rejected by the House of Lords after Canning became Prime Minister. It was passed, with protectionist amendments, after the Duke of Wellington became Prime Minister.

The curious interlude, in which the Canningite Ministers carried liberal measures through the House of Commons with the aid of whigs and Radicals, came to an end with the formation of the Duke of Wellington's Government in 1828. Though the Canningites remained in the Cabinet, they went out after a few months over a minor measure of Parliamentary reform. This did not mean a party alignment on taxation policy. There was some reaction against Huskisson's liberal policy, but every vested interest wanted relief from the burdens from which it suffered; and neither the Government nor the Opposition could judge whether the grievances were general or particular. Because the whigs and the Canningites were in opposition, however, they tended to use free trade arguments against the Government's Budgets. However, this interregnum, too, was of short duration. Roman Catholic relief split the tories in 1829, but they remained in office until after the general election, when they were defeated in the House of Commons and resigned, thus enabling Lord Grey's Government to be formed on the basis of Parliamentary reform.

4. FREE TRADE AFTER THE REFORM ACT

The Reform Act of 1832 is not a dividing line in the history of free trade. As we have seen, free trade was not a 'party political' question in 1830, and it did not become so until the repeal of the Corn Law, when the whigs and the Peelites lined up against the 'Protectionists'. The end of the long period of tory rule in 1830 and the reform of the House of Commons in 1832 is, however, a convenient point to note how ideas had been moving since 1776. It is easy to exaggerate the influence of intellectual movements, because they are often more prominent in our books than in contemporary opinion. The year 1832 was made memorable, it may be said, not so much by a modest and unassuming

[1] *Ante*, p. 352.

Reform Act, as by the death of that great philosopher, economist and 'projector', Jeremy Bentham. Yet Hazlitt wrote in 1825: 'His name is little known in England, better in Europe, best of all in the plains of Chili and the mines of Mexico.... Mr Hobhouse is a greater man at the hustings, Lord Rolle at Plymouth Dock: but Mr Bentham would carry it hollow, on the score of popularity, at Paris or Pegu.'[1]

Allowing for literary exaggeration, it is true enough that the 'hermit of Queen Square Place' had little direct influence on his contemporaries. His 'school' consisted of an assortment of odd characters, most of them not of his generation, who had a remarkable facility for pushing themselves into places where decisions were taken; or perhaps, being in places where decisions were taken, they chose to inform themselves of the principles upon which the decisions should be based. Professor A. V. Dicey, being himself an 'impenitent Benthamite'[2] may have exaggerated, in his *Law and Opinion in England*, the effect of Bentham's ideas upon legislation in the nineteenth century. It is nevertheless true that, wherever one digs into the rubbish heaps of public policy, out slips a scrap of paper—or more likely a whole dog-eared report—which has 'Benthamism' writ large across it. The number of Benthamites in the House of Commons was never very large; and after the death of Ricardo they tended to concentrate mainly on political subjects. On the other hand, they were assiduous in their attendance on select committees, the only means by which the House of Commons could inform itself about economic conditions in the absence of an adequate statistical service. The Benthamites outside the House were, too, almost the only group capable of producing proposals for economic policy which were not evidently founded on group self-interest. The landowners, the West India interest, the East India Company, the shipping interest, the silk manufacturers, and so forth, all had axes to grind. Moreover the Benthamites were strong in the only Ministry which knew anything about industrial conditions regarded from a national standpoint, the Board of Trade. From Huskisson to Gladstone the active officials of the Board were free traders.[3]

[1] C. W. Everett, *The Education of Jeremy Bentham*, p. xv.
[2] A. V. Dicey, *A Fool's Paradise*, p. ix.
[3] Lucy Brown, *The Board of Trade and the Free-Trade Movement, 1830–42*, ch. II.

On the other hand, it is easy to exaggerate the Benthamite influence both in the House and in the Board of Trade. The key to the paradox that the Benthamites were few and their activity not immediately very influential, and that they nevertheless had such wide influence, is that the philosopher of the type of Adam Smith or Jeremy Bentham, the political philosopher who is concerned with the practical problems of his own age, is the child of the prevailing ideas of one generation and the father of the prevailing ideas of the next. Few of those who debated free trade for the next century—and free trade was overthrown, by a political manoeuvre, exactly one hundred years after the first Reform Act—could have quoted chapter and verse, but most of the supporters of free trade spoke the Benthamite language without knowing it. Its principles had become part of the common stock of ideas, and they were put into circulation, as occasion arose, without reference to or acknowledgment of their source. 'It is impossible', said Bentham himself, 'that the bulk of mankind should find leisure, had they the ability, to examine into the grounds of one hundredth part of the rules and maxims which they find themselves obliged to act upon.'[1] This applies *a fortiori* to party politicians, who have 'rules and maxims' provided for them by leaders and party programmes.

Even after 1832 the main political issue was not free trade but the repeal of the Corn Law. Everybody ate corn and nearly everybody used cotton. But the supply of corn fluctuated widely according to the harvest, while the demand was inelastic; prices therefore fluctuated widely and indeed wildly. When the price rose considerably, everybody except the producer and the landowner complained bitterly against the whole landed interest. On the other hand the production of cotton did not fluctuate widely and the demand was elastic. Any farmer who wanted a new smock simply made do with the old one if the price was too high, and did not blame either the duty on raw cotton or the duty on cotton textiles. Moreover, all the workers of all the towns, which were the centres of political agitation, suffered from the Corn Law, while the workers in the cotton towns gained, or thought they gained, from import duties on cotton textiles and did not notice that they lost from import duties on raw cotton. The opponents of the Corn Law appealed

[1] E. Halévy, *Growth of Philosophic Radicalism*, p. 112.

357

to the bellies of the common men; the opponents of tariffs on raw material and manufactured articles had to appeal to the economists, though as soon as a trade suffered from unemployment, its first thought was to petition Parliament.

Political economy was undoubtedly in fashion. It 'penetrated into the University of Cambridge with Prynn in 1816; into Parliament with Ricardo in 1818; and into the University of Oxford with Senior in 1825'.[1] Greville, with his customary exaggeration, remarked in 1826 that 'so great and so absorbing is the interest which the present discussions excite that all men are become political economists and financiers';[2] and Professor Halévy added: 'nobody now talked politics, men talked of nothing but banks, paper money, free trade, and the abolition of the corn laws'.[3]

These political economists were, however, peculiar people. Adam Smith was, by 1832, comparatively respectable. Bentham was not because, in the last fourteen years of his life, he had become a Radical. Ricardo was, until his death in 1823, the high priest of political economy, and his works lived after him: but he was a Benthamite, a Radical, a financier and the son of a financier. James Mill and J. R. MacCulloch were disciples of Bentham and Ricardo. This was not the sort of people from whom the landed interest was prepared to take its politics. On the other hand, the general trend of economic discussion supported the inarticulate major premises of manufacturers and merchants. They wanted more and larger markets and more trade. The removal of restrictions on trade might injure an individual manufacturer or an individual merchant, but a removal of restrictions all round, especially the Corn Law, ought to profit them in the mass, and each was optimistic enough to think that he would get rather more than his share, for successive crises knocked out most of the unsuccessful gamblers, even under the mercantile system. Whatever Ricardo or Malthus said about a particular economic doctrine did not matter, for political economy was becoming an abstruse subject which only peculiar people pretended to understand. The elementary doctrine was simplicity itself.

---

[1] E. Halévy, *Growth of Philosophic Radicalism*, p. 317.
[2] *Greville Memoirs*, I, p. 83.
[3] E. Halévy, *History of the English People in the XIXth Century*, II, p. 237.

If more people had more money to spend they would buy more goods; and there was no need to be subtle about the meaning of 'money'. If people had cheaper food they would either receive lower wages or buy more goods. The restrictive laws were means by which profits were diverted from trade and industry into the pockets of farmers and land-owners. The policies of the political economists, as distinct from their speculations, favoured the expanding economy necessitated by the rapidly developing capitalist system.

The old guard, whig and tory alike, could not accept the argument. It must not be thought, however, that they were prepared to bandy arguments from the text-books. Lord Melbourne, for instance, refused to accept a reform of the Corn Law in 1838, not because he disagreed with the economists—he said the question was both 'difficult and dangerous'—but because the raising of the question would create animosity and discord among social classes and would leave the labouring population dependent upon foreign corn. 'Depend upon it, any advantage that can be gained is not worth the danger and evil of the struggle by which alone it can be carried....'[1] Though a new political balance was achieved by the Reform Act, the landed interest was strongly entrenched, not only by the considerable increase in the number of county members, but also by the continued enfranchisement of many small boroughs in which the landowners had influence. Nor did any of the politicians, except the Radicals, want to diminish its authority. Everybody knew that the British Constitution was founded on property:[2] and to try to diminish the influence of property in order to give more profits to manufacturers was not only unconstitutional but downright immoral. The Corn Law was not intended to enable the landed interest to make *profits*. The very word was anathema to the responsible country gentleman: it savoured of the 'spirit of commerce' which had unfortunately entered into English life. It had depopulated the countryside, deprived the labouring class of its natural leaders, placed a vast population at the mercy of a succession of financial crises, and deprived a large part of the population of the benefits of religion.

[1] *Lord Melbourne's Papers*, pp. 387–8.
[2] But, as Coleridge pointed out, on *unequal* property, so that those who had property had duties: R. J. White, *The Political Thought of Samuel Taylor Coleridge*, p. 231.

The economists regarded labourers as wage-earners and consumers: but labourers were human beings and, so long as they were on the land, they were treated as such. Now the land was being depopulated and it had become difficult if not impracticable for the gentry to maintain their rank and establishments, 'without joining in the general competition under the influence of the same trading spirit'.[1]

This was, of course, the Romantic Movement, the Merrie England school: but in the eyes of many it justified the Corn Laws. Those laws were designed only to maintain the estates of the country gentry, to whom was committed the religious and moral responsibility for their tenants, while at the same time the laws provided for the importation of foreign corn to feed the hordes of people on the poor law when the harvests were so bad that there was scarcity of food. 'During his long life', said Lord Melbourne as Prime Minister, 'it had been his lot to hear many mad things proposed, but the maddest of all mad things to which he had ever had to listen was a proposal to abolish the Corn Laws.' Sir James Graham, in the same year, explained to a deputation from Manchester that:

If the corn laws were repealed great disasters would fall upon the country, that the land would go out of cultivation, that Church and State could not be upheld, that all our institutions would be reduced to their primitive elements, and that the people we were exciting would pull down our houses about our ears.[2]

These arguments did not prevent Sir James Graham from supporting the repeal of the Corn Law six years later.

Moreover, the main task of the Whig Governments, as of all Governments, was to keep themselves in power. From 1832 to 1834 they had, with the Radicals, a firm majority, but their essential concern was to effect the large measures of reform which the agitation of 1830–2 evidently demanded. From 1835 to 1837 they needed Radical support, and from 1837 to 1841 they could not carry on except with Radical or Conservative support. Apart from a rationalisation of the customs and excise laws, which was regarded as a technical operation, the movement towards free trade in this period depended solely on the existence of

[1] S. T. Coleridge in 1817: R. J. White, *op. cit.* p. 203.
[2] Both quotations from Henry Fawcett, *Free Trade and Protection* (3rd ed.), p. 3.

a Budget surplus and the pressure for reduced taxation from vested interests.

From 1832 to 1836 was a period of prosperity. Trade boomed and the revenue was buoyant. It was therefore possible to take off some of the duties which hampered trade but brought in little revenue. A larger reconstruction of the system of taxation was impossible because of conflict between the landed interest and the mercantile interest. This conflict was, more nearly than it had been before 1832, a conflict between Conservative and whig, but there was not a coincidence; most of the whigs were landowners, and in any case they could not contemplate the loss of the rural constituencies. The situation changed at the end of 1836. There was industrial depression and a simultaneous rise in the prices of corn. At the same time the prohibition of outdoor relief under the new poor law of 1834 began to affect the working classes, whose members in increasing numbers turned to constitutional reform as the solution to the disabilities from which they suffered. The middle-class free traders, on the other hand, blamed the Corn Law, though most of the Radicals also had political remedies to urge. The decision to concentrate on an attack on the Corn Law was taken in Manchester in September 1838, when the Anti-Corn Law League was founded.

There is no need to detail the history of this attempt to force a particular proposal through Parliament.[1] It was an agitation which, if it could be kept going long enough, was bound to succeed. It was certain that, at some time, there would be a bad harvest, or a succession of bad harvests, which would raise the prices of corn; and then inevitably the landed interest would be accused of 'starving the people' in order to put unconscionable profits into its pockets. Neither Conservatives nor whigs wanted to lose either the rural vote or the urban vote; but it was certain that, given a sufficient scarcity of food, a parliamentary majority could be obtained for repeal. The Anti-Corn Law League, unlike previous free trade movements, did not produce learned works on political economy: it went into the constituencies with lectures and pamphlets. Moreover, the League did not make the

---

[1] See Norman McCord, *The Anti-Corn Law League*, and vol. II of this work, pp. 102–9.

mistake of attacking the Corn Law and defending the protection of industry. At its initial meeting in Manchester a free trade resolution was passed, and in Parliament the general free trade agitation continued.[1] On the other hand, the League's propaganda was for the most part directed to the single objective of securing repeal of the Corn Law.

The general free trade agitation did not, at this stage, arouse public opinion. In 1840, apparently at the instigation of one of the officials of the Board of Trade,[2] the Radicals secured the appointment of a Select Committee on Import Duties. It was intended to demonstrate, and did to the satisfaction of the Radical members, that by far the greater part of the customs duties were noxious, in that they produced little or no revenue and merely obstructed trade.[3] Nevertheless, the Report aroused little interest. The general problem was too complex to debate. It was easier to concentrate on the single problem of the Corn Law which, according to the League, put up the price of bread.

On the other hand, the whigs were compelled to do something in order to meet the growing deficit in the revenue. To everybody's astonishment, the Budget of 1841 proposed to make a frontal attack on the three great monopolies, timber, sugar and corn. The timber monopoly arose from the heavy, and sometimes prohibitive, duty on Baltic timber and the lighter duty on Canadian timber. In spite of the 'long haul' from Canada, it was cheaper to import Canadian timber, and the shipowners liked the Canadian preference because of the higher freights. It was proposed to decrease the foreign duty and to increase the Canadian duty, which would result in an increase in the revenue. The sugar monopoly arose from the heavy preference on colonial sugar, which gave the West Indian producers a virtual monopoly. It was proposed to reduce the import duty on foreign sugar, which would thus become competitive. Finally, it was proposed, by a

---

[1] According to J. Travis Mills (*John Bright and the Quakers*, II, p. 172) the League's journal stated: 'We hold all legislative interference with the labour market, all attempts of Government to fix the wages of industry, all interference of a third party between employers and employed, to be unjustifiable in principle and mischievous in their results.' No date is given.

[2] Lucy Brown, *The Board of Trade and the Free-Trade Movement, 1830–42*, pp. 70–1.

[3] *Ibid.* chs. 8–12 for a full analysis.

separate measure, to abolish the sliding scale on corn and to impose a fixed duty which would in fact allow foreign corn to be imported except when there was a glut through home production. A good deal of propaganda for free trade was done simultaneously, partly under the inspiration of the Board of Trade.[1] The report of the select committee of 1840, which had almost been ignored in 1840, suddenly received wide publicity, and petitions poured in from the manufacturing districts. The effort failed, because the shipping interests, the West India interest, and the landed interest joined with the Conservatives to defeat the proposed reduction in the sugar duty. The Government did not at once resign, but sought to have a debate on the Corn Law in order to make that law the 'issue' of the inevitable general election. The Government was, however, defeated on a Conservative motion of no confidence.

The Conservatives swept the counties and won half the boroughs; the whigs retained majorities in Scotland and Ireland, but they were reduced. It was, as usual, a complicated election, with a very large number of uncontested elections—213 out of 401.[2] This may have been due in part, as Professor Gash suggests,[3] to the expense involved in successive elections at short intervals. Though the new Parliament was called the 'Bribery Parliament', there is no evidence that there was either more or less corruption in 1841 than in 1837.[4] Probably the electorate, including the landowners who had influence in counties or boroughs, were confused by the sudden change in politics. They had been accustomed to electing reformers and supporters of the established order; they were now asked to elect free traders and protectionists.[5] There were Conservatives who supported a modified Corn Law and whigs who thought, with their late Prime Minister, that any such modification would destroy the foundation of the British Constitution. Most electors, probably, had no notion of the difference between a fixed duty and a sliding scale: one cannot thrust dogma on electors in this way. Anyhow, it had been a weak Government; and in the presence of Chartism it seemed wise to vote for stability. On the other hand,

---

[1] E. Halévy, *History of the English People in the Nineteenth Century*, III, pp. 344–6; Lucy Brown, *op. cit.* pp. 214–15.

[2] N. Gash, *Politics in the Age of Peel*, p. 441.   [3] *Ibid.* p. 239.

[4] G. Kitson Clark, *Peel and the Conservative Party*, p. 482.

[5] *Ibid.* pp. 482–3.

in some of the populous constituencies tories and Chartists combined on a policy of 'No Bastilles', that is, no workhouses.[1] Moreover the Opposition was not wholly whig. Some of the northern constituencies elected candidates, supported by the League, who wanted neither a fixed duty on corn nor a sliding scale, but total repeal of the Corn Law. Among them was Richard Cobden, who early in his parliamentary career described the Corn Law as 'a law that had been baptised in blood, begotten in violence and injustice, perpetuated at the expense of the tears and groans of the people'.[2]

Peel's first effort was a compromise on the Corn Law. He had wanted to leave the question until 1843, but some of his colleagues insisted on a liberal measure, and accordingly he proposed in 1842 a new, but lower, sliding scale. His second effort was more sensational. He proposed to reintroduce the income tax, for a short period of years, and at the same time to remit a large part of the indirect taxes. All absolute prohibitions on import were to be abolished; all duties on raw materials were to be reduced to a maximum of five per cent, all duties on goods partly manufactured to a maximum of twelve per cent, and all duties on manufactured articles to a maximum of twenty per cent. The loss to the revenue was only £270,000, and Peel expected not only to meet that loss, but also to replace the income tax, by increased revenue from trade over the next three or five years.[3]

The Opposition's first reaction was that Peel had stolen their clothes: but debate was in the main concentrated on the three monopolies, timber, sugar and corn. The timber duties were to be lowered, but retaining the Canadian preference. The sugar duties were not to be touched because of the strength of the West India interest. Corn, as we have seen, already had a lower sliding scale. Cobden tried to concentrate the debate on corn, so as to be able to speak for the workers. Peel tried to keep the debate on the lower import duties. The main debate, however, was directed to the income tax, which the whigs had forced the Government to abolish in 1816. It was only a little one—7d. in the £—and the manufacturers, gamblers as always, thought they would be more than compensated by reduced duties on raw

---

[1] E. Halévy, *History of the English People in the Nineteenth Century*, IV, p. 7.
[2] *Ibid.* pp. 12–13. [3] *Ibid.* pp. 19–20.

materials and articles partly manufactured. In spite of the combination of interests, Peel's proposals were accepted.

The League took the question of the Corn Law back to the constituencies. For the moment Parliamentary action was unlikely to be successful. The harvests of 1842 and 1843 were good: that of 1844 was excellent. The League went on with its work, believing that the first bad harvest would compel the Government to repeal the Corn Law. The harvest of 1845 was mediocre; but it was not the harvest but the potato blight which brought success. In November Peel invited his colleagues to suspend the Corn Law, but had the support of only three colleagues. The League redoubled its efforts; and Lord John Russell wrote to his constituents virtually pledging his whig colleagues to total repeal. By 3 December only two Ministers were against repeal; but Peel resigned on 6 December. Lord John Russell was unable to form a Government. The whigs were not enthusiastic, either about repeal or about taking office as a minority Government; and they found various excuses.

Peel reformed his Government and produced forthwith, not a mere Corn Law measure, but a complete scheme for freer trade. He proposed to repeal the duties on almost all raw materials except tallow and timber, on both of which the duties were to be reduced. The duties on textiles were to be either abolished or considerably lowered. The duty on agricultural seeds was to be reduced and those on cattle food abolished. Duties on foodstuffs other than corn were to be reduced or, in the case of meat and live cattle, abolished. The duties on corn were to be reduced gradually until they were abolished in 1849, subject to a registration duty of 1s. per quarter. Other proposals, designed to placate the landed interest, related to local administration.

On the motion to go into committee on the Corn Law, an amendment that the house go into committee that day six months was defeated by 337 votes to 240, there voting in the majority (including tellers) 112 Conservatives and 227 Liberals, while against were 231 Conservatives and eleven Liberals. The Corn Bill passed the House of Commons although, according to Cobden, two-thirds of the members were privately against it. It passed the House of Lords, in spite of an almost unanimous opinion against it, because the peers dared not repeat the experience of the Reform Bill.[1] The Conservative party had, however, irretrievably split. The Protectionists had organised themselves with separate leaders and whips, Lord Stanley leading in the Lords and Lord George Bentinck in the Commons. The other Conservatives, the Peelites, had no organisation, but gradually coalesced with the whigs; and this coalition became the Liberal party, the free trade party. The Protectionists, after a short interval, resumed the name Conservative; and one of Disraeli's main tasks, during the eighteen years in which the Conservatives were, except for two short spells, in Opposition, was to wean them from protection.

The dramatic event was the repeal of the Corn Law; but progress towards free trade had been almost consistent since the younger Pitt took office in 1784. During the long war the essential problem was to find sources of taxation; but afterwards Huskisson's reforms were directed towards free trade. The academic case for free trade, as put by Adam Smith and Ricardo, was fully accepted, especially in the Board of Trade itself. Gladstone had become Vice-President in 1841 and had been convinced by his officials. Peel had become a free trader in principle long before 1846, though as a practical politician he could move no faster than public opinion; and public opinion was moving fast under the influence of the League.

The difference between the parties was, however, a difference of approach. The purpose of free trade, as the free traders put it, was to increase the wealth of the *country* by increasing industry and trade. It was also a moral and humanitarian crusade:

Cobden's thought began with a starving Stockport, and having put a girdle round the commercial globe, came back with gathered treasures of observation to end at Stockport again, while to Bright free trade was a religious passion, sustained by pity and wrath, which he had the gift to communicate in their purest form to thousands of hearers at a time.[2]

The purpose of free trade, as the Protectionists put it, was to increase the profits of manufacturers and traders at the expense of the real people of the country, the landowners, farmers and labourers. 'Protection' was not, as elsewhere, the protection of industry against foreign competition. British industry needed no such protection. It was the pro-

---

[1] E. Halévy, *op. cit.* p. 135.   [2] *Life of John Bright*, p. 56.

tection of the ancient institutions of the country, which were founded on landed property, against subversion by moneyed interests; the protection of the people of the British Empire, especially in Canada and the West Indies, by enabling them to compete with foreign traders; and the protection of the people of Great Britain from reliance on foreign foodstuffs whose export might at any time be prohibited for political reasons. The Protectionists lost the argument because the process of subversion, as they understood it, had gone too far and their control of the situation had been destroyed by the Reform Act. The Conservative party, as a protectionist party, had no future; and Disraeli had to lead them gently towards new pastures, though it took him some time to discover where they were.

5. TARIFF REFORM

Free trade did not come all at once. The Navigation Acts were repealed in 1849; Gladstone combed out the customs duties in 1853, and those which were left were barely, if at all, protective; in 1854 the duties on colonial and foreign sugar were equated, though they were not abolished until 1874; Cobden's French treaty of 1860 did more than abolish protective duties, for it reduced revenue in order to secure a reduction of French protective duties; the duty on paper, the last of the 'taxes on knowledge', went in 1861, though it was barely protective; the duty on flour was removed in 1869, at the same time as the 'registration duty' on corn.[1] John Stuart Mill, whose *Principles of Political Economy*, first published in 1844, went through seven editions before his death in 1873, stated that it was hardly necessary, at least in Great Britain, to do more than state without much argument the falsity of the 'doctrine of protection to native industry'.[2] In the sixties and seventies the problem had completely disappeared from politics. It began to reappear in the late seventies, primarily as a response to trade and agricultural depression. Then it got caught in the rising tide of imperialism, and Joseph Chamberlain jumped on what seemed to be the bandwaggon, though in fact it was going the wrong way.

[1] J. H. Clapham, *Economic History of Modern Britain*, II, pp. 242–6.
[2] *Ibid.* p. 241.

367

British politicians and economists were puzzled that other countries should retain or adopt protection, a 'stupid and impossible proposition', as John Bright called it.[1] The Professor of Political Economy in the University of Cambridge devoted his lectures to 'an inquiry into the causes which have retarded the general adoption of free trade since its introduction into England'.[2] Writing in 1878, he noted that in England, 'where scarcely anyone until lately ventured to utter a dubious word with regard to the benefits conferred by free trade, an inclination is now being shown in many quarters again to lapse into some of the fallacies of protection'.[3] This was a consequence of trade depression.

The new movement had its slogans. Chambers of Commerce passed resolutions against 'one-sided free trade', and there were references to the 'adverse balance of trade', to the need for 'reciprocity' and 'fair trade'. The movement came mainly from the manufacturing districts, which had given so much strength (and so much money) to Cobden's crusade. The 'storm centre', we are told, was Bradford, where the worsted trade was greatly depressed, partly because Victorian ladies would insist on wearing French woollens.[4] A countess started a 'Buy British League' and wrote a pamphlet, of which patriotic Bradford bought six thousand copies.[5] From Bradford, too, came the argument that free trade kept wages down. As Cunliffe Lister, a silk manufacturer, put it: 'No strike committee, no master, not Lister and Co., but the foreigner at Créfeld and Lyons fixes the rate of wages to be paid at Manningham Mills. What he pays, Lister and Co. must pay, as long as his goods come into England free.'[6] So, if there was a tariff on silk goods, there would be higher wages. The difficulty was that if there was a tariff on manufactured articles there would also be a tariff on corn, because British agriculture, too, was depressed, and wanted tariffs on American corn.[7] So, prices as well as wages would go up. On the other hand, Canada did not want tariffs on Canadian corn, but was willing to give Imperial preferences to British manufacturers—

---

[1] Benjamin H. Brown, *The Tariff Reform Movement in Great Britain, 1881–1895*, p. 3.
[2] H. Fawcett, *Free Trade and Protection* (1st ed. 1878, 3rd ed. 1879).
[3] *Ibid.* (3rd ed.), p. 122.   [4] Benjamin H. Brown, *op. cit.* p. 11.
[5] *Ibid.*   [6] *Ibid.* p. 19.
[7] *Ibid.* p. 12.

presumably so as to enable them to compete with American industry but not with Canadian industry, though nobody descended to details. Thus, even at this early stage the tariff reform movement got into its familiar trilemma, the competing interests of industrialists, agriculturalists, and imperialists. Indeed, this is to oversimplify, for the industrialists wanted protection for themselves but not for the industries whose products they used. As Lord Derby said in 1887: 'The strength of our [free trade] position is this, that every free trader is the ally of every other free trader, whereas every protectionist looks with jealousy on those who wish to protect articles in regard to which he is a consumer, and not a producer.'[1]

Those who wanted protection could not expect to get it from the Liberals; and there was no hope of getting it from the Conservatives unless it would demonstrably gain votes. The task was more difficult than that of the Anti-Corn Law League in the forties. The workers of the towns and, after 1884, in the counties, had votes. The Liberal party was highly organised in the towns. It had, until 1886, all the prominent leaders except Lord Randolph Churchill. It had at hand the slogan 'cheap bread'; and, whenever protection was mentioned, 'the cry of cheap bread was heard throughout the land'. The early crusaders for protection were not national leaders like Cobden and Bright, but employers of labour like Cunliffe Lister, Ecroyd, MacIver and S. S. Lloyd, who were hardly known outside the range of their factory whistles. The tradition that the 'bosses' were the enemies of the 'working class' did not begin to arise until late in the eighties, and workers still felt some loyalty to their own sections of industry: but this meant that Ecroyd, the worsted manufacturer, had little appeal outside Bradford.

Nor were these people the sort to become platform orators. Their technique was that of the not very scrupulous pressure group. They 'bought' trade unionists in order to get a footing in the Trades Union Congress. They were more successful with the Conservative associations because those associations, then as now, were dominated by the comparatively wealthy men of the Conservative clubs. On the other hand, the National Union of Conservative Associations had very little

[1] *Ibid.* p. 18.

influence after Lord Randolph Churchill's rebellion had been suppressed. Like the National Liberal Federation, it provided a platform for the little men, who had their brief hour of glory and then went back to their clubs and their houses in the suburbs, leaving Conservative policy in the hands of the professionals.

Moreover the British elector likes his politics in small doses. In 1880 the electors turned out the Earl of Beaconsfield, and in 1885 Joseph Chamberlain swept into the headlines with the *Radical Programme*. In 1886 the issue was Home Rule, and the Conservatives badly needed Liberal Unionist support. The Unionist alliance was precarious until 1892, when Gladstone won a majority again and Home Rule still kept the headlines, in spite of Parnell's divorce. Meanwhile imperialism was rising to its crescendo in the Boer War; and after 1895 Joseph Chamberlain swept into the lead again. Though the National Union of Conservative Associations kept passing protectionist motions, the policy never had a chance of acceptance. Most Liberal Unionists and many Conservatives were free traders. No Conservative leader dared to break the Unionist alliance while Gladstone was leading the Liberals, and to split the Conservative party was, after the time of Disraeli, the only deadly sin. Nor would it be wise to give the G.O.M. an excuse for a rousing 'Midlothian' on the dear loaf. Protection simply was not practical politics until the Conservative party had nothing else to offer after the Boer War; meanwhile it was only partially suppressed because it was popular in the Conservative clubs and presumably—though no evidence is available on this—among those who contributed to Conservative party funds.

Protection, under the euphemism 'tariff reform', came back into Conservative propaganda not as a proposition in economics but as a proposition in imperialism. As we have seen in chapter VI, the great defect of Conservative imperialism was that it assumed a fictitious Empire, a great body of imperial loyalists overseas, dependent on the United Kingdom for defence and external relations, thinking of themselves as citizens of a great Empire of which the United Kingdom was the hub, hoping that that great Empire would, like the land of hope and glory, be mightier yet, and therefore anxious to join with the peoples of the United Kingdom in some sort of union—federal, fighting, or fiscal.

Sir John Seeley invented imperial history and Sir Charles Lucas invented imperial geography, and a generation was taught about the British Empire from wall maps showing the Empire in red and communications radiating from London. What none of the books taught, not even Sir Charles Dilke's, was the strength of colonial nationalism and the diversity of ideas about the Empire possessed by the very different peoples of the several British colonies and the Indian Empire.

The facts of life become a little clearer at the Colonial Conference of 1902, though only a small minority of the peoples of the Empire were there represented because only Canada, Australia, New Zealand, Newfoundland, Cape Colony and Natal had self-government. It can hardly be said that the Conservative politicians realised that, as we now know, all the tendencies were centrifugal. A whole generation of Conservatives had been taught to abhor the alleged doctrines of the 'Manchester School'. Even Lord Salisbury, who was better at sitting on the fence than at reading mythology in the sky, made a speech in which, while warning against forcing the pace, he assumed that there would be 'combinations' which would 'cast into the shade all the glories that the British Empire has hitherto displayed':[1] and this belief, that there would eventually be an integrated Empire, prevailed for another generation.

At the Conference, Chamberlain's reference to imperial federation as being 'within the limits of possibility' and his advocacy of a 'Council of Empire', were quietly ignored.[2] The proposals from the Admiralty and the War Office for increased contributions for imperial defence were coldly received, though small additional contributions to naval defence were made by Australia, New Zealand, Cape Colony and Natal.[3] What the colonies wanted was imperial preference in the British market, that is, tariffs against foreign imports which would allow colonial producers to compete more easily. The Canadian Parliament had, in 1897, given British goods a preference of twenty-five per cent and had in 1900 raised it to one-third. This preference had at first been thought of as a *quid pro quo* for imperial defence, to which the Canadian Government had refused to contribute: but the increased preference of

---

[1] *Life of Joseph Chamberlain*, IV, p. 416.
[2] *Ibid.* pp. 421–2.   [3] *Ibid.* pp. 422–8.

1900 had been criticised by Canadian manufacturers, and Sir Wilfrid Laurier therefore wanted some tariff concession from Britain. Britain had something to concede, because the registration duty on corn, which Sir Robert Peel had left in 1846 and which had not been abolished until 1869, had in 1902 been reimposed by Hicks Beach, for revenue purposes, and Laurier had at once asked for a preference for Canadian corn. Chamberlain and Laurier distrusted each other. Laurier thought Chamberlain 'ambitious, but not for himself alone', and Chamberlain thought Laurier 'not an Imperialist in our sense'.[1] At the Conference, Chamberlain sat on the fence very gingerly, though after much discussion he agreed that preferences should be discussed as a means for increasing inter-imperial trade.[2] It then appeared that the Canadian proposal assumed that, in respect of some articles, an additional preference would be given to British goods by raising duties on foreign imports and, in respect of some other articles, by imposing duties on foreign goods on the free list.[3] This proposal could not be accepted by Chamberlain, because he could not then justify preferences as steps towards freer trade. The other Prime Ministers agreed, however, with the Canadians. The final resolution therefore recognised the principle of preferential trade, agreed that Empire Free Trade was impracticable, recommended the colonies to give preferences to United Kingdom goods and the United Kingdom to give preferences 'either by exemption from or reduction of duties now or hereafter imposed'.[4]

These discussions were valuable to Chamberlain in a double sense. First, he had learned that there was no present hope of any approach to 'imperial unity' except through tariff concessions. Secondly, when the discussions had turned to hard bargaining he found the free trade officials of the Board of Trade ill-prepared to bandy arguments with the Canadian officials. To go into reverse and start a campaign for 'tariff reform' was, however, a serious matter of strategy. This had to be considered from two angles, that of his own career and that of the Unionist parties. When A. J. Balfour became Prime Minister in 1902 there was no longer any question of Chamberlain's succeeding to that office, unless of course Chamberlain somehow persuaded the Con-

---

[1] Life of Joseph Chamberlain, p. 435 [2] Ibid. p. 443.
[3] Ibid. p. 444. [4] Ibid p. 446.

servatives to throw out Balfour. It is unlikely that the as yet unpublished Chamberlain papers will show any such intention. He was at least as ambitious as the average politician; it was an entirely honourable ambition, an anxiety to get to the top of his chosen profession, but he was a political realist; he saw before Lord Salisbury's resignation that he could not hope for the succession, and he must have known after Balfour's succession that there was no hope of getting him out without splitting the Conservative party.

On the other hand, the end of the Boer War left the Unionist parties with no policy except the purely negative one of opposing Home Rule. They had won two elections and could not hope to win a third unless some imaginative policy was produced (and probably not even then, but politicians always exaggerate the influence of their own advocacy). The respective wounds of the Liberal Imperialists and the Pro-Boers would heal and both sections would be moved towards a policy of social reform by pressure from the Labour Movement. Though social reform would have been attractive to the author of the *Radical Programme*, there was no hope of persuading the Conservative party because that party had become, since 1886, the party of the employers. It was, in 1902, very class-conscious because of the development of the new unionism. Like the landowners of the thirties, the bankers, merchant princes and industrial lords thought of themselves as the leaders of the community whom the workers of their respective trades ought to follow because they 'provided employment' and kept the great economic machine working. As the Labour party rose, the Conservatives had to buy votes by increasing social services, but no such idea prevailed in 1902.

Moreover, Chamberlain had broken with his Radical past by supporting, very reluctantly, the Education Bill of 1902, which abolished the school boards and provided aid from the rates for denominational schools. The average voter was not much concerned with either. But the Home Rule Bill of 1886 had split the Nonconformists and other lower-middle-class voters, the right wing going with Chamberlain into the Liberal Unionist party. He could not break up the Unionist alliance on this question, for he and his party had no future except in association with the Conservatives, upon whose votes they were

373

dependent even in Birmingham. The long debates, in which Chamberlain spoke only once, and then only on a closure motion, caused many Liberal Unionists to go back to the Liberal party. From 1902 the Liberal Unionist party was a mere façade, an organisation for controlling what would otherwise have been Conservative seats. If a new policy had to be adopted to win the next election it had to be a Conservative policy. Chamberlain's decision was to continue the imperialist sentiments of the Boer War in a new imperialist campaign: but the Colonial Conference of 1902 had shown that it must be a campaign for imperial preferences. To give preferences there had to be tariffs, and so the new campaign had to be a campaign for protection or 'tariff reform'.

It is plain that the decision had been taken before Chamberlain left for South Africa in November 1902, but the tactics of the campaign had to be carefully worked out lest it split the Unionist alliance. The first step would have to be a very little one, the remission for Empire produce of the registration duty on corn. Chamberlain had decided in August 1902 to press this on the Cabinet.[1] When the matter came before the Cabinet, just before Chamberlain sailed for South Africa, no final decision was taken because it depended upon the Budget proposals of 1903; but tentatively the Cabinet decided to retain the corn tax and to give a remission to colonial corn.[2]

The plan miscarried because C. T. Ritchie, the new Chancellor of the Exchequer, was a firm free trader. Even in November 1902, he had seen that Chamberlain's proposal raised the whole question of free trade, and he had circulated an uncompromising memorandum to the Cabinet.[3] Finding himself able in March 1904 to reduce the income tax, he looked round for an item of indirect taxation for a compensating relief. He chose corn rather than tea because, among other reasons, a corn tax 'lends itself very readily to misrepresentation'.[4] This was from his explanation in the House of Commons, and there cannot be much doubt that one of his reasons was that Chamberlain wanted to treat it as a protective duty so as to give preference to Canadian wheat,

---

[1] *Life of Joseph Chamberlain*, p. 517.
[2] *Ibid.* pp. 518–28. [3] *Ibid.* pp. 520–3.
[4] *Life of the Eighth Duke of Devonshire*, II, p. 299.

374

whereas Ritchie and his predecessor, Hicks Beach, regarded it as a revenue duty.

The Budget came to the Cabinet before Chamberlain returned; but Balfour postponed it until after Chamberlain's arrival. There was now no time to fight the issue of colonial preferences on this comparatively minor aspect of it. Accordingly, the issue was postponed for further examination after Ritchie's Budget was presented. Ritchie's method of defending the removal of the duty, however, led to taunts from the Liberals and protests from the Conservative protectionists. The Cabinet decided that Balfour might mention to a deputation the possibility of reimposing the duty 'if it were associated with some great change in our fiscal system'; and Chamberlain mentioned that he proposed to say much the same at Birmingham 'only in a less definite manner'.[1]

In his speech of May 1904 Chamberlain in fact said little more than he had said in earlier speeches. The question of food taxes had, however, ceased to be academic. It was now a live issue upon which both Liberals and Conservative protectionists immediately seized. L. S. Amery, then a young imperialist of the Milner school (though he had not actually been one of the kindergarten), began to organise the body which became known as the Tariff Reform League.[2] That was an ill-judged venture, but so were Chamberlain's speeches, which he probably would not have made had he been physically fit. In spite of Balfour's efforts at compromise, the tariff reform campaign broke up the Conservative Government and helped to produce the overwhelming defeat of the Unionists at the general election of 1906. They probably would have been defeated even if Chamberlain had secured his modest preference for Canadian wheat. By that time Chamberlain's stroke had caused his retirement from active political life.

Because of the circumstances, nobody really knew what tariff reform was.[3] There were, as we have seen, three approaches, the imperialist, the agriculturalist and the industrialist. The farmers' vote was of no

---

[1] *Life of Arthur James Balfour*, I, pp. 346–7.

[2] L. S. Amery, *My Political Life*, I, pp. 234–9.

[3] See, however, the 'definition' in Tariff Reform League, *Notes for Speakers* (6th ed., 1910), p. 26. Its opponents had no such difficulty: 'the little loaf at home and the apple of discord in the Empire'; quoted by R. B. McDowell, *British Conservatism, 1832–1914*, p. 169.

account because it was in any case Conservative. In politics the prodigal son is the uncertain elector in the marginal constituency, and since 1886 the rural constituencies had ceased to be marginal. In the imperialist code of tariff reform they might get a cut off the fatted calf, because an imperialist tariff would have to be a tax on agricultural products in order to help the colonial producer. On the other hand, there was conflict of opinion among the tariff reformers as to whether or not colonial produce should be taxed so as to protect British agriculture.[1] Naturally the relics of the landed interest, now for the most part large farmers, hoped to profit.

The political problem, however, was to win enough of the industrial constituencies to enable the Unionists to get a majority, and here the imperialists were at a disadvantage. Imperialism was rapidly losing its appeal for the working classes and it could not be denied that taxes on food, with imperial preferences, would put up prices, though the argument was met by a statement that duties on tea, sugar, cocoa and coffee would be reduced. On the other hand, the industrialists' idea of tariff reform, the protection of home producers against foreign competition, was more attractive in the towns because the argument could be put in terms of employment and the appeal to economics had to be used by the free traders. Moreover, the idea of being deliberately hit by other countries (for example, the McKinley tariff in the United States) without being able to hit back was obnoxious; and stories of cartels 'dumping' manufactured articles below cost price, in order to drive British producers out of operation, were readily believed, though the discussion also led to the assumption that tariffs enabled cartels to put up prices on the home market. Balfour tried to keep the argument to what the tariff reformers called 'reciprocity' and the free traders called 'tariff wars'; but this did not suit the imperialists, unless taxes were imposed on food.

The vast collections of tendentious statistics were not produced by the Tariff Reform League and the Free Trade Union until after the general election of 1906. The Liberals made the most of the 'dear loaf' at that election. It may have helped the Liberals to win, though probably the new-found unity of the Liberal party, contrasting with the

[1] Free Trade Union, *ABC Fiscal Handbook* (1912), pp. 204–6.

376

break-up of the Unionists, was more important; and there were other 'issues', like 'Chinese slavery'. Nor did the tariff reformers get a fair run in the general elections of 1910. Lloyd George's Budget of 1909 provoked the Conservative peers to oppose the taxation of land values and enabled the Liberal party to go to the country on the issue of 'Peers *v.* People'.

6. PROTECTION

'Tariff Reform', said the Tariff Reform League's *Handbook for Speakers* in 1910,

is not a revival of the old controversy between Free Trade and Protection. ...Free Trade has always been, and remains to this day, an abstract theory. No such thing exists, since a free exchange of commodities, unhampered by tariff restrictions, has never yet been enjoyed by any country and never seems likely to be enjoyed. On the other hand, Protection, in the commonly understood sense of that term, as a tariff policy designed to raise prices in the home market, is not advocated for this country by any authoritative exponent of Tariff Reform. Tariff Reform, therefore, does not raise any question as to the theoretic advantages or disadvantages of either Free Trade or Protection. It does raise *a question of practical statesmanship*,[1] the question whether or not, in a world of tariffs, a world more and more governed by tariff considerations, this country is to adopt that form of tariff best calculated to raise revenue, to safeguard national industries against foreign State-aided competition, and to afford a means of effective negotiation with other countries for the purpose of extending and developing British trade within and without the Empire.

In other words, Protection was a naughty word, carefully avoided by all tariff reformers until a new generation (or that part of it which was not slaughtered in Flanders) came to the ballot box in 1923, when Baldwin could say, with appalling frankness, that in his opinion the only way of fighting unemployment was 'by protecting the home market'.[2] There was, however, another useful formula in the quotation from the *Handbook*, to 'safeguard national industries'. That formula enabled the Conservative party to revert to Joseph Chamberlain' tactics, though in a different context.

[1] Italics in the original.
[2] Deryk Abel, *History of British Tariffs, 1923–1942*, p. 12.

377

Chamberlain's original proposal, to allow a colonial rebate on a small corn duty, had been a very little one. Of what he would have done next we have no evidence. Instead of defending in the House of Commons a nice little gesture to our Canadian kith and kin, he was compelled by Ritchie to defend himself in Birmingham, where naturally he asserted a general proposition. Thereupon all the Conservative foxes began attacking the hen-roosts and all the Liberal hounds went baying after them. The mistake was to raise the general issue. In 1915 the Coalition Government decided to restrict imports of specified luxury articles, in order to avoid the use of scarce shipping space, by imposing duties upon them. There were no compensating excise duties and accordingly the duties were protective. They were to be repealed as soon as the war was over but, naturally, the Conservative majorities from 1918 onwards did not repeal them. They were repealed in 1924 on Snowden's proposal and restored in the following year on Winston Churchill's proposal. Since he had been first a Conservative free-trader, then a Liberal free-trader, and was now a Conservative Chancellor of the Exchequer, he was careful to explain, 'to some they are a relish, to others a target, and to me a revenue'.[1] Indeed, the duties were subsequently extended to commercial vehicles and motor tyres, apparently for both symmetry and revenue,[2] though much more revenue could have been obtained by an excise or a purchase tax.

Meanwhile the principle of imperial preference had been conceded by the Finance Act, 1919, covering all the items of food, drink and tobacco then taxed: and two years later the formula 'safeguarding of industries' was employed in an Act 'to impose customs duties on certain goods with a view to the safeguarding of certain special industries and the safeguarding of employment in industries in the United Kingdom against the effects of the depreciation of foreign currencies, and the disposal of imported goods at prices below the cost of production'. The 'key industries' thus protected were those considered essential for national defence; but the 'anti-dumping' provisions could be extended, subject to certain conditions being satisfied, to any industry, by an order of the Board of Trade on

[1] Deryk Abel, *op. cit.* p. 26.
[2] *Ibid.* p. 41.

378

the advice of a committee of inquiry. The members of the committee were chosen by the President of the Board of Trade from a permanent panel of persons appointed by him 'who shall be mainly persons of commercial or industrial experience'. By 1926, when the Act expired, the number of classes of goods covered had increased from 39 to 6358.[1] The Act was extended for ten more years. All the articles protected by this Act were covered by imperial preference.

This process of nibbling at free trade might have continued almost indefinitely, for committees under the Safeguarding of Industries Act took an elastic view of its provisions. The process was, however, not fast enough for Baldwin, who became Prime Minister in May 1923. Because of free-trade pressure during the general election of 1922, Bonar Law had undertaken that there would be no fundamental changes in the fiscal arrangements in the next Parliament, and Baldwin regarded himself as bound by this pledge. On the other hand, he held the industrialist's view that the problem of unemployment, which was acute during the post-war dislocation, could be solved only by tariffs, and he so expressed himself in a speech to the National Unionist Association at Plymouth in October 1923. Whether he then intended to advise a dissolution of Parliament is not clear.[2] Since he did not mention the matter to King George V until 17 days later,[3] he probably had not intended an immediate dissolution, particularly on an issue on which not all his colleagues were agreed. In fact, however, he had gone too far to be able to postpone the matter, and the general election was held in December, though some of his colleagues and the King himself thought it inopportune.

From the point of view of the Conservative party it was probably a mistake. Opinion about tariffs was changing. The old Radical opinion that protection was unjust, immoral and ridiculous was held by most Liberals and by older Labour men like Snowden: but the right wing of the Liberal party was becoming more conservative and the left wing of the Labour party was beginning to appreciate that a socialist policy involved control of external trade. In 1923 both Opposition parties

[1] *Ibid.* p. 37.
[2] G. M. Young, *Stanley Baldwin*, pp. 65–6; A. W. Baldwin, *My Father*, pp. 123–4.
[3] Sir Harold Nicolson, *King George V*, pp. 379–80.

adopted strongly free-trade platforms: they might not have done so three years later. The general election put the general proposition in issue, without the 'political education' which should, as a matter of tactics, precede every major change of policy. In order to stave off the 'dear bread' or 'small loaf' argument, it was agreed that tariffs should not be placed on essential foodstuffs. The policy therefore did not suit the imperialists. From the electioneering point of view this did not matter much, for opinion was anti-imperialist, except on the right wing of the Conservative party. Nevertheless, the Government was soundly beaten and the Labour Government, led for this purpose by Snowden, proceeded to cut down tariffs, retaining the principle of imperial preference but not extending its application.

At the general election of 1924 the Conservative programme repudiated a general tariff, but insisted on 'safeguarding' for 'any efficient industry' in which employment and the standard of living were 'imperilled by unfair foreign competition'. Accordingly, the process of 'nibbling' at free trade began again. On the other hand, the general issue of protection was allowed to lie dormant both under the Conservative Government of 1925–29 and at the general election of 1929. The imperialist case was, however, reopened in July 1929 by Lord Beaverbrook, acting through his newspapers. His 'Empire Free Trade' implied British duties on meat and wheat, and free entry into the Dominions for British manufactured goods—at least where they did not compete with Dominion-produced goods, or tariffs were required for revenue.[1] The policy appealed to some sections of the Conservative party, and in February 1930 Lord Rothermere joined in with a proposal to found a United Empire party, which did not in fact mature. The new generation has since discovered that press lords, controlling newspapers with circulations in millions, are not really powerful. The impression that they could control the careers of politicians derived from the belief that Lord Northcliffe had replaced Asquith by Lloyd George in 1916. The persistent advocacy of the 'Empire' by the Beaverbrook press for more than a generation must have had some effect on its millions of readers, but there is no good evidence of it. Except in 1931, the Labour vote increased steadily until 1951 with most of the

[1] Deryk Abel, *History of British Tariffs, 1923–1942*, pp. 53–5.

press against the Labour party. In 1930, however, it was thought that the combined hostility of the Beaverbrook and Harmsworth press might be fatal to Baldwin's leadership, particularly because his right wing had other grievances—his dissolution of 1923, his cross-bench attitude after the general strike of 1926, his alleged laziness while in office, and his failure to give a rousing lead in 1929. Moreover, Empire Free Trade was an old imperialist slogan going back to Joseph Chamberlain; and after 1929 Neville Chamberlain was the 'economist' of the Conservative party. Baldwin was a doughty fighter when roused, and he maintained his leadership, though the position might have been different had it not been for the loyalty of Neville Chamberlain. When Beaverbrook saw that he was being defeated it became possible for Chamberlain to negotiate a settlement, in the course of which Baldwin virtually pledged himself to food taxes.

In fact, however, the Conservatives got their general tariff by the back door. The rapidly developing industrial crisis from 1929 to 1931 brought down the Labour Government and brought in a so-called 'National' Government containing the leaders of the Labour, Liberal and Conservative parties, except Henderson, who led the bulk of the Labour members in Opposition. The original intention of the Conservatives had been to balance the Budget and then to go to the country on the issue of tariffs.[1] When the Budget had been passed many of them were anxious to 'cash in' before the emergency measures became unpopular, though some felt that the National Government should be kept in being to maintain the pound on the gold standard. The aspect of affairs was altered when it was decided to go off gold, and MacDonald thought that there was then no case for an election.[2] The Conservative back-benchers, on the other hand, voted for an immediate emergency tariff and an early election based on the National Government.[3] The Liberals were against an immediate election but were divided on an emergency tariff.[4] The lengthy process by which all three sections of the Government were brought round to the view that it would be best to retain the National Government and go to the country on the basis of a 'doctor's mandate' need not be discussed.[5]

[1] R. Bassett, Nineteen Thirty-One, pp. 188, 246–7. [2] Ibid. p. 252.
[3] Ibid. p. 254. [4] Ibid. p. 256. [5] Ibid. pp. 258–83.

The 'mandate' was: 'The Government must...be free to consider every proposal likely to help, such as tariffs, expansion of exports and contraction of imports, commercial treaties and mutually economic arrangements with the Dominions.'[1]

The result was inevitable. The National Government won a huge majority, with only the truncated Labour party and the Lloyd George group (Lloyd George had been ill the whole time, though able from time to time to send out notices breathing fire and brimstone) against. The Conservatives, having funds and candidates ready, were able to fight nearly all the constituencies not already held by Liberals or the National Labour group, with the consequence that the Conservatives won eighty-five per cent of the Government seats and seventy-seven per cent of all the seats. They could thus do what they liked in the new Parliament, especially because the small band of sixty-eight Liberals supporting the Government were almost equally divided between Liberal Nationals who were prepared to support tariffs and plain Liberals who were not. A temporary Abnormal Importations Bill empowered the Board of Trade to place 100 per cent duty upon selected imports. A Horticultural Products (Emergency Provisions) Bill gave similar powers in respect of fresh fruit, vegetables and flowers. Then came the permanent Import Duties Bill to impose a general tariff of ten per cent *ad valorem*, with additional duties to be imposed by order on the recommendation of an Import Duties Advisory Committee.[2] The Liberals and Lord Snowden threatened resignation, but it was agreed to allow them to remain as Ministers but to oppose the Bill. This Act having been passed, there was an Imperial Economic Conference at Ottawa, attended on behalf of the United Kingdom by protectionist Ministers only, who were led by Baldwin and Chamberlain. The conference was not noted for the 'imperial unity' which was one of the Protectionists' ambitions. At home the free-trade Ministers declared that the Ottawa policy, with its 'hard bargaining', would imperil the harmony of the British Common-

---

[1] R. Bassett, *op. cit.* p. 284.

[2] According to L. S. Amery, Neville Chamberlain had every intention of so constituting and directing the Committee that it would produce 'an effective protective tariff': L. S. Amery, *My Political Life*, III, p. 76.

wealth, that promises not to reduce duties on foreign imports were unconstitutional, that the agreements would prejudice international agreements for freer trade, that the undertakings by the Dominions were inadequate, that taxes and quota restrictions on foodstuffs and raw materials would raise the cost of living, lessen exports, and increase unemployment, and that the agreements had terminated the Anglo-Soviet agreement. On these grounds the Liberals, other than the National Liberals, went into opposition.[1] Lord Snowden did not need so many reasons. He informed the Prime Minister that he could not expect free-traders 'to acquiesce, even passively, in such a policy of national humiliation and bondage'.[2]

The process of slipping protection through under the disguise of a doctor's mandate gave the Opposition, especially the Liberals, the chance to say that it had been obtained by trickery. Having hindsight, we can say that the Conservatives were rather stupid and the Liberals very stupid. The original intention of the Conservative executive committee had been to push the Liberals out before the election.[3] Their difficulty was the modern doctrine (it dates from 1918)[4] that the Prime Minister alone has the right to advise a dissolution. MacDonald did not want to dissolve with only National Labour and Conservative supporters, and on the other hand the Conservatives did not want to be accused of 'breaking national unity' by turning out MacDonald if he refused to advise a dissolution. It is now plain that had they done so, the Conservatives would have won the election on a programme of protection and would have been able to carry out their policies with none of the fictions and subterfuges of the 'National' Governments. Many of the older Liberals, and a few members of the Labour party, were passionate devotees of Gladstonian free trade: the average voter, evidently, had no strong views either way, but simply wanted a strong Government which would keep out the Labour party, and that had to be Conservative no matter what flag it flew.

[1] Deryk Abel, *History of British Tariffs*, pp. 116–17.
[2] *Ibid.* p. 118.
[3] R. Bassett, *op. cit.* p. 258.
[4] Jennings, *Cabinet Government* (3rd ed.), pp. 417–19.

CHAPTER IX

THE WELFARE STATE

I. THE CHARACTER OF THE WELFARE STATE

The theory that 'the country' is something distinct from its citizens is an essential element in nationalism; and in matters which only indirectly affect the material interests of the citizen it has had a long life. When coated with a sufficient layer of sentiment, as in wartime, it will even seem to justify a considerable material detriment: it is a sweet and glorious thing to be taxed and rationed for one's country. Its corollary, that the citizens as a whole should rejoice if the landed interest, or the textile manufacturers, or the coalowners, or the steel barons, acquire more wealth, is more difficult to sustain. On the nationalist assumption it is necessary to prove only that, on balance, the 'country' gains, even if in the process the rich become richer and the poor become poorer. If the Statistical Department shows that the national income has been increased, the nationalist ought not to enquire whose personal incomes have decreased, because clearly the nation, regarded as a unit, has gained. In practice, however, not even the extreme nationalist carries the assumption to its logical conclusion. Few nationalists would agree, for instance, that the enslavement of half the population would be justified if thereby the nation, as a unit, became richer.

The stern individualist often made the same assumption; but in his view the aim of national prosperity could be best and most quickly achieved by every person following his own material interest. Only the internationalist, like Richard Cobden, was capable of seeing that, on his own assumption, the objective was not national prosperity but international prosperity. Only when the whole world was allowed to follow each his own material prosperity, free from laws seeking to benefit nations, classes, groups or individuals at the expense of other nations, classes, groups or individuals, could wealth be maximised and the earth be made most fruitful. On the other hand, nobody except a professional economist who consciously or unconsciously excluded judgments of morals or values (including nationalist judgments) carried

384

this theory to its logical conclusion. Politicians neither could nor did because they had to be concerned with the welfare of classes, groups or individuals and not merely with the welfare of a totality, whether national or international.

In effect, therefore, there has always been a Welfare State, though ideas have varied as to the manner and degree in which the legislature could or ought to intervene to protect or improve the welfare of classes, groups or individuals. That welfare would not be thought of in exclusively material terms. Every chapter in this book has dealt with welfare. Even nationalism is concerned with the welfare of citizens, especially when it is economic nationalism. But the nationalist seldom considers himself bound to show how Bill Bloggs benefits from the fact that 'England' is a 'great power'; Bill ought to be satisfied that his team is in the first division, without asking what it costs him in terms of 'blood, tears, toil and sweat'.

The term 'Welfare State' indicates, however, the development of a more precise idea, that the State should assume the responsibility for providing a wide range of services for its citizens. The services may be self-supporting, like the provision of water, gas, electricity and public transport; but usually they are provided out of, or subsidised by, the revenues produced by taxation. Even the stern individualist recognises that some services should be so provided, like the armed forces, the police, the courts of justice, roads and bridges, and perhaps drains and sewers and scavenging. Opinions may vary, and have varied, as to what services beyond this minimum should be provided. The extreme socialist would 'nationalise' all the means of production, distribution and exchange. Even he usually hedges, for he rarely wants to 'nationalise' religion, sports and pastimes, domestic service, literature, art, music, or journalism. The difference between individualism and socialism is therefore a matter of degree. The extreme individualist is a bit of a socialist and the extreme socialist is a bit of an individualist. In practical politics, however, the extremes are rarely found. Most people want either rather more or rather fewer services than are actually being provided; and in the present century, when all parties have been socialist in the sense of seeking to provide more public services, most people have wanted more but have differed as to how much more.

It has been convenient to think of socialism, in this broad sense, as involving the provision of services. The Welfare State also operates, however, by prohibition and regulation, and even occasionally by enjoining positive action. In this respect the individualist's bare minimum is, speaking generally, provided by the common law. On this foundation have been laid what Lambard called 'stacks of statutes' imposing obligations, positive and negative, on citizens. In the Welfare State the citizen's life is hedged around with statutory prohibitions and injunctions. In the individualist's paradise he may, within broad limits, do as he pleases.

On the other hand, the state of the statute book (and of the vast collections of statutory instruments) is not determined solely by the state of political ideas. Sometimes politicians legislate for the sake of legislation; they fuss around with fussy laws because they wish to give an impression of great activity on behalf of the common weal. They ballot for the privilege of introducing Bills not because there are grievances calling for redress but because, in many cases, the politicians are anxious for publicity. They are congratulated by their fellows because they have made new laws, not because they have repealed old ones. Most legislation, however, comes from the Government Departments. A group of senior civil servants is charged with responsibility for human welfare in the field, let us say, of games and recreation. One of their main objectives must clearly be to produce such a good cricket team that it will score more runs than an Australian team and so recover the 'ashes'. Since there may be an election next spring the Minister of Sports and Pastimes is most anxious to show his zeal; and his civil servants, as in duty bound, produce a Cricket (Encouragement) Bill, whereby all schools are required to have teams playing cricket on Wednesday afternoons and on Saturdays; school and club cricket teams are provided with grants on specified conditions; a cricket inspectorate is established under the control of a chief inspector; subsidies are provided for the production of bats and balls; the importation of foreign bats, balls, pads, gloves, wickets, garden rollers, grass-cutters, and so forth, is discouraged by import duties (though with Imperial preference because it would not be cricket to discourage Australian production); a service of professional umpires is set up; and so forth. In the end the Marylebone Cricket Club may or may not field a better team at Lord's, but the Conservative Government feels justified in going to the country with the slogan 'Conservatives help Cricket'. Unfortunately the Labour party goes one better with 'Socialists support Soccer'; and a glossy pamphlet is produced with pictures of pools winners on the front.

The element of caricature in this saga of a new and fruitful branch of our laws is not as great as may be supposed.[1] It might happen: for the interest of the electorate in competitive sport is greater than its interest in competitive politics, and prime ministers must hold their own against centre-forwards. Incidentally, however, we have slipped back into welfare. The notion that the failure of 'England' to get a gold medal in the Olympic Games might justify a Royal Commission derives from the belief that the State ought to accept wide responsibilities. Only the lunatic fringe supposes that politicians are sent to Westminster to repeal laws, close down Government Departments, and abolish the income tax.

2. THE CONDITION OF THE PEOPLE

To the country gentlemen of the eighteenth century the welfare of the people was primarily a matter of public order. Where they operated, the manorial system in the village and the gild system in the town had kept everybody under control and in his proper station. Already under the Tudors, however, developments in many parts of the country had broken down both systems. The conversion of services into money rents, or even the inclosure of the open fields or parts of the waste, did not in themselves alter the stable village economy. Indeed, improved agriculture might enable more families to settle on the land. The conversion of arable land to pasture, however, caused whole families to migrate to the towns in search of work, to take to the roads, or to squat on waste lands. The parallel development in the towns, the growth of new retail and wholesale trades created by the export trade in cloth and the supersession of the master-craftsmen by capitalists employing journeymen, broke down the gild system.

[1] Since this chapter was written a government committee has advised that £10 million be spent on sport!

Unemployment was not the only problem consequential upon these changes. In a peasant society 'the lame, impotent, old, blind and such other persons as are poor and not able to work'—to quote the words of the poor law—are maintained by their families, often with assistance from the charitable. When labour becomes mobile, however, the modern individualistic family—father, mother and young children— tends to replace the larger community of the static family. The social legislation of the Tudors was concerned with 'idle and disorderly persons' and 'rogues and vagabonds'; it dealt with other indigent persons on the assumption that they were a problem for the charitable. Under the Elizabethan poor law, however, the overseers and church-wardens were empowered not only to set to work all such persons as had no means to maintain themselves, but also to apprentice children and relieve the lame, impotent, old, blind and other persons not able to work.

From the reign of Elizabeth I to the early years of Victoria's reign the poor law was almost the only social service. There were, however, other consequences of the changed economic structure. Developments outside the traditional structure were, even in an age so adventurous as that of the Tudors, regarded with suspicion. The traditional order was self-policing so long as great men did not dispute among themselves. But the growth of trade and industry outside the gild system, the development of new towns in what had been rural parishes or even extra-parochial places, and the spread of the textile industry over the countryside, created a revolutionary situation which required sometimes prohibition, sometimes regulation and control. It was as if the neat and stable social order was bursting apart and spreading itself around like the seeds of a tropical garden. Prohibitions—for instance, of inclosure, of the pulling down of cottages, of erecting new buildings in the towns, of dismissing employees—were ineffective because they could not be enforced. Neither town corporations nor justices of the peace could be induced to undertake the constant supervision required to prevent developments of which they themselves approved in detail, even if they accepted the view that they were bad in general. Methods of regulation were numerous; but most of those, too, were ineffective. The regulation of wages and prices, the enforcement of apprenticeship, the fixing of standards of quality and quantity, and so forth, occupy much space in the justices' manuals of the eighteenth century. Superficially there was a kind of Welfare State, based upon the social hierarchy of landlord, tenant and labourer, or of merchant, clerk and journeyman, or of capitalist, craftsman and workman. It could not, however, be efficiently supervised by unpaid magistrates and constables, who were themselves under no sort of central administrative control after the abolition of the Star Chamber and the enfeeblement of the Council.

The 'industrial revolution' was in fact a slow and partial development which produced what landowners from the agricultural areas regarded as social anarchy; but when anarchy becomes endemic and traditional it is itself a sort of social order. If the individualism of the late eighteenth century could be traced to its roots it would probably be found to derive from the combination of unenforceable legal regulation and de facto anarchy. The occasional efforts by landowning justices to enforce the laws summarised in their manuals would do much to persuade merchants, manufacturers and middle-men that legal regulation was obnoxious in itself, and that 'England' would flourish if the State undertook only its proper functions of maintaining order and providing the machinery for the settlement of disputes.

These matters need not be studied in detail, for the 'condition of England' did not become a matter of party politics until the nineteenth century. The prerequisites of those politics were not, however, mere conflicts of interest between landowners on the one side and merchants and manufacturers on the other. Though the tories are commonly regarded as the country or landowners' party and the whigs as the supporters of the commercial and industrial middle classes, this economic interpretation proves inadequate. The Peels and the Gladstones were tories, while the Cavendishes, the Spencers and the Russells were whigs. In numbers the landowners predominated in both parties, even after the Reform Act. Two other factors, besides the economic, were important. First, in spite of the industrial revolution, the stable English village, with its traditional social hierarchy, was still regarded by many as the normal, while the industrial developments of the midlands and the north were regarded as exceptional. This conservative element was particularly strong because of the heavy over-representation of the rural south and west and because membership of Parliament was a traditional occupation for the sons of landowners. On the other hand, trade and industry forced themselves on public attention after Waterloo, and a whole generation had been able to acquire the individualistic assumptions of Adam Smith. In principle, therefore, the conflict was not between the landed interest and the industrial interest; the landowners were divided by 'ideology' into those who stood by the ancient ways and those who recognised that the people lived by trade and industry as well as by the land and who thought that trade and industry should not be hampered by restrictive laws. There were, in other words, conservatives and liberals, though both were to be found in any Tory or Whig Government. The division of the Conservative party over the repeal of the Corn Law was, in the main, a division among landowners; but it was, in substance, an ideological division. It brought the Conservatives and the Liberals into line as conservatives and liberals, in the true etymological sense, by the late sixties.

Secondly, and even more pregnant of future political developments, there was the growth of a broad social sympathy. The landowners of the eighteenth century were as humane as other people but most of them lived in a sheltered world to which Bradford or Wigan was as foreign as Peking or Valparaiso. As the great industrial towns became larger and more numerous, however, they forced themselves upon public attention, if only as centres of crime and disease. By the end of the eighteenth century all governing authorities, from the Home Secretary to the justices of the peace, were terrified of 'the mob' because it was potentially so powerful and the means of defence were so few. On the other hand, the mob was also a challenge to the religious and the charitable. The dissenters were strong in the industrial towns; and, though they were mostly to be found among the wealthier burgesses, they included many men and women of broad social sympathies, especially among the Quakers. The Methodists, too, went into the industrial towns. Their emphasis upon religious 'conversion' and on the 'sins' of drinking, gambling and Sunday trading, and indeed the general attitude of the Methodist leaders to popular grievances, prevented them from being the instigators of a great movement for social reform; but among the Methodist ministers working in the towns were many who realised that what was wanted was not merely more religion and more charity but also more government. Indeed, the first steps towards a new social order, the policing, lighting, paving, draining and cleansing of the streets, were usually taken by Nonconformist laymen, in co-operation with the Nonconformist ministers and an increasing number of Anglican clergy. They organised themselves as improvement commissioners under powers conferred by local Acts.

The Church of England was ill constituted to give a lead towards social reform. It was essentially a part of the landed interest, from the bishops who hobnobbed with the peers to the country parsons who hobnobbed with the squires. Because of its dependence on tithe and patronage it could not, as an organised body, extend its activities into the new industrial towns. On the other hand many of the clergy, at first mostly evangelicals and afterwards many of the High Church party, took seriously to the task of ministering to the industrial proletariat. Moreover, the general attitude of the Church, like that of the Church of Rome, favoured social reform based upon Christian charity. It was not, like that of the Methodists, inhibited by concentration on 'sin'; it was more a matter of compassion. The concern of the evangelicals with the slave trade is indicative of this general development, though it is also significant that their main interest should be in human beings abroad rather than in human beings at home. In political terms this development implied that while both whigs and tories included persons supporting social reform, they were stronger and more active among the tories. This tendency was of course accentuated by the fact that most of the manufacturers supported the whigs and that exploitation of labour was a means for keeping down the cost of production.

The movement was, however, secular as well as religious, and in this respect it was to be found mainly among the Radicals. Even Bentham was moved by the sight of human suffering.[1] On the other hand neither he nor any other of the prominent Benthamites really understood people. They were moved by a sense of injustice but not by compassion. They assumed a principle of social equality but also assumed that men and

[1] Crane Brinton, *English Political Thought in the Nineteenth Century*, p. 16.

women were rational creatures like themselves. This was consistent with an individualist approach to economic policy and led to the adoption of the 'principle of less eligibility' in the new poor law. They did not realise, until Edwin Chadwick began his investigations, how much unemployment was due to sickness.

Other Radicals were less inflexible, and among them were the founders of British socialism. The Radicals were, however, a miscellaneous crew, something like a lunatic fringe to the Whig party. Each had his own nostrum, though most were agreed on the purely political remedy of Parliamentary reform, which was also the main demand of working-class agitation before the failure of the Chartist Movement.

We distort the movement of opinion, however, when we express it in political terms. It was an emotional development, and therefore was better expressed in literature than in politics. Here were these 'great wens'—to generalise the phrase of one of the romantics, William Cobbett—inhabited by people not quite like us, but lovable characters described by another romantic, Charles Dickens. Cobbett's romanticism was of the Merrie England type. As *The Times* reviewer of G. D. H. Cole's biography put it:

All through his chequered days, as a private soldier and a sergeant-major in New Brunswick, as a refugee in the United States, as farmer, as journalist, as political prisoner, as agitator, as member of Parliament, he was haunted by that notion of an English Paradise inhabited by worthy lords and happy peasants which he seemed to remember in his youth and was sure had existed, if not exactly then, at least some time before, perhaps in the Middle Ages, when the monasteries (so he stubbornly held) were centres of active kindliness, not dismal ruins, blotting the fair landscape, and bishops looked after their flocks, not their families.[1]

The ghost that haunted him was a fiction of his own imagination; but behind the ghost was a ghastly reality, the life of the ordinary family in the disease-ridden and vice-ridden towns. The Methodists prayed for Bradford:

On Bradford likewise look Thou down
Where Satan keeps his seat.[2]

[1] *The Times*, 16 January 1924.
[2] Quoted by E. Lipson, *The Growth of English Society*, p. 149.

Leeds, perhaps, was past praying for; and there were worse places than Leeds.[1]

There was something of the Merrie England theory in Disraeli's *Sybil*, though for the most part the author portrays the contrast between the 'two nations', the rich and the poor. Though for the modern reader it is the best of his novels, it had not the popularity of *Coningsby*, partly because it was too obviously founded on the Blue Books, but mainly because the characters were not real. For realism one must go to Dickens, for his cockneys were live people, only slightly idealised so as to attract his readers' sympathies. Dickens, too, had a much wider audience and therefore contributed more than anybody to the growing social conscience of the Victorian era. The influence of Thomas Carlyle was, however, more direct because he was obviously preaching, and the Victorians liked to be preached at.[2] He relied, said one of his more sympathetic critics, 'on nobility of feeling rather than on continuity of thought'.[3] That he had no political philosophy worth mentioning is therefore irrelevant. While Dickens tugged at the heart-strings, Carlyle rained impassioned blows on his readers' heads. Though he was far from being a democrat, Carlyle's work had more influence on the development of English socialism than any other section of literature. Even now, while its style is more irritating than it was a century ago, it can pile up the emotions. Though Sidney Webb and some other Fabians managed to make British socialism seem almost rational,[4] its foundation was the intense social conscience produced by the condition of the great mass of the people in the decades after Waterloo. It was part of the Romantic Movement, but more closely associated with political conditions than the romantic poets or the romantic history of Sir Walter Scott. It was essentially a surge of social sympathy. Though Karl Marx had some influence later in the nineteenth century, when the Fabian socialists and others sought to rationalise their political pre-

---

[1] Drink was 'the quickest way out of Manchester': E. R. Wickham, *Church and People in an Industrial City*, p. 196.

[2] Crane Brinton, *English Political Thought in the Nineteenth Century*, pp. 165–6.

[3] John Nichol, *Thomas Carlyle* (1934 ed.), p. 188.

[4] As one good Conservative said to another: 'The Webbs carry you on logically and imperceptibly from one point to another; but when you look at the whole, it's moonshine': Sir Austen Chamberlain, *Politics from Inside*, p. 239.

judices, and though Marx used English materials drawn from his reading in the British Museum, his ideas were out of the main stream of British development. British socialism was simply a political programme seeking to redress the wrongs which the early Victorians believed to exist. Its attack on capitalism as a form of economic organisation consistently misfired because it was really directed not against capitalism but against the social consequences of the industrial revolution. British socialism sought a new and juster industrial society rather than a new form of industrial organisation. Accordingly, there has been an emphasis upon progressive taxation and wide social services rather than upon the nationalisation of the means of production, distribution and exchange, which was only the nostrum of a section. British socialism has arrived at the Welfare State rather than at the Socialist State. It has therefore drawn heavily on authors like Cobbett, Disraeli, Carlyle and Ruskin, whose ideas were conservative and romantic because of their intense dislike of the social results of industrialism. The movement of opinion was in the opposite direction during the middle half of the nineteenth century because Victorian prosperity and governmental efficiency had diminished the enormity of the grievance. It arose again at the end of that century because the working class had the vote and realised that they could use it to move nearer to social equality. Socialist policy might be a means to that end and they were prepared to use it: but what the electors wanted, and what all political parties have had to offer them, was the Welfare State.

3. THE NEW POOR LAW

The Poor Law Amendment Act of 1834 was one of the few spectacular pieces of legislation allowed to go through Parliament without substantial opposition. Though revolutionary both in what it contained and in what it implied, it was not 'party political': and, though passed during a political crisis, which involved the substitution of Lord Melbourne for Lord Grey as Prime Minister, the Conservatives helped the whigs to get the Bill through. This is a case of the simplest explanation being the best. The Bill was a means for reducing the burden of the poor rates during a period of agricultural distress. Though based on the doctrines of Malthus and Bentham, its immediate source was the Report of the Royal Commission on the Poor Laws, on which all sections of party opinion had been represented. It was the painful duty of the Commission to report that the money authorised to be raised by the Poor Law Act of 1601 was 'applied to purposes opposed to the letter, and still more to the spirit of that Law, and destructive to the morals of the most numerous class, and to the welfare of all'.[1]

The burden of the poor rates on the landlords was, indeed, the main theme of the Report. Rates were of course collected from occupiers; but it was believed that high rates depressed rents; and it was even suggested that high rates were driving landowners to abandon their lands. The Commission did not argue whether this was good or bad; the belief that the British Constitution was founded on landed property made it obviously bad. On the other hand the farmers also suffered. Under the 'roundsmen' system the parish paid the farmers to employ paupers at rates of wages fixed by the parish, depending on the family needs of the pauper and not on the services he rendered. Also, in many parishes the magistrates had ordered the payment of allowances to labourers at work because the wages were below the level of poor relief. The result of these practices, according to the Commission, was to lower wages and debase the quality of labour. The labourers were becoming, 'not merely idle and ignorant and dishonest, but positively hostile'.[2] Relief in aid of wages was, however, a clear gain to the manufacturer because it enabled him to keep down wages, while the close supervision possible with machinery prevented any deterioration in the quality of the work done.

The most remarkable feature of the Report and of the evidence submitted to the Commission is, however, its middle-class dislike of the working classes. There was nostalgia for the sturdy and independent agricultural labourer, but he had been or was being pushed out by the pauperised and the idle. The reference made by one witness to 'that misery, immorality, want of care and affection for their offspring, attachment to home, respect for themselves and for domestic economy, which are so prevalent among the labouring classes of society'[3] is

---

[1] Poor Law Commissioners' Report of 1834 (reprint of 1905) Cmd. 2728, p. 13.
[2] Cmd. 2728, p. 68.   [3] Ibid. p. 163.

395

typical of the attitudes adopted. 'The Commissioners concentrated their whole attention', said the Webbs, 'on one plague spot—the demoralisation of character and waste of wealth produced in the agricultural districts by a hypertrophied poor law.'[1] The Report was a brilliant piece of journalism, full of interesting and sometimes amusing stories of incompetent and often corrupt administration. It played to the prejudices of a landowners' Parliament and thus persuaded both Houses to accept a new system of administration based upon Benthamite principles which, in a different application, the great majority would have repudiated. It exhibits none of the compassion, or sense of justice, upon which (not without reference to the need to catch votes) the Welfare State was founded. On the contrary, it is a perfect example of the class antagonism which prevailed in the period after Waterloo. 'By 1830', says Dr Kitson Clark, 'Britain had become a miserable, overcrowded, undergoverned country, confronted by the new problems of an expanding, mass-producing industry yet pressed towards higher standards of humanity by the fitful blasts of an extremely articulate public opinion.'[2] Though the Poor Law Amendment Act of 1834 applied to the whole of England and Wales, industrial and agricultural areas alike, the Report of the Royal Commission was really concerned only with some of the incidental effects, in the rural areas, of recent economic developments. The new poor law was virtually the only social service, but it was founded on a very partial examination of a portion of a changing society. The essence of the Report was the protection of the landed interest and the dislike of the landowners for the agricultural proletariat which had not yet been drawn into the factories or had been sent back under the law of settlement and removal.

Humanitarian pressure was in fact against the new poor law. It was in the first instance provided by a few Radicals and Conservatives, among whom William Cobbett was the most vocal. It was wholly emotional and was in fact weakened by Cobbett's characteristic exaggerations. The transition to the new poor law was eased by the good harvests of 1834, 1835 and 1836, but it undoubtedly caused much distress, especially in the bad years of the hungry forties. There

[1] S. and B. Webb, *English Poor Law History*: Part II, 1, p. 84.
[2] G. Kitson Clark, 'Statesmen in Disguise', *Historical Journal*, II, p. 35.

were, too, scandals in the new workhouses, which the newspapers, and especially *The Times*, played up. The Poor Law Commission established by the Act of 1834 had no means of defence in Parliament, and in Edwin Chadwick they had an indefatigable but obstreperous and, in the pursuit of the policy which he believed to be right, unscrupulous secretary. They were therefore attacked by both sides, by the humanitarians who thought they were being harsh to the poor, and by Chadwick and his fellow Malthusians who thought they were—as indeed they were—hedging on the principles of 1834.

There were, too, politicians who were only too anxious to cash in on the unpopularity of the new poor law. The actual and potential paupers had no votes, but they had some sympathisers among the middle-class voters, especially in the industrial towns where the 'Bastilles', as the new workhouses were called, were most unpopular. The members for Liverpool were in the front of the agitation against the new poor law, and even Gladstone at Newark expressed some doubts about it. Perhaps the most significant opponent, however, was young Benjamin Disraeli, who was in transition from his youthful fling as a Radical to his virtual leadership of the Protectionists. His romantic notion of an alliance between the aristocracy and the people (ignoring the great wens) led him to believe that it was possible to revert to the poor law of 1795, that is, the Elizabethan system unperverted by the stress of war.[1] This of course ignored the great social changes consequential upon inclosures and industrial developments. That Disraeli was familiar with the consequences of these changes is shown by the descriptions in *Sybil*, but he had neither the type of mind which delves into the causes of things, nor the capacity to prescribe remedies. What was important was his patrician sympathy, which he shared with many Conservatives, for a somewhat idealised working man—the precursor of the horny-handed, beer-drinking worker who was supposed to oppose Lloyd George's Budget.

The weakness of the opposition to the new poor law was that it was so emotional that it was incapable of being expressed in rational terms. No genuine alternative was suggested, for Disraeli's proposal could not be taken seriously. Nor was Peel prepared to use antagonism to the

[1] *Life of Benjamin Disraeli*, I, p. 478.

397

poor law for 'party political' purposes. The force behind the political opposition was thus very weak. This weakness was a sound argument for the demand of the working class, through the People's Charter, for political reforms which included popular representation. On the other hand, this agitation, too, died down in the fifties as mid-Victorian prosperity began to develop. There was no great popular demand for the extension of the franchise in 1867, still less in 1884. What is more, the agitation against the new poor law diminished. This was due in large measure to the same wave of prosperity, but that same prosperity enabled the administration to be liberalised. In 1847 the poor law came under ministerial control and, curiously enough, the attacks on it became fewer when there was somebody to defend it, though in part this was coincidence.

4. THE FACTORY ACTS

'The safety of the rich', said Dr Ferriar, an associate of the Radical Dr Percival, 'is intimately connected with the welfare of the poor.'[1] Given its origin, there was probably a touch of cynicism in the remark. It was, nevertheless, typical of the attitude of the propertied classes towards the poor late in the eighteenth century. There was a barrier between the rich and those sections of the poor who had become detached from their villages. The new urban centres were, so far as the rich were concerned, centres of crime, vice and disease. As we have seen, however, there was a developing social conscience, more noticeable among the tories of the manufacturing districts than among the landowners of the south; and the landowners themselves were not averse, at least after 1832, from clipping the wings of the factory owners.

The conditions in the factories were appalling, but they can be painted too dark. The employment of whole families, including women and small children, for as long as daylight lasted, and even into the night if candles could be provided, had been and continued to be an incident of production in what a modern writer would call cottage industries. The sweated industries of the late nineteenth century were

[1] Quoted in B. L. Hutchins and A. Harrison, *History of Factory Legislation*, p. 13.

the successors of the domestic industries of the eighteenth century. The conditions in a water-powered or steam-powered factory were not necessarily worse than those at home; in a modern building, under an employer who thought it to be in his interest to pay attention to the welfare of his employees, they might be better. It was, too, easier to regulate conditions by legislation in a factory than in a system of out-work. On the other hand, regulation was contrary to the *laissez-faire* ideas of the time. Free trade was only one aspect of freedom of enterprise.

The main difficulties, as with the new poor law, were not 'party political'. The economy had adapted itself to a system using child and female labour as well as adult male labour, and requiring long hours of work. That it could equally adapt itself to a system in which child labour was prohibited, female labour regulated, hours of work restricted, and factory conditions generally controlled, was not apparent even to economists. Still less was it obvious to members of working families who thought that their incomes would be reduced, or to manufacturers who thought that their costs of production would be increased.

Social ideas, too, had adapted themselves to this system. Fathers who sent their sons to Cambridge and on the Grand Tour congratulated themselves that under the industrial system children were put to useful and remunerative employment, instead of being allowed to run wild and develop idle and dissolute habits. Long hours of work were socially necessary because the workers were under discipline and had no time to indulge in their normally vicious, criminal and unruly habits.

The first attempt at regulation was really an extension of the poor law. In accordance with the Act of 1601 children on relief were apprenticed to employers who generally received their premiums and then regarded the children as expendable. A public opinion against this practice began to develop at the end of the eighteenth century.[1] The employment of such apprentices was regulated by the Health and Morals of Apprentices Act, 1802, whose enactment was due to three enlightened manufacturers, Robert Owen, Nathaniel Gould and, especially, Sir Robert Peel, the father of the Conservative politician. A few provisions applied to all cotton and woollen factories, but

[1] B. L. Hutchins and A. Harrison, *op. cit.* p. 14.

generally the Act applied only to apprentices. The Act was ineffective, partly because it was so limited, and partly because enforcement was left to justices of the peace. Factories using water-power were usually built in rural areas, where apprentices formed a principal source of supply of labour. With the development of steam-power in the early years of the nineteenth century, factories were generally built near the towns, whence children as well as other types of labour could be drawn, so that apprentices ceased to be the main source of supply.[1] The handloom weavers in cottages and cellars did employ apprentices, but they were not subject to the Act of 1802, because it applied only when at least twenty persons were employed.[2]

To meet the new problem thus created, Sir Robert Peel the elder in 1815 introduced a Bill to forbid the employment of children under ten and to limit to ten hours a day the hours of work for young persons. He succeeded only in getting a committee appointed; and, because this committee was considered to be partisan, a second committee was appointed, equally partisan, but in the opposite direction. This agitation produced in 1819 a modest Act, forbidding the employment of children under nine in cotton mills and restricting to twelve, exclusive of meal times, the hours of work in those mills of persons between nine and sixteen, but containing no effective provisions for enforcement. Nevertheless, the two committees succeeded in arousing interest in a social problem which could, in the changing climate of opinion, stimulate a great deal of emotion. It could also, and did, arouse opposition among the manufacturers. Only Robert Owen, on whose initiative the Bill had been produced, and Sir Robert Peel were in favour of limitation of hours for all workers.

There were amending Acts in 1825 and 1831, but they did not go much further than the Act of 1819. Meanwhile a campaign for a shorter working day had been begun in Lancashire and Yorkshire, for the most part by middle-class people who had some knowledge of conditions in the cotton and woollen mills. In 1831 Michael Sadler, Tory M.P. for Newark, crystallised the objective by introducing the Ten Hours Bill. It was read a second time in 1832, but only on the understanding that it

[1] J. L. and B. Hammond, *Lord Shaftesbury*, p. 11.
[2] B. L. Hutchins and A. Harrison, *op. cit.* p. 21.

would be referred to a Select Committee. Because Sadler presided over it, the Select Committee was unusual in the thoroughness with which evidence was collected: it was much more like a Royal Commission. Its Report is one of the classic social documents because for the first time it exposed the effects of the factory system on human beings. The pages of its report 'bring before the reader in the vivid form of dialogue the kind of life that was led by the victims of the new system'.[1] Even if a new humanitarianism had not been developing, the effect of the evidence would have been widespread.

Sadler was, however, defeated by Macaulay at the general election of 1832. The Short Time Committees sent delegates to London to look for a successor and chose Anthony Ashley Cooper, Lord Ashley, afterwards seventh Earl of Shaftesbury. He had had an unhappy home and school life but had been brought up as an evangelical by an old servant of the family. He had been in Parliament, as tory member for the Duke of Marlborough's borough of Woodstock (his mother was a Churchill), since 1826, and he had held minor office under the Duke of Wellington.[2] He was for a short time in Peel's Ministry of 1834, but thereafter he devoted his political life to good causes.

In March 1833, Ashley brought up Sadler's Ten Hours Bill. The employers met the proposal by a motion for the appointment of a Commission, and the motion was carried by 74 votes to 73. The Commission consisted of Thomas Tooke, the economist, Edwin Chadwick, who afterwards became Secretary to the Poor Law Commissioners, and Dr Southwood Smith, the public health reformer. Meanwhile Ashley's Bill had been read a second time without opposition, and the Government's proposal to refer it to a Select Committee, which was opposed by Ashley, was lost by 141 votes to 164. The Report of the Commissioners, however, was critical of the Bill:

The average member wanted his mind set at rest about the children in the mills; he wanted at the same time to be assured that profits would not suffer, nor the country's industries collapse. This desire was accompanied by a deep dislike and mistrust of trade unions and of working class agitation of every kind. The average member was enough in earnest to support Ashley if he

---

[1] J. L. and B. Hammond, *Lord Shaftesbury*, p. 16.
[2] *Ibid.* pp. 2–5.

were given no effective alternative. The Commissioners gave him that alternative, and they satisfied, at the same time, his prejudices, his fears, and his hopes.[1]

The Ten Hours Bill was the product of professional agitators, who had duped the workers. The children were brought into the story for purposes of propaganda. The working day proposed for adults was too short; that proposed for children too long, for they could work in relays. Lord Althorp, for the Government, moved to substitute thirteen for eighteen as the minimum age for night work. The motion was carried by 238 votes to 93, and Ashley surrendered the Bill to Lord Althorp.[2]

The Factory Act of 1833 was nevertheless, from the point of view of employees, a great advance on its predecessors. It applied to all mills except (in some respects) silk mills. It prohibited the employment of children under the age of nine and night work for children under the age of thirteen. No child under thirteen could be employed for more than forty-eight hours in a week or nine in a day, and no person under eighteen could be employed for more than sixty-nine hours in a week or twelve in a day. Children from nine to twelve had to attend school for not less than two hours daily.[3] The great merit of the Act was, however, that inspectors were to be appointed by the Home Office to see to its enforcement. The operatives thought that the factory inspectors would be tools in the hands of the manufacturers: this was, however, the most important provision of the Act. The Government itself was by no means enthusiastic about the Act: and Poulett Thompson, Vice-President of the Board of Trade, said that it was 'an evil forced upon the Government'.[4]

---

[1] J. L. and B. Hammond, *op. cit.* pp. 30–1.   [2] *Ibid.* pp. 31–3.

[3] The first returns from the cotton, woollen and worsted mills showed that the following numbers were employed:

Children under 13	42,181
Males 13–18 years	37,374
Males over 18 years	78,575
Females over 13 years	133,345
Total	291,475

See B. L. Hutchins and A. Harrison, *History of Factory Legislation*, p. 304. The provision for school attendance was unenforceable.

[4] *Ibid.* p. 56.

Still less enthusiastic were the operatives, whose real objective was the limitation of their own hours of work. The sufferings of the children were a genuine working-class grievance; but there was something in the manufacturers' contention that the workers were using the children to play on the sentiments of the philanthropic, and that what they really wanted was less work for the same pay. The whole agitation had to be stepped down, however, in the depression which began in 1838. The real problem then was not to limit the hours of work but to get work for long enough to keep the family alive. The greater grievance was the new poor law, upon which so many textile operatives became dependent. Politically, too, this was the period of the People's Charter. If the workers could get universal male suffrage, vote by ballot, annual Parliaments, payment of members, abolition of property qualifications, and equal electoral districts, they would control public policy and remedy all their grievances. At the same time, too, there was going on the agitation for the repeal of the Corn Law, whereby the manufacturers could retaliate upon the landed interest for the latter's concern with factory conditions.

The cause of factory reform was weakened by the Conservative victory of 1841. With the weak Whig Government in office Ashley had some hope of legislation, for the Radicals and many of the Conservatives would support him. The Conservative victory, in which Ashley took an active part, lost him that section of Conservative support which had used the 'condition of the people' merely as a useful stick with which to beat the whigs. The second Sir Robert Peel had some filial affection for factory laws, but intellectually he was a manufacturer's son who had studied the economics of free enterprise. The apparent success of his efforts to improve trade by relaxing legal restrictions brought him even nearer to the economists' position. When public opinion forced the Government to agree to legislation, Sir James Graham was frankly apprehensive lest they were doing more harm than good. As Sydney Smith said in a different context, the principles of political economy were not generally understood: and according to those principles, as then understood, the limitation of hours of work, even of women and children, would cause more of them to starve.

Nevertheless, public opinion did force legislation. Ashley had in

1840 secured the appointment of a Select Committee on the operation of the Act of 1833 and a Royal Commission on the employment of children in mines and factories outside the Act of 1833. The Report of the Select Committee not only showed the degree to which the Act of 1833 was evaded, but also produced some startling information about conditions in the silk and lace-making industries, which were for the most part outside the Act. The Reports of the Royal Commission were, however, absolutely devastating. What impressed public opinion was not so much the misery and degradation which conditions in the mines produced, as that thousands of little boys and girls spent almost their whole lives in the mines with no knowledge of the elements of Christianity, and that girls above the age of puberty had to work almost naked. Ignorance of religion was not an uncommon feature of working-class life, as General Booth discovered forty years later: but in the evangelical mood of the forties it was startling to be told frankly that the children in the mines were and would inevitably be pagans. For males and females to work in the nude (or thereabouts) in the heat of the mines was as sensible as for them to work in that state in the tropics; and it was less conducive to immorality than the housing conditions in town and country alike: but it shocked the Victorian middle-class, whose convention was that a respectable woman should be clothed from the neck to the ankles.

The Commission's first Report was published in May 1842. Ashley forthwith introduced a Bill to exclude from the pits all women and girls, boys under thirteen, and poor law apprentices; and the Government agreed to support it. Some opposition developed among the coalowners, and Ashley had to meet it by compromise. That compromise was, however, repudiated in the House of Lords by the coalowner whose agent had made it, Lord Londonderry. Fighting coalowners was more difficult than fighting factory owners, for the former were among the great landowners and were strongly represented in the House of Lords. Ashley had difficulty in finding a sponsor for the Bill; and when eventually Lord Devon accepted the task, he felt it necessary to concede amendments in order to secure a majority. In particular, the age limit for the employment of boys was fixed at ten, and parish apprentices were allowed, provided that they were between the ages of ten and eighteen.[1] Women were excluded from the mines, chiefly because the coalowners who employed women were not represented in the House.[2] On the other hand, the inspectors were empowered to report only on the miners, not on the conditions in the mines—a limitation removed in 1850.

The second report of the Commission, published early in 1843, showed that conditions in some of the industries not covered by the Factory Act of 1833 were worse than in the textile factories. The Bill produced by the Government in consequence of this report was from the point of view of the employees a great improvement on the Act of 1833. In spite of strict Government whipping, Ashley persuaded a majority of the House of Commons to support the principle of the ten-hour day for children and young persons. The Government then secured, on another clause, the rejection of both the Government's figure of twelve hours and Ashley's figure of ten. The Bill had therefore to be withdrawn and resubmitted, when the Government obtained a large majority for twelve hours by threatening to resign.

Nevertheless, the Ten Hours Bill[3] was passed in that Parliament, though as it happened its sponsor was not Ashley but Samuel Fielden, the manufacturer, who would be ruined if the opponents of the Bill correctly interpreted its economic effects. Ashley had resigned his seat because he supported the repeal of the Corn Law after being pledged to maintain it, and he had been replaced by a Protectionist. Ashley introduced the Bill before he resigned, but Fielden moved the second reading in April 1846. It was defeated by 203 votes to 193 mainly because of an almost solid Peelite opposition.[4] Six weeks later Peel's Government was defeated on an Irish Bill and the accession of Lord

---

[1] J. L. and B. Hammond, *Lord Shaftesbury*, pp. 69–80.

[2] *Ibid.* p. 80. The provision created hardship, for there was no alternative employment for the women.

[3] I.e., ten hours for children, young men, and women.

[4] The figures quoted by the Hammonds (*Lord Shaftesbury*, p. 116) from *The Ten Hours Advocate* were:

	For the Bill	Against the Bill
Protectionists	117	51
Peelites	7	73
Whigs	71	81
	195	205

John Russell's Government stimulated agitation for the Ten Hours Bill. It was again introduced by Fielden in January 1847 and the second reading was carried by 195 to 87. An amendment to substitute eleven hours for ten was lost by 146 votes to 68. Thereafter the Government supported the Bill and on the only division in the House of Lords it was carried by 53 votes to 11.[1] None of the divisions was 'party political' in the sense that the whips were put on. Opinion in the party groups was divided. The Bill was carried because enough members abstained, among them being Cobden and Gladstone. Disraeli voted for the second reading but did not vote on the proposal for eleven hours.

The fact that, in the modern sense, all the votes were 'free votes' (except those on the Bill of 1844), must not be taken to imply that the controversy was on issues of principle. It is indeed difficult to find principles on either side. By the forties most members believed that some regulation of the conditions of employment in factories and mines was necessary in the interest of the workers. On the other hand most members also believed that interference with the free operation of economic laws was dangerous; and the Parliament which enacted the Ten Hours Bill also repealed the Corn Law. Members on the one side stressed the misery of the workers and thought that the economic argument was being pressed too far. Members on the other side stressed the danger that trade and industry, on which by now a large section of the population depended, would be depressed and mass unemployment created; and these members thought that the harm done by factory conditions had been exaggerated by propaganda. But even this statement of the case gives an excessive impression of consistency. As in all Parliamentary debate, members used the arguments which came to hand, often inconsistently. Since the case for the factory laws rested mainly on emotion or humanitarian sympathy, its strength might vary from year to year, and even from week to week. Though few members depended on working-class votes, they had to pay some attention to opinion among their middle-class electors; and this opinion was, as always, liable to be fickle, especially as the strength of propaganda varied on both sides. Nor could members ignore purely parlia-

[1] J. L. and B. Hammond, *Lord Shaftesbury*, pp. 117–20.

mentary or even party considerations. The case against the Ten Hours Bill seemed stronger when Peel was in office than when Russell was in office: the fact that Peel opposed the Bill was an argument for Protectionist support for it. There were, too, class considerations, the dislike of the landowners for the upstart industrialists, the objection of the industrialists to the outmoded pretensions of the landowners; and there was a sharp change of opinion when the problem related not to factories but to mines.

This was by no means the end of the agitation for factory legislation. The men had not obtained what they really wanted, a ten-hour day for all workers, male and female. The hours of adult males were still unrestricted by law. Since youths and women could be employed for ten hours at any time between 5.30 a.m. and 8.30 p.m., the machines could be kept going for fifteen hours a day by a system of relays which made the checking of evasion difficult. An Act of 1853 forbade the employment of children between 6 p.m. and 6 a.m., but there was still evasion. Also, the Factory Acts applied only to textile mills, not to other industries. After 1850, however, these matters ceased to be of political importance, for the principle of factory legislation had been accepted. There was a stream of legislation consolidated first in an Act of 1878, secondly in an Act of 1901, and thirdly in an Act of 1937. The principle of regulation having been accepted by all political parties, the party differences were few. For most of the nineteenth century the Conservatives were, or at least had the reputation of being, more favourable than the Liberal party to regulation. From 1886, however, there was a tendency to regard the Conservatives as the party of the employers, while the active trade unionists tended (except in Lancashire) to be Radicals, until the formation of the Labour party enabled that party to claim to be the workers' party. In practice, however, neither party dared after 1867 to antagonise the urban workers, for many of them had votes.

5. PUBLIC HEALTH

'One universal atmosphere of filth and stink', was how a medical officer described the environment in which the urban poor lived in 1838.[1]

[1] Sir John Simon, *English Sanitary Institutions* (2nd ed.), p. 182.

In spite of the cholera epidemic of 1831–3, however, the nature and consequences of these urban cesspools were little known. Respectable people did not visit the haunts of crime and vice in the back streets and did not know much of what went on there. Custom had evidently staled the objection to the smell of decaying human excrement.[1] Even the doctors—whose function was to maintain in health those who could afford to pay for their services—'did not get beyond a fluffy sort of generalization... that the disease (cholera) was peculiarly attracted by "needy and squalid" states of life'.[2] Though vaccination had been known as a protection against smallpox since the seventeen-eighties, no public provision for free vaccination was made until 1840; and it has been said that a beautiful woman was a woman who was not marked by the smallpox. Nor was there, until Edwin Chadwick began making a nuisance of himself, any wide notion of the toll of disease, either in misery or in death. The death-rate was known only after the registration of births and deaths was made compulsory in 1836. Misery was not thought of as a justification for legislation; and Chadwick's principal argument was that disease kept up the poor rates.

The public health was capable of becoming a party issue because so many vested interests would inevitably be affected by legislation. Among them were landowners, lessees, speculative builders, water undertakers, owners of common lodging-houses, manufacturers (especially those whose waste polluted the rivers), makers and vendors of iron and earthenware pipes, and ratepayers generally. There was, however, no political dividing line. The pressure for sanitary reform was urban, but so were most of the vested interests. The Conservative party, in so far as it was a country party, or party of rural landowners, was more disinterested than the whigs, since landowners generally let on ground-rent, the lessees taking the rack-rents from the slum property. On the other hand the whigs included many landowners, and the political division between urban and rural really began in 1846. Though the Peelites were, in the main, landowners, there was a tendency, from

---

[1] Some of the refugee camps of Asia can be smelled half-a-mile down wind, yet there is little agitation for their removal, and a few of their inhabitants are wealthy enough to own motor-cars.

[2] Sir John Simon, *op. cit.* p. 175.

1847, for the Conservatives and the whigs to represent different economic interests.

Nevertheless, the public health was a cross-bench problem; proposals for legislation were left to free votes without much whipping. The method adopted was that which had been so successful with the new poor law; and indeed it arose out of that law. In 1838 there was an outbreak of fever in Whitechapel and Bethnal Green. Chadwick moved the Poor Law Commissioners to have it investigated by a team of doctors. Two reports were prepared, the one by Dr Neal Arnott and Dr J. P. Kay on conditions in the Metropolis generally, the other by Dr Southwood Smith on the relation between disease and sanitary conditions in the infected districts. Dr Smith produced a supplementary report in 1839 showing that, of 77,000 persons on relief, 14,000 had had attacks of fever, and 1300 had died from it.[1] These reports were laid before Parliament and published. Stimulated by Chadwick, the Bishop of London (Blomfield) moved an address in the House of Lords praying that the Poor Law Commissioners be instructed to collect information about the causes of disease among the labouring poor in other parts of England and Wales.

While this enquiry (which was extended to Scotland) was in train, there was a debate in the House of Commons on a motion for a Select Committee to enquire into the causes of discontent among the working classes. The three causes, in the opinion of the mover, were lack of sanitary regulation, commercial fluctuations, and lack of religious instruction and education. Other members enunciated all the grievances of the Chartists. The debate was too discursive to lead to a conclusion, but eventually a Select Committee on the Health of Towns was set up. Its report, published in 1840, helped to build up opinion in favour of sanitary legislation.

In 1842 the results of the Poor Law enquiry were published in three volumes, the third being the general report written by Chadwick and published under his name because the Commissioners did not wish to accept responsibility for its conclusions. It is said that ten thousand copies of this report were distributed.[2] Nevertheless, Peel's Government did not feel able at once to introduce legislation which would

[1] *Ibid.* p. 183.　　　　　　[2] *Ibid.* p. 196.

interfere with property rights and would therefore be contentious. They set up a Royal Commission on the Health of Towns, with the Duke of Buccleuch as chairman. Though Chadwick was not a member, he took an active part in the Commission's work. It is therefore not surprising that it confirmed his diagnosis and in substance approved his remedies.

An appropriate Government Bill was introduced in 1845 with the intention that it should be proceeded with in 1846. Two temporary Acts were in fact passed in 1846, the Nuisance Removal Act and the Diseases Prevention Act, but the defeat of the Conservative Government after the repeal of the Corn Law prevented progress with the Public Health Bill. The Whig Government introduced the Bill in 1847, but it was opposed by the vested interests and by those who objected to the centralising tendency of all Chadwick's proposals. The Bill was passed in 1848 with considerable amendments, including the omission of its London provisions; and in the same year the temporary legislation of 1846 was replaced by a permanent Nuisances Removal and Diseases Prevention Act, which did apply to London. Another Royal Commission had been set up in 1847 to consider the public health of the Metropolis, and its reports laid the foundation for an Act enacted in 1848, incorporating the Metropolitan Commissioners of Sewers. Chadwick was a member of this Royal Commission. It is significant that while all this legislation was being passed another epidemic of cholera was on its way from India, and over 54,000 people died of cholera in 1848–9. There was another epidemic in 1853–4.

In all the legislation of the forties there was more fear of cholera than party politics. Nevertheless, the legislation, and above all the tendencies of the General Board of Health set up under the Public Health Act, 1848, did involve political issues which might, had political lines been firmer in the decade after the repeal of the Corn Law, have given rise to party differences. The Board, though not provided with a responsible Minister in the usual sense, had wide powers of interference with local initiative, no doubt because, like the Poor Law Board, its inspiration was Benthamite. Also, it strongly favoured what was later known as 'Gas and Water Socialism' of the 'public utility' type. This principle was put into Victorian language by Sir John Simon:

In the detailed economics of preventive measures, as in regard to the water-service and funeral-services of the metropolis, and in regard to private sanitary improvement-works, the Board favoured a particular principle of administrative interference with freedom of commerce: viz. that, with a view to the improvement or cheapening of certain trade-services to the public, it should be made a function of government...to intervene between buyers and sellers, by converting each local trade-service into a conditional monopoly, which would be conceded by auction or tender to one person, or one body of persons, for each suitable district: so that, in each case, there should be competition *for* the field of service, instead of competition *within* the field of service, and that the service instead of being unregulated should be *under conditions*.[1]

Propagating ideas on these lines, and interfering with the 'rights' of all kinds of vested interests, the General Board of Health created an opposition to itself which was not 'party political' because party politics was still only incidentally concerned with the ordinary men, but which forecast the party politics of the next century, the conflict between the right of property and the pursuit of happiness by those who had no property. When the Public Health Act of 1848 came up for renewal in 1853 the opposition was too strong. The General Board of Health was disbanded and replaced, in effect, by a Minister; Chadwick went into retirement; and the powers of the 1848 Act were renewed only from year to year. Possibly those powers would have disappeared had not another epidemic of cholera been on its way across Europe. Even the separate Ministry disappeared in 1858, the medical functions of the General Board of Health being transferred to the Privy Council and the other functions to the Home Office. This particular Bill was helped through Parliament by the stench from the River Thames. If any obstruction had been offered, said Justin McCarthy, 'the simplest remedy would have been to open the windows'.[2]

The subject of the public health dropped out of politics while Lord Palmerston and Lord Derby governed the country *en société anonyme*, but another epidemic of cholera and epidemics of diphtheria, typhus, yellow fever, cerebro-meningitis and cattle plague reminded those who lived in solid Victorian houses that there was still a problem to be

[1] Sir John Simon, *English Sanitary Institutions*, p. 224 (italics in the original).
[2] *Life of Lord Norton*, p. 167.

solved. The cholera epidemic of 1865 induced the Conservatives to pass the Sanitary Act of 1866 in spite of the fact that the Bill had been introduced by the Liberal Government. After 1867, too, the urban working class was represented in Parliament; and, though the change had no immediate effect on the character of members of Parliament, there developed among many of them a new sensitiveness to working-class misery. The demand for a Royal Commission on the sanitary laws came initially, however, from the medical profession.[1] The Conservative Government acquiesced, but fell before the Commission was appointed; and the Liberal Government which succeeded altered the terms of reference.

It is unnecessary to summarise the recommendations of the Royal Sanitary Commission of 1869–71. Upon them was based the legislation of the period 1871–5 which provided, in substance, our present local health services. Most of it was enacted by the Liberal Government of 1868–74. But the Commission was presided over by a Conservative Privy Counsellor; and Disraeli appropriated the legislation as Conservative policy in his famous 'sanitas sanitatum, omnia sanitas' speech at Manchester in 1872.[2] The final Act, the great consolidating Public Health Act of 1875, was in fact passed under the next Conservative Government.

The fact that the largest invasion of property rights in the nineteenth century was effected without party controversy shows how little foundation has the materialist conception of legal history. There was opposition from vested interests; but it was not worth while for either party to support them because public opinion was skilfully encouraged by a series of public enquiries and confirmed in its views by a series of epidemics. On the whole the Conservative party was more favourable than the Liberal party, partly no doubt because until 1886 there was a tacit alliance between the rural landowners and the urban working class, an alliance which led Disraeli to 'dish the Whigs' in 1867.

[1] Sir John Simon, *English Sanitary Institutions*, p. 325.
[2] His speech was based on a note supplied by the chairman of the Commission: *Life of Lord Norton*, p. 213.

6. EDUCATION

At the end of the eighteenth century the education of the young was no concern of politicians, as such. Generally the aristocracy employed tutors for their sons, who might, however, be sent to Oxford (especially suitable for good tories) or Cambridge (especially suitable for good whigs) as fellow-commoners. The middle classes generally sent their sons to the endowed 'grammar' or 'public' schools, or to the dissenting academies, or to profit-making establishments. Thence they might, if they were prepared to take the prescribed religious tests, proceed to the universities of Oxford, Cambridge, or Scotland. Girls of the upper and middle classes were generally educated at home by governesses, but there were private schools at which they could learn to read and write and be taught the domestic arts, perhaps with a little French or Italian or music to add to whatever other qualifications they possessed for successful marriages.

For the mass of the population there were schools of different types, though their number was small in relation to the population.[1] First, there were the 'dame schools', usually kept by ladies in reduced circumstances, who for a small fee looked after children and provided them with rudimentary education. They were declared by the Newcastle Commission in 1861 to be 'generally very inefficient', and they were not likely to have been more efficient a century or half-a-century earlier. Older children, if educated at all, might be sent to a 'common day school', where a master, again for a small fee, passed on such knowledge as he possessed: and, since he was often a person who had failed in other employments, he might possess very little. The fees in dame schools and common day schools, though small, were sufficient to deter those parents who were very poor, but for their children free 'charity schools' might be available. Schools of this type were opened by the Society for Promoting Christian Knowledge as early as 1698; and generally, as the name and origin indicate, the motives were religious and charitable. The main purpose was to give instruction in the elements of the Christian religion, as maintained by the Established

---

[1] H. C. Barnard, *A Short History of English Education*, pp. 4–13; Frank Smith, *A History of English Elementary Education*, pp. 36–69.

Church. The catechism was heard by the local parson and reading was generally taught. Writing and arithmetic might be added; but, since the children in the charity schools were expected to become labourers, domestic servants and, late in the eighteenth century, factory hands, the main emphasis, apart from that on religion, was upon those handicrafts which created 'habits of industry'. Finally, there were 'schools of industry' in which children were set to work and at the same time taught to read. Since the work produced had to be handicrafts, which found increasing competition from factory products, the schools had no future except as ordinary poor law schools; and it was cheaper to apprentice boys and girls in the factories than to educate them.

In terms of numbers, all this was very little: but the idea that the children of the poor ought to be educated, and even more the idea that the State should undertake the task, were new in the nineteenth century. The labouring classes had been ordained by God to be labourers and domestic servants. For these purposes life and the home were the best educators; and the earlier the children were put to work the less likely they were to acquire idle and dissolute habits and the more likely to develop habits of industry. For the sake of their immortal souls they ought to be taught the elements of Christianity; but this was primarily the business of their parents and secondarily the business of the Church.

The defect to which public attention was first drawn, in fact, was not that the children were uneducated but that they were little pagans. As such they were a danger to the stability of a society in which Christianity, as professed, helped to maintain the dignity of rank and station and to keep the lower orders in a proper state of respectful subservience. For six days a week the children in the factories could hardly make nuisances of themselves. On Sundays they roamed the streets and acquired those habits of begging and thieving which so many in the eighteenth century thought to be natural to children. For the evangelical, too, they had souls to be saved. Accordingly there was from 1780,[1] and especially after the French Revolution showed the

---

[1] There were Sunday schools before Robert Raikes in 1780 opened his school in Sooty Lane: for example, T. Lindsay's school at Catterick in 1764, Hannah More's at High Wycombe in 1769, and Simpson's at Macclesfield in 1778. But it was Raikes' experiment in Gloucester which attracted attention: Balleine, *History of the Evangelical Party*, p. 140.

social dangers of irreligion, a great growth of Sunday schools. They were not always regarded with favour. The extreme right wing, which saw no purpose, other than a seditious one, in teaching the poor, believed them to be Jacobin.[1] A century later they were the means for giving Mother a quiet Sunday afternoon and the children a little of the religious instruction that they did not get at home. But by this time the school boards had assumed the responsibility for elementary education. For the greater part of a century the Sunday schools were the means, and often the only means, by which children could learn to read. Against the cynicism which the Georgian attitude to religion inevitably produces must be set the devoted service of so many parsons, ministers and laymen in the Sunday schools. Sometimes the teachers were paid; but in the factory towns voluntary service was more usual, especially where the schools were Nonconformist.

As the fears inspired by the French Revolution receded, there was a change in the social attitude towards education. Against the disadvantage of educating the poor above their station was set the advantage of teaching them the elements of the Christian religion. Not only did the Sunday schools become respectable, especially if taught by parsons and not by dissenting ministers, but also there was a growth of denominational day schools. They became practicable through the development by Joseph Lancaster and Andrew Bell of the monitorial system, whereby the actual teaching was done in a mechanical fashion by monitors who were first taught the mechanical operation. Lancaster was a Nonconformist and Bell a clergyman of the Church of England. There was accordingly great rivalry between them and between their respective supporters. In 1808 the body later known as the British and Foreign School Society was founded to propagate Lancaster's ideas and use his methods. It was supported by Churchmen as well as Nonconformists, and its intentions were undenominational, but in effect it became a Nonconformist body. In 1811 a number of Churchmen, supporters of Bell, founded the National Society for Promoting the Education of the Poor in the Principles of the Established Church. Though other schools were founded, these two bodies, the British and Foreign Society and the National Society, dominated English

[1] C. S. Carpenter, *Church and People, 1789–1889*, p. 39.

415

elementary education until the board schools were established after 1870.

The concern of Parliament, from the beginning of the nineteenth century, with pauper children and children in factories, has already been mentioned.[1] They were thought of only incidentally as creating an educational problem, because only the exceptional Radical, like J. A. Roebuck, regarded the education of the young as falling within the jurisdiction of Parliament. Even Henry Brougham, whose efforts for education were considerable, thought that the problem could be met, and was gradually being met, by voluntary and charitable arrangements. Nevertheless, it was Lord Brougham who suggested that Parliament help by an annual grant of £20,000 for school buildings. This grant, which began in 1833, went mainly to schools proposed or supported by the two denominational societies; and, after a short initial period, the bulk of the money was used to build Church of England schools.[2]

The belief of members of Parliament that education was no business of theirs was fostered by other beliefs. The clergy, and especially the Tractarian clergy associated with the Oxford Movement, thought that education was emphatically their concern. To say that it was a matter for the Church and not for the State would be to exaggerate the case. Certainly the content of education was a matter for the Church, since its purpose was to enable the poor to lead godly lives. Those who accepted the Established Church as part of the universal Church of Christ, however, thought that it was the duty of the State to help the Church to establish—or perhaps to re-establish—its monopoly: and there could be no nonsense about scruples of conscience because, whatever the parents said, it was the duty of the community to provide for the training of the young in the only true religion. The Churchmen suspected the whigs of flirting with dissent, which was of course heresy, and of favouring secular education, which was not only heresy but also, in a Christian Kingdom, nearly treason.

Conservative laymen, even if they shared in the prevailing anticlericalism—which was enhanced by the sacerdotalism of the High

---

[1] *Ante*, pp. 399–407.
[2] Frank Smith, *History of English Elementary Education*, pp. 138–40.

Church party—reached much the same conclusions, though for different reasons. Education was dangerous because it encouraged the lower orders to develop ambitions inconsistent with their station. There was no harm in taking the young from the streets, where they acquired vicious habits, and teaching them habits of industry by regular work at useful crafts. It was proper that they should be taught the catechism and their duties to their superiors. Under adequate supervision by the clergy, they could even be taught to read the Bible, though there was a danger that, when they became domestic servants, they might also read their mistresses' letters. It was going too far to teach them to write, since their destiny was to become labourers and domestic servants.

What most of the millowners wanted was a supply of child labour to keep the machines going as long as possible, and the economists of the Ricardian school agreed with them. Reading, writing and arithmetic were unnecessary accomplishments for factory workers, indeed literacy encouraged the workers to organise themselves in combinations. On the other hand, the provision of education for the young was not a matter which affected the millowners materially, unless they had to meet the cost; and they approved of Sunday schools as means for keeping boys and girls off the streets. Nor were parents always very keen on education. The eagerness for the 'white-collar' job was a product of the late nineteenth century. Except in the few places where endowed schools, like the blue-coat schools, remained open to the poor, the education given in the schools accessible to poor children was too little to enable those children to aspire to clerical careers. If the child was destined for the factory, the earlier he or she began earning money the better. The figures of school registration early in the nineteenth century tell us very little because the turn-over of pupils was rapid and absenteeism high. The first genuinely literate generation was that born in the seventies, those who swelled the ranks of the 'new unionists' in the nineties. The 'white-collar' workers were, in the main, those provided with secondary education from the beginning of the present century.

The vote of £20,000 in 1833 was, however, the thin end of the wedge. The denominational societies, having got a little money, naturally wanted more. Members of Parliament wanted schools in their constituencies. The few enthusiasts, mainly Radicals, produced a stream of resolutions. In 1834 Roebuck secured a Select Committee on the education of the people. It was unable to produce recommendations, but collected much evidence. There was, too, much agitation outside Parliament for educational development. In part it was associated with the application of the new poor law, for some of the assistant commissioners, notably Dr J. P. Kay (afterwards Sir J. Kay-Shuttleworth), saw in education the solution of the social problems exhibited by the poor law and sanitary enquiries. In part the agitation was associated with the Ten Hours movement; Dr Kay, among others, considered it socially dangerous to enable the urban working class to have leisure unless it was educated to use it.

In 1838 T. Wyse moved an address to the Queen to set up a central Board of Education. It was defeated by four votes in a thin House, mainly because of Church opposition. In the following year, however, a Committee of the Privy Council on Education was set up, with Dr Kay as secretary.

Its first new proposal, to set up a teachers' training college with two model schools, a boarding school and a day school, was strongly opposed by the Church and by members of the Conservative party because 'general religious instruction', common to all denominations, was to be given by an Anglican chaplain and dissenting ministers.[1] Though in fact dissenters' schools had been receiving building grants since 1833, this official recognition of Nonconformity was strongly opposed by the High Church party, and the proposal had to be withdrawn. Indeed the grant for 1839 was carried by two votes only. Nevertheless, the Committee was able to insist that, in future, school grants would involve inspection.

The Conservative Government of 1841 kept the Committee of Council in being but gave its work an Anglican bias. The Factory Bill of 1843 provided for factory schools with Anglican headmasters, though licensed ministers of other denominations might visit the schools one day a week to give religious instruction to children whose parents applied for it. Each school would be maintained out of the

Frank Smith, *History of English Elementary Education*, pp. 174–5.

418

poor rate, and would be governed by a management committee, of which the clergyman and two churchwardens were to be *ex officio* members, with two members appointed by the magistrates and two millowners. These proposals were severely criticised by Nonconformists, who had Opposition support, and the Bill was withdrawn.

The return of the whigs in 1846 enabled Kay-Shuttleworth to secure acceptance of a grant system for pupil-teachers, and the total sum available for grants of all kinds (in Great Britain) was raised to £100,000. When Kay-Shuttleworth retired at the end of 1849 there had been great improvement in the inspected schools, and there were many more schools, though most of the uninspected schools were very bad. Most schools were denominational, and a battle between the High Church party and the evangelicals was raging in the National Society; but most Church schools had committees of management, presided over by the vicar, and he had exclusive authority (subject to his bishop) only over the religious instruction. In effect, the High Church claim to a clerical monopoly of education had been rejected. On the other hand the system of grants-in-aid had mainly helped those who had funds to help themselves, and therefore the Anglicans had derived most benefit from it. Moreover the unified organisation of the Church, in contrast with the sectionalism of Nonconformity, gave the Church the initiative. Nonconformity first became a political force in the agitation against the education clauses of the Factory Bill of 1843; but it was easier for the parson, stimulated by the bishop or the diocesan board of education, to found an elementary school for his parish and obtain a grant than it was for the various Nonconformist ministers or laymen to combine for the same purpose. The Church had therefore occupied a wide field, disproportionate to the number of its worshippers, before the battle for rate-aided schools began.

One must not, however, think of the problem exclusively as one between Anglican and Nonconformist or (what was tending to be the same thing) Conservative and Liberal. The Church was divided between those who favoured clerical control and those who favoured lay control of the schools. Among the Nonconformists and others were several groups. The 'Voluntarists' saw great dangers in State-aided education, not only because, given the narrow franchise of 1832, the Church had predominance both in Parliament and in local government, but also because there was thought to be moral advantage in a system whereby the poor paid small fees and the rich helped out of charity. Both the Church and Nonconformity feared that rate-aided schools would compete on favourable terms with denominational schools and thus drive religion out of education—though this argument appealed more to the Anglicans than to the Nonconformists because the former had more money. At the other extreme were those who regarded religion as a matter for the churches and education as a matter for the State and saw no reason for the State's helping the churches to canvass for recruits among the children.

On the other hand, the old fear of the propertied classes, that elementary education would be socially subversive, had disappeared. There was general recognition that the children of the poor had to be educated; and there were only two difficulties, the cost and the squabble over religious education. The cost to the State in 1851 was £150,000: if provision were made on the same scale for the three million children between five and twelve years of age who were not in employment, the cost to the State would have been three million pounds.[1] There was more chance of getting money out of rates than out of taxes: but any such proposal required a solution of the religious problem. Of the two million pupils in the day schools, one million were in the 10,000 schools built by religious bodies; and 800,000 of the pupils were in Church of England schools.[2]

Various Bills were produced in the fifties, but none had any success. At last, in 1858, the House of Commons passed a motion for an address praying the Queen to establish a Royal Commission. The Newcastle Commission, which reported in six volumes in 1861, was typical of its age. It was no longer thought that working-class children ought not to be taught writing and arithmetic. On the other hand, compulsory education was neither attainable nor desirable; and a minority of the Commissioners considered that the Government had no educational responsibilities save towards those whom destitution, vagrancy or crime cast upon its hands. The existing system, whereby 'almost all

[1] Frank Smith, *History of English Elementary Education*, pp. 222–3.
[2] *Ibid.* p. 223.

the children capable of going to school receive some instruction', was generally sound, but suffered from certain defects, for which the Commission offered remedies.[1]

The recommendations fell to be considered by Robert Lowe, afterwards Viscount Sherbrooke. The office of Vice-President of the Council for Education had been created in 1856, and Lowe had been appointed to it in 1859. An albino with very weak sight, but of great ability, he had suffered as a boy because of his affliction, and had therefore become at Oxford a particularly bumptious undergraduate, his main field of action (apart from the Schools, where he did very well) being the Union Society. His characteristic as a politician, therefore, was his remarkable self-assurance. He paid little attention to the views of his expert advisers, among whom was Matthew Arnold, but devised a grant system, known as 'Payment by Results', which administratively was good sense but educationally nonsense. Though mitigated by subsequent changes, it remained in operation for thirty years. Theoretically the Liberal Government was responsible; and the Cabinet Minister concerned was Lord Granville, Lord President of the Council: but education was still a minor service to which senior Ministers paid little attention. Hence a more than usually heavy responsibility rested upon a junior Minister.

Robert Lowe's ideas on education were expressed in a pamphlet published by him in 1867:

The lower classes ought to be educated to discharge the duties cast upon them. They should also be educated that they may appreciate and defer to a higher cultivation when they meet it, and the higher classes ought to be educated in a very different manner, in order that they may exhibit to the lower classes that higher education to which, if it were shown to them, they would bow down and defer.[2]

Such ideas were common in his generation: but it was a misfortune that English education—Scotland escaped the worst characteristics— was dominated for so long by the ideas of so dogmatic a politician. Even Robert Lowe, however, accepted the idea of rate-aided education in 1870. By leading the 'Cave of Adullam' against the Government, he destroyed Gladstone's Reform Bill of 1866: but thereby he enabled

[1] *Ibid.* pp. 238–43.   [2] Quoted *ibid.* p. 233.

Disraeli to 'dish the whigs' by securing the passing of a more radical measure in 1867. The Reform Act of 1867 in effect put the borough seats under the control of the working-class householders. It was immediately recognised that thenceforth the State could not evade the duty of educating the masses. As Lord Sherbrooke's biographer put it:

Lord Derby and Mr Disraeli had handed over the governing power in the State to vast masses of men who were destitute of even the most elementary education, and...some immediate steps, on a large national scale, would have to be taken to bring the new voters at least within the pale of the non-illiterate.[1]

The phrase which has been attributed to Robert Lowe is 'we must educate our masters'. What Lowe actually said, however, was that it was necessary 'to compel our future masters to learn their letters';[2] and that phrase was a more accurate rendering of his thought. It was not intended that the workers should be educated to be rulers, or in other words that there should be any kind of social democracy. The class structure was to be maintained; and indeed Lowe, in his speeches, produced schemes for the improvement of the education of the upper and middle classes. Those schemes he thought necessary 'if those classes were to continue to have any political influence or even be enabled to maintain their social position'.[3] The working classes were to be forced to learn their letters, and so brought within the pale of the non-illiterate, in order that they might properly exercise the function vested in them by the second Reform Act, of making a choice among those members of the Oxford Union Society who presented themselves for election. It was far from the intention to send the sons of working men to Oxford, since that would be to educate them above their station.

The difficulty of compelling our masters to learn their letters was that the Church of England had acquired a huge vested interest which in places was almost a monopoly. Any reform which substituted secular schools for the voluntary schools would have to be carried over the dead bodies of the whole bench of bishops; any reform which gave increased aid to the Church schools would have to be carried over the

[1] *Life of Viscount Sherbrooke*, II, p. 331.
[2] *Ibid.* p. 330. [3] *Ibid.* p. 331.

dead bodies of the Nonconformists, whose relative political strength had been increased by the second Reform Act. The problem was handed over to W. E. Forster, the Radical member for Bradford, who became Vice-President of the Council. To make things more difficult for him three Birmingham Radicals, George Dixon, Joseph Chamberlain, and the inevitable Jesse Collings, decided to found the Education League to fight for unsectarian, free and compulsory education. Inevitably the opposition formed the National Education Union to defend denominational education.

Forster's task was to produce a Bill acceptable to a whig Cabinet which did not want to split the Liberal party, a House of Commons which was almost exclusively Anglican, and a Liberal party which included a large and aggressive Nonconformist wing. Necessarily the Education Bill of 1870 was a compromise, though it was more fiercely attacked by the Nonconformists than by the Anglicans. In general this fierceness was due to the virulence which Joseph Chamberlain injected into any controversy in which he was engaged. The Bill did not provide for unsectarian, free and compulsory education, but it did provide for the setting up of elected school boards which could build and maintain unsectarian schools and make education compulsory when adequate schools had been provided. On the other hand, the existing voluntary schools were retained, the religious bodies were given twelve months (in the Bill as enacted six months) within which to secure approval for new sectarian schools, and increased financial assistance was provided (originally from the rates, but eventually from taxes) for secular education in sectarian schools.

How acute was the division is shown by the vote on an amendment to the Cowper-Temple clause. This clause, named after the member who moved it, sought to prevent sectarian teaching in board schools, and the Nonconformists wanted to strengthen it. In the division 132 Liberals voted for the amendment; 133 abstained; and the amendment was defeated by 121 Liberals and 132 Conservatives.[1] This gives an exaggerated impression of the strength of Nonconformity in the House of Commons. In a period when electoral organisation was weak, an active body like the Birmingham League could do much damage in

[1] R. W. W. Dale, *Life of Dr Dale*, p. 280.

the constituencies; and borough members feared for their seats. Nor were the Conservatives wholly favourable to the Bill. The National Education Union, usually called the Manchester Union, was less efficient than the Birmingham League and had less money; but the Anglicans had an astute leader in Disraeli, who did his best for the Church, though he had so to manoeuvre as to widen the Liberal split.

The enactment of the Education Act, 1870, was a great step forward. Forster's biographer gives the result in figures:[1]

	1870	1874	1886
Inspected schools	8,281	13,163	19,133
Accommodation	1,879,000	2,861,000	5,145,000
Attendance	1,152,000	1,679,000	3,438,000
Teachers	28,000	48,000	87,000

These figures must be considered in the light of the Act of 1880, under which education became compulsory throughout the country in 1881. The figures for 1874 show a very large increase in the number of denominational schools, especially in the rural areas, where the Church of England, and therefore the Conservative party, generally maintained its monopoly.

The agitation of the Birmingham League did not cease after 1870. It fought against the operation of 'section 25', which enabled school boards to pay the fees of poor scholars in denominational schools. It is generally thought that Nonconformist opposition to Forster's Bill lost Liberal votes in 1874 and helped to return a Conservative Government. There were, however, other factors. In particular, aggressive agitation by any religious sect is apt to bring out the latent anticlericalism of the working class; and some may have voted Conservative in 1874 not because, being Nonconformists, they objected to the Education Act, but because, disliking ministers as much as parsons, they voted against the ministers' party. That astute electioneer, Joseph Chamberlain, dropped out of the religious controversy and founded 'Joe's Caucus' on a policy of social reform generally.

[1] *Life of W. E. Forster*, I, pp. 520–1.

7. THE ACHIEVEMENT OF THE WELFARE STATE

In the long term, Chamberlain was right. Most of the new electors of 1868 had no interest in religious controversy. Only in a few pockets, notably in Yorkshire, the West of England, and Wales was Nonconformity politically strong. Electorally speaking, any strong minority is important, because it may hold the balance between the political parties. In the mass, however, those new electors who wanted education for their children did not much care whether they were taught 'Cowper-Temple religion' in the board schools or orthodox Anglicanism in the Church schools. Even in the Church schools the progressive professionalisation of education since the reign of Kay-Shuttleworth had altered the emphasis. It was no longer a question of teaching the lower orders orthodox religion in order that they might accept the obligations of their lowly station and allow the country to be ruled by and for the benefit of the wealthier classes. Robert Lowe's reforms depressed the quality of elementary education, but at least they recognised that the whole population ought to be taught reading, writing and arithmetic. The teachers produced by the training colleges were, for most of the nineteenth century, a poor lot: but their essential task was to educate, and only incidentally (if at all) to teach religion. Religion was taught in the Sunday schools, which continued to flourish in the first quarter of the twentieth century. In the day schools there were 'periods' for religious instruction at the beginning or the end of the school day (so that those who objected to it could arrive late or leave early): but this made 'Religious Knowledge' just another subject. The main task of the schools was secular education, and it was carried out with increasing efficiency until, in 1902, the London School Board forced the Conservative Government to reform the whole educational structure and to provide secondary education for those who were prepared to pay a little for it, or could win 'scholarships'. After the war of 1914–18 the 'scholarship-wallahs' from the council schools were reaching the universities in increasing numbers.

In the main the achievement of the Welfare State was due to the conflict for votes between the Conservative party and the Labour party after 1918: but the foundations were laid while the Liberal party was trying to adapt itself to household franchise. Historically, the Liberal party of the eighteen-sixties was a combination of four strains, the Canningite tories who had joined the whigs in opposition to the Duke of Wellington in 1830, of whom the last survivor was Lord Palmerston; the whigs, among whom were most of the Liberal peers, including Lord Russell, and also Lord Hartington (a Cavendish); the Peelites, and especially W. E. Gladstone; and the relics of the old-fashioned Radicals, grown old and respectable. This was not promising material for a party based on household franchise. Some new men entered Parliament as Liberals in 1868, among them Sir Charles Dilke: but Gladstone's Government of that year might be described as 'the old gang', were it not for the presence of John Bright and W. E. Forster. The only substantial measure of social reform was Forster's Education Bill which, as we have seen, aroused considerable antagonism in the great cities of the midlands and north. Gladstone was, and remained, a stern individualist.[1] Joseph Chamberlain's view, based upon observation of this Government, was that an appeal must be made to the new electors on a basis of Radical social reform.

The 'Birmingham plan' had considerable success in the great cities, and as a method of organisation it succeeded in establishing itself as a network of Liberal associations federated in the National Liberal Federation. Chamberlain was less successful in influencing Liberal policy. The *Radical Programme* of 1885 had some oddities because of its middle class and Nonconformist background, but it had merits as a series of policies designed to attract working-class voters. On the other hand the Liberal party was becoming dominated by Gladstone, whose mind was less flexible than Disraeli's, and who was apt to go on a frolic of his own in respect of Ireland or foreign affairs. Gladstone was a most persuasive platform politician, but he was not a political organiser or strategist, as Disraeli was. He therefore led the Liberal party into by-roads which did not lead to votes. Moreover the Liberal party had to carry the old-fashioned whigs, who still thought of politics as an upper-class pursuit, and also the factory owners, many of whom were of the second or third generation and were out of sympathy with their men. These disadvantages the party shed in 1886, but it also lost

---

[1] *Life of Gladstone*, III, p. 173.

426

the Radical leaders, Joseph Chamberlain because he could not be persuaded to accept Gladstone's Irish policy, and Dilke because of a divorce suit. John Morley was, in comparison, a lightweight; and new Radical leaders were not produced by the Liberal party until Lloyd George.

It is of course possible that Joseph Chamberlain was mistaken, and that a Radical programme of social reform, accepted by the Liberal party as a whole in 1885, would not have prevented the Conservative predominance which in effect lasted from 1886 to 1905—for the Liberals did not carry Great Britain in 1892 and Ireland was concerned not with social reform but with Home Rule. Political ideas take something like a generation to soak into the minds of an electorate. The middle-class voters enfranchised between 1832 and 1867 were influenced even in the seventies and eighties by the events of the forties, particularly the Chartist Movement and the repeal of the Corn Law. The working-class electors enfranchised in 1867 and 1868 tended to be Conservative in politics because their employers were usually Liberals, because Disraeli was a 'bit of a card', and because, as workers, they were more interested in industrial action through trade unions than in politics. The new rural voters may have been attracted by 'three acres and a cow' in 1885, but the Conservative landowners and farmers were able to re-establish their control of the rural seats in 1886. The result was that the defection of the whigs and the Birmingham Radicals in 1886 was enough to give the Conservatives a majority in Great Britain for nearly forty years.

Nor had the truncated Liberal party any broad popular appeal. In the Newcastle Programme the National Liberal Federation tried to be all things to all men; but it had so many platforms that nobody knew where it stood, except that, because of Gladstone, it was still concerned primarily with Home Rule. The new men, of the stamp of Campbell-Bannerman, Asquith, Grey and Haldane, were not likely to enthuse a multitude; and even Lloyd George (until he learned from experience) thought that the disestablishment of the Church of England had as much appeal in England as it had in Wales. Moreover Joseph Chamberlain, being unable to get much in the way of social reform through the Unionist alliance, kept the Liberals' minds off it by a rousing jingoism after 1895 and Tariff Reform after 1902. The Liberals had to pay some attention to social reform in 1905 because of the threat from the nascent Labour party on their flank.

The really active political group from the nineties were the Fabians, of whom more must be said in the next chapter. Initially, however, they had more success with the Conservatives than with the Liberals, especially in the field of education. They influenced the Liberal Government of 1906–14 mainly through the Report of the Royal Commission on the Poor Laws, and especially the Minority Report. The Webbs' agitation for the 'break-up' of the poor law did not succeed until 1929, and then only partially; but it resulted in proposals for old age pensions, health insurance and unemployment insurance which, though modest at the outset, have in the course of fifty years expanded into the major sources of the Welfare State. The most active of the protagonists in the Liberal party were Lloyd George and Winston Churchill—whose father, Lord Randolph Churchill, had like Joseph Chamberlain realised the importance of providing welfare services for the working-class electors. The Liberal party was, however, unable to become the party of the Welfare State, partly because of the conflict over Home Rule and the Parliament Bill, partly because of the war of 1914–18, but mainly because, for these and other reasons, the Labour party was able to supplant it after 1922.

CHAPTER X

BRITISH SOCIALISM

I. THE CHARACTER OF BRITISH SOCIALISM

The phrase 'British Socialism' is justified by the fact that the article was home-made; and, though its nature and content have been influenced by movements of opinion in other European countries, especially France, Germany and Russia, British socialism has always been as much British as socialist. The word 'socialism' appears to have been first used in 1827. It was in the *Cooperative Magazine*, and it meant co-operation as opposed to competition.[1] It has in Britain always carried that ethical implication, the notion of man's dependence on man, his sympathy with his fellows, and his duty to humanity. The socialist State, if there has to be a State—and genuine socialism is opposed to nationalism because sympathy and moral responsibility are not limited by nationality—is a co-operative commonwealth. Free competition, extolled by the theorists of the industrial revolution, was immoral because it set man against man. Though many British socialists have been atheists, and many more have been agnostics, British socialism has had close associations with Christianity, particularly of the evangelical brand. There have been socialists, like F. D. Maurice and Charles Kingsley, in the Church of England; but they have been comparatively few because the Church has been a landowning hierarchy whose priests were, until recently, drawn from the landowning class. Similarly, the hierarchy of the Church of Rome has generally been anti-socialist, though many British Roman Catholics, recollecting the effects of free competition on the people of their homeland, Ireland, have been staunch socialists. The leaders of the industrial revolution often were Nonconformists, and the views of Nonconformist ministers have usually accorded with those of the men in the rented pews: where Nonconformity had strong support among the working classes, as in Yorkshire, evangelical socialists like Philip Snowden were generally to be found. On the other hand, socialism has often been, as with

[1] M. Beer, *History of British Socialism*, I, p. 187.

429

Lord Snell and Harold Laski, a system of social ethics in substitution for religion.[1]

The evangelical fervour of the socialist missionaries has been a factor of the greatest political importance. It encouraged them to travel by slow and dirty local trains, often on Sundays, to eat their meals out of paper bags, to stand on soap boxes at windy street corners or on rain-swept heaths, and to carry their message to the people where the people were to be found. Their message was usually 'pie in the sky', a message of hope to the depressed and the downtrodden. 'When socialism comes', all would be well; capitalist Huddersfield would be socialist Jerusalem; there would be no more want and no more fear; there would be beauty and loving-kindness where there was ugliness and jealousy. It is easy to caricature, but these socialist propagandists did think of themselves as missionaries. 'Small bands of young crusaders', said Lord Snell, '...carried the glad tidings to the "heathen"...; we worked in the faith that if we cast our socialist bread upon the waters we should see it again after not too many days.... I and others preached the new gospel... with an evangelist's fervour I preached the brother-hood of man.'[2] Lord Snowden quoted Johnny Coe, of Wibsey, who, since he had been 'converted' to socialism understood the old martyrs because he was willing to go to the stake for his socialism. Johnny Coe's advice to the speaker was:

Tha' knows they're an ignorant lot at Wibsey, so don't be trying any of that scientific socialism. We want no Karl Marx and surplus values and that sort of stuff. Make it plain and simple. Tha' can put in a long word now and then so as to make them think that tha' knows a lot, but keep it simple, and then when tha'rt coming to t'finishing up tha' mun put a bit of 'Come to Jesus' in like Philip [Snowden] does.[3]

Harry Snell and Philip Snowden ended their careers in the House of Lords; but Johnny Coe and hundreds of others never had careers, outside the factory.

This political evangelicalism was partly responsible for the 'inexor-able march' of the Labour party from 1900 to 1945. There are relics

---

[1] Laski was a socialist long before he called himself a Marxist.
[2] Lord Snell, *Men, Movements and Myself*, pp. 59–60.
[3] Viscount Snowden's *Autobiography*, I, p. 82.

of it still, as the editor of the *New Statesman* shows when he throws in the odd reference to 'Socialism', with a capital letter. By 'Socialism' he means not the policy of the Labour party, nor even the nationalisation of the means of production, distribution and exchange, but the Paradise towards which the noble army of socialist martyrs is marching. It is, however, difficult to flog an emotion for three whole generations. The young men and women tend to be both curious and sceptical about it. They genuinely want to know where and what this socialism is; and nobody can tell them because it does not exist. It was an aspiration towards something good and beautiful, so different from the back streets of Victorian England, and yet not smug and suburban like the municipal housing schemes of the new Elizabethan era. The Labour politicians are, or at least seem to be,[1] not advocates of a great cause, but ordinary politicians scrambling for offices even more obviously than Conservative politicians, who at least pay lip service to the public school tradition that they play up and play the game for the good of the school, not to get into the team.

Behind this imposing façade of a mythical Socialism, however, lies a very solid body, the Labour party, deliberately set up and deliberately maintained as the manual workers' party, though, like so many of the manual workers themselves, becoming rapidly middle class. Emphasis upon socialist literature, and even upon socialist policies, tends to distort the true character of the Labour party. Fundamentally it is the trade unions' party, the political branch of a substantial entity called the Labour Movement. The socialist literature is not all froth, nor the 'intellectuals' all fringe. In spite of the wrangles of politicians, the vapours exhaled by the lunatic fringe, and the sceptical opportunism of hard-boiled trade-union secretaries, there is in the Labour party a deep sense of social justice, of the dignity of the human being, whatever be his class, colour or creed, which the party has inherited from the evangelicals. If the bleeding hearts of its members sometimes 'go to their bloody heads', there are at least bleeding hearts. Nevertheless, the trade unions provide the money and trade-union votes dominate the Annual Conference. Though the trade unions pay the piper, they do not always call the tune: but they know what they like.

---

[1] Leslie Hunter, *The Road to Brighton Pier*; cf. *Beatrice Webb's Diaries*, p. 295.

2. SOCIALIST THEORY AND THE WORKING-CLASS MOVEMENT

As Professor Tawney has pointed out, it is not the case 'that the classical land of capitalist industry had to wait for an exposition of socialism till a German exile disinterred dusty bluebooks in the British Museum. As Marx himself was well aware, there was an indigenous English socialism which, except for the inspiration to all creative thought given by France, owed nothing to foreign influences.'[1] There has been a small Marxist strand, exhibited at first by the Social Democratic Federation[2] (founded in 1881 as the Democratic Federation), by a few small groups after the Russian Revolution and, since 1920, by the Communist party of Great Britain. There have also been Marxists—or more often people who called themselves Marxists—in the Labour party.

The organised advocacy of socialism was, however, undertaken mainly by the Fabian Society (founded 1884) and the Independent Labour party (founded 1893). Strictly speaking the I.L.P. had no ideology. Its name was chosen, instead of 'Socialist Labour party', because it was hoped to secure the support of the trade unions, many of whose members did not regard themselves as socialists. There were Marxists among the members: but fundamentally its socialism was of the kind described above as 'evangelical'. Keir Hardie's socialism was simply a belief that a better organisation of society than that provided by capitalism was possible: he could not have given a theoretical justification of that belief. Ramsay MacDonald had read widely; but what he called socialism was simply a policy designed to secure social justice. Philip Snowden's background was Nonconformist. Most of the members of the I.L.P. were working men, or self-educated men of working-class background, who were prepared to accept that a socialist commonwealth was possible and considered it equitable, on Christian or ethical grounds, that it should be established. On the other hand, the I.L.P. was not revolutionary. The case for 'physical force', which

[1] Introduction to M. Beer, *History of British Socialism*, I, p. xviii.
[2] The pukka communists say, however, that it 'posed as Marxist': Tom Bell, *The British Communist Party*, p. 13.

had impressed so many Chartists, had disappeared with the extensions of the franchise in 1867 and 1884. If the working class chose to combine in favour of a socialist policy—or, for that matter, any other policy— it could, after 1884, control the House of Commons.

The Fabian Society has had no ideology, in the sense of a dogma which members were expected to accept. It was, however, such a small and compact body that the views of the principal members had a profound effect. The most influential of these leaders, at least until the twenties when young men like Harold Laski and G. D. H. Cole became prominent, were Sidney Webb and Bernard Shaw. It seems odd to say so, but Webb was the political philosopher and Shaw the economist.[1] Webb's philosophy was, however, a frame of reference, a means to an end; and the end was 'the reorganization of society by the emancipation of land and industrial capital from individual and class ownership, and the vesting of them in the community for the general benefit'.[2] Though he had read Marx, Lassalle and Proudhon,[3] his line of thought came from John Locke *via* John Stuart Mill. The latter, as Webb pointed out, moved from the individualist to the collectivist thesis in successive editions of his *Political Economy*.

Nor had Bernard Shaw anything new to contribute. His attention was 'first drawn to political economy as the science of social salvation by Henry George's eloquence, and by his *Progress and Poverty*', which had a large circulation in the early eighties.[4] He was then told to read Marx, and he was so impressed that at first he was prepared to defend him against all-comers, including Sidney Webb. Eventually, however, he was convinced by Stanley Jevons' theory of value.

Fabian socialism was, in short, not founded on a particular theory, as Soviet Communism was alleged to be. It was simply one of the consequences of a general movement of opinion in the nineteenth century. However it be disguised, individualism was founded on the natural right of property.[5] By 'property', the men of the eighteenth century generally meant land, and the landed interest dominated

[1] E. R. Pease, *History of the Fabian Society*, pp. 258–65.
[2] *Ibid.* p. 269.
[3] M. Beer, *History of British Socialism*, II, p. 275.
[4] E. R. Pease, *op. cit.* p. 260.
[5] G. H. Sabine, *History of Political Theory*, p. 661.

English politics for roughly two centuries after the Restoration of Charles II. In the second of those centuries, however, it was increasingly in competition with other forms of capital, at first mainly capital goods like factories and machinery, and later the intangible form of choses in action. The classical economists simply assumed the natural right of capital, including land. On the political plane this implied a conflict between the landowners and the industrial middle classes, since the landowners dominated the political system until 1832. Though the immediate effects of the first Reform Act were small, the tories saw that the eighteenth-century Constitution was being subverted. The suppression of the small boroughs under 'influence' diminished the power of the landowners, and the enfranchisement of the great cities and industrial towns increased the power of the other capitalists. On the other hand, the interests of the great capitalists were more widely diffused than those of the great landowners and therefore less effective politically. Though for the greater part of the nineteenth century political power was in fact exercised by members of Parliament who drew incomes from accumulated capital, whether land or otherwise, few constituencies came under the 'influence' of great capitalists other than landowners. British politics as Marx studied it was dominated by a diffuse and unorganised capitalist class. If political power went by the counting of heads, the middling class, the £10 occupiers and the tenant-farmers, would have governed Great Britain. In fact, however, power was simply shared by the capitalist families. The Peels, Gladstones, Chamberlains and—very late—Bonar Laws and Baldwins joined the Spencers, Russells, Cavendishes, Stanleys, Cecils and Primroses.

Meanwhile, however, the theory of the natural right of property had been weakening not so much by the development of new theory as by encroachments upon the interests of the capitalists through the development of social sympathy. As we have seen in chapter IX, the encroachments by which the nineteenth century reacted against the consequences of the industrial revolution were in large measure contrary to the current economic theory, and were generally not 'party political' at all. The evangelicals in religion and the romantics in literature were part of the same movement, but they were as much consequences as causes. The very ugliness of so much of Victorian Britain was one of the assets of British socialism. The railways made travel much easier, and they took even the most fastidious of travellers into the heart of industrial Britain. The travellers could not help asking themselves what manner of men and women lived in these great wens.

The great reports on conditions in the factories, mines and back streets, referred to in chapter IX, did not surprise the educated peoples of the forties. They merely supplied picturesque details of what was obviously a great social sore, and strengthened movements of opinion which were already taking place. There was, too, a diversity of remedies, illustrated particularly by the acute divisions among the Radicals, though by no means all who produced prescriptions were Radicals. Only a few sought to undermine the capitalist system itself and to vest the instruments of production and exchange in the organised community. For most the solution was to be found in more factories, more machines, more inventions, and freer trade so that, as we should put it, the standard of living would be raised: and this was, in the main, the solution adopted by the Conservative party under Peel and the Liberal party under Gladstone.

Such a solution was not inconsistent with a wide development of social services financed out of taxation. Peel re-established the income tax and Gladstone failed to abolish it, thereby leaving an expanding source of revenue by which large sums could be raised, especially when the wars of the twentieth century accustomed the taxpayers to a high standard rate and graded rates of super-tax or surtax. Harcourt adopted a new social theory when he invented death duties, a theory implying that heirs and next-of-kin had no right to the whole of the estate of a deceased person, and that the State had a right to share accumulated wealth. It was in fact Joseph Chamberlain's theory, that the rich should pay 'ransom' for their privileges—as the natural right of property had become. Lloyd George began the process of putting up taxes on 'beer and baccy' (as well as on port and cigars, though they did not figure in Conservative propaganda), partly for revenue and partly because of his Nonconformist conscience. Later generations have invented new means of extortion. It is indeed a new argument for Socialism that 'when Socialism comes' there will be no tax-collectors, for each person will receive such a portion of the national product as will satisfy his needs—free of taxation because the State will already have retained its slice, for capital development and gratuitous public services. This is part of the 'pie in the sky'; and it does not encourage the surtax-payers to vote Labour, because 'when Socialism comes' there will also be no capital gains, and expense accounts will be on the niggardly civil service scale.

We keep sidling up to socialism and shying away again because in fact the Labour party grew out of the Working-Class Movement, of which the socialist movement was but a fraction. That Movement was un-organised as a whole, though intensely organised in its parts. It became possible through the collection of the workers into towns and industrial villages, where they lived in compact 'estates' erected by speculative builders. Between the back-to-back houses of Prospect Place and the terrace houses of Oxford Mansions was a gulf fixed; there was another between Oxford Mansions and Cambridge Gardens because, as the latter name shows, there was a row of privet bushes in front of every house and therefore the Cambridge women were very superior; the aristocracy lived, however, in Eldorado Avenue, where every house had a bay window, an aspidistra, lace curtains, and a built-in privy. Great though these social differences were, a sense of solidarity de-veloped whenever the rent-collector called or the alderman's lady drove down in her carriage to do her 'slumming'. It was developed in the mine and the factory, and by a common interest in whippets and football. The most important factor, however, was that, thanks to the evangelical movement and the rivalry of church and chapel, an increasing number of workers had learned to read. With the develop-ment of the railways and the penny post, too, the circulation of news-papers, weeklies and tracts became possible. In every shift a few of the men would have their hunks of bread and cheese, or bread and bacon, wrapped in newspaper; and there would be 'literature' in the saloon bar if not in the public bar.

The chapels, and particularly the 'missions', succeeded in drawing in a substantial proportion of the workers, their wives, and especially their sons and daughters—because the chapel was the most efficient of the marriage markets and 'walking out' usually started in Sunday school. The Baptist or Congregational minister in the slums—the Wesleyan chapel was usually on the main road—often developed an acute social conscience and an intense sympathy with the difficulties of his flock. Nor were the Wesleyans and the evangelical and High Church parsons without influence. They were particularly useful where the idea of the co-operative society developed, because they could at least keep accounts.

Potentially, the most important factor was the trade union. Since it was generally a craft union, its members were more likely to live in Eldorado Avenue than in Prospect Place; but among the miners, the weavers and the spinners unionism was more widespread. It is, however, a mistake to assume that the Working-Class Movement was a movement of the working class. It was a movement among the working class, or more accurately a series of movements, led by parsons, ministers, co-operators, schoolmasters, and trade unionists. The only large movement in the first half of the nineteenth century was that of the Chartists, who were mostly middle class but who obtained wide support among the working class. The theory which had provided the motive force for the Reform Bill was carried into the forties. The solution for the grievances of the workers would be found by giving them the franchise, the ballot, equal polling districts, annual elections, and so forth. The fact that the Reform Act had not altered the social composition of Parliament was not entirely ignored, but the causes were misunderstood. The lowering of the franchise and even the redistribution of seats had no effect unless the new electors voted differently from the old. They could not do so immediately for three reasons. First, they did not 'feel' their power. It seemed to them that their task was the same as that of the old electors, to choose between a Cecil and a Cavendish. As between those two the balance might be altered: a safe tory seat might become a safe whig seat or vice versa. Nevertheless, if this example was followed all over the country, the landowners continued to rule though, as Peel realised in 1834, they had to pay some attention to the prejudices of their new constituents. Secondly, there had to be either an organisation to nominate candidates, or a general but unorganised movement which resulted in a series of candidatures of the same type. An attempt was made, by the establishment of the Westminster Club, to provide a Radical organisation, but the Radicals had neither the men nor the money, and eventually whigs and Radicals alike used the Reform Club, thus enabling the whig landlords to retain the greater part of their electoral control. Moreover the Radicals were, ideologically, at sixes and sevens. A Radical was merely a person who wanted new and radical reforms: but there was no consistency among the reforms sought by the Radicals. Finally, there had to be some common element which could form a party basis. The whigs and tories of the thirties were far from being national parties. The electors in a constituency did not choose between a whig and a tory; they chose between the local whig and the local tory; and that was by no means the same thing because the candidate's personality was far more important than his label; and indeed many candidates before the second Reform Act had no labels.

It follows that there had to be a considerable delay before changes in the franchise and the distribution of seats affected the composition of the House of Commons, and even some delay in the development of a policy which suited the new electors. The proposals of the Charter, or some of them—annual parliaments would almost certainly have put elections even more firmly in the hands of the wealthy—would have benefited the working class in the long run, but only very slowly. In any case, however, the Chartist Movement was managed incompetently. There were too many objectives, too many demagogues, too many speeches, too little money, too little organisation, and too little common sense. It was part of the Working-Class Movement, in spite of its middle-class leadership, because it had large working-class support, especially during the hungry forties; but it was led astray. It helped to create a working-class opinion, though a generation elapsed before that opinion began to be politically important. Indeed, the second half of the nineteenth century was the era of middle-class politics. The country gentlemen sat behind Disraeli, and he got a majority in 1874, but that was when some sections of the middle class were moving over to the Conservatives and there joining a large section of the working class enfranchised in 1868. The movement was completed in 1886, but Gladstone, Chamberlain, the Nonconformist Conscience, and Birmingham Radicalism had made the running.

Meanwhile—though we seem to keep forgetting them—there were socialists. Robert Owen (1771–1858) is commonly regarded as the 'father' of British socialism. He was, says Mr Beer, 'distinguished neither by original philosophic speculations nor outstanding literary achievements'.[1] He was a self-made and successful textile manufacturer who had an acute sense of social sympathy. His efforts to improve factory conditions have already been mentioned. His interest in the education of the working class has not been mentioned because it had no permanent results, except as a contribution to the acceptance of the notion that education was a responsibility of the State. He was neither a revolutionary nor a democrat, but his study of social problems in the period of depression from 1816 to 1820 led him to disbelieve the individualist assumptions of the economists. He was particularly concerned with what a later generation called 'poverty in the midst of plenty', that is, by the fact that unemployment and its attendant miseries were caused by over-production. Machinery enabled all men's material wants to be supplied; but, because there was no relation between production and consumption, men and women were starving. His response to that situation was not to develop a theory of State socialism but to suggest the establishment of co-operative communities in which the capital was owned by the communities. The capital was to be found, initially, by the wealthy; but Owen's propaganda was more successful among the working class than among the owners of capital. In this field it led to experiments in co-operation, both in production and in distribution. But the re-establishment of the gold standard after the Napoleonic war also led Owen into the theory of currency. In his view, the use of paper currency during the war had shown that a metallic currency was inadequate because its quantity was determined by the quantity of gold, whereas the true foundation of currency should be labour. A labourer should receive a labour note showing the number of units of value he had produced by his labour.

What is important in Owenism is, however, not the actual theories which Owen and his followers produced, but the development in sections of the working class of the idea that individualistic capitalism

[1] *History of British Socialism*, I, p. 160.

439

was inimical to the workers. It was a small minority movement; it had none of the popular appeal of the agitation in support of Queen Caroline, the agitation for the repeal of the combination laws, the Ten-Hours Movement, or the demand for Parliamentary reform. It produced the Co-operative Movement, which was important in so far as it demonstrated that the individual, profit-making capitalist was not necessary to the economy; and, almost exactly a century later, in 1918, it led to the adoption of a socialistic objective by the Labour party. On the other hand, it would be wrong to express the history of the nineteenth century in terms of a conflict between individualism or capitalism and socialism. The socialists were one of the minor sections of the Working-Class Movement, distinguished from the others by their idealism; for though, like other aspects of the movement, socialism was founded on mutual or class self-interest, the idea of 'each for all and all for each', the idea of men working for each other's benefit instead of for the benefit of a profit-making capitalist, had a considerable emotional appeal because it had, or at least seemed to have, a moral foundation. Owenite co-operation or socialism appeared to be a means for the realisation of the brotherhood of man.

On the other hand, Owen himself was strongly anti-clerical. His ideas had been formed when the Church of England was a branch of 'Old Corruption', described by a Churchman as 'a respectable though little respected department of the State'.[1] It was, in fact, an ally if not a part of the landed interest. A few eccentric clergymen excepted, it had no interest in or concern with the 'condition of England' produced by the industrial revolution. The Wesleyans had gone into the towns, but their neglect of social problems was as great as that of the Church of England. They were concerned with 'sin', and sin, expressed socially, was concerned with sex, drink and gambling. The dissenters were small middle-class minorities, strong among the manufacturers, and believing that free enterprise was ordained of God. A more modern Christian would find it difficult to show how the brotherhood of man, as preached by the early socialists, was inconsistent with Christianity; but it was inconsistent with Christianity as preached in most of the churches and chapels after Waterloo, because it threatened the

[1] Charles E. Raven, *Christian Socialism, 1848-1854*, p. 7.

established order and the incomes of ministers of religion. Those who criticised the established order were equally critical of the churches. Late in life, indeed, Robert Owen criticised what we now know as Victorian social conventions (though he wrote in 1836) and the institution of marriage, as understood by the churches, itself.[1] It was indeed inevitable that socialists, Co-operators, currency cranks, republicans, atheists, Chartists and social nonconformists generally should be classed together as preachers of subversion. Many actually believed in the association: in any event it was a useful line of propaganda and was in constant use by Conservatives up to 1939. Some socialists were atheists; some were republicans; some repudiated Christian sexual morality. The ideas of the first and the last were to be found among Conservatives also; but few of the social nonconformists among the Conservatives published their nonconformity, whereas many of the social nonconformists of the 'Left' enjoyed being notorious. Robert Owen was not the cause of this line of propaganda, for it began with the French Revolution: but he had the misfortune to be, in Leslie Stephen's phrase, 'one of those intolerable bores who are the salt of the earth',[2] and therefore helped.

Most of the ministers of religion have been and are anti-socialist. In this respect they do not differ from men in other professions. They need special mention, however, because their office makes them propagandists; and, though they have not always propagated capitalist religion, they have at least taught religion in a framework of capitalist assumptions. There have always been exceptions. One of the most important was the Christian Socialist movement of the middle of the nineteenth century. It was associated mainly with the names of Frederick Denison Maurice and Charles Kingsley, though it included a number of Anglican laymen, many of them barristers, and among them a substantial leaven of Cambridge men.[3] Their socialism was brought from France by J. M. F. Ludlow, but the movement came into

---

[1] *Ibid.* p. 46.   [2] *D.N.B.* XLII, p. 451; quoted by C. E. Raven, *op. cit.* p. 47.
[3] Ludlow, the founder, was educated in France. Maurice was first at Trinity College and afterwards at Trinity Hall. Kingsley was at Magdalene, C. B. Mansfield at Clare, F. J. Furnivall at Trinity Hall, C. E. Ellison at Trinity College, and F. C. Penrose at Magdalene. Oxford's principal contribution was Thomas Hughes, author of *Tom Brown's Schooldays*.

contact with Owenism, and Christian Socialism developed mainly into producers' and consumers' co-operatives. This was, however, another very small minority movement, middle class in its inspiration and direction. Its permanent effects on the attitude of the Church of England were small.

Nonconformity was almost synonymous with capitalism, though in the course of the nineteenth century, as the manufacturers' sons were sent to the public schools, Nonconformity became increasingly lower-middle-class, retaining its strength among the smaller manufacturers, the contractors and the tradesmen. In Wales and in the west of England and Yorkshire, however, it retained substantial support from the workers; and among them, at least in the industrial areas, socialism of the 'pie in the sky' variety, as well as Co-operation, became popular. It was from these sections, and the industrial population of Scotland, that the Independent Labour party drew a large part of its support in the days when it was the spearhead of the socialist movement. On the other hand the South Wales miners were Liberal until 1909, and the cotton operatives were mainly Conservative until 1923.

3. THE FAILURE OF MARXISM

When Karl Marx arrived in London in 1849 his ideas were already formed, though the revolutions of 1848 caused him to revise some aspects of his theory, and the theory was worked out in full, with much reference to English conditions, in *Capital*, the first volume of which was published in German in 1867, and in English in 1886. His disciple and collaborator, Friedrich Engels, had already, in 1845, published a tendentious book on *The Condition of the Working Class in England*. Engels was then a young man of twenty-four years of age; he wrote the book after eighteen months' experience of England; he used selected secondary sources only, save that he knew Manchester and Salford and had visited other textile towns; and it was intended to be 'a fine bill of indictment' against the English capitalists.[1] In other words, it was 'party political'.

Marx' own work was of much higher quality. His reading was both

[1] W. O. Henderson and W. H. Chaloner in the 1958 translation, pp. xvi–xxiii.

wide and deep. The long delay in producing even the first volume of *Capital* was due partly to his journalistic work, which he had to undertake to keep himself and his family alive (though in fact three of his children died), but it was due mainly to his scholarly insistence on mastering the literature available in the British Museum.

Marxism is, in fact, an abstruse theory of sociology or social philosophy, incapable of being appreciated except by one as learned as Marx in the fields of metaphysics, economic history and economics. Since it was a synthesis of these branches of learning, Marx would not have recognised the distinctions: but few have been as learned as he in the whole of his field, and criticisms have come mainly from scholars expert in the several branches. Except where Marxist theories (adapted, and generally perverted, by Lenin and Stalin) have been prescribed by law or convention, as in the Soviet Union and the so-called 'people's democracies', they have generally been rejected by scholars. That is, few philosophers accept dialectical materialism, few historians accept his materialist conception of history, and few economists accept his theory of surplus value. Speaking generally, his reputation as a scholar is low because, notwithstanding the depth of his scholarship, his conclusions have not been widely accepted in countries in which free discussion is permitted.

The number of genuine 'Marxists' is therefore small. Generally, his conclusions are accepted by so-called Marxists who are not qualified to follow his argument. To be a Marxist, in the political sense, it is necessary only to believe that:

(1) There is a fundamental divergence of interest between the proletariat and the bourgeoisie;

(2) the condition of the working class has deteriorated, is deteriorating and will go on deteriorating until the members of that class realise that there is no solution to their miseries except to take the means of production out of the hands of the bourgeoisie;

(3) the class struggle will therefore lead, sooner or later, to the 'dictatorship of the proletariat', that is, the assumption of power by the working class with a view to the abolition of all classes.

As for dialectical materialism, the materialist conception of history, and the theory of surplus value, the 'Marxist' can accept the remark

443

of William Morris (who called himself a Marxist) when heckled at a Glasgow meeting: 'I am asked if I believe in Marx's theory of value. To speak quite frankly, I do not know what Marx's theory of value is, and I'm damned if I want to know.'[1] Few Marxists are so honest, and indeed many really do want to know but find *Capital*, even the comparatively easy first volume, pretty tough going. The *Communist Manifesto*, produced by Marx with the assistance of Engels in 1848, supplies all that is really necessary and, moreover, sets out a complete programme of political reforms with which few socialists disagree.[2] Even the *Manifesto* contains difficult passages, especially when it deals with socialist literature, for it was really addressed to the German workers of 1848. It is, however, not difficult to ignore these relics of past ideological conflicts and to concentrate on the slogan at the end, 'Working men of all countries, unite!'

Why, then, did Marxism, as a political dogma, fail to strike deep roots in Great Britain, the most highly industrialised of all countries in the second half of the nineteenth century, and the freest from the competition between workers (that is, wage-earners) and peasants? As usual, the answer is complicated.

In England Marx was, and remained, intellectually and socially an alien. He was born in the German Rhineland, which had been incorporated in the kingdom of Prussia by the Treaty of Vienna. He was educated, first, at the University of Bonn and then at the University of Berlin. In the latter university he came under the influence of Hegelian philosophy, whose dialectic he was to 'stand on its head'. German culture, produced in reaction to the sterility of the Thirty Years War, was alive and active, and had diverged fundamentally from the empiricism of England and France. Politically it turned into the extreme nationalism which inspired Bismarck and became foul under Hitler. It also produced, however, various kinds of 'scientific' socialism of which Marxism is one. Late in life Marx, as a working journalist, wrote excellent English; and indeed his German is said to have become tinged with anglicisms. On the other hand, his ideas

---

[1] Quoted by Crane Brinton, *English Political Thought in the Nineteenth Century*, p. 260, from J. B. Glasier, *William Morris and the Early Days of the Socialist Movement*.
[2] *Communist Manifesto* (ed. Laski), pp. 145–6.

always bore the impress of their German mould; his substantial work was written in German; and, like all Hegelians, he had great difficulty in expressing his more fundamental ideas in English. Socialists and potential socialists are, by definition, not nationalists; what mattered to them was not that Marx was a German or that he wrote in German, but that his ideas were formed in a parochially German mould which did not accord with English ideas and habits of thought.

Marxism was addressed to scholars because Marx was a scholar of wide attainments and deep knowledge. His political message, on the other hand, was addressed to the workers of the world who were not and could not be (in the capitalist system as Marx and Engels knew it) scholars. Nevertheless, as chapter I of this volume has emphasised, common political ideas are coloured, if not wholly determined, by assumptions and prejudices which result from intellectual movements. The long English tradition, which is continuous since the sixteenth century, has necessarily given English politics an insular character. English socialists do not speak the same language as German socialists because, though socialism is international, it has in England to be absorbed into a vast complex of inherited political and social ideas, whereas in Germany it is part of a different inheritance deriving, mainly, from intellectual developments after Napoleon.

Marx was not only an alien spiritually; he was in England socially an alien. There was no possibility of his leading an English socialist movement. He was, indeed, not of the stuff from which political leaders are made. He had none of the flamboyance of Lassalle, the eloquence of Ramsay MacDonald (as a young man), or the 'Come to Jesus' evangelism of Philip Snowden. He was not even a good committee man like Sidney Webb. He was a German scholar whose spiritual home was not Hyde Park or Tower Hill but Bloomsbury. He was not the sort to make friends easily; and indeed he was much more efficient at making enemies. His brand of socialism was the consequence of great intellectual effort, and he could not bear the cheery extroverts or ambitious climbers who make good political leaders. His friends, so far as he had any, were the German socialist exiles in London. They were, as one might expect, a group of eccentrics, among whom Marx was one of the most eccentric. The penury of his early years in London, when he was often dependent on Engels' charity, and the poverty in which he continued to live even when he had a regular journalistic income, made him suspicious and bitter. He aspired to lead a great revolutionary movement through educating the workers of the world: he could not, but would not encourage anybody else to do it.

He had one English disciple, Henry Myers Hyndman, who read the French version of the first volume of *Capital* and sought out Marx in 1880. Hyndman made use of these conversations, and of Marx's published ideas, in *England for All*, published in 1881. That book contained no reference to Marx, except a very indirect one, and no reference to *Capital*. Marx's *amour propre* was injured, for he was desperately anxious for recognition. Hyndman's apology probably made matters worse, but it gives one of the reasons for the failure of Marxism in England: 'the English don't like being taught by foreigners, and your name is so much detested here....' The breach with Hyndman did not matter much, for Marx died in 1883: but not even when he was younger could he exercise any personal influence on British socialism. He was not that sort of person.

Marx's writings did influence people. William Morris, for instance, 'accepted Marx, and even tried to read him...'.[1] In fact, however, Morris' socialism was of the eccentric kind, for he disliked the capitalist system, and especially its works, on aesthetic grounds. A good many whiffs of Marxism were exhaled by the propaganda of the Fabian Society and the Independent Labour party. Only Hyndman's Social Democratic Federation, and a few smaller societies, actually claimed to be Marxist. Its paying membership probably never exceeded three thousand.[2] The Communist party of Great Britain has been more successful, though always it has been a small minority movement.[3] It has, of course, followed the party line of the Soviet Communist party, and therefore has never been strictly Marxist; but these niceties of dogma need not concern us.

The real reason for the failure of Marxism in Britain was, however,

---

[1] Crane Brinton, *English Political Thought in the Nineteenth Century*, p. 254.
[2] Henry Pelling, *The Origins of the Labour Party*, p. 243.
[3] It had 9000 members in 1932; 15,000 in 1938; 39,000 in 1947; 40,000 in 1949; 34,000 in 1956.

that the soil and the climate proved to be suitable for parliamentary social-democracy. The workers never have been convinced that under capitalism, as operated in Britain, their condition has progressively deteriorated, because every working-class family knows that it has progressively improved. The great-great-grandchildren of those who suffered in the slums in the hungry forties—and history now tells us that real working-class incomes were higher in, say, 1845 than in 1800—now live in council houses or residential suburbs. The increased productivity, or at least a large part of it, has been passed on to the wage-earners, and the sons of wage-earners have very often become salary-earners. This has come about partly through trade-union action and partly through parliamentary action. Because of his association with the socialist movements in Germany and France, both of which countries were still economically backward in the forties, Marx came to England as a sort of Chartist, and his early English associations were with Chartists. This did not mean that he favoured 'physical force': the lesson that he drew from the revolutions of 1848 was that in a contest of armed force the bourgeoisie would always win. He therefore favoured permeation and education of the trade unions and also parliamentary action, though he believed that at the appropriate time, when the working class was fully alive to the implications of the class war, it would have to seize power because the constitutional machinery was devised by the bourgeoisie for its own protection. The revolution would come about because that machinery had to be overthrown in order to establish the new machinery of a classless society.

Chartism had already failed before Marx reached England. Nor has class solidarity developed into a class war. Through limited companies, building societies, insurance companies, superannuation schemes, and co-operative societies, the ownership of the means of production has been spread so as to include among the owners not only those who can positively be identified as 'capitalists' but also salary-earners and even wage-earners. Indeed, almost every 'capitalist' is a salary-earner who also owns stocks, shares and perhaps land. If the revolution required (and Marx did not say it would) the shooting of the capitalists it would not be easy to identify them, though no doubt a selection could be made *pour encourager les autres*. Nor is it easy to identify the

447

proletariat. It did exist in 1849, but it slowly disintegrated into a complicated social hierarchy rising from the unskilled workers who send their sons to the grammar schools on their bicycles to the unskilled directors who send their sons to Eton in their Daimlers. In between is the great mass of the population, the skilled workers by hand and by brain or, more often, both hand and brain, most of whom have net incomes varying between twenty times and forty times that of Karl Marx. There was a proletariat in Prospect Place, Oxford Mansions, Cambridge Gardens and even Eldorado Avenue, only fifty years ago. Its grandsons live in suburbia and keep up with the Joneses.

Karl Marx could not have foreseen this development because he was imprisoned in his own dogma, an interpretation of history and economics which enabled him to predict the future like an astrologer who had lost a couple of planets and substituted a couple of sputniks. The date of the publication of the first German edition of the first volume of *Capital*, 1867, is significant. The Palmerstonian era had ended and both political parties had decided to gamble on the urban householders supporting them. Marx died the year before the passing of the third Reform Act, which extended the franchise to the rural cottagers (and also the industrial householders outside the boroughs). Had there been class solidarity in 1885 the 'proletariat' could have captured Parliament. Actually, there were almost twenty years of Conservative government. The Marxist ideology no doubt helped to establish not only the Social Democratic Federation but also the Fabian Society and the Independent Labour party. In Marxist language, however, the Fabian Society was 'opportunist' and the I.L.P. 'Utopian'. Marxist theory, too, helped towards the establishment of the 'new unionism' which fought the employers, by collective action, from 1889 to 1914. The war of 1914–18 did not, as Marx had prophesied, result in the 'dictatorship of the proletariat' in Britain, though it did result in the dictatorship of the Communist party (that is, the Bolsheviks who had repudiated the dictatorship of the proletariat) in Russia. In Britain social democracy, represented by the Labour party, consolidated its position as a minority party and continued its inexorable march (1931 notwithstanding) to power in 1945. There is a logic in this history, but it is far more complicated than the materialist conception.

4. THE SOCIALISM OF THE LABOUR PARTY

In the period of Conservative government from 1874 to 1880 the working-class movement was weak and diffuse. The membership of the trade unions represented at the Trades Union Congress dropped from 1,192,000 in 1874 to 464,000 in 1881 and did not again reach a million until 1890 (when it was 1,470,000).[1] In 1868 the London Working-Men's Association had tried to secure labour representation in the reformed Parliament, but without success. In 1874 there was a broader Labour Representation League, but it had petered out by 1880. Two miners were elected as Liberals in 1874; but in other than mining constituencies the middle-class Liberals seemed to prefer Conservatives to working-class Liberals. In some towns there were small labour associations trying to get working-class candidates elected to borough councils. The Owenite tradition, reinforced by the Christian Socialist tradition, perpetuated many of the co-operative societies. There were even new co-operative producers in the seventies.[2] There was, too, an increase in co-operative stores from 927 in 1872 to 1132 in 1880, though there had been many failures.[3] After the Paris Commune of 1871 a number of republican societies was started, but they could seldom agree whether or not they wanted a revolution; and few of them lasted a decade.[4] There were, no doubt, other vaguely socialist groups which history has not recorded; and there were the groups of exiles with which Marx was in contact. The International had met in London in 1863, very casually, and had produced Marx's Inaugural Address to the International, but Marx made it unpopular in England by his tactical defence of the Paris Commune; and after its transfer to Philadelphia it expired in 1876.

Engels said in 1885 that, since the dying-out of Owenism, there had been no socialism in England, because the working class had, to a certain extent, shared in the benefits of 'England's' industrial monopoly. With the breakdown of that monopoly, the working class would

[1] B. C. Roberts, *The Trades Union Congress*, p. 379.
[2] See the lists in Beatrice Potter, *The Co-operative Movement*, pp. 246–9.
[3] *Ibid.* pp. 255–6.
[4] Henry Pelling, *The Origins of the Labour Party*, p. 5.

be brought down to the level of their fellow-workers abroad. Hence there would be socialism again in England.[1] Quoting that passage in 1892, he said that there was indeed socialism again in England. It had become respectable and donned evening dress. More important than this 'momentary fashion among bourgeois circles' was the development of 'New Unionism' through the organisation of the unskilled workers. The leaders of this development were socialists 'either consciously or by feeling'; and the unskilled workers had taken the lead of the working-class movement.[2]

This development was not provided for in the gospel according to Marx. The bourgeois circles which had taken to socialism were, in the main, those surrounding the Fabian Society, which was established in 1884. The references to evening dress and to 'lounging lazily on drawing-room *causeuses*' were something of an exaggeration. They might be used, perhaps, of Beatrice Potter, who married Sidney Webb in 1892: but she had become a socialist not because it was fashionable but because she had worked and done research in the East End of London and other working-class areas.[3] Possibly, however, this was just another sneer at Hyndman, whom Engels had disliked since Hyndman had called on Marx in 1880.[4] In any event, socialism, like all other political theories, was produced by middle-class 'intellectuals' (among whom were Marx and Engels) as a means for achieving what they regarded as social justice. In so far as it was accepted by members of the working class, the explanation is to be found not in the logic of history but in the fact that the workers were persuaded by the 'intellectuals' that the workers would be better off under socialism than under capitalism.

Nor was the 'new unionism' socialist. It is true that most of the organisers were socialists. The London match girls struck work in 1888 of their own accord, though attention had been drawn to their grievances by H. H. Champion and Mrs Besant, who had seceded from Hyndman's Social Democratic Federation. The gasworkers were led by

[1] F. Engels, *The Condition of the Working Class in England* (ed. W. O. Henderson and W. H. Chaloner), p. 370.
[2] *Ibid.* pp. 370-1.
[3] Beatrice Webb, *My Apprenticeship*.
[4] A. W. Lee and E. Archbold, *Social Democracy in Britain*, pp. 75-6.

Will Thorne, of the S.D.F., who had been taught to read by Eleanor Marx. He was helped by Tom Mann and John Burns, both members of the S.D.F., who also helped Ben Tillett with the dock strike of 1889.[1] As Champion recognised, however, it was not for their socialism that they were respected by the workers, but for their willingness to help in the tasks of organisation.[2] The socialists believed, with Marx, in the concept of working-class unity, and therefore were willing to organise the unskilled workers, while the old-fashioned trade unionists were interested in craft unions: but the workers were concerned with conditions of work, not the destruction of capitalism. Engels himself said in 1889 that 'the people regard their immediate demands only as provisional although they do not themselves know what final aim they are working for'.[3] This is Marxism carried almost to absurdity. The 'people', that is, the unskilled workers in the new unions, had an ultimate aim because Marxists said they must have it, though in fact they had not.

The new development of socialist ideas among the middle class and their working-class converts was due to a variety of causes. It was, it must be remembered, a small minority movement. This was the heyday of nationalism, which was degenerating into imperialism. At a lower social level there was a corresponding development of social sympathy for the depressed classes. Joseph Chamberlain produced the *Radical Programme* in 1883–4. After 1886 sections of the Liberal party worked out proposals for social improvement which were incorporated in the Newcastle Programme of 1891. Henry George published *Progress and Poverty* in 1879 and toured Britain in 1881. George was not a socialist but he advocated a tax on land as the ultimate fixed capital. Coming at a time of agricultural depression, his book and advocacy made a great impression upon people who became socialists, from George Bernard Shaw downwards. There was also a literary movement, fostered in their very different ways by Carlyle and John Ruskin. Neither is much read nowadays, but a whole generation was brought up on Carlyle's early work, beginning with *Sartor*

---

[1] Henry Pelling, *Origins of the Labour Party*, pp. 84–8.
[2] *Ibid.* p. 88.
[3] *Ibid.* p. 90, quoting from Marx and Engels, *Selected Correspondence*, p. 461.

Resartus in 1831 and ending with *Latter-Day Pamphlets* in 1850. The fact that Carlyle had no political philosophy which could be put into a party programme is irrelevant: he helped enormously to stimulate the emotional approach to working-class politics which led to the socialist movement at the end of the century. The 'Utopianism' or 'pie in the sky' of the Independent Labour party derived mainly from the evangelism of the Nonconformist sects, ably assisted by Charles Kingsley's books, especially *Alton Locke*, and the propaganda of the Christian Socialists: but its establishment was helped by Carlyle's 'alliance with God'.[1] Providence clearly disapproved of classical economics. So did Ruskin. He supported Merrie England, when the gilds of craftsmen built the great cathedrals and men lived happy and beautiful lives. He, too, was one of the prophets of the New Jerusalem.

Practical politics requires its background of glorious sentiment, but if a political movement is to be successful it must come down to brass tacks. There were plenty of tacks in Marx's *Capital*, but it was very little known in England in the eighties, and not many were either capable or willing to swallow dialectical materialism, the materialist conception of history, or the theory of surplus value. From 1885, when Sidney Webb became associated with it, the Fabian Society supplied the brass tacks.

The influence of the Fabians has been both exaggerated and under-estimated. It has been exaggerated because Webb's technique of 'permeation', whereby Conservative politicians were induced to accept proposals which the Fabians, or more often Webb alone, thought desirable, necessarily gave him a reputation as a 'wire-puller', operating in secret, and therefore suspected of doing far more than he actually did. Those Spartan lunches, at which influential people were attacked over the cold mutton, did produce results; but they were not always very important, and inevitably they were not socialistic in the narrow sense, since they were designed to secure improvements by legislation, especially in education and local government.

On the other hand, the influence of the Webbs has been under-estimated because the nature of that influence has not been fully under-stood. What they really did was to persuade the trade unions that a

[1] Crane Brinton, *English Political Thought in the Nineteenth Century*, p. 167.

452

socialist commonwealth could be created by slow movements on two fronts, the political front and the industrial front. There was no clear distinction until 1926, when the failure of the General Strike, of which the Webbs did not approve,[1] persuaded the trade unions that the strike weapon ought not to be used, and probably could not effectively be used, to secure political objectives. Nor, indeed, was the socialist objective formally accepted until 1918, when the Labour party approved a socialist formula drafted by Sidney Webb. James Macdonald and Keir Hardie, both of whom were prominent in the formation of the Independent Labour party, had secured the passing of a socialist resolution by the Trades Union Congress in 1893;[2] but at this stage it is probable that not more than one-third of the members were convinced socialists;[3] and opposition to the establishment of a socialist party continued until 1918. The trade unions were gradually won over between 1900 and 1918.

It is true that the Webbs, and the Fabians generally, did not take an active part in the process. Sidney Webb was not made to be a leader, and he cut a poor figure when he entered Parliament. The propagandists of the I.L.P., from Keir Hardie to Ramsay MacDonald and Snowden, did the talking and had much effect in the trade-union branches. The trade-union leaders were, however, not very susceptible to propaganda. Their ideas were already fixed. As politicians, they were almost all Radical supporters of the Liberal party; as trade-union officials they were concerned with the interests of their members. They were not the people to take to the barricades. They could not appreciate the argument for the dictatorship of the proletariat. They did not believe that the British workers had nothing to lose but their chains; the skilled workers could lose their comparatively well-paid jobs and what a later generation called their 'differentials'. On the ground the working class was not a homogeneous entity but a series of groups differentiated by their jobs, their conditions of work, their relative social status (all the way from Prospect Place to Eldorado Avenue), their standards of education, and so forth. 'Pie in the sky' was

---

[1] Margaret Cole, *Beatrice Webb's Diaries, 1924–1932*, p. 91.
[2] B. C. Roberts, *The Trades Union Congress*, p. 139.
[3] *Ibid.* p. 142.

attractive to the workers in the sweated trades, and even to some in the new unions; but the more conservative union officials wanted to bring the pie down to earth and to have a look at the contents.

The empirical methods of the Fabians, their concern with practical problems, their repudiation of revolutionary activity, their belief in the 'inevitability of gradualness', and their barely concealed contempt for the propagandists of 'pie in the sky', made socialism seem sensible to sensible men, initially in the trade unions and eventually in the constituencies. The Labour party was built by the trade unions on the basis of Fabian socialism—which was far from concerning itself exclusively with the nationalisation of the means of production—even though, in the early years of the present century, so much of the leadership was supplied by the I.L.P. The practical approach to social problems thus given by the Fabians enabled the Labour party to appeal to the electorate on issues which could be rationally defended, in spite of the froth and foam of the lunatic fringe. Those issues did not in themselves win many votes; but the impression given at successive elections was that most of the Labour politicians were sensible people who had the interests of the workers and others of similar social status at heart, while the 'tories' were rich men engaged in looking after the interests of the 'upper classes'.

Sidney Webb's defects as a student of institutions became obvious as soon as he began producing broad schemes. The *Constitution for the Socialist Commonwealth of Great Britain*[1] was an interesting piece of academic fantasy. Webb lacked a 'feel' for institutions. He was a good chairman of committees and a most expert draftsman of formulae which got what he wanted but also obtained the assent of those who did not want what Webb wanted. He had a remarkable facility for the mastering of documents and for producing perfect summaries. He was almost a walking encyclopaedia on all aspects of English political and economic life, and could produce a competent bibliography almost from his head. In short, he was the model Ph.D. student; but he lacked what most Ph.D. students also lack, the imagination required to understand how people behave. This made him formidable as a critic; being impervious

[1] By S. and B. Webb, 'Printed by the authors for the trade unionists of the United Kingdom, 1920'.

to the emotions which lead most politicians to talk romantic nonsense, he could sort out the sense, if any, from the rhetoric. On the other hand, institutions are people; and to assume that people behave as coolly and as rationally as Sidney Webb is to begin with a fundamental fallacy. Beatrice was more of a romantic, sometimes indeed a mystic; but in this extremely happy marriage and partnership the dominant personality was Sidney's. The Webbs' books—Beatrice's autobiography and diaries partially excepted[1]—are all blue books; and there would be more history in the histories if there were real people in them. The *History of Trade Unionism* and the volumes of *English Local Government* are monuments of research; but they need to be rewritten by a Trevelyan.

The Webbs were not the only Fabians; and indeed Beatrice was not much involved in Fabian activities. Graham Wallas had some of the imagination which Sidney lacked: but he was the student of human nature rather than its manipulator and his positive contributions were small.[2] Bernard Shaw had, of course, plenty of imagination; but he was a dealer in devastating paradoxes, not in imaginative but workable plans.

In the circumstances it may seem surprising that the Fabians did so much. Much of what they did, however, was critical. They turned men's minds away from the Utopian communities of Owenism and Christian Socialism and directed attention to what were, in the nineteenth century, the most successful of the public bodies, the elected local authorities. They also diverted any tendency to follow Marx. They were of course helped by the futilities and schisms of the Social Democratic Federation and the complete failure of the International. But, having repudiated dialectical materialism in theory, they proceeded to ignore Marxism and, indeed, 'studiously avoided any quotations from Marx'.[3] They did not succeed in repudiating the doctrines of the classical economists, and indeed those doctrines flourish, with

[1] Beatrice Webb, *My Apprenticeship* and *Our Partnership*; M. Cole, *Beatrice Webb's Diaries, 1924–1932.*

[2] He is reported to have explained to the Master of Clare how to straighten Clare Bridge: and it should be explained to the reader who does not know Cambridge that this is equivalent to explaining to the Mayor of Pisa how to get the Leaning Tower upright.

[3] Beatrice Webb, *Our Partnership*, p. 106.

Keynesian modifications, in the Faculties of Economics which the Webbs did so much to create.[1] The Fabians simply denied the individualistic assumptions on which economics was based. In the age of collectivism economics would have to be rewritten.

In principle they approved of 'collective ownership wherever practicable; collective regulation everywhere else; collective provision according to need for all the impotent and sufferers; and collective taxation in proportion to wealth, especially surplus wealth'.[2] But a glance at the list of Fabian Tracts in the period 1884 to 1915 and of other publications during that period[3] shows that few were on general issues. Most were concerned with practical and contemporary problems which a Liberal Government might face and a Labour Government, if such there were, would face. A socialist commonwealth was the ultimate objective; but the steps towards that objective must be slow; and meanwhile there were practical problems to be solved in the interests of the workers. These were, in the main, problems with which the Trades Union Congress, and indeed the Conservative Governments of 1895–1905 and the Liberal Governments of 1905–14, were concerned. Hence the Fabians had influence out of all proportion to their numbers.[4] Their propaganda reached few, but those few were important.

The tactical problem for the socialists was whether to 'permeate' the other parties or to form an independent Labour party. On this issue not only the Fabians but also other socialists were divided. A great deal had already been done by Factory Acts, Public Health Acts and 'gas and water socialism' to temper the individualism of the first half of the nineteenth century. On the other hand, it was difficult to get working-class representation through the Liberal machine. The issue was in fact settled by the 'counter-offensive' which, the unions believed, the employers began to conduct towards the end of the century. The Labour Representation Committee from 1899 to 1906 and the Labour party from 1906 to 1918 obtained increasing trade-union support.[5]

[1] They were the founders of the London School of Economics and Political Science and, with (Lord) Haldane, of the Faculty of Economics of the University of London.

[2] B. Webb, *Our Partnership*, p. 107.

[3] E. R. Pease, *History of the Fabian Society*, pp. 273–83.

[4] In the eighties the membership of the Fabian Society never exceeded 150: H. Pelling, *Origins of the Labour Party*, p. 47.   [5] Volume II, ch. VII.

The tactical problem had led to the formation of the Independent Labour party in 1893. Its characteristic was that it was far more working class than the Fabian Society. The literate workers from the board schools in larger numbers took an active part in working-class politics. They had enthusiasm and discipline without the learning of the genuine Marxists or the Fabians. For that reason they added little to socialist ideas but provided a radical left wing for the trades councils and the Trades Union Congress. In the main, too, socialist propaganda was conducted by them. The three societies—the Social Democratic Federation (it changed 'Federation' to 'Party' in 1906), the Fabian Society and the Independent Labour party—joined with representatives of the trade unions to form the Labour Representation Committee in 1899, but the S.D.F. withdrew its affiliation in 1901. Even in 1914, however, the Labour party was not socialist. As Ramsay MacDonald said in 1911:

The Labour party is not socialist. It is a union of socialist and trade-union bodies for immediate political work. . . . But it is the only political form which evolutionary socialism can take in a country with the political traditions and methods of Great Britain. Under British conditions, a socialist party is the last, not the first, form of the socialist movement in politics.[1]

The solid core of the new Labour party was provided by the trade unions. The task of the Fabian Society was to 'permeate' that solid core. The task of the I.L.P. was to propagate socialist ideas in general and to convince the 'rank and file'. In the Labour party it generally acted as a socialist ginger group. It could not be excessively militant, for to do so would be to risk a good deal of trade-union support—and a good deal of trade-union money. Moreover the I.L.P. lost support during the war of 1914–18 because of the pacifist attitudes of so many of its leaders. After 1918, when it lost representation as such in the National Executive Committee of the Labour party (though some of its members were elected in other capacities) it became an increasingly less effective minority movement, until it ceased to be affiliated in 1931.

The war of 1914–18, however, had another consequence, the conversion of the old Radicals of the trade unions to what G. D. H. Cole

---

[1] J. Ramsay MacDonald, *The Socialist Movement*, p. 235.

calls 'socialism of a kind'.[1] Sidney Webb, as usual, was ready with a draft. Henceforth the Labour party was pledged:

To secure for the producers by hand and by brain the full fruits of their industry, and the most equitable distribution thereof that may be possible, upon the basis of the common ownership of the means of production and the best obtainable system of popular administration and control of each industry and service.

This formula left ample scope for interpretation, as Webb intended. It did not rule out the Co-operative movement, nor syndicalism or other forms of 'workers' control'. Those who wanted to achieve socialism within the next few years, and those who thought that, in principle, common ownership was a good idea but that in practice the steps towards that end must be slow, could equally support it.

For the time being, however, there was an official interpretation, also drafted by Webb, in *Labour and the New Social Order*. This may be regarded as fulfilling three purposes. First, it was a statement of Labour objectives. Secondly it was a practical policy for a Labour Government, when it had a majority. Thirdly it provided the substance for an election manifesto for the general election of 1918. In this third aspect it dealt with the temporary problems of the immediate aftermath of the war, which need not concern us.

The fundamental assumptions were those of Fabian socialism. The Labour party would seek to obtain a majority in the House of Commons by ordinary democratic means. There were criticisms of the Representation of the People Act, 1918, and proposals for making it more democratic by means of complete adult suffrage with sex equality, provision for absent voters, and some form of proportional representation. There was no express repudiation of a Second Chamber, but objection was taken to hereditary and *ex officio* members and to any proposal which would result in the Labour party, or any party, being less strongly represented in the Second Chamber than in the House of Commons. Thus the Labour party repudiated revolution; and indeed, in spite of the Bolshevik Revolution, there was no support for it anywhere except in a small affiliated party called the British Socialist party and the left-

[1] G. D. H. Cole, *History of the Labour Party from 1914*, p. 54.

wing section of the I.L.P. British socialism, as propagated by the Labour party, was to be founded on egalitarian democracy, though for another twenty years the Conservative party was to feature the bogy of revolutionary socialism in its propaganda.

The general objective of this democratic party was

the gradual building up of a new social order based, not on internecine conflict, inequality of riches, and dominion over subject classes, subject races, or a subject sex, but on the deliberately planned cooperation in production and distribution, the sympathetic approach to a healthy equality, the widest possible participation in power, both economic and political, and the general consciousness of consent which characterise a true democracy.[1]

Thus the Labour party was committed to 'the inevitability of gradualism'. It was, in fact, a consequence of the acceptance of Parliamentary democracy, and also a consequence of the alliance of the trade unions. In 1918 there was no question of the dictatorship of the proletariat or even of working-class solidarity. Probably these were figments of the imagination in any event: but certainly in 1918 the Labour party was competing against two strongly entrenched political parties, both of which had firm working-class support. To have suggested anything more than a gradual change to a socialist commonwealth would have been political suicide. The trade unions, too, were highly organised, conservative, vested interests, more concerned with the conditions of employment of their members than with the ultimate objectives of social policy. Their leaders had to consider the immediate effects of any particular proposal, and so those proposals had to be put before them in detail and *seriatim*. There was no question of immediate nationalisation of all the means of production and distribution, because the bricklayers wanted to know what would happen to the bricklayers, and the draughtsmen of the Amalgamated Engineering Union what would happen to the draughtsmen. Social equality was a fine ambition, but there must be no interference with the 'differentials' of the skilled workers or of industrially protected workers like the miners and the railwaymen. Every trade unionist wanted to know what would happen

---

[1] Quoted not from *Labour and the New Social Order* but from the first resolution passed by the Labour Party Conference in June 1918 in connexion with the endorsement of that document: cf. G. D. H. Cole, *History of the Labour Party from 1914*, p. 65.

to him under the new dispensation. Hence gradualism was inevitable, as the Fabians had said all the time.

The new programme was strongly reticent on the subject of the social services. About education there was no doubt. Every person had to have the education—primary, secondary, university or technical—for which his abilities fitted him, and in this respect the Education Act, 1918, was deficient. In other respects there was reticence because of pre-war conflicts of opinion. The idea of planning public works and other forms of public expenditure, and of using public control of credit, to minimise a boom and prevent a depression, had occurred to the Fabians before Lord Keynes developed it into the doctrine of 'Full Employment'. But unemployment insurance was to be provided by the trade unions with Government subventions. Nothing was said about health insurance and other forms of social insurance. The agitation for the 'break-up of the poor law', which had been led by the Webbs from 1908 to 1914 because of the recommendations in Beatrice's Minority Report of the Royal Commission on the Poor Laws, led to the assumption that poor law assistance, other than in relief of unemployment, would be provided by the public health authorities. In fact, there was a general emphasis upon local government—due no doubt to the Webbs' own interest in 'gas and water socialism' and the successes of Labour members of local councils—which in the context of subsequent developments seems to be misplaced. It is to be noticed, however, that the Webbs realised the danger of a vast central bureaucracy, clogging up the executive and legislative machines. Not only did *Labour and the New Social Order* assume a considerable extension of local services —whereas in fact there has been a diminution of those services—but also its solution to the Irish problem was 'devolution all round', that is, Home Rule for Scotland, Wales, Ireland and England. This solution was rendered impracticable by the events of 1921, and perhaps it was not a very socialist solution to pander to petty nationalism: but at least the Labour solution sought to avoid an extension of central bureaucracy.

It will be remembered that Fabian socialism distinguished between 'nationalisation' of the means of production and distribution and 'regulation' of private industry. The trade unions were primarily

460

interested in 'regulation' by the fixing of minimum wages, the limitation of hours of work, and the control of factory conditions. It was inevitable that the Labour party should insist upon the fixing of a national minimum wage, without any increase in the hours of work, and should support legislation designed to improve the conditions of labour. In accordance with its socialist aim, however, it also wished to continue the control of capitalist industry which had been established during the war of 1914–18, including the centralised purchasing of raw materials and the rationing of industrial development. This problem was more acute in 1945 than in 1918, but it went against popular prejudice; for the ordinary citizen did not want to go to the town hall to get a licence when he wanted to purchase something or build a toolshed on his allotment. The regulation of capitalist industry implies the regulation of the ordinary consumer, the 'planning' of industry implies that consumers may have to have what the Government thinks proper to let them have, and generally socialism implies a degree of regulation which the ordinary person, accustomed to the 'free for all' of competition, finds obnoxious. 'Controls', and even 'planning', developed into naughty words.

Nationalisation is, in principle, less objectionable than regulation. It implies the establishment of a public authority which is open to criticism. The railways and canals were already under public control in 1918, and it was proposed to expropriate the stockholders 'on equitable terms'. Electricity supply needed rapid development under public control. The coal and iron mines, too, were effectively under public control, and it was desired to expropriate the shareholders. Finally—and in this respect even the Government of 1945 did not dare to go so far—agricultural land should be brought under Government control and cultivated on Government farms, small-holdings, and municipal estates, or leased to co-operative societies and other tenants.

Finally, there should be a system of taxation derived mainly from direct taxation of land and accumulated wealth, income and profits, together with suitable taxes on luxuries and increased death duties and taxes on unearned income. In other words, taxation was to be used as an instrument of social policy in order to bring about the sort of egalitarian society that the Labour party contemplated.

The Annual Conference of the Labour party was not asked to approve *Labour and the New Social Order*. Instead, twenty-one resolutions founded upon it were proposed and passed. The Labour party thus committed itself to Fabian socialism. It should be said, however, that it wanted so to be committed and that by so committing itself it made certain of providing, at some time in the future, a Labour Government.

The organisational reforms of 1918[1] introduced a new element into the Labour party, the hierarchy of local organisations of which the divisional Labour party (called in other parties the constituency party) was the centre. This local organisation has played an important role in the development of party tactics, and it has also provided the Labour party with most of its 'brains'. On the other hand the Labour party was in 1918, and has since remained, fundamentally the trade union party. The British trade unions have performed the remarkable feat of holding together, in what they call 'working-class unity', for nearly a hundred years. The Labour Representation Committee of 1900 and the young Labour party of 1906 were founded on some only of the trade unions, because some unions preferred to keep away from politics and some, like the miners, wished to continue to support the Liberal party. By 1918, however, the unions represented in the Trades Union Congress and the unions affiliated to the Labour party were almost identical. The Labour party of 1918 was the trade unions' party, with a fringe of members drawn from the socialist societies, many of whom were in fact trade unionists. *Labour and the New Social Order* was drafted by Sidney Webb in consultation with Arthur Henderson, who had been a Liberal trade unionist, with the intention of getting it approved by an Executive and a Conference dominated by trade unionists. The trade unions were prepared to accept a socialist objective; but they believed, even more firmly than the Webbs, in the inevitability of gradualism. The Webbs could not have 'sold' anything else.

Labour and the New Social Order was far from being a rousing call to a socialist army. It was a solid pedestrian document, dull and uninspired, like all documents produced by Sidney Webb. There were no

[1] Volume II, ch. VII.

462

slogans in it. It was probably read by few. The provision of a solid, well-reasoned programme did, however, satisfy a large public (most of whom did not read it) that the Labour party was a solid and sensible party. The socialist evangelicals could still stand at street corners proclaiming the proximate arrival of the millennium. The young men, and even some of the young women, could be roused to enthusiasm by the prospect of a society founded on the moral principle of social equality— and emphasis must be laid on 'moral' because, then as now, the young wanted not a programme but a Cause. At the same time, in the 'respectable' working-class house, in which grandfather had solemnly expounded the respective merits of Mr Gladstone and Mr Disraeli, and father had taken sides with or against the Dukes, the Labour party seemed to be more solid and respectable than, say, Mr Lloyd George. One must always remember the continuity of British politics. Some of those who were asked to vote Labour in 1918 had voted for Disraeli in 1868; many had voted for Campbell-Bannerman in 1906. Was the Labour party a respectable sort of party, for which the followers of these eminent gentlemen might be expected to vote? The conversion of these older voters came slowly. Only where trade-unionism was strong could immediate results be obtained. Most older electors continued to vote Conservative or Liberal as they had done before 1914, though the split in the Liberal party encouraged former Liberal voters to vote Labour. The 'inexorable march' of the Labour party was, however, due mainly to the young men and women coming on the registers. *Labour and the New Social Order* had little direct effect, because few read it. The real issue before working-class electors was whether to vote for 'people like us' or for the 'Tories'. The wild Clydesiders of the I.L.P. lost 'respectable' men's votes by their insistence on an immediate social revolution; but *Labour and the New Social Order* affected the behaviour and the arguments of the mass of the Labour politicians, central and local. The 'Village Blacksmith' sort of working man, portrayed in the 'beer and baccy' publicity of the Conservative party in 1910, was not invented in the Carlton Club. What the Conservative publicists forgot to show was his union card, which encouraged him, in spite of his youthful affection for Joseph Chamberlain, to vote Labour.

463

Fundamentally, the policy of the Labour party has not changed since 1918. The greatest change has been in respect of social security. The idea of relying on the trade unions had to be given up, while the Conservative party found various branches of national insurance to be useful as electoral 'carrots'. The Beveridge Plan, produced in 1942 and much publicised by its author in spite of official discouragement, led both parties to be firm supporters of 'social security'. Moreover, the heavy and socially discriminating taxation, which the Labour party anticipated in 1918, came about mainly through the need to finance the war of 1939–45. Large-scale methods of production, as well as death duties, have in any case eliminated most of the old-fashioned 'capitalists'; and capital is spread over a large section of the population, consisting mainly of salary-earners. On the other hand, an almost continually rising standard of production, substantial social services, and heavy taxation have reduced the range of 'differentials' among the social classes. These factors, as already noticed, have eliminated the concepts of 'proletariat' and 'bourgeoisie'; but they have also almost eliminated the concept of 'working-class unity' because a large part of the population considers itself to be 'middle class'.

Nationalisation had to wait until the Labour party assumed office in 1945, except that coal deposits were nationalised in 1938: but under Conservative Governments there was a good deal of regulation, sometimes through what was called 'rationalisation', sometimes through marketing schemes, and sometimes (as in agriculture especially) through conditional subsidies. The Labour Government of 1945–50 nationalised the mines, the railways, goods transport by road, the Bank of England, the production and supply of electricity, gas and water, and the iron and steel industry.

Before 1914 there was a substantial group of socialists who called themselves 'syndicalists'[1] and who favoured control of industries by the persons working in them. The Fabians and most of the I.L.P. were opposed to syndicalism; and *Labour and the New Social Order* condemned it by implication. The method of control of nationalised industries adopted by the Labour Government, following the example

---

[1] The meaning of the word was transposed when the word was imported from France: cf. J. Ramsay MacDonald, *Syndicalism*, Introduction (1912).

set in respect of the London Passenger Transport Board in 1931,[1] was that of the public corporation. This involved the replacement of boards of directors and managers of companies by boards of directors and managers of monopolistic corporations. There were substantial differences which were important, especially to the socialist: but to the consumer and the worker there appeared to be very little change, except perhaps that there was greater freedom to grumble. There is no doubt that in 1945 the Labour party had a 'mandate' to nationalise the industries which it proceeded to nationalise. On the other hand it may be doubted if many electors were enthusiastic about nationalisation. Still fewer, probably, favoured the retention of the wartime 'controls', which the Labour party wished to retain in order to regulate supply and demand. These 'controls' were associated with 'rationing', shortages of consumer goods, and queues.

In consequence of the social changes since 1918 and of the changes in opinion, the Labour party finds itself inhibited from pursuing a socialist programme. The younger generation is less attracted by social equality, or 'fair shares for all' than its parents. It is more concerned to seek careers open to the talents, but realises that such careers, if successful, merely result in heavy surtax. The poor have ceased to be very poor— very largely, of course, because of heavy taxation on the comparatively wealthy, but there is no consistency in politics—with the result that the socialists have lost their high moral fervour. Indeed, they seem to many electors, especially younger electors, to be mere political careerists, like the Conservatives. Moreover the constant threat of a nuclear explosion has tended to induce a return to the Church, not so much because of its dogma as because it represents, or claims to represent, the only element of stability in an unstable world. In current politics, a return to the Church implies a movement towards Conservatism.

The Labour party is still the trade-union party, but the trade unions, except when they are dominated by communists, are conservative bureaucracies. In the industrial field they keep the loyalty of their members; but in the political field they are less successful in inducing the trade unionists, and especially the wives of trade unionists, to vote

---

[1] There were earlier examples under Conservative Governments: cf. Terence H. O'Brien, *British Experiments in Public Ownership and Control.*

Labour. So long as the Conservatives, cynically or otherwise, maintain the essentials of the Welfare State, including full employment, they can attract a substantial portion of working-class votes. This in turn induces the Labour party—which is becoming increasingly middle-class in its personnel—to become more conservative and cautious. In respect of internal politics, therefore, the Conservative and the Labour parties tend to have similar policies; and very largely the choice before the electors is one of persons.

INDEX

Canning, George, 78, 231, 233, 250, 352, 353, 354, 355
Canon law, 21, 26, 31, 36, 87, 132, 133, 150, 199
Capitalism
  definition of, 447
  economics of, 358-9
  government and, 433-4
  Nonconformity and, 442
  ugliness of, 446
  working-class and, 439-40, 447
Carey, William, 236
Carlile, Richard, 164, 168, 169
Carlton Club, 463
Carlyle, Thomas, 276, 393, 394, 451-2
Carnarvon, 4th Earl of, 277, 321-2, 324, 327
Caroline, Queen, 166, 184
Carson, Edward, Lord, 197
Carteret, John, Earl of Granville, 219
Cartwright, Major, 163
Cases
  Alabama, 263
  Amalgamated Society of Railway Servants v. Osborne, 189
  Bate's, 28
  Dr Bonham's, 62
  Bushell's, 139, 148
  Calvin's, 36
  Caudrey's, 24
  Darnel's, 24, 145, 146
  Day v. Savadge, 63
  East India Co. v. Sandys, 173
  Eliot, Holles and Valentine, 157, 158
  Floyd's, 39
  Godden v. Hales, 50
  Joyce v. Director of Public Prosecutions, 176
  Judge Jenkins', 44
  Lumley v. Gye, 188
  Magdalen College, 50
  Dr Peachell's, 50
  Prohibitions del Roy, 33
  Prohibitions, 60
  Quinn v. Leathem, 188
  R. v. Casement, 176
  R. v. William Penn and William Mead, 148
  R. v. Shipley, 158, 159
  R. v. Thistlewood, 150
  R. v. Woodfull, 159
  Seven Bishops', 51, 92, 139, 158
  Sherlock v. Annesley, 309
  Shipmoney, 22, 28, 32, 33, 34, 37-8, 40-1, 58, 60, 138
  Skinner v. East India Co., 44
  Capt. Streater's, 45

Charles Stuart, King of England, 45
Taff Vale Rly. Co. v. Amalgamated Society of Railway Servants, 189
Temperton v. Russell, 188
Wilkes', 159
Castlereagh, Viscount, 78
Caucus, Joe's, 325
Cavalier Parliament, 152
Cavendish, Thomas, 204
Cecil, William, Lord Burghley, 87, 88
Censorship, 157
Central Nonconformist Committee, 126, 127
Ceylon, 210-11, 242-3
Chadwick, Sir Edwin, 392, 397, 401, 408, 409, 410, 411
Chamberlain, Sir Austen, 271
Chamberlain, Houston Stewart, 202
Chamberlain, Joseph, 126, 127, 154, 177, 196, 248, 249, 257, 258, 259, 263, 266, 271, 275, 278-88, 292, 293, 319, 322, 325-6, 327, 328-9, 331, 332, 333, 337, 367, 370, 371, 372-4, 377, 378, 381, 423, 424, 425, 426, 427, 428, 435, 451, 463
Chamberlain, Neville, 381, 382
Champion, H. H., 450, 451
Chancery, Court of, 27, 145, 146, 147, 174
Charters
  corporations under, 172-3
  printing of, 200
Chartism
  Conservative party and, 122
  Corn Laws and, 363, 364
  free trade and, 124
  generally, 72-6, 144, 392, 398
  grievances of, 409
  leadership lacking, 170
  Marxism and, 447
  Methodists and, 106-7
  physical force, 433
  sedition and, 176
  working-classes and, 437, 438
Chatham, William Pitt, 1st Earl of, 66, 78, 213, 215, 216-24, 225, 226, 227, 228, 230, 231, 236
Chatham House, 198
Chesterfield, 4th Earl of, 136-8, 140, 150
Children
  education of, see Education
  employment of, 398-9, 400, 402-6
Chinese slavery, 292, 377
Cholera, 408, 409, 410, 411-12
Christian, Professor Edward, 60, 63, 129
Christian Chartists, 75

479

INDEX

INDEX